INDIA

Dietmar Rothermund is Professor Emeritus of South Asian history, University of Heidelberg, Germany. He is the author of many works on Asian history and politics, including *A History of India* (1986), with Hermann Kulke.

DIETMAR ROTHERMUND

INDIA

THE RISE OF AN ASIAN GIANT

YALE UNIVERSITY PRESS
New Haven and London

For information about this and other Yale University Press publications please contact:

U.S. Office:	sales.press@yale.edu	yalebooks.com
Europe Office:	sales@yaleup.co.uk	www.yalebooks.co.uk

Set in Minion and Gill Sans by J&L Composition, Filey, North Yorkshire
Printed in Great Britain by TJ International Ltd, Padstow, Cornwall

Library of Congress Cataloguing-in-Publication Data

Rothermund, Dietmar, 1933–
  India: the rise of an Asian giant / Dietmar Rothermund.
    p. cm.
  Includes bibliographical references and index.
  ISBN 978-0-300-11309-9 (alk. paper)
  1. India—Economic conditions—21st century. 2. India—Social conditions—21st
century. 3. India—Poilitics and government. I. Title
  HC435.3.R68 2008
  330.954—dc22

                               2007026329

A catalogue record for this book is available from the British Library

ISBN 978-0-300-15827-4 (pbk)

10 9 8 7 6 5 4 3 2 1

CONTENTS

ILLUSTRATIONS

In the text

Source of cartoons: Karoline Schade (ed.), *Indien im Blick: Karikaturen aus Indien* [*India at a Glance: Cartoons from India*]. 2006. Reproduced with the permission of the editor.

MAPS

Cartography: Nittarm, South Asia Institute, University of Heidelburg

PREFACE

This is the account of a witness who has watched India for nearly half a century. I first arrived in India in January 1960 in order to write a book on the Indian freedom movement. In this context I had two long interviews with Jawaharlal Nehru in 1961 and met many other freedom fighters. Studying the freedom movement, I became interested in the fate of the Indian peasantry and then wrote my next book on agrarian relations under British rule. The agrarian distress caused in India by the Great Depression of the 1930s then attracted my attention and I devoted a book to this subject. In the meantime I had been called to the Chair of South Asian History at Heidelberg University in 1968. The South Asia Institute to which this chair belongs provided an excellent base for my teaching and research. One of the projects which I directed for this institute in the 1970s was an interdisciplinary study of an Indian coalfield in Dhanbad District, Bihar. Interacting with colleagues from various disciplines I became an enthusiastic 'interdisciplinarian' and devoted a great deal of attention to the various aspects of India's development. All this was a useful preparation for the writing of the present book.

My aim in tracing the rise of India as an Asian giant is that of understanding the present in terms of its historical background and its future potential. I am convinced that India has a great future. But as a historian I would hesitate to make predictions. In discussing the present germs of potential future developments I also pay attention to the impediments to this development. The people of India have shown great ingenuity in solving problems. They will also overcome the obstacles which are described in some chapters of this book.

By calling India an Asian giant I am juxtaposing it to China, the other Asian giant. So far, China has attracted more attention than India in this respect. I wish to contribute to a more balanced appreciation of the two giants. However, I do not dare to present a comparative study of India and China as I have devoted my life to the study of India, not China. Wherever it seemed to be relevant, I have referred to China in this book. But these references are limited to specific contexts.

In writing this book I have covered many fields of knowledge in which I am not an expert. I have relied on the critical comments and helpful suggestions of many friends and colleagues. I am particularly grateful to those who have been kind enough to grant interviews to me in the course of my present work: Prime Minister Dr Manmohan Singh; Dr Montek Singh Ahluwalia, Deputy Chairman of the Planning Commission; Dr Anil Kakodkar, Head of the Department of Atomic Energy; Jairam Ramesh, Minister of State in the Commerce Ministry; Dr Raghunath Mashelkar, Director General, Council of Scientific and Industrial Research. Amit Dasgupta, of the Indian Foreign Service saw the initial plan of this book and suggested that I should take note of water, energy and infrastructure. I followed his advice and devoted Chapter 11 to these subjects. Dr M. Govinda Rao, Director, National Institute of Public Finance and Policy, has given me advice in his field; Dr Sanjaya Baru, Media Advisor to the Prime Minister, has helped me in many ways. I also wish to thank Mr Mukesh Ambani of Reliance Industries for an interview which gave me valuable insights into the manifold activities of his company. Scholars in the field of Indian economics have informed me about their research. I can mention only a few of them: Dr Ashok V. Desai, Dr Subir Gokarn, Dr Omkar Goswami, Professors Amitabh Kundu, Abhay Pethe and S. D. Tendulkar. The School of International Studies, Jawaharlal Nehru University, New Delhi, invited me for a short-term visiting professorship in the final round of my work on this book. I am grateful to Professor Partha S. Ghosh and Professor Mahendra Lama for arranging this visit and for their hospitality.

Some colleagues not only shared their views with me in personal conversations but also took the trouble of reading specific chapters of my manuscript and sending me their critical comments and helpful suggestions. Dr M. Govinda Rao had a close look at Chapter 3; Dr C. Raja Mohan read Chapters 4 and 5; Professor Suresh Tendulkar read Chapter 6; Dr Sharad Chari read the second section of Chapter 8; and Dr Subramaniam Ramadorai checked the third section of that chapter. Professor Ashok Jhunjunwala had a look at Chapter 9; Dr Sunita Narain checked the section on water scarcity in Chapter 11; Professor Purushottam Kulkarni looked at Chapter 13; and Professor Jean Drèze commented on Chapter 16. Dr Harish Khare read Chapter 17 and found my account of the Indian media 'too romantic'. As an insider, he knows the seamy side of India's media business. Since I am an innocent outsider, I have retained my 'romantic' view, but I have learned a great deal about many subjects from my conversations with Dr Khare. My friend Dr Vishwas Sarangdhar read the whole manuscript and made many helpful suggestions. My wife Chitra has read several chapters and has always helped me with her advice in matters which only someone who has been born and brought up in India could know from personal experience. To all of those mentioned here I owe a debt of gratitude. They are, of course, not responsible for any errors which still remain in the text and for which only the author should be blamed. Last but not least I wish to thank Heather McCallum of Yale University Press who encouraged me to write this book and has accompanied my work on it with helpful advice.

Dietmar Rothermund
Heidelberg, October 2007

PROLOGUE

The Giant's Ascent

The Indian giant is rising like Gulliver after being released from the web of threads with which he had been pinned down. This rise is a laborious process which is still in progress, and it is irreversible. India's captivity was self-imposed; after attaining independence, it experienced a long period of voluntary isolation. This contributed to the development of the inner strength of the nation, but it also fostered an introvert mentality and resulted in a lack of competitiveness. Finally India broke out of this charmed circle of isolation and boldly faced the challenge of globalization. It so happened that this coincided with a technological revolution based on the rapid improvement and global spread of computers. With a large supply of highly educated manpower, India could make a mark in designing computer software and providing IT-related services worldwide. India thus got a head start in the 'knowledge economy' of the new century. This also helped the country to overcome the general 'export pessimism' which had been the result of its isolation. From 1980 to the present the share of exports in GDP rose from 6 to 16 per cent. At the same time the gross domestic savings rate increased from about 20 to 30 per cent. This is the secret of India's ascent.

The mindset of Indian entrepreneurs has changed drastically under the impact of these new developments, as I know from talking to some of them at different times. In the 1960s I met a young businessman on a flight from Mumbai to Kolkata. He told me that his family had owned sugar mills for a long time, but now he felt that he had to go in for modern manufacturing. I asked him whether he knew anything about it. He said no – but he added that one could always buy people who have the necessary knowledge. I told him that quality control is essential in modern manufacturing. His reply was devastating: we can sell any dirt in this country. I guess in those days he must have been very successful with this approach to industrial production. Recently I talked to Mukesh Ambani of Reliance Industries, who is now one of India's most successful entrepreneurs. I told him the story of the young businessman whom I had met in the 1960s and he smiled and said that this man would go down immediately under present conditions. Earlier Indian entrepreneurs lived like frogs in a well; Ambani operates on a grand scale in a competitive market. He represents India's new confidence in a world of great opportunities.

This confidence of Indian entrepreneurs is also based on a stable democratic polity. It is not the stability of an immobile state, but emerges from constantly adapting to new situations. The vibrant nature of Indian democracy is often shown by surprising events such as the recent triumph of Mayawati in Uttar Pradesh. This huge state, inhabitated by nearly 170 million people, has been a bellwether of Indian politics. Only a few years ago it seemed to be a stronghold of Hindu nationalism, but in the assembly elections of May 2007, Mayawati's Bahujan Samaj Party which is backed by the Dalits (Untouchables) captured the absolute majority of the seats – a feat which nobody had predicted. Mayawati, the 'Dalit Queen', had made an alliance with Brahmins and representatives of other high castes; she was also supported by the Muslims. Her success has shown that the democratic process can give rise to new political constellations in a fractionalized society.

Indian society encompasses a spectrum representative of all of mankind, from the desperately poor eking out a living in remote rural areas to metropolitan professionals in the most advanced lines of work and highly talented scientists operating at the cutting edge of research. In tracing the rise of India one has to traverse all these spheres of life. Looking at the evidence of persistent poverty and following the quest for supercomputers, and understanding the arguments of power embodied in atom bombs and rockets, are all relevant in this context. The spheres of Indian life are, of course, much richer and more varied than has been captured by the glimpses provided in the following pages. Observing the ascent of the Indian giant is a fascinating experience for all those who are willing to share it.

CHAPTER I

BUILDING A DEMOCRATIC NATION

Contours of the Indian Nation

India is a state encompassing a civilization. It includes a multitude of ethnic and linguistic groups which share a common cultural background. Its historical continuity is amazing. The art of story-telling has characterized this civilization throughout. It has expressed itself not only in literary genres from great epics to folk tales but also in painting and sculpture and in the performing arts. The lively imagery projected by India has radiated far beyond its boundaries. Creativity has been India's hallmark.

In the recent past India has also become a territorial nation state with defined borders and institutions guarding its territorial integrity. The idea of a clearly delineated territoriality was not prevalent in India in earlier times. The Himalayas in the north and the ocean encircling the country appeared to those living inside it as 'natural' boundaries. In fact the mountain people never conceived of the Himalayas as a boundary and they 'transgressed' it in many ways. Many of the coastal people, on the other hand, participated throughout the ages in maritime trade. The orthodox prejudice against crossing the *kala pani* (black water) was not shared by them. This aversion to seafaring was a relatively late phenomenon in an era when people in India became more introverted and defensive.

The awareness of the 'natural' boundaries of India did not imply a feeling of national identity in territorial terms. Nationalism first found expression among educated people and did not affect the common people for a long time. The poor people from northern India who were transported to Fiji as indentured servants to work on the sugar plantations did not refer to themselves as 'Indians' but as *girmityas*.[1] The word *girmit* was a Hindi neologism derived from 'agreement', the document which bound them to their servitude. Their identity was derived from this common fate. It was only later when emissaries of Mahatma Gandhi reached Fiji that these *girmityas* became Indians.

The nationalism of educated Indians was due to the multifaceted impact of British rule.[2] First of all the British confronted the Indians as a well-organized modern nation. In the eighteenth century Britain was still a very small nation of only a few million people who nevertheless managed to conquer India, the home of about 150 million people. This conquest was the work of Indian soldiers under British command; it was financed by Indian taxpayers under a rigorous British revenue administration. None of the British commanders ever thought of becoming warlords on their own. The solidarity and the corporate memory of the British were far more important than their weapons, which were freely available in the market to all Indian princes who might wish to acquire them. British nationalism was thus not an abstract idea; it was a force demonstrated by the colonial rulers in daily life. Another aspect of British rule was the introduction of educational institutions with their syllabuses and curricula. Initially the British introduced their education in India because they needed personnel for the lower echelons of their administrative service and for the ubiquitous courts of law which soon spread throughout the land. Again, the establishment of these courts was not an altruistic measure. The court fees provided an additional income to the colonial government and the jurisdiction of these courts assured the hegemony of colonial laws.

In designing the syllabuses and curricula for their colonial educational system the British closely followed those of their own schools and colleges at home. Liberal ideas circulating in Britain were thus transferred to India and absorbed by young Indians, who then applied these ideas to the interpretation of their experience in India.[3] This was the third aspect of the impact of British rule, and it proved to be of great importance for the evolution of Indian nationalism. Moreover, the British created careers for educated Indians as clerks, teachers, lawyers and even judges. There was thus an Indian intelligentsia which shared a universe of discourse as a result of their schooling and their daily practice. The circulation of ideas was also promoted by the introduction of the printing press. It had first been sponsored by Christian missionaries, but in due course there were many 'native newspapers' in almost all Indian languages. This Indian journalism alarmed the colonial rulers and they hired special translators who had to prepare 'Reports on Native Newspapers' for them. Due to this vernacular journalism a new type of prose style was introduced into Indian literature which helped to spread the universe of discourse of the English-educated Indians to wider circles.

In the last decades of the nineteenth century British imperial ambition and incipient Indian nationalism became more and more opposed. British ambitions were expressed in visible form at the great Durbar held in 1877 when Queen Victoria was proclaimed Empress of India. There was a conscious attempt at reproducing the trappings of the Mogul empire so as to enhance the legitimacy of British rule over India. The last manifestation of this spirit was the magnificent buildings designed by a British architect for the imperial capital of New Delhi in the 1920s. These imperial vestiges now decorate the national capital of India. Indian nationalism, however, was not entranced by this imperial magic. It concentrated on a reasoned critique of British rule both in its economic and its political manifestations. In the same year in which the imperial Durbar was held, an Indian judge read a paper on 'Free Trade and Protection' to an audience in Mumbai in which he condemned the British policy of free trade which ruined Indian industry.[4] Some years later economic nationalism was even more firmly expressed in Dadabhai Naoroji's book *Poverty and Un-British Rule in India.*[5] The very title showed that the author had learned the lesson taught by the British, of measuring the practical effect of colonial rule in terms of British ideas.

The Indian National Congress which held its first session in 1885 in Mumbai provided a meeting ground for nationalists from all parts of India. Initially the Viceroy, Lord Dufferin, welcomed this congress as he felt that it would provide a sounding board for Indian opinions, but when it passed a resolution condemning Dufferin's annexation of Upper Burma, he changed his mind. He did not prohibit further meetings of the Congress outright but he did not allow Indian government servants to attend. This excluded the Indian judges who had been among the leaders of the Congress from its further deliberations. In general, the delegates of the Indian National Congress were liberal constitutionalists who felt that India was a nation in the making which needed the political framework established by the British.[6] But there was also a group of national revolutionaries, later on called 'the Extremists', who held that India had always been a nation and only needed to break free from its shackles. In order to prove their point, the national revolutionaries glorified ancient India and propagated neo-Hinduism in the interest of national solidarity. This neo-Hinduism gained worldwide attention when Swami Vivekananda attended the World Parliament of Religions in Chicago in 1893. Vivekananda was not a political 'Extremist'; he was an English-educated young man who had become a disciple of the saint Sri Ramakrishna. In his name he founded the Ramakrishna Mission, a modern religious order whose monks preached an enlightened neo-Hinduism. Vivekananda's success abroad greatly enhanced his influence in India. Even liberal nationalists such as Gopal Krishna Gokhale and later on socialists like Jawaharlal Nehru acknowledged their debt to him.[7] Vivekananda himself admitted that he adhered to a kind of traditionalism in order to make his message palatable to his audience. It was, however, a selective traditionalism.[8] He condemned the caste system which was the very opposite of national solidarity, and he highlighted the monism of

Hindu philosophy. Neo-Hinduism had, of course, no attraction for Indian Muslims. Ramakrishna had stressed the equality of all religions and Vivekananda followed him in this respect. But for a pious Muslim an equation of Islam with other religions would sound blasphemous and he would similarly reject Mahatma Gandhi's practice of including Allah in his prayers to Hindu gods. Building national solidarity on a spiritual foundation was, therefore, an impossible task.

When Mahatma Gandhi emerged as the 'Father of the Nation' he took on this impossible task and then tragically failed in his endeavour. He had spent his formative years in South Africa as the leader of the Indian minority. There he had been very successful in motivating both Hindus and Muslims to participate in his non-violent campaigns against colonial oppression. When he returned to India in the middle of the First World War, the draconian Defence of India Act had killed off all political activity. It was not until 1920 that Gandhi saw a chance to lead Hindus and Muslims in a joint non-cooperation campaign against the British-Indian government. Gandhi had argued even earlier that the Indians had practically given India to the British and had ever since kept them there by cooperating with them; if they ceased to do so, the British could not govern India any longer.[9] The Indian Muslims who looked to the Turkish Caliph as the head of all Muslims of the world were greatly incensed by the terms imposed upon him by the British after the war. Their leaders had started a Khilafat movement in India in order to protest against this and Gandhi's call for a non-cooperation campaign greatly appealed to them. Gandhi was glad to espouse a cause dear to the Muslims. He did not know that he had become involved in an orthodox delusion which was soon terminated by the Turks themselves, who deposed the Caliph in 1924. In 1920, however, Gandhi was riding a tide of nationalist fervour.

Not all Indians were as enthusiastic about non-cooperation as Gandhi was. Rabindranath Tagore, India's Nobel laureate, raised his voice against this campaign.[10] Even earlier, he had warned against the dangers of modern nationalism. During the war he had toured Japan and the USA. In his lectures he had stressed the value of universal humanism as against the narrowness of nationalism and had been criticized for taking this stand. Now Gandhi's non-cooperation seemed to Tagore not only narrow but also negative. He and Gandhi were friends, and Gandhi took his criticism very seriously. He replied that he himself also believed in universal values, but first and foremost he had to serve his nation. An India suppressed by the colonial rulers could not bring a message of hope to the world – as Tagore wanted it to do.

The non-cooperation campaign finally collapsed, but it had important though unintended consequences. Those who had forfeited their careers and gone to prison during the campaign now emerged as the first generation of political workers to strengthen the National Congress. Moreover, in revamping the structure of the Congress as a political organization, Gandhi had stressed the recruitment of rural members and the use of Indian languages for political propaganda. He thus broke the charmed circle of educated Indians who had so far monopolized national politics. With the 'prison graduates' as enthusiastic volunteers, the Congress could now penetrate the countryside. This was of great importance in winning the peasants for democracy in the next round of the freedom movement.

Why Indian Peasants Backed a Democracy

In his pioneering study *Social Origins of Democracy and Dictatorship. Lord and Peasant in the Making of the Modern World* Barrington Moore gave more space to India than to any of his other case studies.[11] He did not do this because he could explain the Indian case best, but because he was puzzled by the failure of his theory as far as India was concerned. India should have had an experience similar to that of China where an astute political party used the revolutionary potential of the peasantry and then subjected it to a dictatorship. The Indian peasants, however, made a successful transition to democracy.

Moore's theory is based on Marxist concepts of class conflict and class alliance. The conflict between lords of the land and peasants gave rise to various types of class alliance with the bourgeoisie in Western countries. In China and India there was no such bourgeoisie. In reading the secondary literature available in his time, Moore concluded that the British relied on the landlords throughout their colonial rule. Later research has shown that the British had actually looked for a new social base for the support of their rule by relying on the upper strata of the peasantry whom they protected by means of a plethora of tenancy acts.[12] These acts restricted rent increases by the landlords and defined the 'occupancy right' of the peasants according to the respective provincial conditions. The British hoped that these peasants would support them, as their protection depended on them. In preparation for 'provincial autonomy' under the Government of India Act of 1935, a franchise commission toured the country in 1932 and saw to it that the upper strata of the peasantry would be given the right to vote. Only about 10 per cent of the population were enfranchised at that time, on the basis of property qualifications. The amount of rent or revenue paid by the peasant served as the criterion of enfranchisement. In Bengal a simpler method was used: those who inhabited a proper house and did not live in a mud hut were entitled to vote. In this way the British carefully designed a political arena which they hoped to be able to control. The Indian nationalists whom they regarded as a vocal urban intelligentsia without roots in the countryside would have no chance to capture the votes of the peasants.

The political calculations of the British were upset by the impact of the Great Depression which hit India in the 1930s.[13] In fact, the British intensified this impact by rigidly maintaining an overvalued Indian currency so as to prevent a 'flight from the Rupee'. Being India's major creditors, the British feared that such a flight would affect their own creditworthiness. The Indian peasants whose income was reduced by about half owing to the steep fall in the price of grain and other agricultural produce also experienced an appreciation of their debts due to British monetary policy. The rural moneylenders forced the peasants to part with the gold ornaments of their wives which they would not normally have touched; thus a stream of 'distress gold' left India and supported the pound sterling which floated after the British left the gold standard in 1931. A national Government of India would have imposed a gold export embargo and reflated the Indian currency to ease the plight of the peasantry, but the British did not do this and provoked the wrath of the very same peasants whom they had enfranchised in the hope of getting their support. As the rural moneylenders pounced on the peasants, the British tried to restrain their activities by passing numerous acts imposing controls on them and forcing them to submit to the verdict of debt conciliation boards.[14] This did not help the peasantry very much but it incensed the moneylenders, most of whom had the right to vote as they had enough property to qualify for it.

The Indian National Congress was well equipped to take care of all these rural grievances. Most provincial Congress committees published reports on agrarian distress; some even organized no-rent campaigns. When the election campaigns under the Government of India Act started in 1936 the Congress emerged as a party of the peasantry and carefully geared its programme to those who were entitled to vote. Even the disgruntled moneylenders supported this party, which then swept to victory in the polls in seven out of the nine provinces of British India. These were the provinces with Hindu majorities. The Muslim League, led by Mohammed Ali Jinnah, had hoped to capture for Muslims all the separate electorates which had been introduced by the British in 1909. But the Congress had also put up Muslim candidates and Jinnah had very limited success in those provinces in which the Muslims were in the minority.[15] In the two Muslim majority provinces, Bengal and Punjab, local coalitions swept to victory in the polls and the Muslim League was left high and dry.

Jawaharlal Nehru who had led the Congress election campaign was proud of his success. But he was opposed to the formation of provincial governments by the Congress Party. He interpreted this success in the elections as a plebiscite against British rule and wanted to follow it up by intensifying the freedom struggle.[16] However, the peasants who had voted for the Congress hoped for an immediate relief of their difficulties in terms of amended tenancy acts, debt relief, etc. Their interests prevailed and Congress ministries were formed in the seven provinces concerned but their period of government was cut short by the outbreak of the Second World War when the Congress ministries resigned because the British refused to define their plans for the future of India. Winston Churchill was a diehard imperialist who could not be expected to make any concessions to Indian nationalism.

As far as the peasants were concerned, this early termination of its provincial governments saved the Congress from disappointing their expectations. Under British rule the powers of these governments were limited but the peasants considered the Congress to be their party and believed that democratic elections would lead to its success, an experience which motivated them to back democracy in future years as well. The return of Congress ministries to power in 1946 led to the abolition of the rights of landlords (zamindars). This was the only land reform which the Congress dared to take in hand. The zamindars constituted a very thin top layer of rural society with no political clout under a democratic system. The British were no longer prepared to support them and tenancy acts had long since reduced their rights, so abolishing those rights did not require much political courage. Any further step in the direction of a more equitable distribution of land would touch the interests of the upper strata of the peasantry. The Congress politicians could not afford to go against those interests. These were the obvious limitations of the power of a democratic regime backed by the peasants.

The elections of 1946 that had enabled the Congress party to form ministries once more in the seven provinces, which it had dominated before, also brought the return of the regional coalitions in Bengal and the Punjab. Jinnah's Muslim League had done much better in these elections than in the earlier ones. He had emerged as the sole spokesman of the Muslims during the war when the Congress politicians languished in jail.[17] In 1940 he had strengthened his position by proclaiming his 'Two Nation Theory', according to which Hindus and Muslims were two different nations, 'by any definition of the term'. In territorial terms this could only mean the separation of the Muslim majority provinces from 'Hindu India'. But Jinnah, who had earlier been the leader of the Muslims in the minority provinces, knew very well that the millions of Muslims settled in Hindu India could not be transferred to Pakistan, as the Muslim state came to be called. Moreover, the Hindu areas in West Bengal and in the East Punjab could not be expected to remain attached to those provinces if the 'Two Nation Theory' was applied in territorial terms. For a long time Jinnah kept his cards close to his chest and did not reveal his plans in detail. Having never led an agitational campaign, he knew that he could only win at the conference table and obtain Pakistan as a gift from the British when they decided to quit India. But this also required the acquiescence of the Congress leaders who initially rejected the idea of a partition of India. Gandhi had even called it the 'vivisection of India'. In the final round of negotations, Nehru accepted partition because the alternative was 'Plan Balkan' designed by the British government. According to this plan, independence would be granted to all British Indian provinces separately and they could then see for themselves how to get together in one way or another. From the British point of view, this was an elegant solution as they would not need to partition India. But Nehru saw the real danger of a Balkanization of India if the provinces could not get their act together. He therefore preferred partition by the British – thus providing Jinnah with what he wanted. But Jinnah had to be satisified with a 'motheaten Pakistan' as he called it, because West Bengal and East Punjab would go to India.

The problem of the Muslims who remained in India was aggravated rather than solved by this partition. When Jinnah left Mumbai for Pakistan in order to become its first Governor-General he was asked by his local followers what they should do now. Jinnah admonished them to become good citizens of India[18] – and then left them in the lurch.

Hindus and Muslims: How Riots Disrupt Communal Peace

Partition was accompanied by unforeseen carnage. Large streams of refugees crossed from Pakistan to India, and from India to Pakistan. Jinnah's good advice was of no use in this respect. Finally the millions of Muslims who remained in India tried to come to terms with that country, whereas most Hindus and Sikhs whom fate had left stranded in Pakistan fled to India. Partition became a deep trauma. For the first time Indians had to face the fact of territoriality: they had never given thought to it before. The freedom movement had been directed against British rule; the territory concerned was taken for granted. Tagore had once described territoriality, *rashtratantra* as he called it, as an obession of Western nations whose very being is affected by it.[19] He felt that India was free from this obsession. With Partition, *rashtratantra* descended upon India with a vengeance. Even the 'Father of the Nation', Mahatma Gandhi, was quite helpless when he had to deal with this phenomenon. In 1944 he had held long talks with Jinnah and had even conceded Pakistan to him, provided India and Pakistan would conclude a treaty before partition which would ensure their peaceful coexistence. Jinnah had dismissed this by pointing out that partition had to be the first step, as only separate states could become contracting parties, an argument which

Gandhi had to accept. He was flabbergasted when he was told after accepting partition in 1947 that this would imply the partition of the British-Indian army. He had not thought of this, although it was an obvious consequence of separate territoriality. Once he got the point he said that this would mean that the two armies would fight each other.[20] Unfortunately, his prediction soon proved to be true.

Under the leadership of Jawaharlal Nehru the National Congress tried to do its best to make the Muslims who had remained in India feel at home there. He had to fight against the prejudices of those who saw in those Muslims a fifth column of Pakistan. They spurned Nehru's 'secularism' and accused him of bending over backwards to please the Muslims in order to attract their votes. Under the constraints of the majority election system Indian Muslims did, of course, vote for the Congress party. Separate electorates had been abolished in independent India and a Muslim party would always be marginal under the prevailing system. Moreover, except for the valley of Kashmir where the Muslims are in a majority, they truly formed a diaspora everywhere else in India. Since most Indian Muslims are poor artisans and labourers, they tend to be concentrated in urban areas. For instance, in Uttar Pradesh, India's largest federal state which also has the highest share of Muslims, they account for about 17 per cent of the total population and 44 per cent of its urban population. The concentration of Muslims in a backward state like Uttar Pradesh enhances their marginalization.

In 2005 the Indian Prime Minister appointed a High Level Committee for the Preparation of a Report on the Social, Economic and Educational Status of the Muslim Community of India under the chairmanship of Justice Rajinder Sachar. The so-called Sachar Report, submitted in November 2006,[21] highlights the marginal position of the Muslims. Their social position is close to that of the Untouchables. Most are poor and their access to education is limited. The literacy rate of Indian Muslims is 59 per cent, as against the national average of 65 per cent.[22] The number of Muslim graduates is very small and the rate of their unemployment is higher than that of graduates from other communities.[23] It is generally believed that Muslims are averse to secular education and prefer Madrasahs (Muslim schools), but according to the Sachar Report only 4 per cent of Muslim children attend Madrasahs. More Muslim children do attend *maktabs* – local Koran schools usually attached to a mosque – but *maktabs* only provide additional religious instruction; they are no substitute for regular schools.[24] The Sachar Report shows that the Indian Muslims are part of the mainstream, but that they suffer from acute social and economic deprivation.

In most parts of India, and for most of the time, Hindus and Muslims live as good neighbours. They even share their festivals, though usually not their meals. But proximity also encourages friction particularly whenever interested parties intend to stir up trouble to serve their own ends. Moreover, in India separate religious identities are usually clearly visible in dress and behaviour. Generally one knows the 'other' and can spot him if one wants to hit him. Then there are food habits which are connected with religious sanctions. The Hindu worships the holy cow and the Muslim eats it: at certain festivals the ritual slaughtering of a cow (*kurbani*) is a must for certain Muslims. The Hindu – unless he is a vegetarian – eats pork, which the Muslim considers to be impure. If one intends to provoke and offend, one can easily break a taboo and make the other's blood boil. Indians are gregarious and like to flock together. Usually their crowds are good-natured, but sometimes their mood can change very suddenly. Troublemakers may orchestrate such changes and melt into the crowd without leaving a trace.

Hindu–Muslim riots are not a new phenomenon in India. They have often occurred spontaneously, but in recent times they have been precipitated for political purposes. As will be shown later, election campaigns sometimes have a seamy side and riots may become 'a continuation of politics by other means', as Paul Brass has put it.[25] He has also described 'riot production systems', which may remain latent for quite some time but then spring into action when required by politicians.[26] In his fieldwork he has been able to identify various types of riotmongers who play their respective roles with great skill. Some of them are otherwise respectable citizens who know how to incite others without showing their own hand and do not hesitate to cultivate criminals who do the dirty work for them. Then there are those who hang around in shops and offices and spread rumours which motivate others to take to the streets. The police play a crucial role in all this. If police officers are corrupt or partisan, or both, they can do a great deal of harm. On the other hand, even just a few courageous and determined policemen can nip a riot in the bud by catching those who are eager to start it.

In earlier years the Mumbai police had a reputation for courage and efficiency. Instead of marching into a dangerous locality in great numbers, they would form teams of three policemen dressed like ordinary people. One of them would wear a coat of mail under his clothes and walk ahead. He would be dressed like a Muslim in a Hindu locality, or vice versa. The other two, dressed in a different way, followed him at a short distance. When a rioter rushed to stab the first policeman, the others would nab him before anybody else could interfere. Repeating this performance in various localities, they soon rounded up the most active elements and there was no further trouble. This required a daring and dedication which cannot be taken for granted nowadays. Yet preventive intervention of this kind is crucial for stopping the escalation of violence before it is too late. Rumours often circulate in advance of riots, the insinuation that food is being poisoned by members of the other community being a standard feature of such pre-riot rumours. Paranoia and hatred spread in this way. Once an outbreak occurs there is often an initial tentative phase of sporadic aggression followed by a deceptive pause before an orgy of violence is unleashed. It is this pause which provides the chance for decisive intervention. Sometimes this chance is missed due to negligence, but it may also be disregarded deliberately, as seems to have been the case in Gujarat in 2002. The Indian government maintains a Central Reserve Police (CRP) which is well armed and can be dispatched to federal states when they request it. From the ranks of the CRP a special force was recruited in the 1990s. Called Rapid Action Force (RAF), it is trained in the methods of riot control. RAF troops were dispatched to Godhra in Gujarat in 2002, and were kept waiting in an officers' mess; the local authorities obviously did not want to make use of them.[27]

In addition to a sense of timing, preventive intervention requires an insight into specific local conditions. Some localities may be immune to Hindu–Muslim riots; in others they may be endemic. Lakhnau, for instance, has rarely experienced such riots. As the capital of Uttar Pradesh it has a large Muslim population. Clashes between Shia and Sunni Muslims are endemic here, but Hindus and Muslims live in peace with each other. Lakhnau is known for its *chikan* work, a special kind of embroidery made by Muslim women in their homes. This product is marketed by Hindu traders. Both communities thus depend on each other and must keep the peace.[28] Such symbiotic economic relationships are rare, and in other places economic competition may add to communal tensions. In recent times the spread of anomie in some important towns has led to terrible Muslim pogroms. The tragedy of Ahmadabad in 2002 is a case in point. Earlier Ahmadabad was the home of a thriving cotton textile industry and of the famous textile labour union founded by Mahatma Gandhi. The decline of the mills and the rise of the powerlooms which is discussed in Chapter 7 ruined this industry as well as the labour union which had promoted the solidarity of workers and had provided a social infrastructure in this large city. The decentralized operation of power-looms had emerged in other towns whereas the unemployed remained in the city. Ahmadabad was thus affected by an anomie which destroyed its moral fibre. It succumbed to an orgy of violence abetted by the government and a police which made no attempt to restore law and order.[29] Surat, another large city in Gujarat, was affected by a similar anomie. This city had grown very rapidly. It never had big mills or factories but was crowded with power looms and diamond-cutting workshops. The workers of this 'informal' industry received low wages and slept in hovels, often taking turns in using the same bed. Most of them were bachelors or had left their families in their villages. Without stable social relations they were easy prey for riotmongers.[30]

In most communal riots the Muslims were on the receiving end and generally many more Muslims than Hindus died as a result. But, of course, the Muslims are not a meek community and there are also riotmongers among them. There may even be a convergence of riot production in some places. Solapur, the old textile city in southern Maharashtra, experienced such a convergence in October 2002.[31] In earlier years, Muslims had often pelted Hindu processions with stones and provoked them in many other ways. Congress politicians had then always seen to it that no action was taken against the Muslims. The Hindus had resented this; now, under the influence of the pogrom in Ahmadabad, some Hindu leaders also planned to 'teach the Muslims a lesson' in Solapur. But the riot was ignited by the Muslim editor of a small local newspaper who reported the derogatory remarks made about Muhammad by a Christian preacher in America and combined this with a call for a protest demonstration in Solapur. A Muslim mob then attacked Hindu temples and destroyed some houses. A noted Hindu leader was killed by the rioters. However, at the same time Hindus also took to the streets and destroyed many Muslim shops and homes. The police were not as inactive as in Ahmadabad, but nor did they do a good job. They shot at the wrong people and did not act decisively in places where they should have done so.

In order to cope with communal violence, the new coalition government which emerged from the elections of 2004 drafted a Communal Violence (Suppression) Bill which was submitted to the Indian parliament in 2005. This bill was criticized by human rights activists because it included draconion measures and gave too much power to central government and the army. Critics also pointed out that the measures proposed were only aimed at controlling riots once they had broken out, but did not address their need for their prevention. In some places communal peace committees established by concerned police officers and including important members of both communities had helped to prevent riots.[32] Providing a framework for the activities of such committees should have been a major aim of legislative proposals.

The dark clouds of communal violence will not disappear in the near future, but it is a hopeful sign that the organizations of an emerging civil society in India have taken an active interest in monitoring and preventing this kind of violence. The People's Union for Civil Liberties (PUCL) is the foremost organization of this type. It was founded in 1976 when Indira Gandhi's 'Emergency' threatened civil liberties. After the fall of her government, civil liberties were restored and PUCL remained dormant for some time. It was revived in 1980 and has remained active ever since. Its members have often shown great courage in going to the very centres of violence in order to ascertain the facts, to combat rumours and to lay the blame on those who deserve it. PUCL is proud of its independence. It is exclusively financed by its own members and does not accept funds from sources in India or abroad. The dedication of this organization to upholding the values of Indian democracy is admirable. It has set an example for other organizations of this kind. The men and women who are active in this field support the growth of civil society in India.

Building the Indian nation is a continuous process which needs the support of all Indians. The heritage of the freedom movement and of its dedicated leaders provides the nation with a fund of values and ideals on which future generations can draw, but they must be reminded of it by the activists of the present generation who live by these values.

CHAPTER 2

THE EMERGENCE OF NATIONAL COALITIONS

The 'Congress System'

The Indian National Congress was originally not a political party but a national forum representing all political interests. Its internal organization reflected the evolution of the Indian freedom movement and in the early years this organization was rather loose and rudimentary. After its first session in Mumbai in 1885, the second congress was held in Kolkata in 1886 with subsequent sessions being hosted by all the major cities of India. The local reception committee arranged the annual congress and selected its president whose main duty was to deliver an inaugural address. The delegates who represented their localities were elected at informal meetings. It was only when 'Moderates' and 'Extremists' clashed and the Extremists tried to overwhelm the annual congress by packing it with their supporters that the All-India Congress Committee (AICC) was established in 1908 as a conference of a limited number of delegates properly elected by their provincial associations.[1] This body still exists today and deliberates on the policies to be adopted by the party.

When Mahatma Gandhi took over the leadership of the National Congress in 1920, he revamped its constitution and added a small working committee which could meet at short notice so as to conduct agitational campaigns efficiently. This was the cabinet of the Congress president, nominated by him.[2] Following the earlier tradition, the Congress president held his office only for one year. (Gandhi himself held it just once, in 1924.) Another important step taken by Gandhi in 1920 was the reorganization of the Provincial Congress Committees which had reflected the boundaries of British Indian provinces. He replaced them with 'linguistic provinces' so that each committee could use its regional language. Gandhi insisted that the message of the freedom movement should be conveyed to the people in their own language and not in English, which only the elite could understand.

Gandhi was not interested in the constitutional reforms introduced by the British. To him the Congress as reorganized by him was the national parliament. However, when Congress conducted an election campaign and accepted office under the Government of India Act of 1935 it had to do so as a political party and Gandhi had to agree to this. Nevertheless, when India attained independence, Gandhi recommended that the National Congress should be dissolved or converted into a social service organization.[3] This advice was not followed; on the contrary, Nehru and the other Congress leaders gladly preserved this powerful organization. No other decolonized country inherited a party machine with thousands of political activists, many of whom had spent years in jail for their participation in national campaigns. This dedicated personnel would serve Congress well for another two decades after independence had been achieved.

The 'Congress system' – as it was called by many political analysts – occupied the centre of the political arena for quite some time. It dominated not only the federal government but also the governments of all federal states. The Representation of the People Act of 1951 introduced universal adult suffrage and reconfirmed the majority election system and it was within this framework that the Congress Party won the general elections of 1952, 1957 and 1962. Until 1971, elections for the central parliament (Lok Sabha) and the state assemblies were held simultaneously, which helped to stabilize the Congress system. Members of parliament were carried to victory on the shoulders of the assembly candidates whose constituencies were smaller and who were closer to the people. They were in the forefront of the election campaign. Opposition candidates or independents actually helped the Congress candidates by splitting the vote and thus confirming the central position of Congress.

Under Nehru's leadership, the Congress Party was very active in parliament and was not challenged by a powerful opposition. Nehru attended most sessions of parliament and frequently intervened in the debates. In his time, parliament was in session for about 120 days every year, but in recent years this has unfortunately declined to about 80 days.[4] This is in striking contrast with the British Parliament or the American House of Representatives, which have even more sessions every year than the Indian parliament had in the 1950s. In India, parliamentary debates have become less important. The passing of legislation prepared by the respective departments of government has become the major business of parliament.

Nehru was an astute political strategist. After winning the elections of 1952 he steered a leftist course in order to undercut both communists and socialists. Nehru had been a socialist in the days of the freedom struggle, but in 1948 the socialists had left the National Congress. Accordingly they were in opposition to Nehru and his party, so Nehru had to steal their thunder. Guided by him, in 1955 the Congress Party even passed a resolution recommending joint collective farming. This alarmed the peasantry and the Swatantra Party, which was founded to represent their interests, scored some successes. Nehru promptly veered to the right and nothing was heard of collective farming any more.[5] As long as he was at the helm, the system remained basically unchallenged. His successor, Lal Bahadur Shastri, who took over after Nehru's death in May 1964, could probably have saved the system. Initially regarded as a weak man, he gained in stature when he won the war which Pakistan had forced upon him in 1965. But he died attending the peace conference at Tashkent in January 1966. At this stage a 'syndicate' of regional Congress leaders emerged who were jealous of each other. As they could not agree on a candidate from their ranks, they opted for Nehru's daughter, Indira Gandhi, whom everybody regarded as a weak compromise candidate. Nobody knew that she was an iron lady who would soon show her mettle.

The elections of 1967 which she had to face soon after assuming office revealed cracks in the system. By then, some of the Congress stalwarts who had become chief ministers of federal states after independence had died. Some of their states were captured by opposition parties in 1967 while Congress retained its position in parliament (Lok Sabha) with a narrow margin. Simultaneous elections had obviously outlived their usefulness and Indira Gandhi broke the link in 1971 by holding earlier elections for parliament which otherwise would not have been due until 1972. She conducted the election campaign as a kind of personal plebiscite and won by a large margin.[6] She was then at the zenith of her power and gained even greater glory by winning the war of December 1971 which Pakistan had precipitated. But then her luck left her and the Congress system disintegrated. As she was unable to install reliable and competent followers as chief ministers, she often used the instrument of 'President's Rule' in order to get rid of recalcitrant state governments. This instrument actually derived from the old emergency powers of the British Viceroy which were transferred to the President by the Indian Constitution of 1950. The President can dismiss a state government on the advice of the Prime Minister if the governor of the state reports that it has become 'ungovernable'. Since the governor is appointed by central government, he normally does what is expected of him. After the state government has been dismissed, new elections have to be held within six months, but the performance can be repeated if the central government is not pleased with the result. The Congress system had depended on a proper balance of centre–state relations; the abuse of President's Rule contributed to its demise.

In 1975 Indira Gandhi took a further step in the wrong direction: she practically imposed President's Rule also at the level of the central government. Of course, she did not do this so that the President might dismiss her, but in order to continue in office with emergency powers. This enabled her to postpone the elections which would have been due in 1976. She imprisoned the leaders of opposition parties and then suddenly announced that elections were to be held in March 1977. For this she had to release the leaders of the opposition but she felt confident that they could not organize a successful election campaign at short notice. In this she was mistaken. These leaders decided to break the Congress system by seeing to it that in each constituency only one opposition candidate would face the Congress candidate. Their strategy worked and Congress was defeated with a vengeance. Indira Gandhi was taken aback; she had not expected this at all. Her intelligence service, which should have warned her, had become so used to the fact that only positive news was acceptable to her that it had not dared to report anything else. She did manage to capture power again in the election of 1980, but with the benefit of hindsight one can assert that the Congress system ended in 1977 and that the era of coalition governments began at that time.

The Rise of the Regional Parties

The first regional party that managed to gain power in one of India's federal states was the Communist Party of India which won the elections in Kerala in 1957 under the leadership of E.M.S. Namboodiripad. Of course, the Communist Party thought of itself as a national party and would have liked to come to power in India, not just in a small state. Its success in Kerala was due to the fact that this state was a new creation and that it had never been part of the Congress system. Its main components were the princely states of Travancore and Cochin in which Congress had not been able to operate before independence. Communism had spread there as a clandestine movement. When Namboodiripad was once asked how he had become a communist, he said that it was due to the influence of Jawaharal Nehru who had spread Marxist ideas in India in the late 1920s.[7] The princely states had acceded to India after independence, but they had first been governed separately. It was only when the States Reorganization Commission of 1955, which will be discussed in the next chapter, had recommended the creation of a linguistic state for the south Indian language Malayalam that Kerala came into its own. In addition to the two former princely states, the Malabar District which belonged to the state of Madras was allotted to Kerala because the language of this dictrict is also Malayalam. The new state was a patchwork and it would have been difficult for any party to penetrate it, but the Communist Party had well-trained cadres who worked hard to spread their message. Moreover, that state had the highest rate of literacy in India and the works of Karl Marx had been translated into Malayalam as early as 1903, the earliest translation of his work into any Indian language.

Namboodiripad introduced land reforms and a reform of the education system. He thus alienated vested interests and this led to protest movements. Nehru then resorted to President's Rule and dismissed Namboodiripad's government.[8] Namboodiripad was deeply disappointed in his former mentor. The communist experiment in Kerala seemed to be doomed, but the party retained its influence as a regional party in later years. Playing a game of musical chairs with the Congress Party, the communists managed to recapture power again and again. In the assembly elections of 2006 they triumphed and their veteran leader V.S. Achuthanandan, now 82 years old, became chief minister. The Kerala experiment was repeated in West Bengal where a Left Front led by the communists captured power in 1977 and has retained it ever since. After the assembly elections of April/May 2006 Chief Minister Buddhadeb Bhattacharjee formed the seventh Left Front government of the state.

A completely different type of regional party emerged in Madras (Tamil Nadu). The Justice Party as the political wing of a non-Brahmin movement had been very active in the Madras presidency under British rule. Its name was changed to Dravida Kazhagam in 1944 at the instance of E.V.R. Naicker. While his enthusiasm for a united nation of all speakers of Dravidian languages was not shared by the other Dravidian language groups, it was popular among the speakers of Tamil who were proud of their ancient literary heritage and rejected 'Hindi imperialism'. Naicker had recruited a charismatic young leader, Dr C.N. Annadurai, who later became known as 'Anna' (elder brother) to the people. Anna parted company with Naicker in 1949 and started his own party, the Dravida Munnetra Kazhagam (DMK: *Munnetra* = Progress). Initially he too advocated the secession of the 'Dravidas' from the Indian Union. But when a wave of national fervour swept India after the border war with China in 1962 and the central government banned secessionist parties, Anna renounced secessionism. The Indian constitution of 1950 had stipulated that Hindi would become the national language throughout India after a transitional period of fifteen years. Thus in 1965 the Congress government of Madras enforced this rule which provoked riots. Anna and his party were in the forefront of the Tamil protest movement. The central government relented and a triumphant Anna won the state elections of 1967 by a large margin. The state of Madras was renamed Tamil Nadu. Regional pride had come into its own. But Anna enjoyed his victory only for two years. His death was a blow to his party and his successor, M. Karunanidhi, soon had to face another election, in 1971. He was supported by a popular actor, M. G. Ramachandran (MGR); however, this hero of the Tamil cinema did not want to remain in

Karunanidhi's shadow and stepped into the political limelight after splitting the party in 1972. In 1976 he gave his new party the flamboyant name All-India Anna Dravida Munnetra Kazhagam (AIADMK), 'All-India' indicating that the party wanted to be part of the national scene. By including 'Anna' in the name, MGR stole a march on Karunanidhi, Anna's successor. The two parties attacked each other ferociously until in 1977 MGR finally displaced Karunanidhi, who then had to remain in the political wilderness for thirteen years.

MGR patronized a young favourite, Jayalalitha Jayaram, who then emerged triumphant from the rather fierce struggle for the succession after MGR died in 1987. She defeated Karunanidhi in 1991 after his comeback in 1989. Rajiv Gandhi was assassinated in 1991 when he was conducting an election campaign in Tamil Nadu and it soon appeared that the Liberation Tigers of Tamil Eelam (LTTE) had murdered him. Karunanidhi was supposed to be close to the LTTE and Jayalalitha was able to profit from the wave of sympathy for the slain leader which swept the country. As Chief Minister of Tamil Nadu from 1991 to 1996 she followed the AIADMK tradition of siding with Congress in national affairs. In 1996 she was defeated by Karunanidhi. As an opposition leader controlling several seats in parliament (Lok Sabha) she supported the coalition led by the Bharatiya Janata Party (BJP) in 1998. Prime Minister Vajpayee had a tough time gaining her support and could never be sure of it: in 1999 she toppled his government by withdrawing her support. Having betrayed the BJP coalition which returned to power in 1999, she had created an opening for Karunanidhi, whose DMK now supported Vajpayee. In 2001 the DMK lost the state assembly elections and Jayalalitha returned to power. She had Karunanidhi arrested, further aggravating the tension between the two rival parties. When the Congress-led national coalition government came to power in 2004, Karunanidhi and his DMK supported it. In the run-up to the assembly elections of May 2006 in Tamil Nadu, there were further complications in the political game. Vaiko (V. Gopalaswamy), the leader of a splinter party, the MDMK (Marularchi DMK) was dissatisfied with the seat-sharing arrangement with the DMK and struck a better deal with Jayalalitha. Nevertheless, the DMK were successful in the assembly elections. Karunanidhi, now 82 years old, triumphed once more, this time to lead a DMK–Congress coalition government. Changing tack was a favourite game of the Tamil rivals. Those in power in New Delhi could always find an ally in Tamil Nadu: which of the two parties was available depended on the intricacies of Tamil politics.

The other centre of Dravidian regional assertiveness is Andhra Pradesh, once part of the state of Madras. The Telugu-speakers of Andhra Pradesh did not necessarily love their Tamil neighbours who had been favoured under British rule, the more so as the larger part of the Telugu area was a princely state under the Nizam of Hyderabad. As will be explained in the next chapter, the Telugus were the prime movers in the reoganization of the Indian states. After they had got what they wanted they remained for a long time fairly reliable supporters of the Congress system. Even after Indira Gandhi had been defeated in the 1977 elections to parliament (Lok Sabha), they voted for a Congress government in Andhra Pradesh in 1978. The record of this government was dismal: chief ministers were changed almost annually due to rivalries in the state and among the central leadership.

In 1982, only a few months before elections were due, the famous movie star N. T. Rama Rao (NTR) founded a new party which he named Telugu Desam (Telugu Land), thus emphasizing regional pride. This party swept to victory in the polls in 1983. Some Congress politicians now joined the new party, among them NTR's son-in-law, Chandrababu Naidu. Indira Gandhi, who had returned to power in New Delhi in 1980, resented the rise of the Telugu Desam Party (TDP) and used the old instrument of President's Rule to dismiss NTR. She did not get away with it. A Congress chief minister had been installed, but NTR had convinced the courts: Rao won his case. This gave him more political clout and he could complete his term. But in the state assembly elections of 1988 the pendulum swung back and the Congress Party was returned to power. By the time the next elections were due, an ex-chief minister of Andhra Pradesh, P.V. Narasimha Rao, was Prime Minister of India. He vigorously campaigned in his home state, but Congress was nevertheless defeated and NTR returned to power. In the years when he was out of power, NTR had married again. His second wife was a young woman who had been writing his biography. His family rebelled against the 'stepmother' who gained increasing political influence. Chandrababu Naidu led this rebellion and over-threw NTR in a 'palace revolution'. The majority of the TDP members of the assembly sided with Naidu and he became Chief Minister in 1995. NTR died a tragic hero in 1996, betrayed by his own party. For his part, Naidu proved to be a consummate politician. He acted as a kingmaker in national politics in 1996 and in 1998 the TDP won the majority of parliamentary seats in Andhra Pradesh. Naidu decided to support the BJP-led coalition from 'outside'. For a while he appeared to be the rising star in Indian politics. He championed information technology and even impressed a visiting Bill Gates with his methods of e-governance. But in the elections of 2004, which in Andhra Pradesh happened to coincide with the parliamentary elections, Congress swept the board at the polls and the TDP was reduced to a humble minority. It remains to be seen whether Naidu can stage a comeback in 2009.

Maharashtra, Andhra Pradesh's neighbour, had also been a stronghold of the Congress Party for a long time. It never produced a party comparable to the TDP, but a rather maverick regional party emerged in the great metropolis of Bombay (Mumbai). It was founded by Balasaheb Thakeray, a journalist and cartoonist, in 1966 and adopted the name Shiv Sena (Army of Shiva). This was a reference to the great Maratha king, Shivaji, but it could also be taken as referring to the Hindu god Shiva. Mumbai is the most cosmopolitan city of India, but it is troubled by a combination of ethnic and class conflicts. The city is the capital of Maharashtra, but the Marathi-speakers who live in that city are mostly workers whereas business and industry is controlled by Gujarati-speakers. Moreover, many south Indians from Tamil Nadu and Kerala flocked into the city and competed for jobs with the Marathi-speakers. This provided much scope for the xenophobic propaganda of the Shiv Sena, which became notorious for the *Bandhs* (stopping all traffic and business in the city), which the Party organized. It was certainly a political force to reckon with, but for a long time was unable to make a mark in state politics because its influence did not reach beyond the city limits. In 1995, however, it formed an alliance with the Bharatiya Janata Party and ruled the state until 1999. The Shiv Sena hoped to stage a comeback in the 2004 assembly elections but was defeated, while in the parallel parliamentary elections of that year the number of its seats was reduced from 15 to 12. Having participated in the BJP-led national coalition it now shared its fate. As Thakeray is getting old and infirm and his heirs are at loggerheads, the Shiv Sena does not seem to have a bright future.

In northern India the Samajwadi Party emerged to be for some time the most powerful regional party, dominating India's biggest state, Uttar Pradesh. Samajwadi means 'socialist' and the party has claimed the heritage of earlier socialist parties of India which have long since disappeared from the political arena. Mulayam Singh Yadav, leader of the Samajwadi Party, is an old socialist, but his main asset is that he is a Yadav and thus belongs to the large community of the 'Other Backward Castes' (OBC) which has become very prominent in north Indian politics in recent years. Yadav is a typical representative of the first post-independence generation of Indian politicians. As a young man he was influenced by the Socialist leader, Dr Ram Manohar Lohia. In 1967, the year of his mentor's death, Yadav became a member of the Uttar Pradesh legislative assembly when he was just 28 years old. Ten years later he became a member of the cabinet of that state. For many years he led the Lok Dal (People's Party) of his state which later merged with the Janata Party. In 1989 he became Chief Minister of Uttar Pradesh for the first time and in 1992 he founded the Samajwadi Party. As its leader he once more became Chief Minister from 1993 to 1995. In the brief period of the National Front coalition government he served as Union Minister of Defence from 1996 to 1998. He retained his seat in parliament (Lok Sabha) in 1999 and 2004, but returned to state politics in 2003, serving his third term as Chief Minister of Uttar Pradesh. At the parliamentary elections of 2004, the Samajwadi Party captured 35 seats in Uttar Pradesh and was thus the largest regional party represented in the national parliament, next only to the Communist Party of India (Marxist) which won 43 seats. Unlike the Telugu Desam Party, which is by definition limited to its home state, the Samajwadi Party also fielded candidates in 22 other states, although with hardly any success: it won only one seat in the new neighbouring state of Uttar Anchal. Critics said that Yadav had indulged in a game of vote-splitting by putting up 237 candidates nationwide. In the Uttar Pradesh assembly, which has 403 seats, the Samajwadi Party had increased its strength from 110 in 1996 to 146 in 2002, but in 2007 it suffered a crushing defeat at the hands of the Bahujan Samaj Party (BSP), which gained 207 seats whereas the Samajwadi Party won only 99 seats. Mulayam was replaced by Mayawati (BSP) as Chief Minister. Her rise is discussed in Chapter 12 in the context of Dalit (Untouchable) politics. The Samajwadi Party's sudden decline was due to several factors. First of all, there was the usual swing against the incumbent so often noted in elections, but the party had also lost its hold on some groups which had earlier supported it to the hilt. The Muslims who constitute 16 per cent of the population of Uttar Pradesh had earlier voted for the Samajwadi Party. In the 2007 election only 21 Muslim candidates were elected on the Samajwadi ticket as against 29 fielded by the BSP. It seems that some of the OBC also deserted Mulayam and turned to Mayawati. By now Mulayam appears to be a spent force in Indian politics and would find it difficult to stage a comeback.

In Bihar another Yadav ruled the roost for a long time: Lalu Prasad Yadav. Although both Yadavs have followed a very similar political course, they have always been rivals. Lalu is about eight years younger than Mulayam. He started his political career early, being elected to parliament (Lok Sabha) when he was only 29 years old. In 1990 he became Chief Minister of Bihar but had to relinquish this office when he was accused of massive corruption. The poor of Bihar nevertheless adored him and he was able to get away with installing his illiterate wife as Chief Minister in his place in 1997. In the same year he broke with his party, the Janata Dal (People's Party), and founded the Rashtriya Janata Dal (National People's Party) which later emerged as the main ally of the Congress Party in 2004, having won 21 parliamentary seats. He was rewarded with the important post of Union Railway Minister. But in the state assembly elections of 2005 the Bharatiya Janata Party managed to defeat the Rashtriya Janata Dal. It remains to be seen whether Lalu will be able to stage a comeback some time in the future. Since he is an irrepressible populist, however, he may very well bounce back.

The two Yadav-led regional parties of northern India represent the new type of low-caste social base of mass politics. They are in opposition to the Bharatiya Janata Party which originally had a north Indian upper-caste base and to that extent was also a regional party. It has played the Hindu card to appeal to a wider national solidarity and has done so with considerable success. However, in its main stronghold, Uttar Pradesh, it has recently suffered a severe setback. From 174 assembly seats in 1996, to 100 in 2002, its number of seats then dropped to 51 in 2007. Playing the Hindu card has obviously lost some of its attractions and was by no means a new game. It had been invented by a radical nationalist, V.D. Savarkar, who wrote his manifesto *Hindutva* in 1923. The term 'Hindutva' (Hinduness) was coined by him. He stressed that 'Hindu' originally referred to the people living beyond the Indus River and was thus not a religious but a national epithet. Nevertheless, his interpretation of the term tended to exclude Muslims and Christians. Savarkar emphasized the solidarity of all Hindus and rejected the caste system. In his time, his ideas were far too radical to attract a large following, but in recent years, the BJP has projected Hindutva as its ideology and it has become synonymous with Hindu nationalism. Accordingly the BJP has tried to transcend the limits of a north Indian regional party and has become a national party. However, its recent decline in its former regional stronghold of Uttar Pradesh may not augur well for its prospects as a national party.

In north-western India, the Punjab and Kashmir have been dominated for a long time by two regional parties which in addition to their regional identity are also characterized by a particular type of religious affiliation: the Akali Dal of the Sikhs and the National Conference of the Kashmiri Muslims. The Akali Dal (Eternal Party) is an offspring of the Shiromani Gurdwara Prabandhak Committee (SGPC) which campaigned under British rule for the right of the Sikhs to control their own houses of worship (*gurdwara*). This campaign was successful and the SGPC gained a great deal of influence in Punjabi politics. The partition of India cut right through the region in which the Sikhs lived. Those who were left in Pakistan fled to the Indian East Punjab. Their feeling of deprivation was enhanced by the loss of positions in the army, in which they had wielded considerable influence under British rule. In independent India, this privileged position of one community could no longer be maintained. The Sikhs now demanded a 'Panjabi Subah' , a linguistic state of their own: they could not claim a Sikh state as this would have been repugnant to the principles of the Indian constitution. In 1966 Indira Gandhi did grant a Panjabi Subah by separating the Hindi-speaking South Punjab which was then named Haryana. But the new state Punjab also included Punjabi-speaking Hindus; the Sikhs had a narrow majority in it. The Akali Dal emerged as the party of the Sikhs, but there were also Sikhs in the Congress Party and thus the Akali Dal could not become the dominant party in this state. Radical Sikhs then lobbied for 'Khalistan', a religious state of the Sikhs, and this could only mean secession from India. Indira Gandhi, who had played a game of divide and rule in the Punjab, finally sent in the army to crush the secessionists. She lost her life as a result of this decision. The secessionists were defeated, but Indira Gandhi was shot by her Sikh bodyguards. In subsequent years the Punjab was pacified and the Akali Dal played the role of a democratic regional party. As such it is still of importance.

The National Conference of Kashmir is another regional party with a religious affiliation. It was started by Sheikh Abdullah, the 'Lion of Kashmir', as 'Muslim Conference' in the 1930s. In 1938 he met Nehru and became his friend as they were both inspired by socialist ideas. Abdullah then changed the name of his party to 'National Conference'. Its main aim was the struggle against the autocratic rule of the Maharaja of Kashmir. The Maharaja played a dubious role at the time when India attained independence: he had toyed with the idea of an independent Kashmir and delayed signing the treaty of accession to India – or Pakistan. When threatened by Pakistan, he had appealed to India, but he had to accede to Indian control in order to get this help. Abdullah had a tough time as he organized the defence of Kashmir but was still opposed to the rule of the Maharaja. The National Conference then emerged as the leading party of the state and the Maharaja appointed Abdullah as Prime Minister. In this role Abdullah introduced a land reform which benefited the peasants, who then looked upon the National Conference as their party. Abdullah saw to it that the Maharaja abdicated in all but name in 1949, when the Maharaja's son, Karan Singh, became governor of the state. Kashmir was given special status and Abdullah could be satisfied with his political achievements. However, he espoused the idea of an independent Kashmir and was deposed and imprisoned by his erstwhile friend Jawaharlal Nehru.

After 1953 the National Conference was headed by various politicians who were regarded as stooges of the Indian government. Shortly before his death, Nehru released Abdullah and even entrusted him with conducting talks with the government of Pakistan. These plans died with Nehru. Abdullah then made a pilgrimage to Mecca and during further travels met the Chinese Prime Minister, Chou En-lai, in Algeria in 1965, a move which incensed the Indian government. Abdullah was held again and placed under house arrest in a south Indian hill resort at a safe distance from Kashmir – and from Chou En-lai. Indira Gandhi then released him in 1968 and concluded a 'Kashmir Accord' with him in 1975, after which she made him Chief Minister of his state. She had tamed the 'Lion', who could come into his own only in 1977 when she was no longer in power. His National Conference scored a big success in the state elections and Abdullah ruled the state until his death in 1982. He was succeeded by his son, Dr Faruq Abdullah, a physician who had practised in London and was not at all prepared for the new role which he had to play at home. Fearing Indira Gandhi, who was back in power, he looked for support among other chief ministers who headed regional parties. In 1983 the National Conference won the assembly elections. Nevertheless, Indira Gandhi dismissed Faruq Abdullah in 1984 shortly before she was murdered.

Rajiv Gandhi tried to befriend Abdullah and agreed to an electoral alliance with the National Conference. Unfortunately the heavily rigged elections of 1987 marked the end of democracy in Kashmir, which was soon plunged into an orgy of violence. The Indian government could control the situation only by placing Kashmir practically under military rule. When the Soviets withdrew from Afghanistan in 1989, many unemployed freedom fighters from Afghanistan shifted their operations to Kashmir. Moreover, after Rajiv Gandhi's defeat in 1989, Indian politics were paralysed for quite some time and it was only in 1996 that assembly elections were held once more in Kashmir: these were won by the National Conference, returning Faruq Abdullah to power. In 1998 the National Conference became a partner of the BJP-led coalition government in New Delhi and Faruq's son, Omar, become a minister of state in that government. When in 2002 new elections were held in Kashmir, Omar led the National Conference and it was expected that this party would win. After all, it still had a strong following among the Kashmiri peasants and was a member of the national coalition. Surprisingly the Congress Party, in alliance with a new party, the People's Democratic Party (PDP), made a clean sweep at the polls. This time the elections had been free and fair. The new government headed by Mufti Mohammmed Sayeed (PDP) gave new hope to the suffering people of Kashmir. He remained Chief Minister only until 2005 due to the prior agreement that Gulam Nabi Azad, the leader of the Congress Party in the state, should succeed him during the second half of the term. The transition went smoothly, which showed that the Congress Party had become adept at coalition politics. It had obtained more seats in the assembly than the PDP and had yielded the first innings to the junior party of the coalition.

The 'Far East' of India has also produced a remarkable regional party, the Asom Gana Parishad (Assam People's Conference). Assam had been a rather unwieldy multi-ethnic province of British India. In independent India several hill tribes had been granted federal states of their own, such as Nagaland. The fertile plains of Assam, however, had attracted many immigrants over the years. Since the emergence of Bangladesh, there has been a veritable overflow of its population into the Assam plains. Faced with Bengali competition, the local Assamese had started a xenophobic movement which could be compared to the Shiv Sena of Mumbai. The spearhead of this movement was an association of Assamese students with whose leader, Prafulla Mahanta, Rajiv Gandhi negotiated the 'Assam Accord' in 1985, thus putting an end to a violent agitation. Mahanta became Chief Minister of Assam in 1986. His party, Asom Gana Parishad (AGP), became the main rival of the Congress Party in this state. Initially, the AGP was allied with some small leftist parties, but in 2001 Mahanta suddenly turned around and forged an alliance with the BJP, a move which created a stir both in his own party and in the BJP. Some AGP members left the party and joined the Congress Party. The BJP in Assam split, giving birth to a new party, the Asom BJP. The Congress Party profited from these upheavals. Four years later, Mahanta was expelled from the AGP and started a new party, the AGP (Progressive). While he seemed to be interested in reviving his cooperation with leftist parties, they had not yet forgotten his flirtation with the BJP.

The kaleidoscopic twists of the pattern formed by regional parties in India are rather confusing, but these parties have become an important element of Indian democracy. The struggle for power and patronage has percolated down from the national to the regional level such that Indian nationalists often speak of 'fissiparous' tendencies when commenting on this development. But most of these parties have no interest in disrupting the Indian Union. That they actually provide a new dynamism to political life has been shown by their increasing share of seats in parliament (Lok Sabha). An Indian political analyst has asserted that in recent years even in parliamentary elections the voters have behaved as if they were choosing their state government. If one includes the two communist parties among the regional parties and compares the shares which all regional parties had in the national vote and in the number of parliamentary seats, one sees that in the elections of 1984, 1989 and 1991 the regional parties were still under-represented as they obtained more or less one third of the national vote and captured only one fifth of the seats. However, this changed in the elections of 1996 and 1998 when they received a higher share of the votes, 39 and 44 per cent respectively, and gained the same percentage of seats, a trend which continued in the elections of 2004 when these regional parties captured 47 per cent of the seats. When nearly half of the parliamentary seats are occupied by representatives of regional parties, coalition politics is inevitable. According to political science textbooks, the majority election system should produce a two-party system with no scope for coalitions, whereas proportional representation would always produce coalition governments. The process of the political transformation of India has followed a different course. Starting out as a system of one-party dominance the party regime has gradually shifted to a pattern of coalition governments closely resembling that which would have emerged from proportional representation. There are by now two national parties which get about a quarter of the vote each and similar shares of the seats. This leads to the formation of coalition governments which are headed by a major party and supported by a plethora of small parties. Some of this support may be given from the 'outside' by parties which hesitate to enter a coalition. In view of the plurality of political forces in India this system must be accepted as an adequate reflection of Indian democracy.

Improvisation is a characteristic feature of all aspects of Indian life and is also true of Indian democracy. There is a general lack of the institutionalization of the party system. Election of the office-bearers of the parties is rare with nomination by the party leadership often being preferred, and patronage playing a central role. Candidates are usually expected to cover a large part of their election expenditure to the national parliament or the state assemblies themselves – and these elections are expensive affairs. According to some estimates the parliamentary elections of 2004 cost Rs 13 billion (about US$ 290 million). This contributes to the stability of governments because the candidates would dread elections at short intervals. Cynics may scoff at this political game, but with all its drawbacks it has proved very resilient. Emerging political forces have been accommodated more or less smoothly. Violent clashes of interests have been avoided and the legitimacy of the state has been maintained. The rise of coalition governments fits into this pattern of political accommodation.

The Emergence of National Coalitions

The first national coalition government was the one headed by Prime Minister Morarji Desai in 1977. Some of its members were Congress dissidents like Desai himself, who had been Indira Gandhi's Deputy Prime Minister until she dismissed him in 1969. But there were also the two socialist parties and the right-wing Bharatiya Jan Sangh as it was called at that time. Having broken the 'Congress system' by putting up only one candidate against the Congress candidate in each constituency, the new coalition transformed itself into a party, the Janata Party (People's Party), so as to build a proper two-party system. However, there was a great deal of distrust in this new party. Democracy within the party was conspicuous by its absence. No elections of the office-holders of the party were ever held and everyone else was afraid of the cadres of the Jan Sangh who might get the upper hand in such elections. Nevertheless, Desai was proud of heading a unified party. When asked whether his government was not just a replica of the rather tenuous coalition governments which had been formed in several Indian states after the elections of 1967, he stressed that the Janata Party was now a united party. Desai was a competent administrator. He had been a district officer under British rule and had left the service in order to join Gandhi. He often mentioned that he regretted ever having served the colonial masters, but when asked whether he had not acquired his administrative skills while serving them, he had to admit that this was true.[9] Desai was a stern taskmaster rather than a skilful politician and resigned in 1979 when the Janata Party disintegrated. The party's name was then inherited by a smaller party which valiantly tried to oppose the Congress Party after its return to power. Its name was also appropriated by the Bharatiya Janata Party, which did not revert to its earlier name.

The next attempt at coalition building was made even before the elections of 1989. V.P. Singh, who had been first Finance Minister and then Defence Minister in Rajiv Gandhi's government, parted company with him and then engineered a campaign aimed at defeating the Congress Party. He forged electoral alliances for this purpose, trying to repeat the strategy which had proved so successful in 1977. In this process he yielded a large number of seats to the BJP which would not be contested by any other candidate standing against the incumbent Congress member. In this way he greatly aided the rise of the BJP which had won only two seats in 1984 but gained 86 in 1989. However, when V.P. Singh formed a minority government after defeating Gandhi, the BJP did not join his coalition but supported his government from the outside; so did the communists. In suspended animation between these two poles, Singh's government could not survive for long. The BJP withdrew its support and an even more precarious minority government led by Chandrashekar, a former Socialist, replaced Singh's government in 1990. This government was supported by the Congress Party from the outside, which then withdrew its support when it felt confident of winning an election in 1991.

The Congress Party had remained opposed to coalition politics because it had hoped to regain its central position but in this it narrowly failed and had to form a minority government under Prime Minister P.V. Narasimha Rao. This government attained a majority of seats in the course of its term of office by attracting some splinter parties. When Rao lost the elections of 1996, Congress was still the biggest party and he could have remained in power by forming a coalition government. But true to the old Congress policy of avoiding coalitions, he did not do so and left it to the BJP to make an attempt at coalition building. When this attempt failed a third force emerged. As mentioned earlier, the regional parties had come into their own in this election and they formed a 'National Front' which depended on outside support from the Congress Party. The National Front looked for a leader among the chief ministers. Jyoti Basu, the Communist Chief Minister of West Bengal, would have been an appropriate candidate, but his party did not permit him to accept the offer. Chandrababu Naidu, who had just come to power in Andhra Pradesh, had not yet consolidated his position there and did not want to become Prime Minister at this stage. So the job had to be taken by the relatively unknown Chief Minister of Karnataka, H.V. Deve Gowda. After barely a year in office he clashed with the leadership of the Congress Party, which withdrew its support. However, there was no intention of precipitating an election. Election expenditure involves enormous amounts – often large donations of 'black money' – and the party coffers had been emptied at the time of the last election. The National Front was therefore asked to replace Deve Gowda with another prime minister. Naidu acted as the kingmaker and saw to it that the External Affairs Minister, Inder Kumar Gujral, took on the job. Gujral was a man of integrity and had a great deal of experience as a minister in the central cabinet, but he did not have the political clout of a leader in state politics. Moreover, he was at the mercy of the Congress Party, which withdrew its support yet again in 1998.

This time coalition building got into full swing. The BJP as a right-wing party was not squeamish about coalitions, as the Congress Party still was, and did not scruple to invite anybody to join a 'coalition of the willing'. It had narrowly missed the boat in 1996 but in 1998 it was at the peak of its electoral success, winning 25.6 per cent of the national vote and 182 parliamentary seats.[10] Since this was not enough to form a government, it therefore offered attractive terms to coalition partners by restricting the number of its own cabinet ministers and offering important ministries to its allies. As mentioned earlier, Jayalalitha and her AIADMK were of crucial importance in this respect. She first supported and then toppled Prime Minister Vajpayee. At this stage Sonia Gandhi, the new President of the Congress Party, could have made a bold move, constructing an alternative coalition. Sonia, the widow of Rajiv Gandhi, had initially avoided the political limelight. An Italian by birth she was branded a 'foreigner' by Hindu nationalists. However, Congress politicians had often consulted her and had encouraged her to take a more active role in Indian politics, which is why she finally consented to become President of the Congress Party. Being used to the fact that politicians would come to her, whereas she would not go to them, she was not prepared for the task of forging a new coalition. She waited too long for others to contact her rather than wooing them. New elections were held in November 1999. Vajpayee officiated in the meantime and thus had both the drawbacks and the benefits of an incumbent. He won the 'Kargil War' which Pakistan had forced upon him and impressed the electorate. The BJP retained its 182 seats and coalition building proved easier this time. Vajpayee now could serve a full term until 2004. He expected another victory at the polls, but this time had no success, a failure he later explained by stating that the Gujarat pogrom may have given the party a bad name. Perhaps he also realized that the slogan 'India Shining' which the BJP had used for the election campaign did not reflect the experience of the poor.

The change in the fortunes of the two national parties was actually less dramatic than it appeared at a first glance. The BJP had lost 44 seats and the

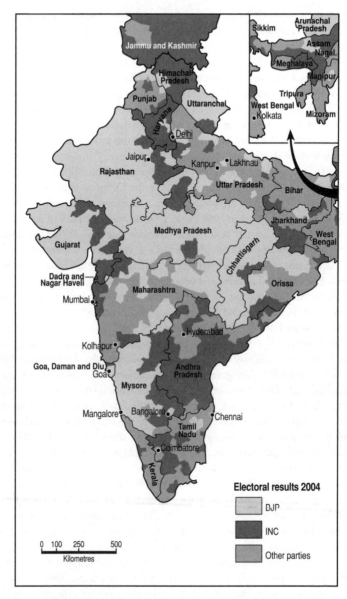

Map 1   Strongholds of Major Parties in the Elections to the Federal Parliament (Lok Sabha), 2004
Source: Election Statistics, Government of India
Cartography: N. Harm, South Asia Institute, University of Heidelberg

Congress Party had gained 31 as compared to the previous election. With 145 seats the Congress Party was only slightly ahead of the BJP, which had captured 138. The BJP had, indeed, lost some seats in Gujarat, but even more damaging were the losses in Uttar Pradesh. Here the party leadership had made a crucial strategic mistake by backing the ex-Chief Minister Kalyan Singh in an attempt to appeal to the Other Backward Castes.[11] This annoyed a large segment of the upper castes but did not attract enough of the OBC vote as the Samajwadi Party was the more authentic OBC party. Another error of judgement which affected the fate of the BJP was the decision to drop the DMK as a partner in Tamil Nadu and to rely once more on the AIADMK which was now ruling the state. It so happened that the AIADMK did not capture any seats in the parliamentary elections.[12] Another BJP ally, the Telugu Desam Party, which had supported the coalition from the outside, suffered a crushing defeat at the polls. With 24 TDP parliamentary seats lost, the BJP-led coalition was at the end of its tether. This meant that the Congress Party now had to try its hand at coalition building, at which it showed considerable skill. The year 2004 thus marked the definitive turning-point in the history of Indian democracy as both national parties were now obliged to think in terms of coalitions.

The emergence of coalition politics has increased the importance of the Election Commission of India. This institution is based on Article 324 of the Indian Constitution which provides that the President of India may appoint a Chief Election Commissioner. Actually for a long time this was a one-man commission. The qualifications of the commissioner were not specified, but by convention a high-ranking retired civil servant has been appointed to this office, an office which no politician has ever held. As long as the Congress system lasted, the election commissioner had only a ceremonial function: he was never called upon to make crucial decisions. In the period of political instability after 1989, the election commissoner became an umpire whom all parties respected. The unique leadership of T.N. Sheshan, who held this office from 1991 to 1996, helped enhance the stature of the Election Commission. He had been cabinet secretary and also a member of the Planning Commission and while his abrasive manner alienated many politicians, his supreme self-confidence intimidated all critics. He saw to it that paramilitary troops were deployed to guarantee the security of the elections and identity cards were introduced by him to reduce the practice of voter impersonation and other types of electoral fraud. Further, he imposed a code of conduct on the parties and candidates participating in the elections. Due to Sheshan's activities the Election Commission gained a reputation which surpassed even that of the judiciary. J.M. Lyngdoh, who was Chief Election Commissioner from 2001 to 2004, was more diplomatic than Sheshan but equally firm in his decisions. The free and fair elections in Kashmir in 2002 are to his credit. The emergence of the Election Commission into the limelight at a time of vital political change shows the resilience of India's democratic institutions.

In the summer of 2007, coalition politics was tested in the presidential elections which led to the victory of Pratibha Patil, the first woman to hold this high office in India. She had emerged as a candidate in this hotly contested election only at a fairly late stage. The incumbent, Abdul Kalam, could have opted for a second term and would have had a good chance of winning the election, but he decided not to stand. The Vice-President, Bhairon Singh Shekhawat, entered the contest. In earlier days under the 'Congress System' vice-presidents had almost invariably succeeded the president and their election was more or less a ceremonial affair. But in 2007, Shekhawat, an old BJP-stalwart was supported only by the opposition. The victory of the candidate of the ruling coalition seemed to be preordained, but the coalition did not immediately agree on a candidate. Some leading Congress stalwarts were not endorsed by the other members of the United Progressive Alliance. All of a sudden the name of Pratibha Patil emerged. She was strongly backed by Karunanidhi, the boss of the DMK. Governor of Rajasthan and a Congress politician for many decades, she was born in Maharashtra, had become a member of the legislative assembly of that state at the age of 25 and had remained a politician ever since. Once she was nominated as the candidate of the ruling coalition, she campaigned vigorously and had to put up with fierce attacks launched by the opposition. Electioneering was as intense as for a parliamentary election, even though the president is not elected by the people but by an electoral college consisting of all members of parliament (Lok Sabha and Rajya Sabha) and all state assemblies. The total number of the electoral college is 4,896. In order to account for the population represented by its members, they get a quota of votes which indirectly reflects the size of their constituencies. This adds up to a total number of 945,875 of which Pratibha Patil got about two-thirds. Shekhawat was trailing behind; in the left-dominated states West Bengal and Kerala he did not get a single vote.

As a consequence of this electoral contest there was a serious split in the BJP-Shiv Sena alliance. Bal Thakeray, the Shiv Sena leader, had always complained that no Maharashtrian had ever become President or Prime Minister of India. He could not afford to oppose a Maharashtrian candidate now and was bitterly criticized by the BJP for betraying the common cause. This illustrates the relevance of regional parties in national politics.

The rise of regional parties and of national coalitions drawing their strength from such parties has provided a new foundation for Indian democracy. A clear-cut two-party system is more suitable for homogeneous nations. The broad spectrum of political interests in India requires different methods of arriving at national consensus. Political analysts speak of 'nested games' played by politicians under these circumstances. This refers to multiple trade-offs: concessions in one arena are compensated by gains in another. A flexible party system as well as a suitable federal structure are essential if such games are to contribute to political stability. Just as the Indian party system had to evolve under changing conditions, so the federal structure had to adjust to the process of political transformation.

CHAPTER 3

THE TENSIONS OF FEDERALISM

Federalism and the Devolution of Power

Federalism was introduced into India by the British to enable them to proceed with a limited devolution of power while retaining central control.[1] Due to its origin, this was a 'federalism from above' in which the federal units were endowed with circumscribed powers. It was thus the very opposite of the normal type of federalism initiated 'from below' by the respective units which then determine which powers they wish to transfer to a central government. The Government of India Act of 1935 accordingly contained both a standard constitution applicable to all federal units, the British–Indian provinces, and a separate part for central government. The Viceroy remained as 'irremovable executive', but he would head a federal government in which the Indian princes were supposed to play a decisive role. This part of the constitution would only come into operation if at least 50 per cent of the princes joined the federation. A majority refrained from doing so, probably fearing that they would have to make financial contributions to the federation. The provincial part of the Government of India Act came into force nevertheless and the Viceroy gained greater powers than ever before.[2]

Indian nationalists detested the federation as a conservative stratagem designed to frustrate their endeavours. Jawaharlal Nehru proclaimed that the constitution of India would have to be framed by a constituent assembly based on universal suffrage and unfettered by British designs. But this did not happen. The Independence of India Act hurriedly passed by the British Parliament in 1947 was only a revised edition of the Government of India Act of 1935. The Indian Constitutent Assembly was not based on universal suffrage and it more or less endorsed the existing constitution while also introducing a list of fundamental rights and a special section of 'Directive Principles of State Policy'. The Indian National Congress had compiled a long list of such rights in 1931. As Congress was not in power at that time, the list could include rights such as the right to work, the right to free education, etc. If the state could be sued to provide this, it would be unable to foot the bill. Therefore these rights were relegated to the 'Directive Principles' which are not justiciable.[3] Some critics said in the Constituent Assembly that these were pious wishes which might as well be excluded from the constitution, but subsequent experience has shown that the Indian Supreme Court can refer to these 'Directive Principles' in its judgments even though citizens cannot base any claims on them.

The Indian constitution is thus an amalgam of British colonial practice and the aspirations of the freedom movement tempered by political prudence. The great powers of the Viceroy were vested in the President, but exercised by the Prime Minister. As this office did not exist under the Government of India Act of 1935, it was introduced in the new constitution by the laconic statement, 'There shall be a Council of Ministers with the Prime Minister at the head . . .'. British precedent – based on the unwritten British constitution – seemed to determine what the powers of the Prime Minister would be. They are enormous – and in order to protect his powers from undue interference, a paragraph was added which stipulates that the advice given by the Prime Minister to the President may not be subject to any court of law.

The standard constitution of the Indian federal states was retained practically unchanged. There was discussion in the Constituent Assembly about whether the governor should be elected, but those who argued for central control prevailed and the nomination of the governor by the Government of India was retained.[4] As mentioned earlier, the instrument of President's Rule, reflecting the emergency powers of the Viceroy, was also enshrined in the Indian constitution. Occasionally there were debates on the question of whether President's Rule was compatible with the principles of federalism. When the National Front formed the government in 1996, there were expectations that this strange instrument would be abolished, for the National Front was after all a government of chief ministers who had always resented this type of central interference. The National Front left President's Rule untouched, as did the subsequent BJP-led coalition. In the meantime the Supreme Court had thrown a spanner into the works of President's Rule by its 'Bommai judgment' of 1994. This referred to the case of a chief minister of Karnataka whose government had been dismissed in 1993. The Supreme Court ruled that a state government must be given a chance to prove its majority on the floor of the house and that central government has to warn the state government well in advance. Referring to this judgment, in 1997 and 1998 President Narayanan rejected plans by the BJP-led coalition to impose President's Rule. This made it almost impossible to dismiss an undesirable state government as long as it could be expected to prove its majority.[5] The

Gujarat government headed by Chief Minister Narendra Modi was not dismissed in 2002, even though it abetted the murder of thousands of Muslims. This was certainly an emergency, but Modi would have been able to prove his majority on the floor of the house. There was no problem with President's Rule in the event of inconclusive elections when there was no majority. It has continued to be used in such cases, demonstrating the power of 'federalism from above'.

The Council of States (Rajya Sabha), the upper house of the Indian parliament, is supposed to be representative of the federal states with a total of 220 of its members being elected by the legislative assemblies of those states. It has remained a rather harmless body more or less like the British House of Lords, providing berths for senior politicians who have had their innings in the lower house (Lok Sabha) or are distinguished persons nominated by the President. Nehru created a National Development Council which included all chief ministers and was mainly used to discuss ideas of the Planning Commission, also created by Nehru. It has continued to meet ever since, but it has rarely been used for solving structural problems of federalism. For this the constitution had provided for an Inter-State Council. The President had the power to create such a council, but for a long time was not asked to do so. It was finally established in May 1990 when V. P. Singh was Prime Minister of India. The council has a permanent secretariat headed by a senior civil servant. It held some sessions but then remained more or less dormant[6] owing to the rise of the regional parties described earlier. These parties could drive their bargains under the new dispensation of national coalition building. Such bargains are of temporary relevance; they may be superseded by subsequent bargains. The central government can live with this and the individual states are usually only interested in solving their current problems, which is why no fundamental reform of the federal structure has been attempted so far although several voluminous reports have been written which are advocating such a reform.

The Process of 'States Reorganization'

There was only one basic reform that could not be postponed: the reorganization of states along linguistic lines. The old boundaries of British–Indian provinces reflected the development of colonial rule and had no particular historical sanctity. Moreover, the integration of the princely states had changed the contours of the old boundaries. Mahatma Gandhi had set the pattern of linguistic provinces by reorganizing the jurisdiction of the Provincial Congress Committees (PCCs) in 1920,[7] but his new units remained within the boundaries of the British-Indian provinces: for example the huge

Bombay Presidency had a Marathi PCC and a Gujarati PCC, among others. He introduced similar linguistic subdivisions in the Madras presidency where there was an Andhra PCC and a Tamil Nadu PCC.

After independence the Andhra linguistic region gained greater weight due to the addition of the Telugu-speaking princely state of Hyderabad. Andhra was the name of an old dynasty which had once ruled the region of the Telugu-speakers. They were proud of their heritage and campaigned for Andhra Pradesh to be carved out of the Madras presidency. As a northerner Nehru had no sympathy for these southern aspirations and feared that they would endanger national unity. Reluctantly, he assented to the claims of the Andhras when one of their leaders died in a hunger strike in 1953. After yielding to the Andhras, he could no longer refuse to heed the claims of the other linguistic provinces and a States Reorganization Commission was appointed in 1954 which submitted its report in 1955.[8] According to its recommendations, Andhra Pradesh was carved out of the state of Madras, which was left to the Tamil-speakers. The princely state of Mysore was amalgamated with the Kannada-speaking districts of the Bombay presidency to form a new state called Karnataka. Kerala was also established at that time, as mentioned earlier. To facilitate cooperation between the new states, Nehru created zonal councils in 1956 which included states adjacent to each other. This construction was not limited to the south; there were also Northern, Central and Eastern Zonal Councils. In 1956 it seemed as if the new order was well established, but there was some unfinished business: the division of Gujarat and Maharashtra. Nehru had postponed dealing with this matter, because the city of Bombay (Mumbai) created an intractable problem. The Maharashtrians claimed it as their capital and the Gujaratis, who controlled the business of this metropolis, did not want to let it go. In fact, they were not very eager about getting a separate Gujarat. Gandhi had solved the city's problem in his day by establishing a Bombay PCC.[9] This could have led to the creation of a city state, but such a state did not fit into the Indian political landscape. The late 1950s were a time of violent agitation among the Maharashtrians, who demanded their own state with Mumbai as its capital. This was finally granted in 1960. In 1963 Nehru also granted the status of a federal state to Nagaland, an area inhabited by fiercely independent tribes.

After Nehru's death subsequent Indian governments showed greater flexibility in the delineation of new federal states. Indira Gandhi partitioned the old Punjab in 1966 and created the new Punjab and Haryana. Her son Rajiv granted federal statehood to a group of territories in 1987: Arunachal Pradesh, Goa and Mizoram. Prime Minister Vajpayee added another round of three states to this category in 2000: Chhattisgarh, Jharkhand and Uttaranchal.[10] This was supposedly done to accommodate tribal populations, but there may also have been some partisan politics involved. Chhattisgarh and Jharkhand are adjacent states in the central Indian tribal belt. Chhattisgarh was carved out of Madhya Pradesh, which was the largest Indian state in territorial terms. Jharkhand was separated from Bihar, which lost about half of its territory, one third of its population and all its mineral wealth. The Jharkhand movement was an old one, but former central governments had rejected its claims and the Bihar government was naturally not in favour of this separation. Vajpayee's government was opposed to Lalu Prasad Yadav and his party, and was eager to cut him and his state down to size. Lalu's political base was in northern Bihar and he had little influence in Jharkhand, which is why the new state could be created. Uttaranchal had a rather different story. It was not a tribal region but was inhabited by high-caste Hindus who resented the growing influence of the Other Backward Castes in Uttar Pradesh, fearing that the reservation policy which favoured the OBCs would reduce their own prospects if they remained in that state. Vajpayee's government was in sympathy with them.

The creation of three new states in 2000 may not yet be the end of reorganization. There are suggestions that the unwieldy state of Uttar Pradesh should be carved up into three manageable units with a population of 50 to 60 million people for each new state. K. M. Panikkar, a member of the States Reorganization Commission of 1955, had irked Nehru by suggesting such a division. At that time Uttar Pradesh was a bastion of the Congress Party and the irreverent suggestion was not heard of again. In recent years the Congress Party has lost ground in this state and would no longer object to its break-up.[11]

Also in recent years, a problem concerning India's federal equilibrium has arisen which had not been apparent in earlier times; it is owing to the much faster population growth in the northern states which is discussed in Chapter 13. The Indian constitution provides for an adequate reflection of the population in terms of the number of parliamentary seats. If this is taken seriously, adjustments would be due after every decennial census. In the 1970s an agreement was made that rearrangements should be postponed until the census of 2001, by which time it had become obvious that the northern states were entitled to many more seats than had been allocated to them so far. The BJP, which headed the coalition government at that time, would have profited from this new allocation, but under pressure from the southern states the 84th amendment of the Indian constitution was adopted in 2001: this stipulates that the matter will be postponed until 2026.[12] In the meantime the number of seats allocated to the different states will remain the same and only intra-state adjustments in the delimitation of constituencies may be made.

In general, federalism, as handled by the Indian government, has proved a flexible instrument for the control of the vast Indian Union. National unity has not suffered under the system of states reorganization, as Nehru had feared, but has actually been strengthened by it. Resistance from below has every so often been subdued by federalism from above. The field of federal finance has proved to be the the the most difficult area of centre–state relations, for when states are governed by regional parties which are not represented in a national coalition, financial bargaining can become a bitter contest.

The Problems of Federal Finance

The constitutional instrument for the adjustment of centre–state relations is the Finance Commission, appointed by the President every five years. It consists of a chairman and four members. After submitting its report, which has to be laid before both Houses of Parliament, the Finance Commission ceases to exist. It does not have a permanent secretariat and its members are eminent experts who revert to the positions they held earlier. The recommendations of this commission are not binding; they will be implemented by the legislature according to its own judgement. The sharing of taxes between the centre and the states is the main issue considered by this commission.

The Finance Commission had a precursor in the Niemeyer Award of 1936. Sir Otto Niemeyer was an officer of the Bank of England sent to India in order to settle centre–state financial relations under the Government of India Act of 1935. He had a tough time trying to accommodate the claims of the various provincial governments.[13] The proportion of the sum of the budgets of all provincial governments to the total budget of the central government which emerged from his recommendations was about 1:1.6, a proportion that has been more or less preserved by all finance commissions. In Niemeyer's time income tax was the major tax which had to be shared by the central and the provincial governments. In recent years customs duties, which were once exclusively reserved for central government, have dwarfed all other revenues. As long as protectionism prevailed in India, customs duties played a minor role since a tough protective tariff naturally yields no revenue income, but as soon as tariffs were lowered in the 1980s and imports grew, customs duties increased by leaps and bounds. By 1980 customs duties had already surpassed income tax. Whilst income tax also increased in subsequent years, customs attained even higher levels. In 1992 the total revenue income of the central government and states amounted to Rs 1,153 billion; this includes Rs 155 billion due to income tax and Rs 252 billion to customs duties.[14] The states could only watch this windfall gain of the central government with envy and frustration. If the Finance Commission allocated any additional funds to the states, it was not a matter of entitlement but of magnanimity. However, a new departure was made with the 80th amendment to the Indian constitution adopted in 2000 which stipulates that 29 per cent of the net proceeds of Union taxes should be transferred to the states.

Customs duties were a prime example of a buoyant tax, whereas land revenue which had long since been given to the states was its very opposite. Ever since the Great Depression, which broke the back of the British–Indian land revenue system, this revenue had not been increased and had practically dwindled to insignificance under the impact of inflation. In some areas the cost of its collection surpassed the revenue income. But the peasants did not want the abolition of this tax, because the revenue receipts were often their only proof of legal possession of their land as the official record of rights was defective and did not secure land titles.

The usual approach of the states to the Finance Commission was that of a mendicant highlighting his poverty. In fact, Niemeyer had coined the term 'centripetal mendicity' when describing the attitude of the provincial governments of his time.[15] Meeting the demands of the states, the various finance commissions have always resorted to the method of 'gap filling', that is, granting amounts which cover particular shortfalls in the state's revenue income.[16] The relationship of the states with the Finance Commission is thus totally different from their relationship with the Planning Commission. This latter commission was not mentioned in the constitution: it was created by Nehru in 1950 by means of a Cabinet Resolution. It drafts the Five Year Plans which are only indicative and do not have the force of law, but as the Prime Minister is the *ex officio* chairman of the Planning Commission, his political fate is linked to the implementation of the plans. The Planning Commission nowadays has a huge permanent staff and its influence is far greater than that of the Finance Commission. Planned expenditure has considerably increased over the years and accordingly it has become an ever more important element in centre–state relations. The states are in no position to match the expertise of the Planning Commission and depend on the funds which they get under the plans.

The approach which the states adopt when dealing with the Planning Commission is different from that of asking the Finance Commission to fill the gaps in their budget. In order to impress the Planning Commission, they must show that they can finance projects for which they will then receive matching grants under the Five Year Plan.[17] One might expect that when submitting their requests they would state how they would meet the costs arising out of such projects in the future, but the counterproductive distinction between planned, and non-planned expenditure upsets such calculations.[18] Completed projects require proper maintenance, otherwise they become liabilities rather than assets. However, the cost of maintenance is considered to be non-planned expenditure. For filling the gaps in that type of expenditure the states turn to the Finance Commission. There have been suggestions that for better co-ordination the Planning Commission should be amalgamated with the Finance Commission. But the functions of the two commissions are so different that this would not work. The Planning Commission is an integral part of the government and its deputy chairman has the rank of a cabinet minister. The Finance Commission is a body of experts who are regarded by the states as impartial umpires, whereas the states would see the Planning Commission in different light.[19]

In spite of 'gap filling' and the allocation of funds under the Five Year Plans, the fiscal position of the states steadily deteriorated; it is only recently that larger transfers from the central government and an increase in revenue income have improved their position.[20] As far as expenditure is concerned there are two major liabilities with which the states are saddled: the huge losses of the state electricity boards (SEBs) and the steadily rising salaries of government servants. The SEBs are discussed in Chapter 11; here we shall only refer to the problem of paying the increased salaries of the civil servants. Although the majority of them are on the payroll of the states, the increases in salaries are recommended by pay commissions appointed by central government. The recommendations of the fifth Pay Commission (1998) have been a big blow to the state governments; indeed, critics have stated that the central government damaged the Indian economy by accepting the recommendations of that Pay Commission.[21] Initially, these recommendations had been quite reasonable. Nevertheless, the government servants had threatened to go on strike. Prime Minister Gujral lost his nerve, said that he wished to avoid a strike at any cost and then appointed a group of ministers and empowered them to revise the recommendations. These ministers toned down the recommendations concerning retrenchment, etc. and increased the rise in salaries from 20 to 40 per cent,[22] which meant that central government had to face a rise from Rs 218 billion to 435 billion. The combined states experienced a rise from Rs 515 to 898 billion.

The Pay Commission had originally recommended the retrenchment of government staff by about 30 per cent and a reduction in the number of pay scales so as to reduce the financial burden on the states. But retrenchment is politically dangerous. 'Jobs for the boys' are at stake when a government takes retrenchment seriously, so state governments were reluctant to cut back on their staff. The total number of government servants employed by 21 federal states amounted to 7.9 million in 1994 and remained at that level until 2001. Their salaries had risen by 114 per cent in this period. In 2002 a modest attempt at retrenchment could be noticed. It amounted to about 10 per cent of the staff, but as salaries went up by around 5 per cent during that year, the effect of this rentrenchment was insignificant.[23] The sixth Pay Commission is expected to make new recommendations in the near future that will be a further blow to government finance. On the other hand, the rapid rise in incomes in the private sector necessitates an increase in the salaries of civil servants. In any case, corruption is rampant in India; if civil servants are underpaid they will be even more tempted to accept bribes. However, it is only in the higher echelons that the pay scales of the private sector provide a challenge to the public sector; the majority of government servants are better off than corresponding staff in the private sector – more so if one takes job security, pensions and so on into consideration.

The income of the state governments does not measure up to these liabilities. The insignificance of the land revenue has already been mentioned. Sales tax, the mainstay of the finance of the states, can be levied on goods but not on services, which nowadays account for a much larger share of GDP than the production of goods. The 95th amendment of the Indian constitution introduced a welcome change in this respect in 2003. It permits the centre to levy service tax which will be collected and appropriated by the centre and the states. Another measure which will simplify tax collection and enhance the revenue of the states is the introduction of a uniform value added tax (VAT) to replace various sales taxes. It was adopted and implemented by 22 states in 2005; the others will follow suit soon. The revenue derived from VAT had already surpassed that derived from the old sales taxes in the first year of the operation of this new scheme.[24]

Next to the taxation of goods and services, the taxation of immovable property proved to be a major problem. The widespread undervaluation of such property means that the taxation of property or of its transfer does not yield sufficient revenue. State governments are often admonished to do more about mobilizing resources, but the tax structure does not permit them to do so. They would also hesitate to commit political suicide by burdening their voters with taxes. Only central government can save the state governments by tightening up the entire system of taxation and allocating some buoyant taxes which surge due to economic growth exclusively to the states. Alternatively the power of collecting such buoyant taxes could remain with central government while a larger share of the revenue is allotted to the states.

The finances of local government (village councils, municipalities, etc.) are even more of a problem than those of the states. These local bodies have very limited capacities to raise their own taxes and are dependent on transfers 'from above'. There are about 250,000 units of local government in India, but their share in total government expenditure amounts to a mere 6 per cent.[25] This includes major cities whose tax base is rather precarious. The Mumbai Municipal Corporation is a case in point. Its main income is derived from a tax on urban property and from *octroi*, a tax imposed on goods entering the city. Due to undervaluation the ratepayers do not contribute as much to the municipal budget as they should and the income from this tax is dwarfed by *octroi*. The expenditure on staff collecting rates is far higher than that on the swarms of petty *octroi*-collectors, who have an additional source of income as they can hold traders to ransom. The scope for extortion has been increased by an ingenious innovation introduced in the 1980s: piece rates on goods were changed to an *ad valorem* assessment. The municipality's income from *octroi* was doubled in this way, while that of the petty collectors may have risen even more as their powers of discretion were now much greater. The pay of the *octroi*-collectors is very low; the municipality seems to take into consideration that they have additional income from their peculiar work. One could describe them as licensed highwaymen who share their loot with the municipality. *Octroi* is a very obnoxious tax that distorts the working of the market.[26] It could easily be replaced by a surcharge on the sales tax, but this is collected by the state government on which the municipality in any case depends for 'transfers from above'. It is understandable that the municipality should jealously guard its independent sources of income. However, the large investment required for the improvement of a metropolis can neither be derived from *octroi* nor from the budget of the state government: it can only be taken care of by the central government.

Local bodies such as village councils (*panchayats*) are even worse off as far as financial resources are concerned. Their political rights have been enhanced and elections have been held every so often, but there are hardly any local taxes under the jurisdiction of these bodies. Rajiv Gandhi introduced the 73rd and 74th amendments to the Indian constitution which strengthened *panchayats*, but these amendments did not refer to the transfer of central funds to the *panchayats*. The amendments were designed so as to extend federalism from above to the village, circumventing the influence of the state governments; nevertheless federalism was stymied by those governments. The general argument against entrusting more financial responsibilities to the village councils is that they lack the capacity to deal with such matters. Of course, this is a flawed argument, as capacity building can be done only by entrusting such work to the people concerned.[27] Proper monitoring would help to check their performance. Essential services such as the construction and maintenance of local roads, the provision of primary education and basic public health, including the supply of drinking water, should be in the hands of local government. As a case in point, the control of the village schoolteacher may be mentioned. In rural India it is a common complaint that teachers who are servants of the state government often shirk their duties. If they received their salary from the village council they would be under local supervision and would not fail to show up for their classes. The above discussion of problems arising at the various levels of government has shown that financial reform still has a long way to go in India. There is no dearth of competent academic advice on these matters, but the political will of bureaucrats as well as of the elected representatives of the people is often lacking. The dead weight of inherited institutions cannot be easily overcome, the more so as they provide a reliable framework for the daily routine of governance. But as India grows in many respects, it faces challenges which it must meet.

CHAPTER 4

A ROLE IN WORLD AFFAIRS

India, China and Pakistan

Indian foreign policy under the guidance of Jawaharlal Nehru reflected the ideas of the Indian freedom movement. For Nehru, this movement was aimed at securing not only the freedom of India but the emancipation of the colonial world. India was, indeed, a pacesetter in the process of decolonization and acted as the spokesman of what came to be known as the Third World. The other two worlds had staked their claims soon after the Second World War and there was an Iron Curtain which divided them. The Cold War which emerged from this polarization did not tolerate a Third World as such: allegiance to one side or the other was taken for granted. Nehru, however, stressed that India did not wish to sacrifice its newly won independence. As decolonization progressed, other new nations also took this stand. 'Afro-Asian Solidarity' and 'Nonalignment' emerged almost simultaneously as common denominators of the views adopted by the new nations. The Bandung Conference of 1955 marked the rise of the first movement, while the meeting of Nasser, Nehru and Tito on the island of Brioni in 1956 prepared the ground for the second.[1] There was a difference of emphasis between these two movements. Afro-Asian Solidarity was invoked in order to complete the unfinished business of decolonization. In this endeavour, nations such as China, which was an ally of the Soviet Union at that time, could fully participate. The second movement, however, was by definition restricted to those nations that had not concluded pacts with either of the Cold War powers. At the first conference of the nonaligned nations in Belgrade in 1961, Nehru stressed that the nonaligned must remain nonaligned among themselves. This meant that except for refraining from military pacts with the superpowers they were free to conduct their foreign policy according to their own national interest. Owing to this simple principle the movement continued for a long time whereas Afro-Asian Solidarity disappeared fairly soon.

The big blow to this solidarity came in 1962 when China invaded India in order to settle a border dispute. Nehru had assumed that China was an anti-imperialist power just like India and that such powers would live in peace with each other. Moreover, he had supported China's control over Tibet, which was supposed to be an autonomous region. Unfortunately, he had failed to get from China a definitive statement concerning the India–China border in return for this support. The treaty which Nehru concluded with China in 1954 only mentioned some passes through which the trade between the two countries might flow. It also contained the five principles (*panchshila*) relating to mutual benefit and non-interference in each other's internal affairs which Nehru henceforth regarded as the cornerstone of his foreign policy.[2] However, none of this could prevent a clash with China. In 1959, the Dalai Lama, Tibet's priestly ruler, fled to India and Nehru granted asylum to him but did not permit him to establish a Tibetan government in exile. In the following months border clashes increased and notes were exchanged which Nehru did not publish until he was forced to do so by the Indian parliament.[3] In 1961, the Chinese Prime Minister Chou En-lai visited India for border negotiations. Nehru had collected all relevant maps and was surprised that Chou En-lai did not wish to look at them but immediately proposed a deal: China would recognize India's eastern border as delineated by the McMahon Line of 1914 if India would leave the Karakoram Pass and Aksai Chin (north-east Kashmir) to China. China had secretly occupied most of Aksai Chin in the 1950s, so India would simply have to acquiesce in this loss. The access to the Karakoram highway was of great strategic importance to China for the control of its western provinces. However, Nehru as head of a democratic government could not deal with national territory as easily as Chou En-lai had expected. The deal was not accepted and border clashes continued. Finally, China forced the deal on an unwilling India by means of a well-planned military offensive. When the USA and the Soviet Union were busy with the Cuban Missile Crisis in October 1962, a division of Chinese troops crossed the McMahon Line in the east and soon reached the Assamese plains. But this was a diversionary move. These troops withdrew before their supply lines could be cut. In the meantime the Chinese also launched a massive offensive in the west to capture the Karakorum highway – and they did not withdraw as this was the area which really interested them. Subsequently, there was a conspiracy of silence between India and China as to what had happened there.[4] India was not willing to admit its losses and China would not reveal its illegitimate gains. China has adopted an attitude of superiority ever since and sometimes this has even been expressed quite openly. When China invaded Vietnam in 1979, Deng Xiao-ping compared this to what China had done to India in 1962. Atal Bihari Vajpayee, who visited China at that time as India's Minister of External

Affairs in order to 'normalize' relations with China, got this message and immediately returned home. 'Normalization' had to wait for a long time.

The clash between India and China had sounded the death knell of Afro-Asian Solidarity even before 1962, but anti-colonial solidarity still motivated Nehru, who was sensitive to appeals from leaders of countries which were involved in their freedom struggle. In September 1961, Kenneth Kaunda, the future President of Zambia who had attended the Belgrade Conference of the Nonaligned Nations, visited New Delhi and gave a lecture in which he blamed Nehru for tolerating Portuguese colonial rule in Goa.[5] He argued that rather than setting an encouraging example which the Africans could follow Nehru obviously wanted to wait until the Africans had overcome Portuguese colonial rule, whereupon Goa would then fall into his lap like a ripe fruit. Kaunda was clearly quite right in assessing Nehru's motives and his speech stung him into action. Goa was liberated by the Indian army in December 1961; it proved to be a walkover but this could not have been predicted. As a member of NATO, Portugal was well armed and had a strong garrison in Goa. It could also rely on support from Pakistan. If the Portuguese Governor-General had decided to defend Goa seriously, the liberation could have ended in a bloodbath. Fortunately, he only blew up a few bridges and surrendered gracefully as he was aware of the far superior power of the Indian army. This was Nehru's last great triumph, but he experienced it with mixed feelings. He lost his reputation as an apostle of peace and was berated by every Western power. This he could live with, but the humiliating defeat he suffered at the hands of the Chinese in 1962 broke his heart. He must have felt very deeply that he had failed as architect of India's foreign policy.

Nehru's successors adopted a more realistic approach: India's regional position was more important to them than its role in world affairs. The twin challenges of China and Pakistan converted India with a vengeance into a self-conscious territorial state concerned with its defence. A retired Indian general had once said that the colonial legacy of a huge army embarrassed India's political leaders as much as inheriting a brewery would embarrass a teetotaller. Nehru did not invest much money in armaments; however, this changed after India's defeat by the Chinese in 1962. Defence expenditure was stepped up, which alarmed Pakistan. The Chinese had shown that India could be beaten and had thus set Pakistan an example, but due to India's rapid armament, the window of opportunity for Pakistan seemed to be closing fast. Pakistan's military dictator Ayub Khan was pushed by his young Foreign Minister, Zulfiqar Ali Bhutto, to attack India in Kashmir. Bhutto had forged a military alliance with China in 1963 and Pakistan had yielded a large part of territory to the west of the Karakoram Pass to China at that time. Nehru's successor, Lal Bahadur Shastri, was considered weak and inexperienced. Pakistan tested his reaction to a border intrusion in the Rann of Katch in the summer of 1965. Shastri requested the then British Prime Minister Harold Wilson to arbitrate in this matter, which only served to encourage Ayub Khan to launch his Operation Grand Slam in September 1965[6] and he sent his tanks to cut the only connection between India and Kashmir. If Shastri had again called for arbitration, Ayub Khan could have finished his business in Kashmir and then negotiated from a position of strength. But this time Shastri ordered his troops to launch a counter-attack on Lahore. He also refused to listen to a Chinese ultimatum which referred to their threat to cross the border of Sikkim. Pakistan had hoped that China would open a second front in the east, but the Chinese did not follow up their ultimatum and bitterly disappointed their Pakistani allies. China had encouraged Pakistan in the hope that it would do some damage to India, but it was not interested in investing anything in this war as it had reached its aims in 1962. The same Chinese stratagem was repeated in 1971 when Pakistan lost its eastern half and the Chinese supported Pakistan, but did not give the Pakistanis help when they needed it.

Shastri's steadfastness greatly enhanced his stature, while at the same time Ayub Khan lost face. At a peace conference organized by the Soviet Union in Tashkent, Ayub had to sign an agreement that he would never use force again, otherwise Shastri would not have returned the territory to him which the Indians had captured during this short war. The Indian army enjoyed this triumph: it could now forget about its defeat three years earlier. Ayub Khan, however, was soon confronted with the demand for autonomy of what would soon become Bangladesh. The people of East Pakistan had realized that Ayub would not have been able to help them if Shastri had sent his troops to the east as well. Moreover, the West Pakistanis had all along behaved like an occupying power in East Pakistan and they became even more obnoxious in the run-up to the secession of Bangladesh. Millions of East Pakistanis fled to India. By then, Indira Gandhi was India's Prime Minister. She toured the capitals of the world but nobody would help her by putting pressure on Pakistan. Finally, she concluded a Treaty of Friendship with the Soviet Union in August 1971 and liberated Bangladesh by sending in Indian troops in December. The Soviet treaty had been advocated by Leonid Brezhnev for a long time, but she had hesitated to sign it. Now she signed it in a hurry so as to have some support in the risky venture in Bangladesh.[7] The Soviet Union advised India not to intervene. President Nixon had sent an American aircraft carrier armed with nuclear warheads into the Bay of Bengal; later, he stated that he would have used them if the Soviet Union had helped India. A third world war could have begun right then and there. Fortunately, the Indian army was quick and successful and the Pakistani troops in Bangladesh quickly surrendered. Indira

Gandhi could be proud of achieving this victory single-handedly, even defying Nixon whose sabre-rattling had been quite useless.

In 1972, Indira Gandhi met Bhutto who had become President of the rest of Pakistan and had to retrieve the 90,000 Pakistani prisoners of war from her. The only assurance she got from him in return was that henceforth all conflicts between India and Pakistan would be settled bilaterally and that he would see to it that the ceasefire line in Kashmir – now called the Line of Control – would be recognized as the international boundary between India and Pakistan. She could have insisted that he agreed to this immediately instead of making vague promises, but he argued that he would not survive such a concession politically and that this could not be in her interest.[8] General Zia-ul-Haq murdered Bhutto five years later and thus India lost the partner of the Simla Agreement of 1972. Had the question of the international border been settled in 1972, India could have insisted on its validity.

India had now emerged as the leading regional power in South Asia and it was tacitly recognized as such by both superpowers. In subsequent years, it tried to 'normalize' its relations with China. This was not easy, as the tactless remark of Deng Xiao-ping showed in 1979. India swallowed its pride and tried to get along with China as best it could. A real breakthrough came with Prime Minister Narasimha Rao's visit to China in 1993 when an agreement was signed that both sides would respect the 'Line of Actual Control' between India and China. Since again there was no indication of where this line was supposed to be, there was thus no progress beyond Nehru's treaty of 1954 which had proved to be insufficient. Just as in that earlier period, the Indian side again stresssed that it approved of China's control of Tibet. Whether China really appreciates India's 'good behaviour' is an open question. China's behaviour was not 'good' at all as it continued to aid Pakistan in terms of nuclear armament and rockets such as the Chinese M-11, which was called 'Shaheen' in Pakistan and was first tested there in 1999. Obviously, China has an abiding interest in propping up Pakistan against India without taking any particular risk in so doing.

India's relations with its smaller South Asian neighbours have been troubled by various tensions which arose from the fact that they perceived India as the 'big brother' who often made them feel his superiority. Since all these neighbours had common borders with India but none with each other, they could make common cause in warding off Indian influence. India then felt that these neighbours were ganging up to confront it, which is why India preferred to deal with them bilaterally rather than thinking in terms of regional cooperation. SAARC, the South Asian Association of Regional Cooperation, emerged from a plan of Ziaur Rahman, the President of Bangladesh, who felt that it would be easier to deal with India in such a context rather than in bilateral negotiations. Bangladesh actually owed a debt of gratitude to India for India's help in liberating it from Pakistan. But nations usually do not like to owe such a debt and resent their benefactor's insistence on it. Ziaur Rahman, however, was a consummate diplomat and converted India to SAARC. In fact, at the first meeting of the heads of government of SAARC in Dhaka in 1985, the Bangladeshis were surprised when these heads agreed to meet every year because they found their informal contacts beyond the rather inane official agenda very useful. Numerous sources of minor friction among the neighbours could be discussed in such informal talks.

Nepal, India's neighbour to the north, also owed a problematic debt of gratitude to India. In 1951 India had helped to end the autocracy of the Ranas, a clan of feudal lords, by supporting King Tribhuvan in recovering his royal authority and installing a democratic government. Unfortunately his successor, King Mahendra, put an end to democratic rule in 1961 and introduced his own model of guided democracy and royal autocracy. Moreover, he played the China card so as to counteract Indian influence. All this was deeply resented by India, but it refrained from open interference. When King Birendra succeeded Mahendra, relations with India improved, but there were neverthe-less quarrels about landlocked Nepal's trade via India. When India was governed by the National Front, Inder Kumar Gujral, who was first Minister of External Affairs and then Prime Minister, announced the 'Gujral Doctrine' which implied that India should step forward unilaterally and approach its neighbours rather than expecting them to please India. In this period, relations with Nepal improved, but they deteriorated once more later on.

Sri Lanka created a very special problem for India owing to the separatist movement of the Tamils there. These Tamils could appeal to the Tamils in India who granted a safe haven to those who rebelled against the government of Sri Lanka. In 1987 J. Jayewardene, the President of Sri Lanka, cleverly concluded a treaty with Rajiv Gandhi, the then Prime Minister of India, and invited him to send an Indian Peace Keeping Force (IPKF) to Sri Lanka to disarm the Tamil rebels. Rajiv Gandhi thought this could be easily achieved, but sending the IPKF proved to be a costly mistake. At first he dispatched only 5,000 troops, but in due course there were 50,000 Indian soldiers stationed in Sri Lanka where they behaved like an occupation force without being able to subdue the rebels. Finally Jayewardene's successor, R. Premadasa, demanded the withdrawal of the IPKF. Rajiv Gandhi's successor, V. P. Singh, who was not politically committed to the treaty which Rajiv had signed, readily agreed to this withdrawal. India had lost much money and its reputation in this futile venture and Rajiv lost his life when he was assassinated by Tamil rebels in 1991. When Chandrika Kumaratunga became President of Sri Lanka, relations between that country and India improved once more. But India would never forget the humiliating experience of the IPFK. From now on it would hesitate to interfere in the troubles of its neighbours.

New Orientations after the End of the Cold War

India had all along deplored the Cold War, but in fact this calamity had provided a reliable framework for India's foreign policy. Moreover, while always stressing its nonalignment, India had found a very reliable partner in the Soviet Union on which it had depended almost totally for all its modern armaments since 1963.[9] The Western powers had actually pushed India into the arms of the Soviet Union by refusing to supply India with weapons. They feared that such weapons would be taken apart by Soviet military advisers in India and copied by Soviet engineers. India supplied to the Soviet Union large amounts of consumer goods which were in short supply there. In this way, India could easily pay for Soviet weapons.

The Soviet invasion of Afghanistan upset India's relations with the Soviet Union as Afghanistan had been a member of the nonaligned movement and had been of some benefit to India as a counterweight to Pakistan.[10] All this changed in 1979 and, to make matters worse, Pakistan emerged as a 'front-line state', receiving enormous amounts of American military aid. The Soviet withdrawal from Afghanistan and the subsequent end of the Cold War in 1989 were welcomed by India. However, the sudden change of world affairs in the wake of these unexpected developments left India in the position of a voyager who has lost his compass at sea. At this juncture, India was confronted with the first Gulf War, which affected it very badly. Thousands of Indian workers whose remittances helped to improve the Indian balance of payments had to be repatriated at short notice. Iraq which, next to India, was the only other important power which had a treaty of friendship with the Soviet Union, had been on friendly terms with India as it was considered to be a secular state. The Indian Minister of External Affairs, Inder Gujral, rushed to Iraq and embraced Saddam Hussein, a gesture which was rather undiplomatic in the circumstances of that time.[11] The defeat of Iraq and the triumphant rise of the only remaining superpower forced India to reset the coordinates of its foreign policy, the first visible effect of this reorientation being the establishment of full diplomatic relations between India and Israel in 1992 under Prime Minister Narasimha Rao. There had been secretive attempts at an earlier time to establish relations with Israel. Vajpayee had worked for this while he was Minister of External Affairs in 1978, and Prime Minister Morarji Desai had even arranged for a secret visit by Moshe Dayan at that time.[12] But there was no follow-up then. India had so far always sided with Arab nationalism and had shunned Israel. Arab nationalism was obviously a casualty of the first Gulf

War. India decided to opt for the winners and – at that time almost unnoticed – the axis USA–Israel–India emerged as a new element in world affairs. Israel had emerged as India's second-largest arms supplier after Russia. It had also become India's biggest trading partner in western Asia.[13]

India's adjustment to the hegemony of the one remaining superpower would probably have progressed much faster if the troubled 1990s had not intervened which were characterized by many counter-currents in Indo-US relations. To begin with, there were the increasing tensions in Kashmir which burdened India. As mentioned earlier, in the aftermath of the Soviet withdrawal from Afghanistan, many Afghan freedom fighters who were now 'unemployed' turned their attention to Kashmir. Pakistan was glad to make use of them and India had to send ever more troops into the troubled state. There was a vicious circle of terrorism and repression. The USA had no sympathy for India's position and Pakistan was an American ally, after all. It was only in 1999 when Pakistan overplayed its hand in the Kargil War that the USA sided with India.

General Pervez Musharraf who later emerged as Pakistan's military dictator had indulged in a remarkable exercise of brinkmanship by launching a secret commando operation across the Line of Control in Kashmir in the spring of 1999.[14] During the winter, the Indian troops guarding this line are concentrated in a few fortified outposts. Musharraf's commandos could penetrate the line unnoticed. They were supposed to capture some territory before the thaw set in and Indian troops could march from Srinagar to Kargil to relieve the small contingents stationed in the isolated outposts. The commando operation was brilliantly planned, but it proved to be a political disaster. The thaw set in early and the Pakistani intruders were defeated. Musharraf had started the first conventional war between two atomic powers. He was sure that India would not cross the Line of Control because of the threat of nuclear escalation. India refrained from crossing the line on the ground but did deploy Mirage fighter planes, which attacked Pakistani positions successfully. By June 1999, Musharraf knew that the game was up and when his old friend General Zinni, the American Chief of Staff, visited him in order to urge him to withdraw his troops, he immediately agreed but also played a trick so as to pass the buck on to the Pakistani Prime Minister, Nawaz Sharif.[15] He asked Zinni to see to it that President Clinton would receive Sharif in Washington, to negotiate the withdrawal at the highest level. Musharraf sold this plan to Sharif by telling him that President Clinton was taking a personal interest in the matter and that this would amount to an internationalization of the Kashmir issue, which Pakistan had aimed at all along. The simple-minded Sharif swallowed the bait and rushed to Washington uninvited.[16] He did not realize that by doing so he was assuming sole responsibility for the withdrawal and that Musharraf could pass the blame for it on to him. Once he realized, he tried to get rid of Musharraf but was then overthrown by him.[17] President Clinton was compelled to take a 'personal interest' in this matter, but not an interest which would be favourable to Pakistan. He saw that he had been used by Musharraf and was not amused. This contributed to his dramatic visit to India in March 2000, discussed in the last section of this chapter. After spending several days in India, Clinton only stopped over in Pakistan for a few hours in order to give Musharraf a piece of his mind. The general had sown the wind and reaped the whirlwind.

Indo–US relations were muddied not only by the Kashmir issue in the 1990s but even more by India's defiance of American nuclear policy. The Non-Proliferation Treaty (NPT) which India had never signed came up for renewal at that time. At the same time there were negotiations concerning a Comprehensive Test Ban Treaty (CTBT). India resented both treaties, on the grounds that they would endorse the position of the nuclear powers and foreclose the options of the nuclear have-nots. As is explained in Chapter 5, India had planned to conduct nuclear tests in 1995 and then sign the two treaties as a recognized nuclear power, but it refrained from doing so under American pressure. This did not augur well for Indo–US relations, which deteriorated even further after the Indian tests of 1998 and the American imposition of sanctions against India. The year 1998 thus marked the nadir of Indo–US relations. It was a blessing in disguise that Musharraf started the disastrous Kargil War in 1999 and provided a starting-point for a rapid improvement in the relationship.

In the 1990s, India also tried to intensify its contacts with the European Union. Arjun Sengupta, the Indian ambassador to the EU, had even proposed that India should apply for associate membership. This bold suggestion was not appreciated by the authorities in Brussels or by the Indian government. The EU was not prepared for it because it could have served as a precedent for other Asian nations and the Indian government was still wedded to the idea of nonalignment, which could not be reconciled with such close ties with Europe. Nevertheless, Sengupta's initiative led to the Cooperation Agreement between the European Community and the Republic of India on Partnership and Development which was ratified in 1993.[18] In spite of this agreement, the EU remained a rather shadowy phenomenon for India, albeit older diplomatic relations with the major nations of Europe still prevailed. Among those relations India's contacts with Great Britain used to be most important. The transfer of power in 1947 had not been accompanied by a political rupture; on the contrary, the Indian elite had an almost nostalgic attachment to Britain. Moreover, Britain remained for a long time India's most important trading partner. But this changed after the 1970s when other nations also intensified their trade with the country.

In the late 1990s, participation in the ASEM process (Asia–Europe Meeting) would have been desirable for India, but this was precluded by the Asian members, who obviously did not want to admit India. China, Japan and the members of the ASEAN states as well as the members of the European Union participated in the first ASEM summit in Bangkok in 1996 and in subsequent annual summits in various Asian and European capitals. When Portugal held the presidency of the EU in 2000, it inaugurated a special India–EU summit; subsequent annual summits were held in New Delhi and in the capital of the state then holding the EU presidency and it seems that this special treatment has reconciled India with its exclusion from ASEM.

A rather peculiar task for Indian diplomacy was the rebuilding of the relationship with Russia as the successor to the Soviet Union. In the summer of 1991 the Treaty of Friendship with the Soviet Union was to be renewed after twenty years of existence. There had been some criticism of this treaty in India. It had been concluded by Indira Gandhi only as a kind of reinsurance at the time of her action in Bangladesh. After that it had lost its usefulness and it was seen as not quite compatible with Indian nonalignment. However, in 1991 Gorbachev was still in charge of the Soviet Union and India certainly wanted to be on good terms with him. So the treaty was renewed shortly before the Soviet Union disappeared. Subsequently, India established good relations with all the Soviet Union's successor states.

A Strategic Partnership with the USA?

Indo–US relations had experienced many ups and downs between 1947 and 2000. For most of the time political relations had been strained, whereas social relations were very good. Indian immigrants have settled in the USA in great numbers; at present they amount to nearly two million. Most middle-class Indian families have relatives in America and there are frequent visits in both directions. Politically, however, relations between the two countries have not been very cordial. Whenever the USA took any note of South Asia it was usually due to some regional crisis, and then it always backed Pakistan. Even when America provided aid to India it was often administered in such a way that India felt humiliated. A case in point is President Lyndon B. Johnson's food aid to India at a time when India was in great need of it. His policy of administering this aid was nicknamed 'ship to mouth' as each shipment used to be sent so as to arrive at the last minute before starvation took hold.[19] He wanted to teach India a lesson as he felt that the Indian government was not doing enough as far as reforming its agrarian policy was concerned, and he was also afraid that in due course the USA would not have enough agrarian surplus to feed India. But the lasting impression this policy had on Indira

Gandhi and her government was a feeling of deep humiliation. India's later policy of keeping unnecessarily high buffer stocks was probably due to a feeling of 'never again' which lingered on long after Johnson's term of office. Similarly, Nixon's treatment of Indira Gandhi had left bad memories. Nixon not only tilted towards Pakistan, but was much more interested in China than in India. In fact, his sending an aircraft carrier into the Bay of Bengal in 1971 was not only meant as a threat to India but as a message to China that the USA was a powerful ally ready to take action when it is needed.[20]

President Carter's period of office was a time of Indo–American *rapprochement* after years of hostility and indifference. His visit to India in 1978 was the first by an American President since Eisenhower's visit in 1959. The interval between this second and the third presidential trip to India was even longer: twenty-two years, which is why President Clinton's visit in March 2000 was such an extraordinary event. Moreover, Clinton's message to India was much more positive than anybody had dared to hope for he seemed to have realized that 'the world's largest democracy' had a natural affinity with the USA and that India would be its best partner in Asia.

President Bush's call for an 'Alliance against Terror' after the events of September 11, 2001 met with an immediate positive response from India. Of course, India hoped that its own struggle against terror in Kashmir would be supported by such an alliance. In this India was soon to be disappointed, and it too became a target of even more daring terrorist attacks when Maulana Masud Azhar, a prominent Pakistani terrorist, orchestrated an attack by suicide bombers on the Kashmir legislative assembly in Srinagar in October 2001.[21] Whereas in earlier times the authorities would have maintained that the attackers were Kashmiri freedom fighters, Azhar deliberately broke a taboo and published the names and places of origin of the terrorists, showing that they were all Pakistanis. He thus intended to sabotage the Alliance against Terror which General Musharraf had somewhat reluctantly joined. The Indian government realized this and refrained from giving publicity to this incident, but in December 2001, Azhar and his companions launched an attack against the Indian parliament which almost succeeded. The terrorists, disguised as Indian policemen, were shot only at the last minute. If they had entered the parliament building they could have killed ministers and MPs with impunity as even the guards inside are not permitted to carry arms. The Indian government could not play down this dastardly attack as it had done in the case of the earlier one in Srinagar. Prime Minister Vajpayee deployed Indian troops along the border with Pakistan although it was obvious that while the terrorists were from Pakistan, Musharraf and his government were political targets rather than the instigators of this attack. The problems involved in taking action against non-state actors were clearly revealed in this case. A war between India and Pakistan seemed to be imminent in the summer of 2002 and it was only due to American mediation that it was avoided.[22]

Even before this crisis had been resolved, the USA and India intensified their cooperation in the field of military security. There was a conference in New Delhi in September 2002 in which details of India's request for an anti-missile system were discussed. India wished to acquire the Israeli Arrow system, but this could be done only with American approval, as American technology was involved. It appeared that the USA could not deny this system to India. There were also joint Indo–US naval exercises in the Indian Ocean in 2002. This was a shot in the arm for the Indian navy, which had so far played a minor role among the Indian armed forces. In 1995, the Indian navy had 55,000 men and could deploy only a few dozen ships, including two small aircraft carriers with 64 fighter planes as well as 15 submarines and 40 speed-boats.[23] For a blue water navy this is certainly insufficient and even for guarding India's coastline of about 7,600 kilometres it is a very small force. Moreover, India has a large continental shelf with offshore oil and gas resources and groups of distant islands which must be protected by the Indian navy. With American cooperation, this navy could achieve its full potential. The arrangement was mutually beneficial, for the USA would certainly need help in the vast Indian Ocean which encompasses sea lanes of great importance for the supply of goods, oil and gas for many nations.

The arrival of President Bush in India in March 2006, only six years after President Clinton's momentous visit, highlighted the new intensity of Indo–US relations. Prior to this visit, Prime Minister Manmohan Singh had prepared a nuclear deal on a trip to Washington in July 2005. This deal implied that India, without signing the NPT, would nevertheless be treated as a responsible nuclear power with full access to American technology in respect of non-military use of nuclear power. Detailed negotiations followed this initial announcement. The Indian atomic energy establishment feared that it would lead to a dependence on American technology which could harm India in the future. Bush was aware of these reservations but when talking to Prime Minister Manmohan Singh during his visit he said that he wanted the deal and was not interested in the small print. The final deal that arrived at in New Delhi at Bush's behest was obviously not a very precise agreement, but it opened the door for American companies to sell items to India which had been banned before, and it confirmed that India now is in all but name a member of the exclusive nuclear club.

India's partnership with the USA is at present of central importance to its foreign policy. In future years, this bilateral partnership must be integrated into a 'Concert of Asia' which is essential for keeping the peace in this region.[24]

In addition to India and the USA the major players in this game are China and Japan, and to some extent Russia. India is destined to play a constructive role in this new diplomacy, because it has good relations with the USA and Russia and is about to have closer ties with Japan. Its relationship with China is burdened by earlier conflicts, but in recent years the two Asian giants have arrived at a *modus vivendi*. As participants in a 'Concert of Asia' they can be expected to tune their instruments to avoid any discord.

CHAPTER 5

THE ARGUMENT OF POWER: ATOM BOMBS AND ROCKETS

The Symbolism of the Atom Bomb

Soon after India had conducted its first nuclear tests in 1998, Raja Mohan, a leading Indian defence analyst, asserted that India had so far relied on the power of arguments: now it trusted to the argument of power. There is more to this assertion than meets the eye. The Indian atom bomb is, in fact, an argument rather than an operational weapon. It has been developed entirely by civilian agencies in a process from which the Indian military has been deliberately excluded. India has announced that it will never use its atom bomb for a first strike, and even a retaliatory second strike would take some time under present conditions, because the warheads would first have to be transferred from civilian control to the military guardians of the weapon's delivery systems. From a military point of view, this sounds odd, but if one regards the bomb as an argument rather than as a weapon, it does make sense.

Initially it seemed that India would never adopt this argument. When the atom bomb was dropped on Japan in August 1945, Mahatma Gandhi was so shocked that he did not comment on the terrible event at all. He would have liked to condemn this inhuman act, but he did not dare to do so as he was thinking of India's immediate future; he saw that armed with this bomb, the Allies who had won the war could suppress the Indian freedom movement and extend colonial rule indefinitely. Many people expected a statement from Gandhi and some statements were attributed to him. He therefore sent a short message to *The Times* of London in September 1945 stressing that he had never commented on the atom bomb.[1] Ghandhi subsequently kept quiet about the subject for almost a year. Stray remarks showed that he was deeply perturbed by the challenge of the bomb, which embodied a violence against which *satyagraha* would be completely ineffective. The aggression he had combated with non-violent means could be met in a human encounter; the violence of the bomb, however, was anonymous and was subject to remote control. Its reign of terror could paralyze all political action. It was only after the British showed definite signs of wishing to end their colonial rule that Gandhi dared to speak out. He then condemned the dropping of the bomb as 'the violence of cowards' and predicted that humankind would curse the man who had invented this bomb.[2]

Unfortunately, Indian political leaders and scientists did not curse this man but tried to emulate him. Nehru had ambivalent feelings about the bomb: on the one hand he did not want it, but on the other he was attracted to the idea that India should have the capability of producing it. This was reflected in his relationship with the brilliant Indian physicist Homi Bhabha, whom he encouraged and supported and who obviously felt that Nehru expected him to produce the bomb. Bhabha had made a name for himself in the field of cosmic rays and he had succeeded in gettings funds from the Tatas, India's premier magnates, to establish the Tata Institute of Fundamental Research (TIFR) in Mumbai in 1945.[3] Nuclear physics was an important subject for TIFR from the very beginning. Bhabha impressed Nehru, who made him the first chairman of the Atomic Energy Commission (AEC) in 1948 and in the same year the passing of the Atomic Energy Act cemented the alliance between the Prime Minister and his star scientist. The Act shrouded policy and scientific research in this field under a veil of official secrecy.[4] Nehru, who was also his own Minister of Atomic Energy, was protected from political interference in this field and Bhabha obtained a monopoly of research on atomic energy. His colleagues outside the charmed circle of the AEC could not scrutinize what he was doing, nor did they have access to the ample funds provided by the government. In due course the AEC absorbed more than a third of the annual government grants allocated to all fields of scientific research.

Nehru knew that India's industrial development would require a great deal of energy supply and he hoped that Bhabha could provide for this. For his part Bhabha led him to believe that this was possible, but the scientist was well aware of the technical problems involved and would gladly have made use of President Eisenhower's Atoms for Peace programme under which states that agreed to international control would be provided with fissile material.[5] Nehru publicly stated that India would not accept controls and thus precluded such access to American technology. Bhabha was in a fix, the more so as his illustrious colleague, Meghnad Saha, a nuclear physicist who had once been close to Nehru but had then been sidelined by Bhabha, had turned into a bitter critic. Saha had been elected to the Indian parliament in 1952 and in 1954 he attacked Bhabha publicly, emphasising that he obviously did not know how to build a reactor.[6] For Bhabha it was not only the technology of the reactor but also the supply of fuel which caused problems. India had no indigenous sources of uranium, so Bhabha had to think of alternatives for producing fissile material in India. Opting for enriched uranium as a fuel would have meant that India would have been dependent on a foreign power for its supply. Since India had ample resources of thorium, Bhabha planned a fuel cycle which would lead from thorium to plutonium and then to uranium 233.[7] This would require a fast breeder reactor and India did not even have much simpler reactors at that time. Realizing that he was facing an impasse, Bhabha suggested to Nehru that India should unilaterally renounce the production of atom bombs. He obviously hoped that this would give him access to foreign technology. But Nehru replied that such a renunciation would make sense only if India was actually able to produce a bomb,[8] an argument which Bhabha could not contradict. Now he had to pretend that he could make the bomb. The long and tortuous road which led to India's tests of 1998 began with Bhabha's dilemma in 1955. He did not want to admit to Nehru that he needed access to foreign technology to provide India with nuclear energy and was thus trapped into making the even taller claim that he would be able to produce the bomb single-handedly. Subsequently, Nehru tested Bhabha's credentials in a conversation with a retired American general who had been involved in the making of the American bomb. Nehru asked Bhabha in the presence of the general whether he could make the bomb and Bhabha asserted that he could do so within a year. Nehru then asked the general whether he believed that Bhabha could do it, and the general confirmed it.[9] The general, who had come as a salesman to Bhabha from an American company, was not an objective judge. As an expert, he probably knew that this claim was false, but he could not contradict Bhabha in front of Nehru.

In the meantime Bhabha had managed to get the blueprints of a small research reactor of the 'swimming pool' type from his British colleagues.[10] It went critical in August 1956 and was named Apsara. As it had actually been built in India, Bhabha could claim that it was an indigenous product. Finally Bhabha landed another coup by talking the Canadians into selling a reactor to India without attaching conditions concerning the control of the plutonium which would be a by-product of the working of this reactor. By 1964 India thus possessed an unsafeguarded reactor and could extract plutonium from the fuel rods after replacing them; by 1965 an Indian plant for the extraction of plutonium was in operation and the country soon had enough material to produce a bomb.[11] In order to protect the AEC's new type of activity, a new Atomic Energy Act had been passed in 1962. It was rushed through parliament without being submitted to a select committee.[12] One MP participating in the debate on the bill compared its draconian provisions to the laws of Fascist Germany. Nehru supported the bill very strongly and Bhabha emerged with greater powers than he had had before. Early in 1965 he informed the American Department of State that he could produce an atom bomb within eighteen months and if he could get American blueprints for it, he could do it in six.[13] He assumed that because of China's going nuclear, both superpowers would aquiesce in India following suit. Actually he had good reasons to be quite sure of this. But the window of opportunity was soon closed and India missed its chance. Nehru had died in 1964 and his successor, Lal Bahadur Shastri, was as yet not prepared to endorse a test. Moreover, Bhabha was not yet ready to conduct one. To gain time he suggested the idea of a 'nuclear umbrella' which the USA or the Soviet Union should provide for India to protect it against China,[14] an idea which Prime Minister Shastri endorsed. There was a futile debate in the Indian cabinet at that time which ended in a resolution that no attempt should be made to build a bomb now but that this decision could be revised later on if necessary. However, Shastri agreed that India should aim at a 'peaceful' underground test.[15] In 1966, Bhabha died in an air crash when an Air India flight hit a mountain in Switzerland. He had not been able to provide India with nuclear energy or with a bomb but his legacy was a huge research establishment. The centre which he had built up at Trombay near Mumbai was named Bhabha Atomic Research Centre (BARC) after his death and the nuclear physicists working there inherited Bhabha's ambition.

His successor was Vikram Sarabhai, the scion of a family of Gujarati textile magnates who were friends of Mahatma Gandhi. Sarabhai was also a brilliant physicist, but he had concentrated on the exploration of outer space with rockets and satellites. If India had had an operational interest in nuclear armament, Sarabhai's interest would have been a perfect complement to Bhabha's ambition. Nuclear warheads are useless without delivery systems. It was important to develop suitable rockets and guidance systems in parallel to the quest for the bomb. But this was not Sarabhai's idea. He was opposed to the bomb,[16] and instead thought of the communications revolution which would be due to the deployment of satellites. He would have been thrilled by the export of Indian software via satellite; that was the kind of achievement he cherished, not the delivery of bombs. Thirty years later, Bhabha and Sarabhai's legacies converged, but in 1966 Sarabhai's policy was an obstacle to those who wished to pursue Bhabha's path. Moreover, as far as nuclear energy was concerned, Sarabhai pleaded for the construction of bigger reactors using enriched uranium as they would provide energy more cheaply.[17] This, of course, would have raised the old spectre of foreign control once more and was anathema to the scientists who were bent on building a bomb based on plutonium, which has remained India's favoured technology ever since. By now the nuclear research establishment was so huge that there were niches in which work on the bomb could continue. Raja Ramanna, a brilliant physicist and great piano player, was able to go ahead with his work on the bomb.

Sarabhai died suddenly at the age of 53 in December 1971. Now Ramanna and his colleagues had a free hand in preparing for a nuclear test.

The scientists were eager to prove that they could now do what Bhabha had wanted to do but could not accomplish. However, they depended on Prime Minister Indira Gandhi's decision, which was determined by factors other than scientific endeavour. In 1974 she was ready to listen to their appeals. At the zenith of her power in 1971, she had almost reached its nadir in 1974. The sudden increase in the oil price had plunged India into an imported inflation. Labour became restive; a huge strike of railway workers and other government employees emerged as a dangerous challenge to Indira Gandhi's power. She had also been unable to assert her control over recalcitrant federal states. At this juncture, a successful nuclear test would help her to improve her image. She had not given much thought to the political consequences of the test and initially fully enjoyed its success. She stressed that this was the test not of a bomb, but of a 'nuclear device' tested for peaceful purposes. It was, indeed, only a device which proved that Indian scientists knew how to conduct nuclear fission. But, of course, it was also interpreted as a signal that India could now claim to be a member of the 'Nuclear Club'. In this respect, it was a Pyrrhic victory as the club did not welcome India but instead tightened its controls so as to prevent India from making further progress along these lines.[18] The American Secretary of State, Henry Kissinger, organized the Nuclear Suppliers Group in London in 1975 and saw to it that India could not gain access to foreign technology in this field.[19] Bhabha's old dilemma re-emerged with a vengeance. Political turmoil in India meant that the scientists could no longer count on further attention for quite some time. Indira Gandhi's 'Emergency' was followed by the rise of the Janata government under Prime Minister Morarji Desai, an old associate of Mahatma Gandhi and a man totally opposed to the bomb. He deplored the test of 1974, but he also rejected the NPT which the USA would have liked to impose on India. His period in office amounted to a nuclear moratorium.[20]

When Indira Gandhi returned to power in 1980, India's nuclear establish-ment hoped to be able to convince her once more of the need for further tests. In the meantime Pakistan had made enormous strides in this field. Bhutto had paid great attention to Pakistan's nuclear armament. He had advocated an 'Islamic Bomb' in 1972, and after India's test in 1974 had adopted a double strategy to move ahead with it. He supported A.Q. Khan, who had pirated Dutch plans of nuclear centrifuges and had also pioneered the enrichment of uranium in Pakistan, whereas India relied on plutonium. In addition Bhutto established close links with China in the field of nuclear research. In his prison cell, he wrote in 1977 that establishing this Chinese connection was perhaps the greatest service that he had done for his nation.[21] After having murdered

Bhutto, General Zia wholeheartedly embraced the former president's nuclear legacy and brought it under military control. Before Zia was killed in 1988, he had seen to it that Pakistan was practically a nuclear power. Threats based on this capability were conveyed to India in 1987 when Operation Brasstacks, an Indian military manoeuvre near the Pakistan border, appeared to be too close for comfort to the Pakistan military.

Indira Gandhi was wary of repeating her decision of 1974 which had landed India in a dead end. However, in 1982 she was almost prevailed upon to sanction another nuclear test. Her political predicament was similar to that of 1974. After her success in the elections of 1980, her star was sinking again and she urgently needed to improve her image. The scientists were happy when she permitted the preparation of the tests, but they were even more disappointed when Indira Gandhi called off the tests at the last minute in 1983. Some influential civil servants must have persuaded her that the tests would have the same counterproductive consequences as in 1974.[22] Moreover, the record of BARC was not yet very encouraging. It was a white elephant showing few results for enormous expenditure. It had 32,000 employees, yet its output was meagre. Due to India's dependence on plutonium, the fast breeder reactor was essential, but it became critical only in 1985, nine years behind schedule.[23] Of course, the scientists could proudly point out that they had managed to get ahead without foreign know-how. Nevertheless, they badly needed a test as a demonstration of their competence in these circumstances. Indira Gandhi's advisers could see through this and warned her accordingly. Moreover, premature tests could have adversely affected the Indian Integrated Guided Missile Programme which Indira Gandhi launched in 1983 and about which more will be said later.

Rajiv Gandhi, who had to shoulder the political burden left him by his mother, was initially rather reluctant to get involved with nuclear policy, the more so as he was not on good terms with Raja Rammana, the most ardent and knowledgeable supporter of further tests. Rajiv was eager to lead India into the twenty-first century on a path of technological progress. His first visit to the USA in 1985 – where he was denied the Cray XMP-24 supercomputer which President Reagan had at first wanted to give him – confronted him with the 'dual use' problem. He must have realized that new Indian nuclear tests would have exacerbated this problem and would thus have impeded Indian technological progress. As a diversionary move, he appointed a small secret committee in September 1985 composed of K. Subrahmanyam, India's foremost defence analyst and advocate of the bomb, with Raja Ramanna representing the scientists and three Vice-Chiefs of Staff representing the army, the navy and the air force. At the same time, Rajiv also asked his economic advisers to calculate what a mimimum deterrent would cost. They concluded that it would be much too expensive.[24] Except for signing a treaty with Pakistan in 1985, agreeing that they would not attack each other's nuclear establishments, Rajiv Gandhi did not do much to advance India's nuclear policy. Nevertheless, he seems to have given the green light for the assembling of nuclear weapons at the end of his term of office. But after his defeat in the elections of 1989, India once more faced a period of political turmoil in which no important decisions could be taken. Prime Minister V. P. Singh, who was also Defence Minister, appointed Raja Ramanna as Minister of State of Defence in 1990. While this certainly enhanced the importance of that brilliant scientist, it did not enable him to start the tests for which he had waited so long.

Political stability returned to India in 1991 under Prime Minister Narasimha Rao who seemed to be more amenable to the pleas of the scientists. As a former Minister of External Affairs he was well versed in the diplomatic game posturing of NPT and CTBT and was resolved not to succumb to American pressure in this field. He was certainly not interested in acquiring the atom bomb as an operational weapon, but valued it as an argument in a diplomatic game. He wanted to conduct the tests and then sign the two treaties as an 'atomic power' in 1995. This should have been acceptable to the USA, but keeping India 'non-nuclear' was more important to the American policy makers than getting the treaties signed. Accordingly President Clinton called Narasimha Rao personally and asked him to refrain from conducting the tests.[25] After initiating economic reforms which were just beginning to show some positive results, Narasimha Rao did not wish to jeopardize the success of this policy by defying the USA. Once more the tests were shelved, to the great disappointment of the scientists.

The Bharatiya Janata Party had stated in its election manifesto that it would carry out the tests if it came to power. It wanted to put an end to the policy of 'nuclear ambiguity' which had so far been followed by the Indian government and intended to put the nuclear card on the table. But beyond this it did not spell out the operational consequences accruing from such a decision. It also looked upon the bomb as an argument just as Narasimha Rao had done. When Atal Behari Vajpayee tried to form his first coalition government in 1996, the scientists started their preparations for the tests immediately but had to call a halt when Vajpayee failed to form a government. The National Front which then governed India from 1996 to early 1998 depended on the outside support of the Congress Party and could not be expected to conduct the tests. It was only when Vajpayee was able to form a government in 1998 that the tests could take place. Everybody concerned listened to his first speech explaining the aims of his government, but he remained noncommittal about the bomb. This was probably also due to the fact that the preparations for the tests were conducted in such secrecy that even American intelligence agencies were caught napping.[26] It seems that the scientists had carefully calculated the breaks they would get whenever the American satellite had passed their site and would not return for several hours. In the event, Vajpayee announced the tests only after they had been carried out. This time there were not just 'devices' but actual bombs of various sizes, including a hydrogen bomb. The hydrogen bomb based on fusion rather than fission was of particular interest to the Indian scientists. It was tested at a separate site at some distance from the other bombs so as to prevent mutual interference. However, as that site was only at a distance of 5 kilometres from a village only a small hydrogen bomb could be tested. The seismic impact of this test was not very impressive and analysts doubted that India had really tested a genuine hydrogen bomb. But the Indian Department of Atomic Energy confirms that a hydrogen bomb has been tested and that no further tests are required to prove this point.[27]

Pakistan carried out its own tests a few weeks later. This was expected, as were the American sanctions which President Clinton had to announce as he was compelled to do by law. The Americans then surprised the Indian government by asking for India's 'Nuclear Doctrine' a doctrine that deals with the operationalization of nuclear weapons. Since the Indian government was interested in the bomb as a political argument but not as an operational weapon, it did not have such a doctrine. The Americans argued that not having a nuclear doctrine was worse than having a bad one, because without it there would be uncertainty and this could turn a crisis into a catastrophe.[28] The Indian side was annoyed by these American promptings. Finally the National Security Adviser, Brajesh Mishra, convened a group of experts who prepared a draft doctrine. It looked very much like its American counterpart, involving a triad of air, land and sea forces equipped with nuclear weapons. The Americans were aghast, for this meant that India would need an arsenal of at least the British or French type. The External Affairs Minister, Jaswant Singh, who had been in continuous dialogue with the officials of the American State Department, could have told his American interlocutors: 'You asked for it!' Instead he emphasized that this was not an official government statement but merely a draft prepared by experts.[29] Once Jaswant Singh left his post and became Finance Minister in 2002, Brajesh Mishra submitted a new nuclear doctrine which was very similar to the draft of 1999. However, in the meantime Indo-American relations had much improved owing to President Clinton's visit of March 2000. It was a strange paradox that Clinton could turn a defeat at home into a triumph in India.[30] The Senate had killed off CTBT, for which Clinton had campaigned incessantly, also twisting Vajpayee's arm to make him sign it. Now this was no longer an issue and Clinton's visit was a huge success. Nevertheless the definition of a 'minimum credible deterrent' remained on India's agenda and is considered in the third section of this chapter. Since a nuclear deterrent depends on an adequate delivery system which would mainly consist of guided missiles, the availability of such missiles must be discussed before turning to the analysis of the deterrent.

The Quest for Satellites and Rockets

Vikram Sarabhai had started India's quest for satellites and rockets, and India's impressive record in this field owes much to his legacy. Just like Bhabha, Sarabhai had first worked in the field of cosmic rays at the Indian Institute of Science during the Second World War. He was thus close to Bhabha in many respects. But as has been mentioned earlier, Sarabhai was opposed to the bomb and he was not at all interested in creating delivery systems for it. Moreover, he was aware of Bhabha's dilemma with regard to access to foreign technology. Space research was dependent on international cooperation and Sarabhai was eager to avoid any identification of his programme with nuclear ambitions. Sarabhai had initially set up the Indian Committee for Space Research (INCOSPAR) with TIFR. One of his early associates in this organization was Abdul Kalam, later President of India. INCOSPAR established a rocket launching facility at Thumba in Kerala in 1962 where the first launch was of an American-built rocket by Sarabhai's Indian team which had been trained in the USA.[31] He then ventured to construct an Indian satellite launch vehicle. Various experiments conducted in the 1960s proved very successful and a second launching station was set up at Sriharikota near Chennai. Finally, in 1969, INCOSPAR was transformed into ISRO – the Indian Space Research Organization under the Department of Atomic Energy (DAE). In keeping with his interest in international cooperation, Sarabhai wanted to disentangle ISRO from the nuclear establishment which he himself led at that time. Accordingly a separate Department of Space was created by the Indian government in 1972 soon after Sarabhai's death.

Sarabhai's successor at ISRO was the equally brilliant and dynamic Satish Dhawan, an acronautics engineer who had done a stint of practical work in the factory of Hindustan Aircraft Ltd in Bangalore before going for further studies to the USA. There he had specialized in aeronautical fluid dynamics, a field to which he later on made important scientific contributions as Professsor of the Indian Institute of Science in Bangalore. Dhawan combined the skills of an engineer with a deep interest in basic research and often constructed the apparatus for his experiments himself. He was also a dedicated teacher. In 1962, he became Director of the Indian Institute of Science and remained in charge there until 1981. When in 1972 Indira Gandhi asked him to head ISRO, he accepted on condition that he could retain his post at the Indian Institute of Science. He managed to do justice to both institutions and turned out to be one of those rare leaders of scientific research and engineering who get the best from their staff by inspiring them with their own innovative work. The rapid advance of the Indian space programme was due to him. ISRO cooperated closely with the Soviet Union and in 1975 the first indigenous Indian satellite, Aryabhatta, was launched with Soviet technological help. The first launch of a completely indigenous satellite launch vehicle was accomplished in 1980.

In spite of India's attempt at carefully dissociating ISRO from the nuclear establishment, the USA prohibited technology transfer to ISRO in 1992. Under pressure from America, Russia also had to suspend its technology transfer to ISRO. This concerned cryogenic engines which were essential for satellite launch vehicles.[32] Neverthelesss, ISRO scored one success after another in the 1990s with its polar satellite launch vehicles and geostationary launch vehicles. The INSAT series of satellites were very useful for the development of communications; today ISRO even produces satellites for European customers. In addition ISRO also made great strides in the field of remote sensing, technology that has mutiple uses as 'spy in the sky', for the monitoring of agricultural production and to determine the impact of natural calamities and so on.

A triumph of Indian satellite construction and the development of indigenous launch vehicles was achieved in 2000 when an Indian satellite weighing 2,000 kilograms was put into orbit by a powerful Indian rocket. Even the second-stage engine of this launch vehicle would have suffced to propel an intercontinental ballistic missile over a distance of 8,000 kilometres. 'Dual use' is no doubt always implied by this kind of research, but satellite launch vehicles are by no means ballistic missiles and cannot be easily converted into them.[33] They are huge, heavy and immobile, whereas missiles must be light and mobile in order to be deployed by rail or road or even in submarines. Nevertheless, the experience gained in civilian rocketry concerning engines with solid or liquid fuel as well as nose cones permitting re-entry into the atmosphere can be transferred to missile technology: personnel trained in one field can easily move to the other. The career of Abdul Kalam is a case in point.[34] As a young aeronautics engineer he had joined the newly established DRDO (Defence Research and Development Organization) in 1958. His project there was to design a hovercraft. This did not succeed and he left DRDO and started working with Sarabhai for INCOSPAR. He was stationed at Thumba, where he concentrated on the launching of rockets. In 1963, he was sent to the USA to do advanced work in aeronautics with NASA. Sarabhai appreciated his work and so did Dhawan, who relied on him for the production of satellite launch vehicles. After two decades of work in this field, Kalam returned to DRDO in 1982 and took up the Integrated Guided Missile Development Programme in 1983. This included short-range and long-range missiles and the programme was termed 'integrated' because the work on these various types of missile was supposed to proceed simultaneously. The programme started with a short-range ground-to-ground missile called Prithvi with a maximum payload of 1,000 kilograms; the second was Trishul, a short-range maritime missile. The third one was an anti-tank missile Nag, and the fourth, Akash, was a medium-range ground-to-air missile. The fifth one was a long-range (approx. 2,500 kilometres) ground-to-ground missile, Agni I.

Kalam worked on all these missiles and launched several of them successfully, a new task his twenty years of practical experience with satellite launch vehicles helped him to perform. All his missiles were indigenous products. Sometimes the second-best solution had to be adopted in order to make any headway. Prithvi, for instance, was powered with liquid fuel although Kalam would have much preferred solid fuel. Filling a rocket with liquid fuel is a laborious process which requires a great deal of preparation, but the ignition is easy. Solid fuel can be transported and the missiles can be deployed quickly, but its ignition sometimes causes problems. Prithvi was first launched in 1988, and Agni I followed in 1989. While Prithvi went into production, Agni I was euphemistically called a 'technology demonstrator'. It was equipped with a first-stage engine powered by solid fuel and a second-stage engine with liquid fuel. Thus, Agni I was basically a satellite launching vehicle in the new garb of a guided missile.[35] It was then replaced by Agni II, powered exclusively by solid fuel and having a range of 5,000 kilometres. Its first successful test flight was conducted in 1999. As a further step ahead, Agni III was launched in 2006. Kalam had become the head of DRDO in 1992 and had also been directly involved in the nuclear tests of 1998 when he had sat in the bunker while the tests were conducted. His presence was kept a closely guarded secret. He had to don a Gurkha cap and was referred to as 'General Prithviraj', a suitable pseudonym for the maker of the Prithvi missile. Kalam was a 'general' only in terms of his pseudonym; otherwise he was a civilian scientist and as such completely innocent as far as strategic considerations were concerned. Admiral Raja Menon, an eminent Indian strategist, has referred to the Integrated Guided Missile Programme as a classic instance of the absence of strategic guidance for Indian scientists. Menon pointed out that all short-range missiles could have been procured in the world market, but not the long-range ones on which the Indian scientists should have concentrated.[36] He was particularly critical of the deployment of the Prithvi rocket which did not serve any useful purpose and became an irritant in a tense moment. Eventually these rockets were parked near Hyderabad from where they could not reach any target outside India.[37]

In spite of India's arsenal of bombs and missiles, the problems of nuclear targeting and similar operational details had not yet been solved. The missiles were 'arguments' just as much as the bombs. Nevertheless, India considered bombs and missiles a deterrent which would prevent potential enemies from attacking the country.

The Relevance of a 'Minimum Credible Deterrent'

After the nuclear tests of 1998 the Indian government announced that all that it was interested in establishing with its newly revealed power was a 'minimum credible deterrent'. This prompted the USA to ask for a specification of the 'minimum' in concrete terms. Prime Minister Vajpayee then stated in the Indian parliament that numbers do not really matter in this field.[38] He was also reluctant to pronounce any hard and fast 'doctrine' except for the assurance that India would not launch a first strike. India obviously hoped that the argument of power would be accepted without any further specifications. The earlier policy of nuclear ambiguity, which meant that potential adversaries were kept guessing whether India had a bomb or not, was now taken to a higher level. India had a bomb: but the adversaries were kept guessing what the country would do with it. Whereas the government wished to keep its cards close to its chest, there were military experts in India who enthusiastically put their cards on the table. General Sundarji, a retired army officer who had been known for his bravado in active service, published a detailed estimate of what he considered to be an adequate deterrent. He felt that the capability to attack five cities in Pakistan and ten in China with three warheads each of 10 to 20 kilotons would constitute a sufficient deterrent.[39] The 45 warheads required for this were already available in India. Keeping missiles with warheads stored in bunkers would be too costly: General Sundarji would rather keep them mobile in the railway system. Moreover, the storage of warheads before they are mounted on missiles could be highly decentralized as the Department of Atomic Energy and DRDO have about a hundred facilities all over India. With the strong traditions of the separate services in India, it would come as no surprise that the navy should have different ideas from those projected by General Sundarji. Admiral Raja Menon, a submarine officer, would rather have a sea-based deterrent, preferably missiles in nuclear-powered submarines.[40] There are some snags in this which make India's strategists shy away from such a deterrent. First and foremost, the warheads could no longer be retained under civilian custody but would have to be handed over to the submarine commanders well in advance. Secondly, targeting is a problem; barrage firing would be the most suitable mode of nuclear warfare by submarine and this would involve a massive strike covering a fairly large area.[41]

It seems that Indian strategists would at the most arm submarines with cruise missiles, for example, the new Brahmos, a joint Indo-Russian product named after the rivers Brahmaputra and Moskwa. They are propelled by Russian engines and guided by Indian software and have a range of 300 kilometres.

Much more important for a 'credible deterrent' than counting missiles and warheads is the structure of the military command which must act in an emergency. As mentioned earlier, the military has been more or less excluded from nuclear planning in India. The musings of retired officers may provide food for thought, but for a credible deterrent it matters what happens after the Prime Minister pushes the proverbial button. India's military tradition with its different Chiefs of Staff for the three services is not very well suited to the nuclear age. At least there has been an attempt to create a special central command for nuclear warfare. The respective systems of control, communication and the processing of intelligence will also have to be created.[42] A nuclear state requires higher levels of internal security and this may impinge on the civil liberties of the people. Guarding bombs and missiles as inert national assets is already quite a challenging task: making them operational at short notice is far more difficult.

Some Indian strategic thinkers have argued for a 'recessed deterrent' which in practice would mean the renunciation of a rapid retaliatory response to a first strike, but would still assure the adversary of such a response after some time. The recessed deterrent would preclude the existence of a ready arsenal controlled by the military. However, this may delay a retaliatory response very much and therefore it has been suggested that a nuclear 'force-in-being' should be kept ready to receive the warheads kept in civilian custody at very short notice. But whether a deterrent is somewhat recessed or not, it still requires the same elaborate infrastructure and efficient control and command as a nuclear arsenal, otherwise the response to a first strike might have to be postponed indefinitely. Concentrating on the bomb as an argument, the Indians tried to avoid as far as possible the dirty business of 'weaponization'. As Raja Menon has put it: 'weaponizing is like entering a long sewer. It is dirty and the exit is only at the other end. The only alternative to wading through the dirt and coming out at the other side is to retrace one's steps.'[43]

Ashley Tellis, the Indian scientist turned American defence analyst, has advised that American aims with regard to the Indian instruments of nuclear deterrence should be to keep them small, stealthy and slow.[44] Such instruments would suffice for India's purposes and would also prevent an arms race and the dangers of escalation. Tellis has worked hard for an American nuclear *rapprochement* with India. From 2001 to 2003 he was adviser to Robert Blackwill, the American ambassador to India.[45] He has written an in-depth report on India's nuclear posture for the RAND Corporation, the think-tank of the American air force, which was published in 2001. It seems that he was also behind President Bush's 'nuclear deal' with India in 2005 which accepts India's political argument and quietly shelves the issue of signing the NPT, which India has consistently refused to do. India's nuclear scientists have been sceptical about this deal, because they feel that since they have achieved so much after years of 'denial-driven' work, the Americans may succeed in subjecting India to some kind of international control after all. Dr Anil Kakodkar, the present head of the Department of Atomic Energy is a reactor engineer who appreciates international cooperation for the civilian use of nuclear energy. But he feels that the old mindset of 'arms control' still exists in Washington.[46] Therefore he also belonged to the sceptics. However, the debate in the American Senate in November 2006 may have convinced the Indian sceptics of the American intention to see the deal through without changing its terms. The Republican Richard Lugar and the Democrat Joseph Biden, respectively the outgoing and incoming chairman of the Senate Foreign Relations Committee, joined forces in defeating several 'killer amendments' which would have forced the Indian parliament to cancel the deal. These amendments concerned a cap on fissile material and a condition that India should stop cooperating with Iran on matters of energy.[47] After this debate the bill was passed by both houses and the act was signed by President Bush on 11 December 2006. The bipartisan support of the nuclear deal would also signal the end of the cartel of the Nuclear Suppliers Group which Henry Kissinger had organized after India's first test in 1974. Of course, all this is also due to the economic interests of all those suppliers, as they will be glad to do business with India in this field. It is interesting to note that the Chinese President, Hu Yintao, also offered to cooperate with India in the field of the civilian use of nuclear energy when he visited New Delhi in November 2006 only a few days after the debate in the American Senate. The long period of India's isolation has finally come to an end. Bhabha would have rejoiced at such a solution to his dilemma.

The Indian communists did not see the deal in this light. They feared that India would become subservient to the USA and threatened to withdraw their 'outside' support of the government if it did not agree to put the deal on hold. A special committee comprising representatives of the government and the left parties held several meetings to discuss the deal. Both sides were not interested in precipitating an election over this issue. The Indians in the USA who had lobbied for the 'nuclear deal' were disappointed and hoped that the BJP would vote for it with the government. But the BJP refused to do so and insisted on a renegotiation of the deal. For the first time India's foreign policy emerged as a hotly contested issue in public debates.

CHAPTER 6

LIBERALIZING A HIDEBOUND ECONOMY

The Legacy of the Wartime Economy

The doctrine of free trade was a creed to which the British firmly adhered when their imperial power was at its zenith. Accordingly, the British–Indian government was not supposed to interfere with the forces of the market and this was reflected in the structure of that government. Its departments were small. They were geared to the maintenance of law and order, the collection of taxes and revenues, etc. Only the procurement of goods required by the government for its own use was an activity which was directly connected with the market. Most of these goods were procured 'at home', that is, in Great Britain, a fact which was often criticized by Indian producers. The turbulence of the world economy in the 1920s and 1930s compelled the British to betray their free trade principles and 'imperial preference' was introduced to protect British trade against outside competition. As far as India was concerned, this was first practised with regard to steel.[1] The Tata Iron and Steel Company (TISCO) had supplied steel for the British war effort during the First World War and had rapidly expanded subsequently. But then it was faced with Belgian and German competition which could have ruined it in no time. The British intervened and introduced a protective tariff which shielded Indian steel against continental European competition but also included preferential rates for British steel. In this way a strategy of 'market sharing' was inaugurated in India. When the Indian cotton textile industry was hard pressed by Japanese competition in the 1930s, this principle was extended to that industry.[2] Thus free trade had been practically abandoned, but except for the administration of customs, the British–Indian government was not yet actively interfering with the Indian market. This changed with the impact of the Second World War in two vital spheres: food supply and procurement of material for the British war effort. The war years happened to be years of good harvests in India. Food availability was thus not a major problem. But prices rose and speculative hoarding increased. At first the government introduced price controls which it could manage with its law and order administration. However, it soon found out that such controls only encouraged an expanding black market. The acquisition of buffer stocks by the government was the only alternative.[3] This required an agency which could buy and store grain – the precursor of the Food Corporation of India which still exists and guards enormous buffer stocks even today.

The other vital sphere of government economic activity during the war was the procurement of Indian industrial products for the war effort. The rather modest procurement machinery of pre-war times was literally put into reverse gear. Earlier goods required by the British–Indian government were mostly bought in Great Britain and shipped to India. Now huge amounts of industrial products were bought in India and sent abroad. Two million Indian soldiers served the British in Europe and Asia. Their uniforms and boots, their arms and ammunition were mostly produced in India. Many other items needed by the British were also supplied by Indian industry. This was a windfall for Indian industrialists, who profited immensely from the war. Government procurement meant, of course, that they were faced with a single buyer. Prices were dictated rather than left to the law of supply and demand. The British procurement agency imposed a 'cost plus' rule. The cost of production was calculated by the British bureaucrats and a margin of about 10 per cent added for the benefit of the industrialists, for whom this was a risk-free business. Indian industry got so used to this comfortable straitjacket that it was going to miss it once hostilities ended.

Under the Government of India Act of 1935, industry was a provincial subject. But this changed during the war, when procurement and price control were managed by the central government. As will be discussed later, industry should have become a provincial subject again after the war, but this was prevented by the new Indian government after the attainment of independence. Centralized control of Indian industry was thus an important part of the legacy of the war. After the provincial governments had taken office in 1937, the Indian National Congress had created a National Planning Committee headed by Jawaharlal Nehru. He saw to it that in addition to the political representatives of the provincial governments a number of experts were recruited to contribute to the committee's deliberations. When the Congress governments resigned at the beginning of the war, the work of the National Planning Committee ended prematurely and Nehru could submit its report only in 1940 shortly before he was arrested and put into jail for the rest of the war. The report was more or less a list of industries which India needed and while it did not specify the investment required or the methods of raising the necessary funds, as a preliminary exercise it set the pattern for Nehru's later industrial policy and his establishment of a Planning Commission in 1950.

The Report of the National Planning Committee introduced the discourse on Indian development which was to dominate all subsequent debates.[4] An emphasis on state intervention, a vague type of socialism and traces of Keynesian economics converged to create a general consensus on what ought to be done in India. Industrialization was stressed as a necessary means to redeem the country from the fate of a traditional agrarian economy. The impact of the Great Depression had shattered the complacent assumption that economic development would take care of itself; the need for planned intervention was accepted even by many British officials working in India. Their suggestions sometimes sounded progressive although their actions usually reflected the seamy side of imperial policy. As far as the rhetoric of development was concerned, there was a broad spectrum of agreement. The only dissenting voice was that of Mahatma Gandhi,[5] who disliked economics as a science of social determinism. From John Ruskin's work he had derived the idea of *Sarvodaya* (The Rise of All) with individual self-restraint its essential source. Accordingly Gandhi was opposed to state intervention, which was regarded as a necessity by almost everybody else at that time.

During the war while the Congress leadership was still in prison, a group of Indian industrialists drafted the Bombay Plan of 1944.[6] Most of the authors were capitalists and the others were intellectuals in their pay. Nevertheless, the rhetoric of their plan was more or less the same as that of the report of the National Planning Committee of 1940. However, they went beyond that earlier report by calculating the investment needed over a period of fifteen years (1947–62) in order for per capita income to be doubled. A total of Rs 100 billion would be required for this plan; out of this Rs 10 billion were to come from the sterling reserves accumulated in the Bank of England during the war, Rs 40 billion could be expected from national savings during the plan period, Rs 6 billion could be derived from exports and Rs 3 billion from the sale of hoarded gold, Rs 7 billion could be received in the form of foreign aid or loans. There would still be a gap of Rs 34 billion, but this could be covered by 'deficit spending' – as recommended by Keynes, who had claimed that printing money in order to revive the economy would not lead to excessive inflation until full employment was achieved. The Bombay Plan also recommended a division of labour between a public and a private sector. The former would take care of heavy industries which required 'capital deepening' and the latter would produce consumer goods. Marxist critics called this a 'Fascist Plan',[7] but to Nehru it must have seemed that the capitalists were not deviating too much from what he had in mind.

While Nehru was still in prison, the Viceroy, Lord Wavell, took note of the Bombay Plan. Instead of debunking it, he appointed Sir Ardeshir Dalal, one of its authors, as a minister for reconstruction and planning in his government.[8] Dalal had been a civil servant and then a director of Tata; he was eminently suited for the new post and took it up with enthusiasm. However, he resigned within a year as he could not do anything for Indian industry in his new position. He realized that his appointment was meant to provide an excuse for the government. As a kind of political testament he drafted the official Statement of Industrial Policy of April 1945. It contained important elements of the Bombay Plan and committed the Government of India to continued state intervention after the war. The statement also drew attention to the fact that central control of Indian industry would cease with the end of the war, as industry was a provincial subject under the Government of India Act of 1935. In order to retain central control, specific legislation was required and the statement contained an outline of this. It also advocated industrial licensing and state ownership of industries 'for which adequate private capital may not be forthcoming', such as aircraft, automobiles, chemicals, iron and steel. There was no reference to socialism in the statement but it recommended that 'the unhealthy concentration of assets in the hands of a few persons' should be avoided. This statement of 1945 foreshadowed the future industrial policy resolutions of Nehru's government.[9]

When Lord Wavell appointed Nehru as interim Prime Minister in August 1946, Nehru had to face turbulent times and could give no thought to industrial policy. It was only in 1948 that his government adopted a new Industrial Policy Resolution which demarcated three sectors: a public sector, a private sector and one in which both public and private investment would be permitted. This resolution more or less echoed the statement of 1945. Nehru still had to share power with the conservative Home Minister, Vallabhbhai Patel, who also had a say in the appointment of the Finance Minister, seeing to it that this ministry would not go to a socialist. Nehru had to wait until Patel died in 1950 before he could determine economic policy on his own. Patel was against the socialists, but he was nevertheless a centralist and would therefore go along with a proposal to retain control by the Government of India over industrial policy. Accordingly a bill to this effect was introduced in 1949, but there were long debates before the Industries (Development and Regulation) Act of 1951 could be passed. The wartime legacy of state intervention was thus firmly entrenched in independent India.

While the Act was still being drawn up, Nehru established the Planning Commission by cabinet resolution in 1950 as has been explained in Chapter 3. In 1956, the government passed another Industrial Policy Resolution which was the definitive statement of Nehru's vision and has very often been cited as such in subsequent years.[10] It enhanced the role of the public sector, which was not only to occupy 'the commanding heights of the economy' but was given great scope to compete with the private sector in many other fields. The state governments were practically excluded from decision making in the field of industrial policy; they could only make a mark by suggesting projects for which they would get matching grants from the Planning Commission. The state governments had hardly any staff that could equal the power and the expertise of the Planning Commission, which was much bigger and more influential than any of the ministries of the Government of India. With the subsequent growth of the Prime Minister's Office (PMO) in Indira Gandhi's time, the Planning Commission and the PMO became the two arms of the Prime Minister, who could dominate Indian politics in this way.

The tightening of central control and the system of industrial licensing unfortunately contributed to a fossilization of Indian industry. Nehru believed that competition would lead to a waste of scarce resources which a poor country like India could not afford. He did not realize that in the long run the excesses of bureaucratic control would be much more wasteful than competition. Licensing was not the only method of control; in addition the Planning Commission specified physical targets of production, that is that the number of machines of a given type was dictated by the planners. Moreover, in the public sector the top managerial positions were filled by senior civil servants who often had no idea of industrial production. All this added up to a suffocating atmosphere which would stifle all creative initiatives. This atmosphere could only be maintained behind the walls of protectionism which shielded the Indian economy from all outside influences. If no competition was permitted inside India, it was necessary to eliminate foreign competition as well.

Protectionism and Import Substitution

Protectionism had grown in India in the interwar period when imperial preference was gradually introduced by the British. Protective tariffs have been justified by the German economist Friedrich List (1789–1846), who was often quoted by Indian nationalists. Such tariffs were supposed to protect infant industries and were to be reduced or abolished as soon as these industries could stand up to international competition. It was agreed that protective tariffs would always hurt consumers, but that nevertheless they would benefit in due course from the growth of their national industries. Imperial preference could not be justified in this way; it would hurt the consumer but only provide an imperfect protection for national industries. Under British rule, Indian industrialists had to accept this system, otherwise they would have received no protection at all.[11] It was only natural that they should strive for perfect rather than imperfect protection.

When market sharing under the regime of imperial preference was introduced into India, the Indian socialists feared that a 'Fascist Compact' between Indian and British capital would ruin the Indian freedom movement.[12] But the Indian capitalists saw that they could not hope to prosper under imperial rule and supported the freedom movement. Protectionism became a common denominator of capitalist interests and socialist ambitions and the mixed economy of independent India was based on this common denominator. Market sharing now applied to the relationship between the public and the private sector in India with indigenous production of goods which had been imported under British rule now the main aim of both sectors. Since India had a large home market, there was great scope for this import substitution, but due to the limited purchasing power of the Indian masses, import substitution was not as attractive an option as many had hoped. Moreover, it was valid only for industries such as the cotton textile industry of western India which had produced for the home market even before independence. The export industries of eastern India – jute products, tea – would not benefit from protectionism. As far as jute was concerned, partition had severed the connection between the East Bengal districts producing raw jute and the jute mills of Kolkata. The rise of the Ahmadabad–Mumbai–Pune region and the decline of eastern India were thus predetermined by the convergence of political and economic developments.

Nehru's economic policy resulted in a trebling of Indian industrial production during his period in office.[13] He had hoped that this would bring about the 'take-off into self-sustained growth' which the American economist W. W. Rostow had proclaimed as a vital stage of economic development. However, Nehru had neglected agriculture, which was hardly amenable to state intervention as it was in the hands of innumerable peasants. He had advocated joint collective farming, but this was resented by the peasants and he had then shelved this policy. Nevertheless agricultural production increased during the Nehru years, but this was entirely due to the extension of cultivation rather then to an increase in yield per acre. Marginal soils had been cultivated which would not yield anything if the rains failed hence the two successive droughts after 1965 affected agricultural production, and with it the Indian economy, very severely.[14] A 'plan holiday' was proclaimed and this ushered in a prolonged industrial recession which lasted until the early 1980s.

The stagnation of India's protected industry after 1965 was caused by several factors.[15] The agricultural crisis was only one of them; since it was soon followed by the Green Revolution of the 1970s it could not be blamed for the continuation of the industrial recession in later years. The declining opportunities for import substitution and India's insufficient exports impeded industrial growth. Indira Gandhi had devalued the rupee by half under

American pressure in 1966. According to the universal recipe of the World Bank, this devaluation would curtail imports and foster exports. However, this recipe did not work as far as India was concerned as the demand for its exports was inelastic and its imports were mainly essential ones such as investment goods and petroleum.[16] The prices for these imports increased in India while the rise in petroleum prices after 1972 only served to exacerbate matters and led to an imported inflation in India. Indira Gandhi had given in to American pressure in 1966 because President Johnson had promised a substantial amount of American aid as a reward for her compliance, but the aid did not come and India had to suffer from this betrayal. India's balance of payments was badly affected, but this was partly compensated for by the remittances of Indian workers who had migrated in great numbers to the rich oil states around the Persian Gulf.

The Indian economy was adversely affected by several internal factors at that time. The substitution of imports as an engine of growth had begun to falter in the mid-1960s. Demand for durable consumer goods had receded. The rise in food prices reduced the funds available for other purchases. The Green Revolution mainly benefited rich peasants whose demand for industrial goods would not immediately increase. Moreover, industrial innovation was inhibited by a policy of inward-looking self-reliance. In many fields India still depended on the import of foreign technology and this was severely curtailed during this period. In addition, a Monopoly and Restrictive Trade Practices Act (MRTPA) was passed in 1969 and a Foreign Exchange Regulations Act (FERA) in 1973. Both acts vastly increased the powers of the bureaucracy, which had a stranglehold on the activities of industrialists. The ceilings imposed by these acts impeded industrial growth. Under the MRTPA licences could be denied to companies once they had more than Rs 200 million gross capital assets, and under FERA foreigners could hold at most 40 per cent in an Indian firm. The MRTPA–FERA regime thus provided a procrustean bed for Indian industry and stunted its growth.[17] Actually, at a time when plan expenditure on industry was insufficient, the government should have tried hard to encourage the private sector to go ahead and increase its share of industrial investment, but instead it stifled the initiatives of the private sector in many ways. In Indira Gandhi's time, India was the most comprehensively regulated market economy in the world[18] and many features of this economy survived deregulation in 1991. A case in point is the reservation of many products for small-scale production. Such industries were favoured by the government because they created employment and acted as a counterweight to big industries in the private sector. As late as 2005 hundreds of products were still reserved for these small-scale operations. In the meantime imports had been freely admitted which competed with these reserved products while large Indian industries were still prohibited from manufacturing them.[19]

Planned expenditure on industrial investment had become of major importance since the second Five Year Plan of 1956–60. The volume of this plan amounted to 12 per cent of GNP and one fifth of it was allocated to industry; this relationship also prevailed more or less during the third (1961–6) and fourth (1969–74) Five Year Plans. But during the plan holiday (1966–8) there was practically no such investment. The fifth Plan (1974–8) which amounted to 17 per cent of GNP allocated a quarter of plan expenditure to industry. This was obviously intended to break the spell of industrial stagnation, but it did not yet succeed. Further planning was upset when Indira Gandhi was defeated in the elections of 1977. After her comeback in 1980 she faced a balance of payments crisis and had to ask the World Bank and the International Monetary Fund (IMF) for help. They considered India a good risk and in the period from 1980 to 1984 IMF loans of a total of Rs 41 billion were made available to the country; these loans were repaid from 1985 to 1989.[20] In 1980 Indira Gandhi resisted American pressure to devalue the rupee once more, but she accommodated American interests by toning down the FERA regime. This was the first hesitant step towards a liberalization of the Indian economy. In her second period of office from 1980 to 1984 she tended to encourage the private sector as against her earlier reliance on the public sector. However, this did not mean that she was converted to the creed of neo-liberalism; rather it reflected a new perception of the role of the state in the process of development.

The Slow Process of Liberalization

After the 'lost decade' of the 1970s, the 1980s were a time of increasing economic growth which quickly transcended the 'Hindu rate of growth'. (The witty Indian economist, Raj Krishna, had introduced this term for the meagre annual growth rate of 3.5 per cent which had prevailed for a long time.)[21] This rate more than doubled in the 1980s, a period that also witnessed an increase in the share of the state in the GNP. This larger share enabled the state to step up plan expenditure, which must have contributed to economic growth. The sixth and seventh Five Year Plans illustrated this trend very clearly. The expenditure on the sixth Plan (1980–5) was roughly 17 per cent of GNP and that on the seventh (1985–9) roughly 24 per cent. At the same time a liberalization of the economy was gradually achieved. Protectionism was reduced and tariffs were lowered though the effective tariff rates still remained quite high. The lowering of tariffs and the subsequent increase in imports provided central government with a windfall in terms of rising revenue from customs duties.[22] Customs duties amounted to

Rs 18 billion in 1977 when income tax yielded Rs 22 billion. By 1986 customs duties had risen to Rs 180 billion while income tax stood at Rs 98 billion. Customs duties which were entirely reserved for the central government thus amounted to almost a quarter of the total tax revenue of the central government and the state governments. If the central government had invested all these windfall gains in productive economic activities it would have been of great benefit to the Indian economy. But much of this additional revenue income helped to finance the creation of more jobs in the public sector, where the number of employees increased from 15 million in 1981 to 19 million in 1991. Only 10 per cent of them were employed in manufacturing. This massive public employment programme was to some extent compensation for the 'jobless growth' in the private sector in the 1980s. Substituting capital for labour by installing new machinery had been a general strategy of private entrepreneurs in this period as they considered labour a liability rather than an asset. Creating 'jobs for the boys' is always important for politicians, but overstaffing greatly burdened the public sector and could not easily be reduced in subsequent years. Meanwhile the salaries and wages of public sector employees strained the resources of both central and state governments.

The 1980s were a period of rising prosperity but also of alarming trends which culminated in a crisis at the beginning of the following decade. Imports had increased much faster than exports. The deficit in the balance of trade was for some time compensated by 'invisibles' which improved the balance of payments, but these invisibles also included liabilities. Commercial loans from abroad had helped to finance economic development in India but this also meant increasing debt servicing. In addition, the government incurred massive fiscal deficits. Critics pointed out that this Keynesian policy followed by the government stimulated growth in the short run but was not sustainable: it was bound to precipitate a crisis.[23] This crisis would have overwhelmed India even without any external shocks.[24] But in the event, these financial upsets provided a catalyst for the onset of the crisis. There were several such upsets which added up to a veritable financial tsunami. The non-resident Indians (NRIs), whose role is described in Chapter 18, had 'parked' large amounts of money in India: the government had assured them of high interest rates on their accounts in India and that they could re-convert their money into foreign currencies at any time. The remittances of Indian workers in the Persian Gulf region were also among the substantial invisibles. If there was any doubt about India's creditworthiness, commercial loans would no longer be available and the NRIs would withdraw their money. The Gulf War of 1990–1 resulted in a sudden loss of remittances. The invisible liabilities then turned into a nightmare. Political instability in India added to this predicament. The balance of payments crisis was so severe that the Indian government was even compelled to airlift all its gold reserves to London in order to obtain a British loan. This was such a humiliating experience that India's subsequent quest for high foreign exchange reserves can be seen as a reaction to this trauma. Foreign exchange reserves are, after all, like credit given to the government whose currency one holds. Accumulating such reserves beyond reasonable limits is a luxury which India cannot afford. But in view of the trauma, India's attitude is understandable.

A crisis can also be an opportunity if it is overcome in a constructive way. The new Indian government which took office in 1991 proved this point. Prime Minister P. V. Narasimha Rao appointed a very competent Minister of Finance: Dr Manmohan Singh. By working together they became a powerful team. As one member of Manmohan Singh's staff quipped: 'Narasimha Rao has the courage of Manmohan Singh's convictions.' This was very important, because Singh was an expert with no political power base of his own, whereas Narasimha Rao was powerful but had never given much thought to economics. Singh introduced comprehensive reforms. He devalued the rupee by about one fifth, deregulated the economy to a large extent and pursued a programme of structural adjustment. Such a programme is expected to result in a J-curve: after an initial recession the economy will recover and grow at a healthy rate. Usually the lower part of the J covers a few years and its stem may lean to the right, indicating a slow ascent. The Indian J corresponded much more to the actual form of the letter: after a short dip in 1992 it rose steeply and reached its peak in 1995. Unfortunately, the curve did not then level off but declined to a much lower level. While the industrial growth rate was 10.3 per cent in 1994 and 12.3 per cent in 1995, it came down to 3.8 in 1997 and in 1998, returning to rates of only about 6 per cent in 2002 and 2003.

There were several reasons for this decline. The private sector had gone on an investment spree, which led to the creation of overcapacity. The stock market had boomed, but had then declined. There was also a setback in the speed of further reforms. Narasimha Rao had to think of the elections of 1996 and tended to adopt populist measures. The equation of courage and conviction mentioned above did not work any longer. Singh had wished to forge ahead with the privatization of substantial parts of the public sector but by October 1995 he had to admit that the cabinet was against this policy.[25] As Suresh Tendulkar has pointed out, there were only a few reformers with conviction in the government; many others were merely reformers by convenience.[26] There had never been serious debate on the reforms in the Congress Party. When elections approached the reformers by convenience would jettison their reformist stance and adopt populist policies. In January 1996, however, Manmohan Singh could survey his achievements with some satisfaction – perched on top of the J-curve, so to speak.[27] He had restored the balance of payments and removed the foreign exchange constraint which had always handicapped the Indian economy. He had drastically reduced import duties while at the same time the competitiveness of Indian exports had increased and more foreign direct investment had been attracted. The fiscal deficits had been reduced and inflation curtailed for his policies had proved to be more employment friendly than those of earlier governments. The macro-economic framework was sound and further progress could be made along these lines.

Unfortunately the government was defeated in the elections of 1996 and a new period of political instability began. The National Front whose fate has been discussed earlier was not in a position to continue the reform agenda. The BJP-led coalition which took office in 1998 could have been expected to support the reforms, since in earlier years the BJP had advocated economic liberalism. The Congress Party had then stolen the BJP's thunder by opting for liberalization. By 1998 some Indian industrialists had come to fear foreign competition and would rather advocate *swadeshi* (national) produc- tion because they did not want to encourage foreign investors who could challenge them.[28] The BJP sided with these industrialists. In any case, the new government had other priorities. It conducted the atom bomb tests of 1998 which automatically led to the imposition of American economic sanctions. India was not cowed by these, but they certainly did not improve the country's economic prospects. The Kargil War of 1999 which was imposed on India by Pakistan was another setback. During Prime Minister Vajpayee's tenure of office there were some encouraging signs such as the export of computer software and of cut diamonds which is discussed in Chapter 8, but there was no repetition of the dramatic upswing of the mid-1990s.

The return to power of Dr Manmohan Singh in 2004 seemed to herald another period of vigorous reforms. Now that he was Prime Minister he could have the courage of his own convictions. But the coalition government he headed was in a different position from the Congress government led by Narasimha Rao. In addition to the coalition partners whose views had to be respected, there were the Communists who supported the government from the outside. They had captured many more parliamentary seats in 2004 than in earlier elections and were opposed to any attempts at privatizing public sector enterprises. In fact, even the earlier government had avoided the dirty word 'privatization' and had replaced it with 'disinvestment'. The Communists, of course, would not support disinvestment either. They would not risk toppling the government, because that would mean a return of the BJP to power. Therefore Manmohan Singh could dare to call their bluff in many ways. But a test of strength in matters concerning the public sector would be rather dangerous.

Manufacturing has shown encouraging growth rates in India in recent years.[29] After a dip from 7.1 per cent in 1999 to 2.9 per cent in 2001, the growth rate increased rapidly to 9.2 per cent in 2004. Capital goods and consumer goods showed higher growth rates than other products. There was, however, a noticeable shift in the rates of value added in various industries. Textiles declined further for reasons which will be discussed in the next chapter. The chemical industry progressed speedily. Pharmaceuticals were particularly prominent both in terms of domestic supply and in exports. In 2004 this industry produced goods worth US\$ 8.3 billion, of which 45 per cent were exported. Steel production increased rapidly, from 34 million tonnes in 2002 to 40 million tonnes in 2004. India's industrial growth also attracted more foreign direct investment (FDI). From US\$ 3.45 billion in 2002 the inflow of FDI increased to US\$ 5.34 billion in 2004.[30] Compared to the FDI flows to China, these are still very small amounts; the figures for China for the years in question were US\$ 52 and 63 billion. In contrast with the very modest amounts of FDI, India has recently attracted much more foreign institutional investment (FII). This type of investment is attracted by the booming Indian stock market. It enjoys full convertibility on capital account whereas Indian funds are restricted to convertibility on current account for purposes of trade. FDI, which is usually invested in factories and so on, cannot be withdrawn at short notice, whereas FII-portfolio investment is highly volatile. In recent times the Indian government has been very confident of the robust nature of the Indian economy. India may even introduce full convertibility on capital account and let the rupee float freely, which would then lead to an appreciation rather than a depreciation of the Indian currency. With strong economic growth, such a scenario is very likely, whereas only a few years ago when the 'Asian Crisis' had shocked the world, India was very reluctant to think of adopting such a policy. Convertibility on capital account requires a robust and well functioning banking system. During the Asian Crisis the banking systems of several Asian countries had proved to be very fragile, because Asian banks had indulged in short-term borrowing in international markets and used these funds for long-term lending at home.

When Dr Manmohan Singh was Finance Minister in the 1990s he had proposed the introduction of convertibility on capital account. The Tarapore Committee which was appointed by the Reserve Bank of India in 1996 to look into this matter had designed a road map which should have led to full convertibility in 2000. The intervening Asian crisis derailed this plan. In March 2006 Dr Manmohan Singh took up this matter again and the Tarapore Committee was revived. It prepared a road map of a more cautious type which should lead India to full convertibility in 2010. It also admonished the government to reduce its debts and its fiscal deficit as convertibility would make

India very vulnerable if this was not done.[31] The Indian government relies on financial repression in its fight against inflation. It also parks its deficits in public sector banks. Neither of these practices goes well with full convertibility. It seems that the government has now adopted a gradual approach to this aim by raising the amounts which Indians may transfer abroad at a moderate rate.

While India's macro-economic scenario once more looks very encouraging, the internal differentiation of the country has increased and regional disparities have become conspicuous. Whereas Gujarat and some other rich states have advanced at a rapid pace, India's poor states such as Bihar and Uttar Pradesh have fallen back since 1991. In the 1980s Gujarat's growth rate of 5.7 per cent had been slightly above the national average of 5.6. Even Uttar Pradesh had scored 5.8 per cent in this period and Bihar was only slightly below average, at 5.2. In the period from 1990 to 2004, Gujarat achieved 8.9 per cent whereas Uttar Pradesh stood at 3.7 and Bihar at 4.2. The national average was 5.9 for this latter period. The discrepancy between the two periods is obviously due to the fact that investment by the state was very substantial in the 1980s whereas it was scaled back in the reform period. Gujarat then benefited from a surge of private investment which was not available in states like Uttar Pradesh and Bihar.

The latest initiative of the Indian government for the encouragement of private investment is the establishment of Special Economic Zones (SEZs). This idea was first propagated by Murasoli Maran, a minister in the BJP-led coalition, who had visited China and came back with great enthusiasm for the special economic zones which he had seen there. Suggestions for the adoption of this Chinese model had been made to the Indian government even earlier, but the model did not seem to fit into the Indian political landscape. Prime Minister Narasimha Rao had shown no interest in it when it was recommended to him. But in 2004 the new Congress-led coalition took up the scheme and passed the Special Economic Zones Act in 2005.[32] This was followed in February 2006 by the publication of an elaborate set of rules.[33] The Act contains many details of the procedure for approval of such zones, the exemption from customs duties and taxes, etc. but it is silent about the land which has to be converted into such special zones. The rules provide some more information on this point, but even this consists of stray references. It is stipulated that the land concerned should be vacant and unencumbered and that the developer of the zone is not permitted to sell this land. Such requirements are justified because the privileges enjoyed by the developer would enhance the value of the land enormously and it would become an object of speculation.

Reading the specimen application form which has to be signed by the developer is very illuminating. He is asked to show proof that he owns the land in question, otherwise he should explain how he intends to acquire it. He is also asked to state how he is going to rehabilitate displaced persons. This is a surprising question, as the land is supposed to be vacant according to an article of the rules. Neither the Act nor the rules contain any reference to the method of land acquisition. A developer applying for an SEZ could very well buy the land at market rates and the state should not be required to help him in this transaction. When asked about this, Prime Minister Manmohan Singh confirmed that the government should not interfere with the forces of the market in this respect.[34] Nevertheless, the colonial Land Acquisition Act of 1894 has been resorted to for this purpose, an expedient which has led to intense debate in India. Agriculture Minister Sharad Pawar joined the ranks of its critics and stressed that the government should have no role in the acquisition of farmland.[35]

The Land Acquisition Act is very useful for developers. First of all, it explicitly refers to the acquisition of land by companies in addition to the needs of government. Furthermore, it empowers the district officer to make an award concerning the payment of compensation. If the expropriated landowner challenges this award in a court of law, the burden of proof of the correct market price is on him. The court is debarred from taking the future value of the land into consideration. The establishment of an SEZ would, of course, raise the value of the land enormously. But the court must turn a blind eye to this.

A recent lawsuit brought by the peasants of Jamnagar District in Gujarat against an enterprise of the powerful Reliance corporation highlights this issue. They argued that the Land Acquisition Act was misused so as to deprive them of their land. The peasants lost their case in the High Court of Gujarat and appealed to the Supreme Court, which upheld the High Court's verdict. The powers given to the executive by the Land Acquisitions Act are clearly defined, so the courts cannot provide any help in this matter. The Supreme Court gave leave to the Jamnagar peasants to approach it concerning the amount of compensation for the land, but as this is already laid down in the Act, only an amendment to the Act could prevent its unfettered application to the creation of SEZs. Hundreds of large and small SEZs have been approved very speedily. Cultivated land has been expropriated in spite of the original intention to use only 'vacant' land for SEZs. When looking at this new procedure one is reminded of the British establishing colonial economic enclaves in India: they also found the Land Acquisition Act helpful for this purpose.

Defenders of the use of the Land Acquisition Act argue that there are good reasons for resorting to it. Mukesh Ambani of Reliance Industries thinks that it should not be used for purely commercial purposes, but that industrialists who establish factories which provide employment should be entitled to invoke it.[36] He is about to build a second Mumbai as an SEZ and he proposes to return one eighth of the land fully developed to the former owner, thereby converting him into a stakeholder in his project. Montek Singh Ahluwalia, deputy chairman of the Planning Commission, adduces a practical reason for making use of the Act. In establising a large SEZ the developer would have to deal with hundreds of owners and this would discourage him from investing in it. But Ahluwalia agrees that the old colonial Act may have to be revised.[37]

Critics have pointed out that the creation of SEZs may lead to investment diversion wherever relocation costs are lower than the tax benefits available in those zones. Moreover, there may be massive welfare losses due to the displacement of the expropriated people. There are estimates that about a million people may be affected by displacement. Furthermore, the special privileges of those who move into the SEZs will be in striking contrast to the outside entrepreneurs who have worked hard without getting such benefits. Revenue losses will be of such proportions that the government must shift the tax burden to others, a scenario that will further complicate a tax structure which ought to be broadened and simplified rather than riddled with unnecessary concessions.[38] This latest attempt at 'patchy' liberalization seems to be as faulty as the earlier attempts at imposing ill-considered schemes on the Indian economy. The story of the Indian textile industry, which is related in the next chapter, is a case in point.

CHAPTER 7

SICK MILLS AND STRONG POWERLOOMS

Sick Mills: The Consequences of a Misguided Textile Policy

Once upon a time, India was the world's leader in cotton textile production. Such textiles were exported even by the weavers of the Indus civilization. When the Dutch and the British arrived at the shores of India, they soon found that the trade in Indian textiles would bring them great profit. They first shipped those textiles to other countries around the Indian Ocean, but then they also included them at auctions in Amsterdam and London and discovered that there was a great demand for them in Europe. The Indian cotton prints were beautiful and solid, but they did not change with the fashion. In the European markets new, attractive designs were essential. The London cotton printers were pioneers in this field in the early eighteenth century.[1] Since a reliable supply of white cotton cloth was often a problem, spinning and weaving were done in England where labour was scarce.

The English woollen industry complained about the damage done by competitors, but in fact that industry also expanded and could not release labour. In the latter half of the eighteenth century, labour-saving devices for spinning and weaving cotton were invented in England and spread rapidly – but not to India. The devices were cheap and easy to make, but India had plenty of labour and did not need them. In fact, even when British mills inundated India with cotton cloth, the handloom weavers in some regions could still compete with them as long as food and raw cotton were cheap.[2] Only the weavers of Bengal who had mainly worked to export white cloth which was needed by the London printers faced starvation and death when the East India Company no longer bought their products. Their bones then bleached in the plains of Bengal, as Lord Bentinck had observed and Karl Marx later repeated.

The Industrial Revolution bypassed India, but in the mid-nineteenth century when silver once more poured into the country for the financing of railway construction and the prices of food and raw cotton rose, the hand-loom weavers found it difficult to compete with industrial production. In the meantime, British textile machinery had been exported to many countries and it also reached India, where the first modern cotton textile mill was set up in 1854. When the American Civil War interrupted the supply of raw cotton to British mills, the price of Indian cotton rose and cotton cultivation expanded. This was a tough time for the young Indian textile industry, but once the war was over, cotton prices fell and many new mills were started in Mumbai and then in Ahmadabad. Initially most Indian mills were spinning mills, supplying the handloom weavers of India and other Asian countries with yarn. At the end of the nineteenth century, there was a glut in the market for yarn. This is when composite spinning and weaving mills became popular in India, because yarn which could not be sold could be used in the weaving department of the same mill. The composite mill then became the standard type of Indian cotton textile mill.[3]

In the years of the Great Depression, the Indian textile industry was partially protected under the regime of imperial preference. Production for the home market expanded, but there was hardly any investment in new machinery.[4] Moreover, India had no textile machine industry of its own. During the Second World War, no machinery could be imported, but the mills worked around the clock under the regime of government procurement. By the end of the war, spindles and looms were worn out and mill-owners would have liked to have invested in new machinery. However, foreign exchange was scarce as India had no immediate access to its reserves accumulated in the Bank of England. At this stage something happened which had terrible conse-quences for the future of the Indian textile industry. Mahatma Gandhi had compelled the Indian government to abolish the food-grain controls intro-duced during the war. Prices fell after the controls had been abolished – as Gandhi had predicted.[5] His followers then tried to apply the same rule to cotton texiles, which had also been subjected to controls. The mill-owners warned the government that they would not be able to cope with the rising demand with their decrepit looms. Nevertheless, the controls were abolished and prices rose. Controls were then re-imposed in August 1948.[6] At the same time positive discrimination in favour of the products of handloom weavers was introduced. These weavers were dear to Gandhi as he regarded them as the paragon of the type of cottage industry which he preferred to the mills. The well-meaning protectors of the handloom weavers did not notice that these weavers had to a large extent been replaced by powerloom weavers, whose rise will be described below. The mills were now prevented from modernizing their equipment and expanding their production. They were turned into living fossils. The mill-owners continued production halfheartedly. There seemed no longer to be any future for this industry. Some mills were closed down as early as the 1950s and 1960s. To make matters worse, a prolonged strike of textile labour in Mumbai in the 1980s sounded the death knell for the industry in this metropolis.

It was quite natural that textile labour should be frustrated under these conditions, but resorting to a strike in an industry which was already doomed proved to be counterproductive. The workers turned to Dr Datta Samant, an independent labour leader who had organized a very succesful strike for the workers of the Premier automobile factory in Mumbai. This strike ended with a substantial increase in wages, which were tied to a productivity index. Samant was a medical doctor who knew nothing about economics and thought that his recipe would work in the textile industry just as it had done in the automobile industry. He was a charismatic leader and inspired the workers to continue their strike, which started in 1982, for eighteen months. (His life ended tragically when he was openly gunned down by gangsters in 1997.) The result of the strike which he had led was perverse: the workers shifted to the powerlooms in order to earn a living and the mill-owners procured cloth from these power looms and marketed it.[7] By the time the strike ended the powerlooms had taken over most of the production and the mills were 'sick'.

The phenomenon of a 'sick mill' can only be understood in the Indian context. Elsewhere a sick mill would go bankrupt and close down. In India, however, where there are no unemployment benefits, laid-off workers are politically dangerous and therefore the government will nurse sick mills to keep them alive even if they cease to produce anything. The mill-owners soon learned to make a profit out of being sick. The Reserve Bank of India sanctioned favourable loans for such sick mills. Clever manipulators could siphon off enough money from such loans and use it for other purposes. The production of mill-made cloth declined steeply under such conditions, from about 3.4 to 2 billion metres in the decade of the 1980s. In the same period the production of powerlooms increased from 5 to 11.4 billion metres.

In 1985 the government headed by Rajiv Gandhi announced its New Textile Policy, which was supposed to turn the industry around. For the first time the government acknowledged the existence of powerlooms and excluded them from positive discrimination, which was now exclusively reserved for genuine handlooms. In 1986 a Textile Modernization Fund was introduced and in 1987 the government established a Board of Industrial Finance and Reconstruction (BIFR) as an instrument to turn around sick mills. BIFR was vested with considerable powers. It could order a change of management, arrange for the merger of mills or put them up for sale. The officers in charge had judicial powers, but as they were 'generalists' of the Indian Administrative

Service (IAS), they hardly knew how to use those powers. BIFR remained ineffective and often saved bankrupt firms 'in the public interest', imposing 'sacrifices' on the creditors and enabling the mill-owners to profit from such measures.[8] By the end of 2004, BIFR had handled nearly one thousand cases of textile mills, which had accumulated Rs 190 billion losses, and had 662,000 workers on their payroll. Actually no remedial devices could cure the ills of mills. Having crippled them for years, the government merely offered them some crutches.

Mumbai, the textile metropolis of India, was deeply affected by the demise of this industry. Moreover, a dynamic adjustment to new conditions was prevented by the government: whereas it had earlier discouraged investment in the mills, it now obstructed the sale of their land. About half of this land was private property while the other half was in the hands of the National Textile Corporation, the receiver of sick mills. Some of the mill-owners sold off their land surreptitiously, forging links with the Mumbai underworld. In some cases this involvement led to the murder of prominent mill-owners by gangsters whom they had patronized and who had then turned against them. The extent of urban land locked up by the mills is enormous.[9] In addition, 730 hectares of valuable urban property are controlled by Mumbai's inefficient Port Authority, which earns most of its money from demurrage charges due to the slow handling of cargo. The map of Mumbai which shows these locked-up lands looks like a pockmarked face. Some shopping malls have been built wherever clever entrepreneurs have managed to get hold of such land, but drastic surgery is required to provide Mumbai with a much-needed facelift. This would also require a relocation of the workers who populate the large slums of the metropolis. Powerlooms and workshops for ready-made garments can be more cheaply accommodated outside city limits; in fact, many of them are already located there. But the planning for this urban transition has been haphazard.

The Amazing Progress of Powerloom Production

Powerloom production is a typical example of the thriving activity of the informal sector of the Indian economy. It started out with a few discarded looms from the mills which were put in sheds and operated by workers who could be hired and fired at any time and had to be satisfied with low wages. Powerloom operators had emerged during the Second World War. In 1941, the Government of India had appointed a Fact-Finding Committee (Handlooms and Mills), which also took note of the existence of these powerlooms, indicating that by 1939 there were about 2,500 of them and that they were spreading with great rapidity.[10] Policy makers of independent India

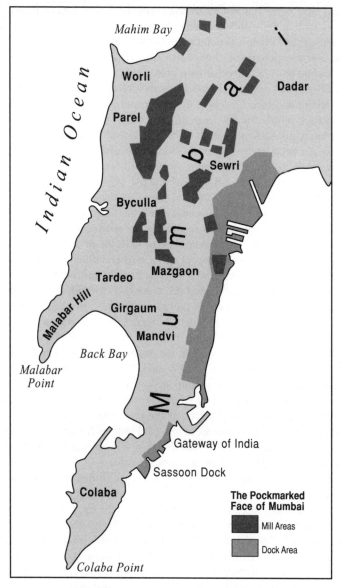

Map 2 The Pockmarked Face of Mumbai: Mills and Docks
Source: Two separate maps in D. D'Monte (see bibliography)
Cartography: N. Harm, South Asia Institute, University of Heidelberg

should have noted this report. By the 1960s there were already powerloom centres such as Bhiwandi in Maharashtra where thousands of looms were running day and night. The point when the amounts of cotton cloth produced by mills and by powerlooms were nearly equal, at about 4 billion metres each, was reached by 1975. After that date, powerloom production trebled over the next fifteen years while mill production dwindled into insignificance.[11] The government had tried for a long time to encourage the spread of industrial production outside the few large urban centres. In this respect, the rise of powerloom production seemed to be a welcome development. But these looms need electricity and transport connections and tend to form clusters, as in Bhiwandi. About half of them operate in Maharashtra and not in the economically more backward states of India.

The new textile policy of 1985 did not affect the powerloom sector very much as it was unregistered and could hardly be controlled. The only government measure which was deeply resented by the powerloom operators was an order issued in 1986 that reserved the production of saris and dhotis to genuine hand looms. The output of cheap saris and dhotis for the masses is the mainstay of powerloom production; the hand looms could not cope with this demand. Whoever had drafted this order had obviously no idea what he was doing. There was a wave of protest which soon subsided, presumably because it was impossible to impose the order. Another ill-conceived measure was the exemption of handlooms from the tax on yarn. This was easily subverted in such a way as to benefit the powerlooms. Handlooms use hank-yarn whereas powerlooms need reeled yarn. This gave rise to another illegal industry which specialized in putting hank-yarn on reels and selling them to the powerloom operators. Under government regulations, the spinning mills are obliged to reserve 25 per cent of their production for hank-yarn, the winding of which they outsource to low-paid women. It is absurd that a large part of it then ends up in the workshops where it is reeled for the powerlooms – a job which the spinning mills could do directly.

Whereas powerlooms were originally those which had been discarded by the mills, nowadays most are manufactured specially for the powerloom operators. The spinning mills have also benefited from the rise of the powerlooms, among them the spinning mills of Coimbatore which had never been composite mills. Coimbatore is also the home of India's most modern factory producing spinning machinery, the Lakshmi Machine Works (LMW).[12] It started production in 1966 with the close cooperation of a Swiss firm which not only supplied the machine tools but also provided technical training and continuous technology transfer.

The powerlooms run by small-scale operators are almost exclusively shuttle looms. Weaving technology has moved on and shuttleless looms have replaced the old shuttle looms in modern mills. In these new looms air jets blow the woof through the warp. For man-made fibres, water jets can be used. The new looms have much higher rates of productivity and their output is of higher quality, which is particularly important for export production. Accordingly a new stratification can be noticed in the Indian textile industry. The home market for cheap cloth is left almost entirely to the powerlooms whereas the production of high-quality cloth has become the preserve of modern composite mills which have survived the general demise of the mills. According to recent statistics (2004) the powerlooms have the lion's share of 83 per cent of textile production, about 12 per cent is left to the handlooms and the rest is taken care of by the mills.

Present Challenges and Future Prospects

Fewer than a dozen modern mills dedicated to the production of cloth of high quality are the pacesetters for the revival of the Indian textile industry. Among them there are two famous mills in Mumbai, Bombay Dyeing and Standard; another two are located in Bangalore, and one each in Ahmadabad, Solapur and Banswara (Rajasthan). The eleven mills account for only 5 per cent of the weaving capacity, but their share in total mill production amounts to 20 per cent. As far as sales are concerned, they control 50 per cent of mill production, which reflects the high value of their products.[13] A large share of their production is sold to the makers of ready-made garments, which will be discussed later.

In addition to garments, there are many other textile products which require new skills and technologies. Shoe uppers, for instance, are among such new products. India is a leading supplier of leather shoe uppers, but with the global spread of sneakers, textile uppers are also in great demand. Seatbelts are another product that sells well. The textile parts of tyres also belong in this category (Chinese exports to the USA consist to a large extent of this material). There are many more 'technical' textiles which nowadays claim a large share of world textile production. With the rising demand for cotton products in the export market, the cultivation of raw cotton has also increased very fast in India in recent times. Moreover, bad harvests doubled the world market price of cotton from late 1993 to May 1995 when it reached 115 US cents/lb, an extraordinarily high price that soon declined to 66 US cents/lb, in 1998. At present it tends to be even lower. However, the price signal of the mid-1990s had enticed Indian peasants in areas where the soil was not suited for cotton cultivation to switch to that cash crop. Many of them were in debt and were doubly affected by poor harvests and the fall in prices in subsequent years. The first wave of suicides of Andhra peasants was owing to this calamity.

From 1980 to 1996 the production of raw cotton almost doubled in India and reached 2.4 million tonnes. In this period yield per acre had only increased by 60 per cent. This meant that the area under cotton had to be expanded in a big way. Whereas in the early 1990s the area under cotton had amounted to 7.5 million hectares, it suddenly increased to 9 million due to the price rise of 1994. Many peasants were new to cotton cultivation and had given up the cultivation of millet (*jowar*) in order to grow this cash crop which fetched such a good price. When the cotton boom left them in the lurch, they could not even fall back on their humble millet. The total amount of *jowar* harvested in India dropped from 11.7 in 1990 to 7.5 million tonnes in 1997, a level at which it has remained ever since. The production of raw cotton, however, which stood at 1.6 million tonnes in 1990, has continued at about 2.3 million tonnes from the second half of the 1990s to the present.[14]

A new challenge to India which actually should prove to be a great opportunity was caused by the expiry of the Multi-Fibre Agreement on 1 January 2005. Before this date the markets of developed countries were protected by a quota system. This enabled those countries to make special concessions to poor countries, which depended to a large extent on export earnings from textiles. Bangladesh is a case in point; it benefited a great deal from such concessions. With the abolition of quotas, free competition will prevail and there is general agreement that this will be to the advantage of China and India, whereas countries such as Bangladesh will suffer. Prices will fall as a result of this competition. The consumers in importing countries will profit while the exporting countries will have to cut their costs. China is far ahead of India in textile exports and this means that the Indian textile industry will have to improve its performance in many ways in order to catch up with its giant competitor. Whereas India increased its share of the world textile and clothing market only marginally from about 3 to 4 per cent in the period from 1990 to 2003, China's share expanded from about 7 to 19 per cent. The growth of exports of textiles and clothing to the USA after 1 January 2005 is revealing. While India increased its exports to the USA by 34 per cent, Chinese exports expanded by 242 per cent. China has been requested to impose some voluntary restrictions on its exports, but even if restrictions were to be imposed India would hardly be in a position to catch up with China in the foreseeable future.

There are many constraints which impede India's competitiveness. For instance, Indian labour productivity amounts to only one third of that in the USA whereas in China it reaches 55 per cent of the American level. Energy costs much more in India than in any of the countries competing with it in this field. Delivering Indian goods to the USA takes on average 24 days, whereas Chinese goods reach their American destination within 15 days. The quality of Indian goods is often inferior to that of Chinese goods. Moreover, the quality of Indian consignments often varies unpredictably. Much of this is due to the highly fragmented structure of the Indian textile industry. It is not easy to remove all these constraints very quickly. Many are owing to the historical conditions described above and concerted efforts are needed to overcome the legacy of misguided policies. The National Textile Policy announced in 2000 heralded a bold new departure. It is aimed at raising the level of textile and clothing exports from US$ 11 billion (2001) to US$ 50 billion (2010). In 2004 the value of these exports amounted to about US$ 9.4 billion. High hopes were raised by the abolition of the quotas, which should have led to a substantial growth of Indian textile exports in 2005,[15] but in 2005 these exports registered a negative growth rate of about minus 2 per cent. This was a big disappointment; it cast doubts on the ambitious figure projected for the year 2010. It seems that India's competitors were able to exploit the new opportunities much faster, something which China's exports to the European Union demonstrated very clearly. They surged by 80 per cent in 2005 in spite of a slight appreciation of the Chinese currency by about 2 per cent. Perhaps this will force India to make a desperate effort to overcome the constraints that are blocking its growth in this field.

The policy of reserving the production of many textiles for the small-scale sector had impeded Indian exports for a long time. It could be maintained in a protected home market, but it strangulated export production in a highly competitive world market where economies of scale are essential. In March 2005, this reservation was scrapped, but it took some time before this led to a massive increase in export production. The export of ready-made garments, which had amounted to US$ 6. 2 billion in 2004–5, reached US$ 8.6 billion in the following year and showed further growth throughout 2006.[16] As will be shown in the next chapter, this contributed to India's success in stepping up its exports, but the textile component still did not quite measure up to the expectations raised by the termination of the Multi-Fibre Agreement.

CHAPTER 8

DIAMONDS, GARMENTS AND SOFTWARE

The Magic of Diamond Processing

When India had shielded its economy behind tariff walls, its share in world trade had dwindled into insignificance. As mentioned earlier, 'export pessimism' was the prevailing mood at that time. It was not easy to change this mood so only new branches of export production could escape it. Nowadays three new types of commodity account for more than half of India's total exports. Diamond processing was the first and the most unexpected success story of them all. Of course, India had been known as a source of beautiful diamonds in ancient times, but in modern times South Africa has been the leading producer of raw diamonds and the processing is done in Western Europe in places such as Antwerp. Only a few decades ago Jewish merchants controlled almost the entire diamond trade and Jewish artisans participated in the processing of these precious stones. Suddenly a community of Gujarati merchants from Palanpur cut into this trade and made use of cheap and skilled labour available to them in places such as Surat and other towns of Gujarat as well as on the outskirts of Mumbai.

India has to import the raw diamonds; the contribution of its export industry is the value added by expert processing. A breakthrough was provided to this new industry by the creative use of industrial diamonds. Only about a quarter of all diamonds mined are normally fit for jewellery; the rest are passed on to the makers of machine tools for cutting and grinding. Most industrial diamonds are small. Gujarati entrepreneurs knew how to get these tiny stones processed and adopted novel designs of jewellery which sparkled due to the collective effect of many small stones rather than the individual radiance of larger and very expensive diamonds. This created a new market of middle-class consumers who could not afford expensive jewellery. But the Gujarati entrepreneurs also ventured into the market for very precious stones.

They even created new brands such as the Nakshatra diamonds endorsed by the Indian actress Aishwarya Rai, a former Miss World.

The buying of diamonds in places like Antwerp is done by the so-called 'sightholders', experts entitled to inspect raw diamonds and select them for their respective companies. Earlier these sightholders were a charmed circle of insiders, but the Gujarati merchants gained access to the circle and now almost dominate it. Eleven of twelve diamonds processed in the world are now processed in India.[1] This, of course, means that the fast growth which this Indian industry registered in recent years is bound to level off. The value of Indian exports of precious stones – mostly processed diamonds – has expanded by leaps and bounds. In 1966 the value of these exports was a mere US$ 25 million; by 2004 it amounted to US$ 14 billion.

India's greatest advantage is the low wage paid for the rather demanding job of diamond processing. The fixture in which the diamond is held during processing is called a *dop*. With a semi-automatic dop a worker can polish 800 to 1,000 diamonds per day. The wages of Indian workers in this line are about 10 per cent of those earned by their colleagues in Antwerp. This is why more than 800,000 workers are employed in the various workshops in Surat whereas in Antwerp there are only about 30,000 still active in this field. Surat is just one of the Indian centres of diamond processing, though perhaps the largest. The conditions of the workers are generally quite miserable and children are also recruited for this work. Large profits are reaped only by the entrepreneurs, who have now extended the scope of their work to other Asian countries and even to Russia.

Although India now has the lion's share of diamond processing, Indian jewellers still control only about 3 per cent of the world market in jewellery. Whereas Indian exports of processed diamonds may have peaked, there is much scope for further growth in using those diamonds for Indian-designed jewellery and creating new markets for it, albeit for such up-market activities more skills and higher education are required than for mere diamond processing. Some Indian companies have already demonstrated their abilities in this field, but much remains to be done. India depends to a great extent on the American market whose retailers usually accept Indian consignments which they can return if they are unable to sell them. Marketing is thus of crucial importance to the Indian producers. Exploiting cheap labour as the sole source of profit has its limits; moreover, there is plenty of cheap labour in Asia, and China may also challenge India in this field. Moving ahead is essential here as in so many other fields. In order to encourage new initiatives and advanced training the Indian government established the Indian Institute of Gems and Jewellery in Mumbai in 2005.[2] It is located close to the Special Economic Export Processing Zone (SEEPZ) where many jewellers as well as computer software and hardware producers have set up workshops. Surat is about to overtake Mumbai by building a 72-hectare Gems and Jewellery Park at the cost of about US$ 900 million.

Moving up-market and going global is a must for India's jewellers. Establishing a reputation by producing famous brands is important in this field and in this line Mehul Choksi and his firm Gitanjali Gems Ltd have blazed a trail which others may follow. The company was established in 1966 and became one of the first sightholders in India. Around the year 2000 its business seemed to stagnate, but under Choksi's dynamic leadership it has forged ahead in recent years. He saw to it that production and retail sales of the company expanded together. In addition to production centres in Surat and Mumbai he developed a Special Economic Zone in Hyderabad with the support of the Government of Andhra Pradesh. But the most dramatic expansion has been in the field of retail sales. The company already had about 800 retail outlets in India, and it then started a partnership with a leading retailer in Saudi Arabia which owns 38 shops specializing in diamond jewellery. Choksi's greatest coup was the acquisition of Samuels Jewellers, an American retail chain which operates 97 stores in 18 US states. The deal was concluded in December 2006 and Choksi had to pay about US$ 40 million for the company.[3] This provides Gitanjali Gems with outlets for its famous diamond brands such as Nakshtra, Asmi and Gili. The USA encompasses 35 per cent of the world jewellery market; an entry into this market via a well-established retail chain is thus a coup for Choksi's company. He is also experimenting with new designs, matching diamonds with metals other than gold, that have a special appeal to young people. The traditional Indian market is still dominated by diamonds set in 22 to 23 carat gold – and most of this traditional market is in the hands of local jewellers and goldsmiths. In fact, the organized sector controls only about 7 per cent of the Indian jewellery market. There is thus much scope for entrepreneurs like Choksi to capture a larger share of the market both in India and abroad.

In the meantime new trends have also emerged in global diamond trading. Much of it has shifted to Dubai, where the government has granted a tax holiday of fifty years to the traders and sponsored the construction of a skyscraper with 65 floors exclusively dedicated to the diamond trade. It is said that all of the office space was taken up by the traders as soon as it was made available. This was a severe blow to Antwerp, which had been the hub of the global diamond trade for such a long time. For some years it seemed as if the sky was the limit for India's booming diamond processing industry, but in 2006 there was a deceleration of Indian exports in this field.[4] It remains to be seen whether this is a temporary setback or the first sign of a levelling off of the ascending curve of Indian diamond exports.

The Attraction of Ready-made Garments

The discovery of the world market for ready-made garments has also been a fairly recent phenomenon as far as India is concerned. Indian tailors were not used to the production of such garments; 'tailormade' items made to measure for the individual consumer were what they usually produced. Cutting cloth for mass production according to strict specifications was the kind of work to which Indian tailors could not easily adjust. However, the demand for ready-made garments increased not only for export but also in the Indian home market. By now about 70 per cent of the production of such garments is taken up by Indian consumers, which means that garment production has a strong base at home and does not depend exclusively on the export market. In the period from 1995 to 2003, India's exports of cloth and of ready-made garments had been of approximately the same value and had shown similar growth rates. In 1995 India exported cloth worth US$ 4.4 billion and garments worth US$ 4.1 billion; the respective figures for 2005 were US$ 4 billion and US$ 8.6 billion.[5] This shows that garment exports have expanded at a much faster rate in recent years, a trend that may continue in the near future. China is India's greatest competitor in this field. It more than doubled its garment exports from US$ 24 billion in 1995 to US$ 52 billion in 2003, dwarfing India's export performance. As mentioned earlier, the Indian government had announced a National Textiles Policy in 2000 and had announced that by 2010 India should be able to export textiles worth US$ 50 billion, half of which should be due to the export of garments. In order to achieve this goal a fund for technological upgrading was established and the reservation of the production of garments for small-scale industries was abolished as it was realized that India had to achieve economies of scale if it was to compete internationally.[6] Investment in the textile industry was nevertheless sluggish in subsequent years. It was only after the international textile quota system had expired that Indian entrepreneurs stepped up their investment, but decades of misguided textile policies and technological constraints could not be overcome within a short time. Nevertheless, Indian textile and garment exports have registered an encouraging increase in recent years. It remains to be seen whether the ambitious target announced in 2000 will be reached by 2010.

Most ready-made garments are made of woven textiles, but knitwear has also played an important role in recent years. Originally, the main items of cotton knitwear produced in India were vests (men's undershirts); then T-shirts and sweatshirts were introduced and their production increased rapidly. Vests are white and need no dyeing, just bleaching, but the new items require dyeing and printing. Knitted products include velour, towels and designer form-fitted clothing, which added many new elements to the labour process.

Indian producers have adopted these changes and have supplied an expanding export market. Small-scale enterprises in the 'informal sector' are controlling this field which is quite similar to powerloom production. However, while powerlooms weave more or less uniform types of coarse cloth, the knitwear producers must deal with knitting, cutting, stitching and dyeing or printing. The control of labour is crucial to these operations, and labour relations accordingly differ from those prevalent in other branches of the textile industry. Tiruppur, a town near Coimbatore in Tamil Nadu, has emerged as a major centre of knitwear production and Sharad Chari has made a fascinating study of the mode of production in this town.[7] He has described the emergence of 'fraternal capital' as a typical form of cooperation among small-scale entrepreneurs in this field. Most of the owners of the small workshops and even a large number of their employees belong to the Gounder caste of peasants who have made a successful transition to industrial production. The Gounder peasants are used to hard work in intensive agriculture where the landholder and his labourers are working together and this style of operations has been transferred to the shop floor where the owner is always present, usually controlling the stitching table where the cloth is converted into garments. Gounders who want to emphasise the special features of their work often make it appear as a kind of 'work ethic'. Actually it helps them to justify the control of labour in their small-scale industry. They do not strive for economies of scale as these would be diseconomies under the official rules favouring small-scale enterprises. Accordingly, successful entrepreneurs do not invest their capital in expanding their production, but in setting up 'fraternal' enterprises run by other members of the Gounder caste, albeit these people are not necessarily related to them in terms of family ties. Total production has thus grown very quickly and whereas earlier only men worked in this industry, more and more women have been recruited in recent years. Most workers are paid by piece rate or they work under various types of contracts rather than receiving regular wages.

When production for export increased, a new elite of export merchants arose from the ranks of these small entrepreneurs. Smart young men in business suits, wearing sunglasses, can be seen chatting with their relatives on the shop floor who provide them with the material which they market in New York or elsewhere.[8] Many of these exporters are assemblers rather than producers. The links of fraternal capital connect all these people and make it difficult for outsiders to penetrate this business. In this way fraternal capital provides horizontal and vertical linkages which are otherwise only found in big corporations. Decentralized supervision – and exploitation – of labour is an asset in this type of business organization. Contracting in and out enables the small entrepreneurs to respond to changing demand. Such an organization helps to defend the class of entrepreneurs against labour unions, which have a strong tradition in this area.

Another interesting example of the control of labour in this region is the putting-out system practised by a producer of rag carpets in the adjacent Erode District. He uses rags from the hosiery industry and gets carpets woven for the big Swedish firm IKEA. Initially it was traditional weavers who got involved in this business, but soon the putting-out system was extended to villages whose supply of labour was of a very different kind. In a Gounder village affected by water scarcity, the peasants took up carpet weaving in order to survive. In another village inhabited by migrant construction workers, the women who had also participated in this work shifted to carpet weaving, which they could do at home.[9] Tapping labour resources of different kinds for export production is a characteristic feature of the informal sector of India's economy.

Similar features of decentralized production and exploitation of labour can be observed in the garment industry of Ahmadabad, a city once famous for its large composite textile mills, most of which have long since closed down or are 'sick'. But in the 1990s hundreds of small workshops producing ready-made garments sprang up. Their production is supplemented by home-based women who stitch garments for entrepreneurs who operate a putting-out system.[10] These women had been used to stitching petticoats and children's wear; they own very simple sewing machines. When they were required to stitch more complicated garments for export their skills and their machines often proved insufficient for the new tasks. They usually earn piece rates which amount to about 2 to 5 per cent of the value of the articles they produce. With such low wages they can hardly afford to invest in add-ons to their sewing machine for new lines of production. Nevertheless, they somehow managed to get on with their work. This area of Gujarat is also famous for its embroidery, which has been successfully adapted to the requirements of export production, a line of production in which India is ahead of China.

Whereas the type of operations described so far would indicate that garment production is located only in the informal sector, it should also be mentioned that there are a few highly sophisticated modern companies in India which are moving ahead very fast in the manufacture of world-class garments for export. Raymond is a case in point; it is a company which was once known mainly for its woollen suits. At present it is believed to control about 60 per cent of the world production of worsteds and has also ventured into making cotton shirts and denim for blue jeans.[11] Some of the denim is then sold to the makers of famous brands of jeans; in addition Raymond manufactures jeans under its own brand, Everblue.[12] The ready-made suits and trousers of this company are marketed in India and abroad while the company's stores in many Indian towns provide retail outlets for ready-made garments. Computer-aided manufacturing has been introduced in the new plants set up by Raymond in Bangalore. The ambitious management of this great Indian company aims at making it a global billion-dollar fashion house. Arvind Mills of Ahmadabad is a close rival of Raymond. One of the very few traditional Indian cotton textile mills to have made the transition to modern production in a competitive global environment, it has become a world leader in the production of denim, being the fourth largest producer worldwide and producing four times as much denim as Raymond. It also provides cotton shirting to the makers of Arrow Shirts. In recent years Arvind Mills have entered the field of ready-made garments in a big way, clearly emerging as one of the chief protagonists of India's expanding manufacture of cotton garments. Realizing that ready-made garments fetch higher profits than cloth, Arvind Mills is investing heavily in their manufacture in its mills in Ahmadabad and in Bangalore.[13] The company has also adopted a clever stratagem for winning over India's local tailors by providing them with kits for making jeans. Such a kit costs the equivalent of just US$ 6 and contains the required length of denim cloth plus zippers, rivets, etc. Mass manufacturing is thus reconciled with the old tradition of wearing tailor-made clothes. Since the kit includes a patch with Arvind's brand name, Ruf and Tuf, the wearer can also follow the current trend of parading a well known label, a marketing ploy that shows the ingenuity of Indian entrepreneurs in responding to new challenges.

The Triumph of Software Design

The type of export product for which India has become best known in recent years is computer software. This is not the kind of software marketed by Microsoft, but customized software for individual processes of CAD (computer aided design) and CAM (computer aided manufacturing). The production of this software is very labour intensive and requires highly qualified experts. Only a few years ago it was assumed that the investment required for hardware and software would be 70:30; by now it is the opposite – the expenditure on software has far surpassed that on hardware. In the late 1980s the Indian government under Rajiv Gandhi adopted a wise policy concerning information technology: the import of the latest computers from abroad was freely permitted. This was a major reversal of policy; in the early 1980s the import of computers had been prohibited in order to protect the home market for the infant industry of Indian manufacturing of hardware. The few Indian companies which had started making computers had to close shop or convert their operations to assembling the cheaper type of foreign computer for Indian consumers – or they had to forget about hardware and turn to software production. Wipro, described in detail later, experienced this transition at that time.

After the new policy had been implemented, Indian software programers and systems analysts had access to the most modern hardware and could start the highly profitable business of producing customized software for clients at home and abroad. Parallel to this, the outsourcing of computer-enabled business operations from Western countries to India also progressed very fast with many American and European companies shifting their IT departments to India where bookkeeping, ticket reservations and similar services could be done so much more cheaply than at their headquarters. 'Body shopping' also became a lucrative business for Indian IT companies: they would hire and train experts whom they would then send abroad to work for their foreign clients. Such experts would receive an Indian salary and a limited allowance for living in a more expensive foreign country and would have to sign a bond obliging them to return to their Indian employers. This did not completely prevent such experts from looking for greener pastures abroad; those who were similarly qualified and had watched what had happened to others avoided the trap of 'body shopping' and made a beeline for the USA or other Western countries. But in due course, salaries for qualified personnel increased in India. Moreover, in terms of purchasing power parity an Indian salary amounting to only 20 per cent of an American salary would still enable a programer to live very comfortably in India.[14] This has helped to retain experts in India and to entice those who had settled abroad to return home and start their own software production. The 'brain drain', which had been criticized earlier turned into a 'brain gain' as the returnees had acquired a great deal of valuable expertise during their stay abroad.

At first Indian programers had simply solved specific problems for their foreign clients. The quality of Indian IT work and the speed of its transmission via satellite attracted more and more such clients. Satellite communication not only helped to exploit the benefits of the time difference between India and the USA, it also protected the Indian IT firms from government interference. As Dewang Mehta, President of NASSCOM (National Association of Software and Services Companies), once put it, there is no customs official sitting in the satellite.[15] This, of course, also implies that official statistics hardly reflected the growth of software exports. Only NASSCOM could provide the relevant information based on the voluntary reports of its members. It is also the only source of figures on the size of India's IT labour force, which amounted to 813,500 in 2004.[16] The absence of customs officials in satellites was not the only factor which saved the young IT industry from being troubled by the Indian government: IT business was considered to belong to the service sector and was not recognized as an industry. There are more than 400 statutory provisions designed for the control of industry in India; IT did not come under their purview and this was a great help. As far as satellite transmission was concerned, the Indian IT business benefited from the rapid decrease in costs of access to the required bandwidth. In 1984 monthly payments of US$ 1.2 million were due for 2Mb bandwidth; by 2002 this had come down to US$ 3,800 and there was a further decrease by about 40 per cent in the subsequent three years.

While satellites had initially been the main transmitters, the worldwide spread of fibre-optic cables contributed even more to India's connectivity. Both the boom and the bust of the new economy contributed to India's rapid progress in this field.[17] The boom encouraged enormous American investment in fibre-optic cables, which reduced the cost of transmission; the bust then cut IT profits in America and precipitated outsourcing to India. Due to India's earlier success in fixing the problem of Y2K, that is, the relapse of computers to the year 1900 at the beginning of the year 2000, the country was fully prepared for new challenges. Under such favourable conditions India's IT firms grew at a fantastic speed. Giants such as Wipro and Infosys in Bangalore and Tata Consultancy Services (TCS) in Mumbai soon had thousands of highly qualified employees and rapidly moved up-market in the IT business. Brief accounts of these three largest companies and their directors will provide an insight into the rise and growth of the Indian software business.

TCS is the oldest company in the field. Established in 1968, at first it was a normal consultancy firm, employing about 300 people in the 1980s. But TCS had already entered into a partnership with the American computer firm Burroughs in the 1970s and Subramaniam Ramadorai, who later on became the visionary head of TCS, having joined the company as a young computer programer in 1972. He was born in 1945 and had studied physics at the University of Delhi and electrical engineering at the Indian Institute of Science, Bangalore, adding a degree in computer science from the University of California. He had a brilliant career in TCS and became its CEO in 1996. By that time TCS had already made their mark in designing and marketing computer software, but now the company started offering whole financial systems as well as systems for industrial production such as aircraft engineering. TCS introduced the Integrated Quality Management System and the Customer Banking System. Ramadorai is a sensitive and self-effacing head of the company; nevertheless TCS has a rather centralized command structure and it is only in recent years that he has started to think about transforming its infrastructure. For this a special transformation officer with the rank of vice-president has been appointed. TCS has grown extremely fast and attained a global reach; transforming its organization in keeping with these new dimensions is an urgent task. In 1993 TCS had about 4,000 employees and a revenue of approximately US$ 50 million. By 1998 the number of employees and the amount of revenue had almost doubled. In 2005 there were 46,000 employees and a revenue of about US$ 2 billion. The ambitious aim of TCS is to reach US$ 10 billion by 2010 and past performance seems to indicate that this goal will be achieved. TCS has made its name for its excellent banking and financial service programmes which account for 38 per cent of its business. Its other major field is application development and maintenance. In its new research laboratory in Hyderabad TCS has developed Bio-Suite, a software program for the simulation of molecular reactions. Companies which develop new medicines can screen large numbers of potential reactions in order to find out those which they need for their product. Moreover, the Hyderabad centre also houses a language laboratory which helps to develop computer literacy in various Indian languages. This lab can be used to design software for customers who use languages other than English.

Recently TCS has taken the interesting step of appointing the Harvard professor Clayton Christensen as one of its directors, whose work is discussed in the next chapter. It seems that his theories will contribute to the transformation of TCS. One of the company's assets is the spread of its worldwilde activities, which makes it less dependent on the ups and downs of the US market: this accounts for only 60 per cent of its business while about 12 per cent is in India and the rest in many other countries. TCS has also been active in China. Working in different markets insures TCS against occasional setbacks, one such being the loss of a major contract approved by the governor of the state of Indiana in 2003. TCS was supposed to reorganize the unemployment administration of this state. It had submitted the best bid and the administration greatly appreciated working with TCS, but political pressure led to the cancellation of the contract.[18] The state of Indiana incurred a heavy loss, but the move pleased those who wished to retain such work in American hands. Actually just 65 American jobs were saved for four months, whereas the loss to the state amounted to US$ 8 million.[19] TCS received compensation and could forget about this unfortunate venture since its international business increased very rapidly. No private client of TCS could afford to waste money for political reasons as the state of Indiana had done. While TCS is still head and shoulders above its Indian competitors, the two other giants, Wipro and Infosys are catching up fast.

The rise of Wipro has been a quite unusual success story. About 80 per cent of the company is owned by one man, its founder-president, Azim Premji, who was for some time the richest man in India until Mukesh Ambani surpassed him. Wipro was originally started by Premji's father as a company producing vegetable oils. In 1966, when Premji was studying electrical engineering at Stanford University, his father suddenly died and Premji had to return to India to take charge of the company. He was only 21 years old and one of the shareholders of the company advised him to sell his shares and leave it to more experienced managers. Premji later called this the defining moment of his life. He rejected the advice and in due course led the company in such a way that it attained world class status in his lifetime. He started manufacturing computers, which seemed to be a promising venture in 1980 when the Indian government prohibited the import of computers to encourage their production in India. Wipro was hit by Rajiv Gandhi's change of policy but then quickly made the transition to software production. It closely rivalled TCS and then managed to transform its structure before TCS started thinking about restructuring. Premji 'verticalized' his company by creating four divisions which are managed like independent companies, thus avoiding the pitfalls of centralized direction and being able to adjust flexibly to new demands made by customers in different fields. The four divisions are Telecom Service Providers, Product Engineering Solutions, Finance Solutions and Enterprise Solutions. Wipro relies heavily on the American market, earning 80 per cent of its revenue in the USA. In 2005 WIPRO had 42,000 employees and a total revenue of about US$ 1.6 billion. It was thus catching up with TCS and could be expected to reach the same ambitious goal of US$ 10 billion by 2010.

Wipro has a special relationship with General Electric (GE), the huge American company, which accounts for about 50 per cent of Wipro's export earnings. Jack Welch, the legendary boss of GE, visited India in 1989 in order to explore the Indian market for medical equipment. But he then discovered that India could be a source of low-cost software production for his firm. GE's ties with India have grown steadily, making it India's greatest foreign employer. The GE–India relationship was further strengthened by the setting up of the John F. Welch Technology Centre in Bangalore in the year 2000 with a staff of about 2,000 scientists of various disciplines. It concentrates on Research and Development (R&D). This is crucial as the Indian IT industry is often blamed for not investing enough in R&D and should be inspired by this initiative. Wipro will certainly benefit from this new development.

The third Indian software giant, Infosys, is the youngest company of the three, having been established as late as 1981. Its great CEO, Narayana Murthy, is a contemporary of Ramadorai and Premji, as he was born in 1946. Murthy's father was a poor schoolteacher and although he did well in the IIT (Indian Institute of Technology) entrance exam, he could not afford to study there and took his first degree at a local engineering college in Mysore. He then did a Master's degree in electrical engineering at IIT Kanpur in 1969 and worked for Patni Computer Systems before he founded Infosys, as whose CEO he served from 1981 to 2002 when he turned over this job to the company's co-founder Nandan Nilekani. Murthy remained as Chairman of the Board and 'Chief Mentor' – a unique designation which accurately reflects his service to Infosys. The early years of the company were not very promising; the real chance of growth and progress came only after 1991 when the new policy of the Indian government opened India's doors and enabled Infosys to become a global company with offices in the USA, Canada and Great Britain; it also became the first Indian-registered company to get listed on the American stock market (NASDAQ) in 1999. At that time Infosys had a modest annual turnover of US$ 100 million, but within five years it attained the US$ 1 billion level. In 2005 Infosys had 32,000 employees. Its annual revenue was about 30 per cent less than that of TCS, but its net profit was only about 9 per cent less than that of TCS, and 12 per cent higher than that of Wipro. Considering the much smaller number of employees at Infosys, these figures indicate that in 2005 it was the most profitable of the three big companies. One of the secrets of its success is that the staff share in the company's profits. Murthy distributed shares among the staff members as he was not interested in amassing a personal fortune but wished to see that the people he worked with did well. By 2000 he could proudly report that Infosys had created 1,913 rupee millionaires and 235 dollar millionaires in this way. Like its competitors, Infosys sells a wide variety of customized software, but it has also entered the market for packaged applications with its Enterprise Solutions Practice. Its financial program, Finacle, has been very popular with bankers worldwide and has proved more than four times faster than the program of its nearest rival.[20] In 2006 Infosys was ranked as the fastest growing technology and service provider (TSP) in the USA. This was due to its using the Global Delivery Model (GDM) for a portfolio of solutions offered to the financial services industry. Infosys has been a GDM pioneer for quite some time. The secret of this stratgey is global co-sourcing and finding the right partners for it. Tasks are split into sub-modules that are internally cohesive and require as little as possible interface with other modules. One can then concentrate on some essential modules and get others from partners who can produce them more efficiently and at a lower cost. The international fame of Infosys has attracted thousands of young Americans, who flock to its campus in Bangalore as interns.[21] This shows that the days when the transfer of technology was a one-way street are definitely gone.

Next to the big three there are two other promising Indian IT firms which may soon enter the 'big league'. One is Satyam Computer Services of Secunderabad which was founded in 1987. By 2005 the company had 25,000 employees and had crossed the US$1 billion line. Another is Patni Computer

Systems of Mumbai, founded in 1978, which was Narayana Murthy's first employer. It has 12,000 employees and an annual revenue (2005) of US$ 450 million. Altogether these five major companies accounted for about 40 per cent of India's software exports in 2005, a phenomenon which indicates that there are many others in this field that also contribute to India's success as a software exporter. Their success is not just due to low-cost production, but also to the high quality of Indian software. There is an international standard measuring the capability of firms in this field called the Capability Maturity Model (CMM) administered by Carnegie Mellon University, Pittsburgh. Its has five levels, the highest of which is 5. Of all firms and institutions graded worldwide according to CMM, 72 per cent of those which have achieved Level 5 are located in India.[22] This shows that India is by far the most advanced country in this field. Only nine firms worldwide had achieved this standard by 2000 and five of them were in India. By now there are more than a hundred, but India has maintained its lead and will probably do so for quite some time to come. Encouraged by their success, many Indian companies have started posting their earnings as per the US GAAP (Generally Accepted Accounting Principles) so that their shares can be listed on the American stock market.

In addition to the big Indian IT firms discussed above, there are by now many small firms doing pioneering work in specialized fields. MindTree in Bangalore has been asked by an American firm to cooperate in providing programs for corporate governance. Ashok Soota, the founder of MindTree, was earlier Vice-President of Wipro. When he started his new company in 2000, he aimed at more challenging tasks of software design like network planning and systems integration and he has been quite successful in these. He attracts clients who are not interested only in cutting costs but also in new ideas.[23] Another pioneering company is Dhruva Interactive, also in Bangalore, which concentrates on computer games.[24] HeyMath! in Chennai produces teaching programs which enable children everywhere to do their maths more effectively and enjoy it. The company was started by a husband and wife team, Harsh Rajan and Nirmala Sankaran, who had worked as bankers in London. They got in touch with the Millennium Mathematics Project of Cambridge University and decided to use computer animation for teaching mathematics. They then set up a research lab at IIT Chennai and after having perfected their program, they first tested it in Singapore. Schools in this city state are innovative and ambitious and adopted HeyMath! enthusiastically. After this success in Singapore, HeyMath! was soon in demand in many other countries.[25]

Another field in which Indians have launched a successful new enterprise is the copy-editing and production of scientific books and journals. This has to be done by highly qualified editors. TNQ in Chennai has forged ahead in undertaking such work for European and American publishers. The company was established in 1998 with 15 employees. By 2006 it had a staff of 600, among them many experts holding Ph.D degrees in the sciences with which they have to deal. Several Indian firms are nowadays active in knowledge process outsourcing (KPO). This includes data searching in various fields and the monitoring of R&D in sciences such as biotechnology and pharmaceuticals. KPO is expected to grow at a very rapid rate.[26] It requires highly qualified manpower and signals an important move ahead in the value chain. India has no dearth of skilled manpower, but it still suffers from a very low teledensity and there are only seven PCs per 1,000 persons (2005) as compared to 37 in China. The continuous recruitment of highly qualified personnel depends on a broader base of skills in the nation.

Of the three types of thriving export discussed in this chapter, software occupies the leading position, earning about US$ 17 billion, closely followed by diamonds at US$ 16 billion; ready-made garments then come behind at some distance with about US$ 7 billion. Altogether this amounts to US$ 40 billion, or more than half of India's total exports. The fastest expansion is to be expected in software exports. If the predictions of India's major players in this field prove to be correct, a total of at least about US$ 80 billion can be expected by 2010. According to a rough estimate, about 20,000 employees are required to generate US$ 1 billion in export revenue. This would mean that by 2010 about 1.6 million Indian IT experts will be required for this business. Naturally, the creation of these new jobs in India would imply a loss of such jobs in the USA and other Western countries. Not only does the loss of these jobs generate fears in the West, but the growing dependence of Western countries on India in this field worries Western industrialists. On the other hand, Indian entrepreneurs are also aware of the enormous loss they would have to suffer if a sudden rupture put an end to India's connectivity. At the time when the confrontation of India and Pakistan reached its climax in May 2002, the State Department urged American citizens to leave India. The Confederation of Indian Industries (CII) then appealed to the Indian government to adopt a more moderate stance and this may have contributed to the subsequent easing of the situation and the success of American mediation.[27]

In 2005 the total turnover of Indian IT and IT enabled services (ITES) amounted to about US$ 30 billion, nearly half of which was spent on salaries. The average annual salary of an Indian IT expert was about US$ 12,000. The multiplier effect of IT employment was substantial: for every employee working in this field there would be four employees in supporting and related types of work. This meant that by 2005 more than 5 million Indians owed their employment to the rapid rise of IT/ITES.[28] While India benefits very much from its booming IT industry, the growth of the industry has not contributed to a more even distribution of industrial activity; instead it has accentuated regional disparities. Actually, software production should encourage decentralization as access to satellites is available throughout the country, but as this business requires a critical mass of intellectual interaction and contact with research institutes etc., birds of the IT feather have eagerly flocked together and built their nests close to each other. A look at Map 3 below which indicates the major IT centres in India shows the prominence of the quadrangle Mumbai–Hyderabad–Chennai–Bangalore. More than two-thirds of all Indian IT firms are located within this quadrangle. The only other major concentration is in the Delhi metropolitan area (including Noida and Gurgaon). In the vast region of eastern India, IT firms are conspicuous by their absence. Only Kolkata has a tiny 3 per cent. This concentration was noticeable even in 1995 when there were only 262 firms of which 34 per cent were based in Mumbai and 26 per cent in Bangalore. As the number of firms

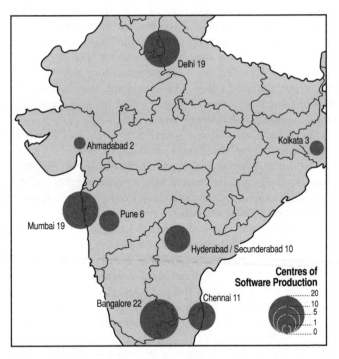

Map 3   Regional Distribution of IT companies. The figures refer to percentages of the total number of firms
Source: Data provided by M. Fromhold-Eisebith (see bibliography)
Cartography: N. Harm, South Asia Institute, University of Heidelberg

more than trebled by 2004, the shares of Mumbai and Bangalore were some-what reduced, but the pre-eminence of the 'charmed' quadrangle remained unchallenged.[29]

The other two stars in the field of export production, diamond processing and the production of ready-made garments, also show a great deal of regional concentration. Diamond processing is concentrated in coastal Gujarat, while ready-made garments are manufactured in western and southern India and in the Punjab. Nevertheless, the success of the new export industries may encourage similar activities elsewhere once the ghost of 'export pessimism' which has haunted India for such a long time has finally been exorcized. The Federation of Indian Chambers of Commerce and Industry predicted in December 2006 that by the end of the fiscal year 2006–7 the total value of Indian exports would amount to at least US$ 125 billion. It also reported that the majority of Indian entrepreneurs are confident that exports will continue to increase in 2007.[30]

CHAPTER 9

THE QUEST FOR
SUPERCOMPUTERS

Indian Supercomputers: From PARAM to ANUPAM and KABRU

When Rajiv Gandhi wanted to acquire a Cray supercomputer for India, the US government vetoed the sale because it was feared that the computer could be used for constructing an atom bomb. This embargo prompted India to build its own supercomputer and Indian scientists coined the term 'denial-driven innovation' in this context. Innovation meant that the Indian computer had to be different from the one built by Cray. India's indigenous supercomputer PARAM actually turned out to be a good example of 'disruptive technology', a term introduced by the Harvard economist Clayton Christensen when analyzing the process of fundamental technological change. He pointed out that new technologies tend to disrupt established ones, which then become obsolete sooner or later.[1] The defence of 'sustained technologies' – as he calls the established ones – consists of incremental improvements which help to postpone obsolescence for some time. Denial-driven innovation would naturally aim at disruptive technology as it could not be called innovation if it consisted only of reinventing the wheel. The story of the PARAM super-computer illustrates the phenomenon of disruptive technology since it outperformed the contemporary Cray supercomputer – and at a fraction of the cost of Cray's expensive machine.[2]

The new technology which enabled PARAM to succeed was massive parallel processing (MPP). This type of processing was not unknown: it had been debated as an alternative of vector-type sequential processing for a long time. The legendary Gene Amdahl who had first worked on the IBM mainframe computers was involved in lively debates on the merits of parallel processing in the late 1960s and in subsequent years. Most computer experts agreed that parallel processing was a good idea but thought that it was difficult to control. Therefore sequential processing prevailed for a long time. This type of processing uses an imperative instruction language which does not work in

MPP machines. When Seymour Cray started his Cray Research Corporation in 1972, he opted for sequential processing. In 1984 he delivered the first Cray supercomputer X-MP to NASA.

In the meantime a young doctoral student at MIT, Daniel Hillis, had started a company called Thinking Machines, in 1983. He had worked in the field of robotics and artificial intelligence and was fascinated by MPP because he felt that it was similar to the operations of the human brain. He was fortunate in getting help from a retired physics professor, Nobel Laureate Richard Feynman, who joined the project of constructing the 'Connection Machine'. Feynman was a genius; he had worked on quantum electrodynamics and was also a pioneer of nanotechnology. Hillis asked him to design the routers, i.e. the actual connections in his machine. CM-1, the first Connection Machine, was ready in 1985. The American Defense Advanced Research Projects Agency subsidized it. Hillis's interest in artificial intelligence and the military quest for image and speech recognition coincided. But the machine was not aimed at ordinary number crunching and therefore failed as a business proposition. While the going was good, work was progressing fast. The CM-5 was such a fascinating machine that Spielberg featured it in his film *Jurassic Park* in 1993. But a year later Thinking Machines went bankrupt.[3] However, the Connection Machine had served as a technology demonstrator for MPP. Four years before Hillis had gone bankrupt, Cray had jumped on the MPP bandwagon, launching a crash programme to produce a marketable MPP machine as soon as possible. Hillis was not the only one who made Cray MPP-conscious. Somewhat later than Hillis, but more successfully, the Indian computer scientists had started working on a supercomputer based on MPP.

Rajiv Gandhi, who wanted to lead India into the twenty-first century, was interested in obtaining the latest Cray supercomputer for India: this was the Cray X-MP 1205. It still had the old technology of sequential processing but it was the fastest machine available at that time. When the US government denied this machine to India, as an immediate reaction the Indian government established the Centre for the Development of Advanced Computing (C-DAC) in Pune in 1988. Its director, Vijay Bhatkar, opted for MPP and created the PARAM supercomputer within three years. Bhatkar was lucky in getting a particularly suitable RISC (reduced instruction set chip) for his new machine, the 'Transputer', which had been marketed by the British firm Inmos in 1985. The transputer (from transistor + computer) is a chip which includes its own RAM (random access memory) and is good at communicating in an MPP environment. The PARAM supercomputer was not only very efficient but also surprisingly cheap. Professor D. Popovic of the University of Bremen in Germany, a friend and colleague of Vijay Bhatkar, was able to buy a PARAM for his university for US$ 20,000, whereas the Cray computers cost about US$ 5 million or more.

Progress in this field is so fast that the marvellous PARAM became dated within a few years. By the end of the 1990s even IBM-PCs could perform the tasks for which a PARAM had been needed only a few years earlier, as Professor Popovic found out. In the meantime C-DAC had not rested on its laurels and had produced a PARAM Padma, which secured the Centre a place of honour in the 'Teraflops' League of the world's fastest computers. Cray, however, had accelerated its MPP programme with a vengeance in the 1990s. In 1993 the Cray T3D, a very robust MPP machine, had come on to the market and two years later the T3E appeared, which became the world's best-selling Teraflops machine. The Tata Institute of Fundamental Research bought one of these machines rather than relying on PARAM any longer. C-DAC, as a government research institute, could not compete in the long run with a highly resourceful private company like Cray. Denial-driven innovation has its limits once the denial ends and disruptive technology does not kill the protagonists of sustained technology if they abandon the path of incremental improvements and adopt the disruptive technology at the right moment. Cray had shown this by opting for MPP in 1990 and thus remaining a leader in the field of supercomputing. Vijay Bhatkar perhaps thought that C-DAC could not progress as fast as he would have wished. In 1998 he left the institute which he had created after a decade of exciting work.

In the meantime the Bhabha Atomic Research Centre (BARC) had started to develop an MPP supercomputer of its own.[4] The work on this project was started in the early 1990s just when Cray had also opted for MPP. Seymour Cray had died following a car accident in 1996 but his company continued his work and was far ahead of BARC. In 2002 BARC produced Anupam, a 43-gigaflop supercomputer which was soon upgraded to 72 gigaflops. In 2003 BARC unveiled Anupam-Aruna with a computational speed of 360 gigaflops. All this was not yet in the Teraflops League which C-DAC and Cray had joined some years earlier. The real breakthrough came with Anupam-Ameya, which achieved a sustained performance at 1.7 teraflops in 2005. Anupam – which means 'incomparable' – was also unique because of its low-cost construction as it was made with off-the-shelf components. In addition, BARC provided Anupam with user-friendly software. It was installed in several major research institutes in India.

Even though Anupam proved to be very successful, the Department of Atomic Energy also funded another supercomputer: Kabru.[5] For a few years Cray had been ahead of its Indian rivals: now his company faced a new challenge which emerged from the Indian Institute of Mathematical Sciences in Chennai (Madras). Professor Hari Dass, a physicist interested in lattice gauge

1 Prime Minister Dr Manmohan Singh.

2 Pratibha Patil, elected President of India in July 2007, is the first woman to achieve this position. As a member of the Congress Party, Patil won a seat in the Maharashtra Legislative Assembly in 1962 and has been involved in politics ever since. She was Governor of Rajasthan before becoming President of India.

3 Mayawati, Chief Minister of Uttar Pradesh, addressing a meeting. The 'Dalit Queen' is the leader of the Bahujan Samaj Party which won an absolute majority in the legislative assembly of Uttar Pradesh in 2007.

4 The Chief Minister of Tamil Nadu, Karunanidhi; his son, Stalin; and his nephew, Dayanidhi Maran, who was a minister of the Government of India.

5 Kapil Sibal, Minister of Science, Government of India, during his election campaign. The decorated car is called a 'Rath', after the chariot of ancient Indian heroes.

6 Pavement bookstall, Rajiv Gandhi Chowk (Connaught Place), New Delhi.

7 The new Metro is the pride of New Delhi, running as an underground in the city centre and on elevated tracks in the suburbs.

8 A motorbike being towed in New Delhi. Due to heavy traffic in the city, obstacles must be removed as quickly as possible.

9 BrahMos cruise missiles, jointly produced by India and Russia, at a Republic Day parade. The missiles' names refer to the rivers Brahmaputra and Moskwa.

10 An Indian soldier undergoing tough military training.

11 Mukesh Ambani, Reliance Industries, and his life science advisor, Dr Vishwas Sarangdhar.

12 The old Phoenix Mill of Mumbai has been converted into the department store Big Bazaar.

13 'Bombay the City' by Mario Miranda (1996).

14 A member of the Boda tribe of Northeastern India. Tribal people account for eight per cent of the Indian population.

15 Schoolgirls of Northeastern India, wearing their school uniforms.

16 The Simputer (Simple, Inexpensive, Multi-Lingual Computer) is able to convert text into oral messages in Indian languages, turn pages with a twist of the wrist and possesses many other attractive features.

17 A diamond necklace of Indian design. The diamond industry is one of India's most important export industries.

theory with reference to fundamental particles such as protons, needed an extremely powerful supercomputer and decided to design one himself with the help of his colleagues. He chose the name Kabru for his project: this is the name of a mountain in the Himalayas which has never been climbed by a mountaineer. He opted for constructing a cluster of 144 ordinary, inexpensive computers with Intel-Xeon chips working with the Linux operating system. They develop an extraordinary capacity by cooperating with each other. This requires the right type of connections and suitable programing. Kabru thus is a new type of 'connection machine'. It is interesting to note that the essential work on the connections was done by a young private company, Summation Enterprises, Mumbai, which used a Norwegian device called Wulfkit to integrate the cluster. The company aptly describes its business as 'systems integration'. Another young company, Netweb Technologies of New Delhi and Bangalore, also participated in this work. The existence of such companies is an encouraging sign of India's 'take-off' in this field.

Kabru stunned everybody concerned by reaching a speed of 1.382 teraflops when it was inaugurated in 2004. It was surpassed in India by Anupam-Ameya in 2005 and by a new IBM machine in Bangalore which is, of course, enormously expensive. The total development budget of Kabru, funded by the Department of Atomic Energy, was only about US$ 500,000. Kabru provides evidence of Indian ingenuity and it is to be hoped that PARAM, Anupam and Kabru are just stepping-stones to even more inspiring future achievements.

Social Inclusion: Bringing the Internet to the Village

The term 'denial-driven innovation' can also be applied in a somewhat different sense to the task of bridging the digital divide in India. The denial in this case is not that of access to advanced technology by a superpower but denial of the access to modern communication because of poverty, illiteracy and the lack of rural infrastructure. Technological innovation is essential in this field, but it is not sufficient; it must be accompanied by new approaches to social organization. Such efforts at achieving social inclusion are highlighted by the annual Stockholm Challenge Award, an award that arose from an initiative of the European Commission which was originally confined to Europe. It then became a global challenge and in 1999 the Mayor of Stockholm announced that there would be an annual international convention of the finalists competing for the award. Indian organizations have participated in this competition and won awards which will be mentioned below. In India, the Bangalore Declaration on Information Technology for Developing Countries in the Global Village of November 1998 had addressed the same points as the Stockholm Challenge at about the same time. It had stressed that agriculture, primary health care and low-cost communication should be priority areas for the application of information technology in developing countries.

Social inclusion is the main aim of all these initiatives. Therefore Indian scientists and engineers are particularly interested in technological innovation which would help to extend connectivity to the villages and they have devoted a great deal of attention to the transfer of information via satellite to the remotest parts of India. The main operative parts of satellites for the transmission of information are called transponders. These are very expensive devices: the international rates for hiring a transponder may amount to more than a million US dollars per year. The Indian National Satellite Systems (INSAT) helps India to save a great deal of money so that more than a hundred Indian transponders are in operation by now. Information in a 'packetized' form can be dispatched by digital transmission in split-second intervals, thus permitting multiple access to the transponder. This mode of transmission is called time division multiple access (TDMA). A public sector firm, Gujarat Communications and Electronics, established in 1975, has done pioneering work in this field. On the ground the messages sent by the transponder can be received by a very small aperture terminal (VSAT) which is then connected to local phones via wireless in local loop (WLL). However, the VSAT is still a very expensive device. WLL does not depend on satellite support as it can link up with the telephone system. In recent years almost all Indian towns have been connected to the fibre cable network. WLL can operate as a wireless extension of this network, using a small town as the hub of the local loop and reaching villages up to a distance of about 35 kilometres. Assuming that the next town is at a distance of not more than 70 kilometres, the countryside could be fully covered by WLL; only remote areas would depend on VSAT.

The scientist who introduced WLL and its applications is Professor Ashok Jhunjhunwala of IIT Madras (Chennai).[6] He has formed with his colleagues a team called TeNeT (The Telecommunications and Computer Networking Group), which is an organization that has helped young scientists who have graduated from IIT Madras to launch their own enterprises. One of these new companies is Midas Communications Technologies, founded in 1994, which manufactures the equipment for WLL. The system is called corDECT and consists of a DECT (digital enhanced cordless telecommunication) interface unit (DIU) which is linked to the telephone network and the internet. The DIU uses wireless transmission to reach a number of compact base stations at a maximum distance of 10 kilometres. These base stations transmit their signals to the wall sets in the village kiosks where a PC and a telephone are connected to the wall set. Further equipment for video conferencing or a digital camera and an apparatus for measuring blood pressure can also be added. Doctors can do a preliminary check-up at a distance in this way. By using repeaters the reach of WLL can be extended from 10 to 25 or 35 kilometres. corDECT deserves to be called a 'disruptive technology' as it blazes a new trail in rural telecommunications.

Another young company sponsored by TeNeT is n-Logue, a rural service provider which looks after the village kiosks and their equipment.[7] Founded in 2000, it has made rapid strides first in Tamil Nadu and then in Gujarat and Maharashtra. The company's charter prohibits it from working in urban areas so it is exclusively devoted to rural service. The kingpin in this organization is the local service provider. Located in a town close to the villages he serves, he is responsible for maintenance and business supervision, recruiting suitable kiosk operators in each village. These operators as well as the local service providers are not employees of n-Logue; they are entrepreneurs who work on their own account and only pay some fees to the parent company. n-Logue supplies the equipment and organizes the training of operators. It cooperates with Midas as far as WLL technology is concerned.[8] The TeNeT team at IIT Madras advises both companies free of charge. n-Logue is active in over 40 districts and has introduced many novel features such as video-conferencing and remote medical diagnosis. Under the brand name Chiraag (Spark), n-Logue also provides educational modules for various subjects and different grades of proficiency. The TeNeT team's dream is to nurture many micro-enterprises in the villages and to double rural GDP in the near future.

While these activities were spearheaded by engineers interested in rural social inclusion in southern and western India, some initiatives in northern India such as Gyandoot (Knowledge Messenger) and Drishtee (Vision) were sponsored by activists of a different type. Gyandoot, which was started in Dhar District, about 60 kilometres to the west of Indore in Madhya Pradesh in January 2000, owed its existence to some officers of the Indian Administrative Service who were inspired by the idea of e-governance. Accordingly, they first thought of enabling the villagers to procure copies of land records or other official papers speedily without having to visit district headquarters. Other items, such as price information, were then added. Since Gyandoot had a head start in setting up kiosks in the villages it attracted a great deal of media attention in India and abroad. It was also one of the first winners of the Stockholm Challenge Award, in June 2000. Unlike n-Logue it continued to be guided by government officials who controlled the Gyandoot Samiti, its central board of control.

A report of the Indian Institute of Management, Ahmadabad, which was commissioned to examine the working of Gyandoot in the field, pointed out that the service attracted fewer users than originally claimed. It also found that while the front end of the information chain was computerized, the back end, i.e. the district office, was not. The clerks were still handling papers manually in their leisurely way and, of course, bribes were not transmitted by the computer. In fact, the reduction of corruption was one of the virtues of Gyandoot. In due course, Gyandoot teamed up with n-Logue and MIDAS to improve its system, but organizationally it remained attached to its 'official' connection. Drishtee, however, was from the very beginning a private venture, started about a year after Gyandoot by a young man, Satyan Mishra, who had worked for UNICEF in north Indian villages. He followed more or less the business model of n-Logue, the kiosk operators being private entrepreneurs and not employees of Drishtee. Within a few years he had established about a hundred kiosks in five states, after having initially concentrated on Haryana. An international firm, Boston Consulting, had helped to set up the business operations as a social service and an Indian firm manufacturing tractors came in as a sponsor. Drishtee spread almost as rapidly in the north as n-Logue did in the south and west of India. A unique private venture of a similar type is Computer on Wheels (COW) in Andhra Pradesh. It does not set up kiosks but relies on itinerant operators with laptops and motorbikes who visit the villages in their circuit about twice a week, take and deliver messages and see what else they can do for the villagers. The operator is also equipped with a camera and a portable printer powered by solar cells. COW was started in seven villages of Mahbubnagar District in 2002. The project is supported by Digital Partners, India, an NGO which helps those who take initiatives in this field. With all these interesting projects it is not surprising that India has emerged as the country which has the largest number of competitors for the Stockholm Challenge Award.

Whereas Gyandoot, Drishtee, Computer on Wheels and n-Logue are primarily motivated by the idea of social inclusion, a major trading company, Indian Tobacco Company (ITC) launched a similar network called e-Choupal (e-Meeting Place) in June 2000.[9] This is aimed at cutting out middle men and establishing direct links with the producers. ITC is one of India's biggest traders of soy beans and other cash crops. Buying produce directly from the farmers is good business for the company as well as for the farmers, who get a better price for their crop. The e-Choupal kiosks provide current price information and enable the farmers to place orders for seeds, fertilizers, etc. Of course, ITC highlights the social benefits of e-Choupal. Being a rich company it can afford to invest in equipment like VSATs which are too expensive for most other organizations. ITC recovers the cost of equipment for a new kiosk within one year of its operation. In 2003 e-Choupal had reached more than a million farmers in about 11,000 villages. The local operator, or *sanchalak*, has to contribute to the operating costs but also receives commission on all services which he provides. He also gains a great deal of prestige in his village. It is encouraging to note that all organizations mentioned here have been able to recruit good local operators, often even energetic young women who are empowered by the new role they have adopted.

All the activities discussed here have proliferated only in the last few years. Eventually more than a hundred organizations of Indian civil society formed a National Alliance for Mission 2007 with the motto 'Every Village a Knowledge Centre'. This informal forum was chaired by the renowned agricultural scientist Professor M. S. Swaminathan. He was supported by NASSCOM and a large number of IT specialists. They aimed at achieving connectivity of all Indian villages by 2007. The Indian government pledged to invest Rs 1 billion annually (about US\$ 200 million) for three years in this scheme which should be sufficient to reach 100,000 villages. The Telecom Authority of India (TRAI) promised that tariffs would be reduced for this purpose. Instead of having a kiosk in each of India's 600,000 villages, Professor Swaminathan recommended a 'hub and spokes' design whereby a centrally located village would serve several villages in its neighbourhood. The social inclusion of the people of rural India could thus be achieved relatively quickly.

Simputers and 'Thin Clients': Future Connections for the Indian Masses?

Even more rapid progress could be expected if Indian engineers and entrepreneurs succeed in transforming the Simputer into a tool which is affordable for the Indian masses.[10] The Simputer (Simple, Inexpensive, Multi-lingual computer) was invented by a team of four professors including Vijay Chandru of the Indian Institute of Science in Bangalore, and three engineers of Encore Software Co., Bangalore. They formed the Simputer Trust and decided to take the unusual step of making their construction plans available on the internet as public domain hardware. Everybody could download the plans and build their own Simputer free of charge. Only if they manufactured it for commercial use would they have to pay a fee to the Simputer Trust. The unique hand-held Simputer has many attractive features. It is able to convert text into oral messages in Indian languages and can 'talk' to the illiterate. A few buttons and a touchscreen help to operate it. It also flip-flops, i.e. turns pages with a twist of the wrist. It is equipped with a smartcard-reader and can be shared by many users, who insert their personal smartcards. Vinay Deshpande, founder chairman of Encore Software Co. and managing trustee of the Simputer Trust, promoted the idea very vigorously. A private company, Picopeta, was established for manufacturing the Simputer, but it had great difficulties with commercially viable production. A public sector firm, Bharat Electronics Ltd (BEL) then agreed to include the Simputer in its programme as a niche product. BEL is a very succesful firm which was started in 1954 with the main task of supplying electronic equipment to the Indian defence forces. It has also made a mark in manufacturing useful devices for civilian use. One of its other niche products is the highly acclaimed Electronic Voting Machine which was used throughout India in the elections of 2004. The BEL PicoPeta Simputer, which was soon renamed Amida, at first seemed a very promising product when it entered the market in 2002 but only three years later its 'obituary' was published in various newspapers. Only a few thousand Simputers had been sold – the price range of US\$ 200 and above was beyond the reach of those for whom it had been designed. Imported handhelds such as the Palm Pilot were in a similar price range. Of course, they could not talk to the user in Indian languages, but the more affluent users who could afford such gadgets did not need such features. It was obvious that the Simputer could neither bridge the digital divide nor attract customers who preferred imported gadgets.

Meanwhile Deshpande's Encore Software Co. which had also started manu-facturing Simputers had faced the same difficulty of not being able to offer them at a price below US\$ 200. It then decided to move up-market and started producing more sophisticated handheld computers in 2005. One of these was the SATHI (Situational Awareness and Tactical Handheld Information) devel-oped in cooperation with the Indian Army. It had the same features as the simputer but added GPS, enabling soldiers to locate their position. For main-taining wireless connections without any disturbance SATHI is equipped with a new omnidirectional antenna produced by the British firm, Sarantel. Particularly when soldiers are deployed in small groups in difficult terrain, SATHI proves very useful, enabling these groups to exchange encrypted messages and avoid the hazard of 'friendly fire'. But the Encore team also found civilian uses for its improved technology. Its new Mobilis computer rivals all notebooks available in the market by being cheaper, lighter and more versatile.[11] Various models costing about US\$ 250 offer an integrated monitor and keyboard and several useful features inherited from the Simputer. Relying on flash memory rather than on a hard disc and on the Linux public domain operating system, MOBILIS is inexpensive and weighs only about 750 grams. It still remains to be seen how successful these new products will be in capturing a market share which will enable them to survive. Even then these products will not be able to bridge the digital divide, which was the original aim of the Simputer Trust.

A different approach to breaking the price barrier is the production of 'thin clients', i.e. computers containing only bare essentials and relying on servers to which they must be attached. This line was taken up by a young company Novatium in Chennai run by Rajesh Jain, who could rely on the advice of Professor Jhunjhunwala and of an American engineer and entrepreneur,

Raymond Stata, chairman of Analog Devices. Nova NetPC which was launched by Novatium in 2005 is an ideal 'thin client' priced at US$ 100. It is a small box, 6 inches by 8, and contains a web browser, handles e-mail, allows for word-processing and even has an MP3 player. At its heart is a chip like that in a cell phone. It has no disc drive, no monitor and no keyboard, but such devices can be attached to it and a TV set can be used as monitor. It relies on a server which has the software and internet connections. In its present shape it would be a good addition to TV sets, which can be found in millions of Indian homes. But it would not easily reach the rural people whom the Simputer Trust had in mind. At any rate, both the simputer and the Nova NetPC are testimony to the ingenuity of Indian pioneers in this field who may still come up with a low-cost device which can really bridge the digital divide.

CHAPTER 10

AGRICULTURE:
CRISIS OR PROMISE?

The Current Crisis of Indian Agriculture

Two-thirds of the Indian people depend on agriculture for making a living, but the industry contributes only about one fifth to India's GDP. In recent years agricultural growth has slowed down to about 2 per cent.[1] The Punjab, India's premier agricultural state, has experienced this decline in a dramatic way. In this state agriculture accounts for 40 per cent of GDP as against the Indian average of 20 per cent; this trend indicates a crisis for the Punjab. But the crisis is not limited to the Punjab. Other parts of India are also affected by the phenomenon of low agricultural growth. As Finance Minister Chidambaram has pointed out, agriculture must grow by 4 per cent and manufacturing and services by 12 per cent each if India is to reach a total growth of 10 per cent per year.[2]

The Indian government is alarmed by this slow growth in agriculture. In the recent paper outlining the approach to the eleventh Five Year Plan, the Planning Commission speaks of an agricultural crisis and asks for an initiative to regain agricultural dynamism. It recognizes that small farmers face special problems but states that agricultural deceleration actually affects farms of all sizes. The growth rate of agriculture must be doubled so as to lead to a rise in real wages and an increase in rural employment.[3] Rural non-farm employment which increased in earlier years has not grown in recent years. At the same time the migration of surplus labour from the countryside to the urban areas has also declined. This has saved the cities from being swamped by migrants but it has exacerbated the problem of rural unemployment.[4] Unemployment not only affects landless labourers but also smallholders who must work for others as their land does not support them throughout the year. Population increase has precipitated the fragmentation of landholdings, which leaves no scope for agricultural regeneration.[5] Some smallholders would probably wish to sell their land and leave the village. However, problems in the Indian land market prevent them from doing this. A proper record of ownership which makes land a marketable commodity is missing in most Indian villages. The British revenue authorities usually recorded the land but not its owner: they did not need to know the name of the owner because the law of land sale applied to revenue defaulters assured the authorities that the revenue would be paid regardless of the actual conditions of ownership.[6] Without a record of rights there is no title insurance to protect the buyer of land. It would cost a huge amount to establish an adequate record of rights throughout India, but this expenditure cannot be avoided if India wants to create a land market which would permit consolidation of economically viable holdings.[7]

Smallholders are usually unable to adopt new methods of production. They have to avoid risks and the success of richer neighbours fails to inspire them. I saw a striking example of this when I visited a rich farmer in eastern Maharashtra in the 1960s. He lived in a huge old mansion in the countryside which was shared by the families of his sister, a medical doctor, and his brother, a lawyer and member of the state legislature. The farmer had been teaching mechanical engineering before he had to take over the farm from his father. He had introduced large-scale sprinkler irrigation and produced rich harvests. The fields of his neighbours looked poor and barren and I asked him why they did not follow his example. He said that they would not do so because they knew very well that they could not emulate him. He was rich and resourceful and well connected to the authorities due to the political influence of his brother. This gave him easy access to government subsidies and special lines of credit. His poor neighbours lacked all these advantages and continued to eke out a living as they had done before.

When I visited that farmer, the Green Revolution had not yet reached India. In any case this revolution helped the big farmers much more than the small peasants. Economists used to say that the impact of the Green Revolution was neutral in that everybody should have benefited from it. But in fact those who could afford to take risks and therefore adopted the new methods of production left behind those who were poor to begin with. The Green Revolution in India was not the result of careful planning but was forced upon the country by a great calamity. In the Nehru era, agriculture had been neglected. Nehru wanted to promote industrial growth and to achieve this he tried to keep industrial wages and food prices low. The massive importation of American wheat in the early 1960s was solicited in order to support this policy. Nevertheless, agricultural production increased in the Nehru years, but this was achieved by extending cultivation to marginal lands which would not yield anything when the rains failed.[8] This is what happened at the time of a double drought in 1965 and 1966 which marked a turning-point in India's agrarian history. After this prices rose and the cultivated area was reduced as marginal lands were given up. Irrigation was extended, hybrid varieties of grain were introduced and fertilizer was applied in increasing quantities. India has a total cultivable area of 1.6 million square kilometres, which amounts to about half of its territory. In due course irrigation was extended to 40 per cent of the cultivable land; the rest is rain-fed and thus subject to the vagaries of the monsoon.

Initially the Green Revolution was almost exclusively a wheat revolution and as such limited to northern India.[9] The area under wheat expanded from 18 to 24 million hectares between 1970 and 1990 and then more or less remained at that level. The yield of wheat (kg/ha) rose from 1,300 in 1970 to 2,700 in 2004, but compared to Western Europe where the yield is usually more than thrice this amount, the yield of Indian wheat is still at a very low level. Rice has performed less well: its cultivated area expanded from 37 to 43 million hectares from 1970 to 1990 and has remained at about that level. The yield of rice has risen from 1,120 kg/ha (1970) to 2,020 (2004), but in the USA it amounts to 7,370. The modest performance of rice is due to the fact that only 53 per cent of the area under rice is irrigated as compared to 87 per cent of the area under wheat.[10]

The Green Revolution relied on the application of chemical fertilizer. In the 1970s much of this had to be imported until domestic fertilizer production caught up with rising demand. In the years from 2001 to 2005 average annual consumption of nitrogenous fertilizer amounted to 108.4 million tonnes, of which 0.18 million had to be imported; for phosphate the respective figures were 3.8 and 0.33.[11] Potassic fertilizer cannot be produced in India and therefore 1.6 million tonnes had to be imported. In the early years of the Green Revolution, the peasants had concentrated on nitrogenous fertilizer as it increased yields immediately, but its one-sided application contributed to the deterioration of the soil and it was realized that a balanced mix of fertilizers was required. The government subsidized the application of fertilizers. This was a heavy burden on the budget and after the economic reform of 1991 attempts were made to reduce such subsidies, but since the peasantry had got used to them, it was politically hazardous to do this.

The reform of 1991 did not help agricultural growth because it led to a severe curtailment of agricultural credit. Most Indian peasants are indebted and depend on local moneylenders who charge usurious rates of interest. After nationalizing the commercial banks in 1969, the Indian government adopted a policy of social and development banking and instructed the banks to establish rural branches. In 1969 there was a total of about 8,000 branch offices of banks; by 1993 there were 60,000 of which more than half were in rural areas. However, the credit made available in this way usually benefited the richer farmers who knew how to deal with the required formalities. In 1975 additional regional rural banks had been established which were supposed to provide credit to the 'weaker sections' of society. This had been followed up with an Integrated Rural Development Programme (IRDP) in 1978 which was aimed at enabling the poor to earn an income and to foster rural employment by means of subsidized credit. Politicians were tempted to use their control over subsidized credit in order to reward their voters, the worst abuse of this being the announcement of debt waivers in election campaigns. This spoilt the chances of repayment once and for all. It is understandable that the reformers should try to curtail this misplaced generosity. In the meantime the example set by the Grameen Bank of Bangladesh had shown the virtues of managing micro-credit by NGOs. India tried to follow this example in a big way, but it turned out that the transaction costs of the NGOs were high and the interest rates they had to charge were only slightly less than those charged by the traditional moneylenders. In fact, these moneylenders benefited most from the reforms for they quickly expanded their business when government credit dried up.[12]

Under the influence of these policy changes, agricultural production in the post-reform era did not grow as fast as in the pre-reform decade. In the 1980s agricultural growth had been fostered by increases in productivity whereas in the 1990s it had been propelled by high support prices for rice and wheat. This had more or less reached its ecological limits because there are large regions in India which are unsuitable for the cultivation of rice and wheat. On the Indian highlands rainfall as well as irrigation are scarce and neither wheat nor rice can grow there. The humble millets (*jowar* and *bajra*) are the major food grains in this region. Their yield is, of course, much less than that of rice and wheat: 841 kg/ha for *jowar* and 876 for *bajra* (2004). Moreover, the area under these types of millet has receded from 30 to 18 million hectares (1970 to 2004).[13] This indicates that peasants have turned to cash crops such as oilseeds and cotton. But in this way they have become more vulnerable and when the new crops disappointed them, they could no longer fall back on the millet with which they had traditionally fed their families.

The area of cotton cultivation expanded from about 7.6 million hectares in 1970 to nearly 9 million in 2004.[14] There has also been a remarkable increase in the yield of cotton: from 106 kg/ha in 1970 to 225 in 1990, and to 324 in 2004. This latter spurt is probably due to the introduction of genetically modified 'Bt Cotton'. Bt stands for *Bacillus thuringiensis*, a micro-organism found in the soil from which a gene has been inserted into cotton, making it resistant to the bollworm which affects this plant. The seed is marketed by Monsanto, and Indian peasants pay a good price for it as it helps them to save on pesticides and to increase the yield of the cotton crop. There has been an acrimonious debate on this introduction of genetically modified cotton. It is pointed out that there are side-effects such as the spread of root rot. Other adverse effects may be apparent only after some time. Moreover, in some regions of India, the new seeds did not produce good results and the peasants suffered. When cotton prices rose suddenly in 1994 many peasants shifted to cotton cultivation even if the soil which they cultivated was not suitable for this crop. When the crop failed, many of them committed suicide as they were heavily in debt. The introduction of Bt Cotton seems to have precipitated a new wave of suicides, though in other regions peasants praised the new variety. The Indian government has permitted the spread of Bt Cotton seeds and seems to be very optimistic about the results.[15] Time will tell whether the sceptics were right to warn the peasants.

The manipulation of genes enhances the control of the giant firm Monsanto over the Indian market. It has absorbed its greatest competitor, Cargill, and has thus become even more powerful. Monsanto now produces seeds with a built in 'terminator' which makes the second generation seeds sterile, thus forcing the peasant to buy new seeds for every harvest. This destroys the tradition of selecting seeds carefully for the next harvest. Of course, the peasant can stick to his old seeds and escape Monsanto's domination. But very often he is not free to make a decision. Government agencies, moneylenders and grain dealers force the peasant to opt for the new seeds which guarantee higher yields.

Next to food grains and cotton, sugar-cane plays a major role in Indian agriculture. India is the world's largest consumer of sugar and the second-largest producer of sugar-cane (after Brazil); 4.5 million cane growers are involved in its production, not to mention the millions of seasonal labourers who cut the cane. Sugar-cane covers 3 per cent of India's cultivated area. It is a very thirsty crop and depends on intensive irrigation. There are 571 sugar mills throughout India, many of them owned by cooperatives. In the triennium 2001 to 2003 the average annual production of sugar-cane amounted to 274 million tonnes.[16] The production of one tonne of sugar requires about 10 million tonnes of cane. While the per capita availability of sugar has steadily increased from 6 kilograms in the 1970s to 16 in recent years, this yield is still very modest when compared to Brazil's 50 kilograms. India has also exported sugar and molasses, but this business is subject to frequent variations. From 1990 to 2003, a period of high sugar prices in the world market, India exported a substantial amount of sugar, but in 2004 sugar exports declined dramatically.[17] The Indian government feared that rising sugar prices would fuel inflation and saw to it that there would be enough sugar available in the home market. In July 2006 it even imposed a ban on the export of sugar. The sugar price in India declined by 30 per cent within a few months and the Indian cane growers pleaded with the government to lift the ban.[18] In January

2007 the Indian government reversed its policy and decided to encourage the export of sugar because there was a glut in the Indian market. A rich harvest had yielded 24 million tonnes of sugar of which only about 19 million tonnes were required for domestic consumption. The production of ethanol was also taken into consideration by the Indian government.[19] India could emulate Brazil in this respect where about 50 per cent of sugar production is used for making ethanol, a product for which flex-fuel engines in Brazilian cars have created a growing demand. In Brazil, sugar has become an energy commodity rather than a food product, and India may follow this trend.[20] But so far India is still at the very beginning of exploring this alternative to the export of sugar.

An essential part of Indian agricultural production is the cultivation of oilseeds and pulses. They are required for a balanced diet, particularly for vegetarians, that is, the majority of Indians. The quinquennial averages of the production of foodstuffs for 2000 to 2004 were 84.7 million tonnes of rice, 70.5 of wheat, 32.5 of millet, but only 12.8 of pulses and 21 of all oilseeds plus 7 of groundnuts. The daily per capita availability of food grains amounted to 400 grams in this period, but the availability of pulses was just 32 grams.[21] Before the great drought (1965–6) the daily availability of pulses was about twice that amount. The Green Revolution bypassed pulses. Earlier the peasants had grown pulses in between the food-grain crops: the Green Revolution did not tolerate this 'disorder'. However, pulses are easily attacked by pests if they are grown close together. Whereas India is otherwise more than self-sufficient in food crops, it must import pulses. In 2004 this import had a value of US\$ 382 million. A much larger item on the import list was that of vegetable oils, which amounted to US\$ 2.4 billion.[22] Imported vegetable oils nevertheless attract a customs duty of 70 per cent, the duties being kept at a high level in the interests of domestic producers. Actually, world market prices of oilseeds increase due to the additional demand created by the conversion of vegetable oils into bio-diesel.[23]

The cultivation of food grains, pulses and oilseeds is carried out by millions of peasants, most of whom are smallholders. Big landlords in the Western sense of the term have never existed in India. Under the tyrannical regime of the monsoon, the risks of agriculture have to be shouldered by many small cultivators. The so-called zamindars whose tenure was abolished in the late 1940s were orginally revenue collectors whom the British had converted into rent receivers.[24] They appropriated the surplus of peasant cultivation – usually without providing any 'inputs'. In some regions they did supervise the maintenance of local irrigation works, but this was about all they contributed to Indian agriculture. Sometimes they also took part in rural moneylending, but in general this business was left to local traders who provided credit to the peasants so as to have a claim on their produce after the harvest. The local trader and moneylender occupies a strategic position in Indian agriculture as he conveys the signals of the market to his debtors in no uncertain terms. If the crop fails, however, he does not bear the risk and at the most grants a moratorium on the debt, as the survival of the debtor is in his interest.

A very peculiar feature of Indian agriculture is the large-scale procurement of food grains by the government. This practice was started during the Second World War, when the predecessor of the Food Corporation of India was established to store buffer stocks so as to prevent man-made famines caused by speculative hoarding by private traders. Later on this practice was re-inforced when India was subjected to the humiliating 'ship to mouth' policy of President Johnson, mentioned earlier. The cruel lesson had its effect: the Indian government decided that it would never have such a humiliating experience again and started procuring buffer stocks with a vengeance. Procurement also proved a useful political instrument as it pleased the rural voters. Since this procurement yielded much more than was needed for buffer stocks, these stocks were managed like a revolving fund and surpluses were sold at subsidized rates in 400,000 Fair Price Shops, to benefit the poor. However, it was not easy to target the poor in this way. An official committee estimated that the government had to spend Rs 3.65 in order to get one rupee to the poor. Direct cash transfers would have been more efficient. But abol-ishing the Public Distribution System would also mean reducing procure-ment, as a buffer stock of about 16 million tonnes would be sufficient for an emergency. Actually the whole system of procurement and distribution has gone completely awry in recent years. In earlier times the amounts of grain procured and distributed were more or less balanced, but between 2001 and 2003 average annual production of grain amounted to 170 million tonnes, of which 38 were procured and only 18 distributed via the Public Distribution System.[25] Beyond that system the government devoted another 11 million tonnes annually to a variety of welfare schemes. This still left a large amount of stock with the government. The cost of maintaining this stock dwarfs all other public expenditure on Indian agriculture.[26] If the government dumped this surplus on the world market, the prices of rice and wheat would collapse. The perverse functioning of procurement is also demonstrated by the fact that market prices are nowadays often below the so-called minimum support price.[27] This means that the minimum becomes a maximum and the government has to bear a high cost. Moreover, while distribution is a nation-wide operation, procurement benefits very few states. In the triennium 2003–5, the Punjab had the lion's share of procurement; 57 per cent of the procured wheat and 41 per cent of the procured rice came from the Punjab. Haryana accounted for 31 per cent of wheat procurement and Andhra Pradesh for 17 per cent of rice procurement. As the government admits, only rich farmers who produce a large amount of marketable surplus actually benefit from this policy.

In addition to the vast area of peasant cultivation there is a small plantation sector of Indian agriculture. This is more or less restricted to tea gardens and coffee plantations which occupy ecological niches as they thrive where other crops do not grow. Neither tea nor coffee is indigenous to India; they were introduced by the British colonial rulers. The British had become addicted to tea in the eighteenth century when they imported it exclusively from China. At the time of the Opium War of the late 1830s they became aware of the hazards of relying only on China for the supply of their tea and tried to find suitable places in India for growing Chinese tea (*Camellia sinensis*). The foothills of the Himalayas in Assam appeared to be best suited for tea gardens but the first experiments with the Chinese variety were not very successful. By chance the British then discovered that the tribes of Assam prepared tea from a different type of plant (*Camellia assamica*). Subsequently both varieties were cultivated in India. The Chinese variety was grafted on to the Assamese one and this new variety was then grown in the hills around Darjeeling. Indian tea exports grew rapidly in the late nineteenth century and throughout the twentieth. India surpassed China in this respect. In the early twentieth century tea was still an exotic drink for most Indians, but in due course domestic consumption relegated the export of tea to a relatively minor position. Between 2000 and 2004 India produced annually 845 million kilograms of tea, but in this period domestic consumption increased by 12 per cent from 653 to 735 million kilograms.[28] China is once more ahead of India in terms of tea exports and Sri Lanka and Kenya have filled the gap left by India. The story of Indian coffee is quite similar to that of tea although the dimensions of production and export are much smaller. In the quinquennium 2000–4 the average annual production of coffee amounted to 280 million kilograms and domestic consumption increased by 25 per cent from 60 to 75 million kilograms.[29]

The dimensions of Indian agricultural production discussed so far have only encompassed the commodities which can be stored and sold even after a considerable time. In recent years, however, India has also made a mark in the production of perishable commodities such as fruit, vegetables and milk, which must be consumed or marketed as soon as possible. Their marketing requires logistics which are different from those for handling other types of produce. The 'godown' of the grain trader is not suited for these perishable foodstuffs, which have to be collected and transported very fast. They may even require cold storage. Technological progress has ensured that all these commodities can be handled efficiently. The Indian peasants have responded to these new possibilities very well and many have greatly improved their income in this way.

The Promising Growth of Horticulture,
Animal Husbandry and Fisheries

The products of these sectors of Indian agriculture had reached the market only in a limited way in earlier times. The heat of the day would quickly spoil vegetables and turn the milk sour and women who carried such products on their heads to nearby local markets would have to sell them there as soon as possible. Trucks carrying vegetables to more distant markets were rarely available, but occasionally unique linkages did develop, such as the transport of vegetables to the large market of Jharia in the biggest Indian coalfield in what is now Jharkhand. Trucks delivering coal would return full of vegetables for the miners. Big towns also had their networks of supply of perishable commodities. The lack of rural infrastructure has impeded the proper marketing of such commodities. However, some progress has been made in recent years and the production of fruit and vegetables has increased. Between 2002 and 2004 the area under fruit and vegetables amounted to 10.5 million hectares and altogether about 136 million tonnes were harvested annually.[30] In 2005 the Indian government launched a National Horticultural Mission, the aim of which is to double production by 2011. But production should not only be enhanced: it should also be diversified. India has always been famous for its spices, and their production has also grown in recent years. In the period from 2000 to 2005 the area under spices remained more or less the same, at about 2.5 million hectares, but production increased from 3 to 4.4 million tonnes.[31] India's unique biodiversity encourages horticulture as there are varieties of fruit and vegetables suitable for different types of soils and micro-climates. The Indian Institute of Horticulture in Bangalore has done pioneering work in this field, but to apply the knowledge gained by research, the peasants need adequate training. In Maharashtra, where horticulture is of great importance, the state government has launched schemes which benefit peasants who wish to turn to this field of activity. If they reclaim new land for horticulture, the government will pay the wages of the labour required.

In the field of animal husbandry, milk production has shown amazing progress in recent years. India is home to 57 per cent of the world's buffalo population and 16 per cent of the world's cattle. Nevertheless, milk production remained for a long time rather limited. In recent years, dairy farming has become an important source of income for landless labourers and cooperatives, which now have about 13 million members, have been established in many places and help in marketing milk. Operation Flood has worked wonders in getting this 'white revolution' started. Initially supported by marketing surplus milk powder donated by the European Union, this supply was then gradually replaced by Indian milk. In 1990 milk production had amounted to

80.6 million tonnes: by 2006 it had risen to 100 million tonnes.[32] Accordingly, per capita availability of milk increased during this period from 176 grams per day to 245. The installation of bulk coolers in the villages has helped to preserve the milk until it is transported to a dairy. By now, there is a National Milk Grid encompassing more than 100,000 village cooperatives in 265 districts and modern methods of testing the quality of the milk on the spot facilitate immediate payment to the producers, making it possible to step up production even more. Operation Flood was limited to the more accessible parts of the countryside, but then an Intensive Dairy Development Project was launched which stimulated milk production in the more remote, backward areas. The recent 'White revolution' has matched the earlier Green Revolution, and has benefited many people whom the Green Revolution had bypassed. Well-organized animal husbandry could also provide the material for the large-scale production of biogas for which the modern technology is now readily available. Moreover, after yielding gas the material can still be used as manure and is even more beneficial in this form than before treatment in the biogas plant.

Poultry is another item of animal husbandry which is growing very fast. It also generates income for landless labourers, both male and female, and is therefore of great social importance. It is estimated that it gives employment to about 2 million people. The total value of the output of poultry amounted to US$ 3.3 billion in 2004 and included the production of 1.65 million tonnes of chicken meat and 45 billion eggs.[33] Considering that only 21 billion eggs were produced in 1990, this increase is even more phenomenal than the increase in milk production.

Fisheries have also shown a very promising development in recent years. Traditionally, river fish have been in greater demand in India than sea fish, although India is surrounded by the Indian Ocean which supports immense numbers of fish both in the Bay of Bengal and on the continental shelf near the coast of western India. From only 2.4 million tonnes of fish caught in 1980, the total catch rose to 6.5 million in 2005.[34] It is interesting to note that the contribution of inland fisheries to the total catch has risen much faster than that of marine fisheries: from less than 1 million tonnes in 1980, the catch of inland fisheries rose to 3.5 million tonnes in 2004, a rise that probably reflects the increasing demand of domestic consumers. Sea fish have perhaps contributed more to the exports of marine products. In the triennium 2002–4 an average of about half a million tonnes of marine products were exported annually, fetching a price of US$ 1.4 billion.[35] In 2004 a Marine Fishing Policy was launched in order to ensure further progress in this area. About 11 million people are earning their livelihood as fishermen or by working in ancillary activities in India.

Exports from the World's Largest Hothouse

India's climate ensures the country grows fruit, vegetables and flowers for the whole world, particularly those varieties which do not grow very well in the temperate zones of the north. The sun and the monsoon make India a natural hothouse. There are indigenous Indian fruits such as mangoes which are in great demand in Europe and elsewhere, but most of the mangoes found in European markets come from Kenya or South America. They are poor substitutes for the much tastier Indian mangoes and yet they fetch a good price. Then there are Indian fruits like the delicious *chikku* (sapota) which are hardly known in Europe but would certainly find a market there once people discovered their taste. Proper marketing and logistics are the main problems which must be overcome in order to get the Indian fruits to customers abroad. Israel has solved this problem for products of this kind and could well serve as a model for India in this respect. Some sensitive fruits like mangoes require air freight, as they must be consumed within a month of being harvested. However, if kept at a constant temperature of 15°C mangoes can last longer. This requires careful cooling. Other fruits could be transported in containers by sea – if the Indian ports could handle such perishable freight with the necessary speed. The Indian government predicts that exports of agricultural produce which currently amount to US\$ 7.5 billion will grow to US\$ 20 billion by 2015. If this goal is to be reached, the processing of fruit and vegetables must progress. So far only 2 per cent of fruit and vegetables are processed in India, whereas in many other developing countries processing amounts to 80 per cent.[36]

The expansion of horticulture for export faces difficulties as far as some fruits in specific regions are concerned. Nagpur has been known for its delicious oranges (*santra*) for a long time and the Nagpur Orange Growers Association (NOGA) has done pioneering work in the marketing of oranges. It has also done much for the processing of oranges (canned juice, marmalade, etc.) But now this legendary centre of orange cultivation is threatened by a lack of water; many trees have died and replanting is impossible as long as water scarcity persists. Otherwise this region would be in the forefront of production for export. In the meantime Tropicana has started manufacturing orange juice in the Punjab on a massive scale.

The highlands of Maharashtra as well as similar regions in India are well suited to the cultivation of grapes. Mahagrape, an organization of 25 farmers' cooperatives encompassing altogether 2,000 grape farmers, has taken a lead in exporting grapes[37] and their example has stimulated other fruit growers to establish organizations, such as Mahamango. Maharashtra has about half a million hectares under grapes, producing more than half a million tonnes.

Other regions are also taking up this profitable business and there is a national organization, the Grape Growers' Federation of India. These activities could be expanded, particularly if India also produces more wine, which would easily find an export market. There are some excellent Indian wines available already, but they have hardly reached connoisseurs abroad. Wine cultivation in India is handicapped by the lack of a national wine culture and the consumption of alcohol is frowned upon by the majority of Indians. Those Indians who drink usually do so in order to get drunk – and thus confirm the prejudices of others. The drunkards prefer hard liquor and have no taste for wine. Moreover, Indians generally drink water with their meals, although there are varieties of wine which go very well with Indian food. Perhaps part of the rising Indian middle class will acquire a taste for wine in due course. A reduction in the heavy taxes on wine would also help to make wine more popular; taxing wine to the same extent as hard liquor tends to discourage wine drinkers. An indigenous wine culture supports the export of wine: its absence makes wine production for export a rather vulnerable business. India's potential for the cultivation of grapes and the making of wine is great and will certainly be explored to an increasing extent in future years.

Some enterprising Indian winemakers have already established a reputation in the export market and have impressed foreign consumers with the high quality of their products. Grover Vineyards in Bangalore, established in 1988, has been able to sell wine even to the French[38] and in 1996 the famous French firm Veuve Clicquot Ponsardin acquired a minority stake in this company. Even before Kanwal and Kapil Grover started production, the Chougules from Goa were making wine in the highlands of Maharashtra. Later they teamed up with another famous French firm, Piper-Heidsieck, producing an Indian 'champagne' named after the Marquise de Pompadour. They also offer an attractive range of red wines. The youngest company in this field is Sula Vineyards of Nashik in Maharashtra, founded in 2000, which has won international prizes for its fine wines. Indian wines sell abroad at prices of about US$ 15–18, which is relatively high. With an increase in production and aggressive marketing more sales at somewhat lower prices could easily be achieved so that India could at least rival Chile in terms of wine exports.

Another candidate for growing export production is floriculture. India produces some very beautiful flowers which are in demand worldwide. One such is *Helicona rostrata*; its magnificent red and yellow blossoms, which form a broad ribbon, immediately attract attention. There are many other amazing flowers which India has to offer and in 2006 it earned US$ 66 million from their export. But India faces stiff competition from Africa and has sometimes disappointed its customers by the low quantity and quality of its exported blooms. The methods of floriculture must be modernized and intensified in India so that it can reap a rich harvest and earn a great deal of foreign exchange.

India's most prominent export crop has for a long time been processed cashew kernels. The cashew nut tree is related to the mango tree and thrives in the same climate. The Portuguese discovered the cashew nut tree in Brazil in the sixteenth century and brought it to India and East Africa. The processing of the cashew nut is very labour intensive. The outer shell is hard to crack and if this is not done properly, the kernel will be broken and then fetch a much lower price in the market. Moreover, between the shell and the kernel there is a caustic substance which causes blisters if it touches the skin. Roasting is required to reduce the caustic oil (cardol) and even then the nut must be handled with caution. The processing is mostly done by women who receive rather low wages for their work. Kerala is the centre of cashew processing and the Kerala State Cashew Association is the largest exporter of cashew nuts in the world. In addition to processing its own production of about half a million tonnes, India imports another 250,000 to 400,000 tonnes annually from Africa. The value added by processing these nuts is very substantial, but India has to compete in a rapidly changing global market in this area. There has been a relatively steep increase in the volume, accompanied by a drastic fall in the value of imports and exports. The price per tonne of imported nuts fell by 19 per cent from US$ 844 to US$ 676 and the price per tonne of exported kernels by 27 per cent from US$ 4,904 to US$ 3,567 in recent years. Output doubled worldwide from 1994 to 2003 and cashew nuts have surpassed almonds in world production. At the same time there was a change in the ranks of cashew producers: Vietnam has replaced India as the number one country for cashew nut production, contributing 28 per cent to world supply as against India's 25 per cent. Vietnam's rapid rise is due to careful horticulture and high cashew yields. Having been a leader in this field for a long time, India cannot afford to rest on its laurels and must apply new methods to the production, processing and marketing of this valuable crop.

Avocados and olives can also be grown in India, but their cultivation is still in the experimental stage. In the meantime, the inconspicuous gherkin (*cornichon*) has started a triumphant march across southern India. It is almost exclusively grown for export as it attracts few Indian consumers. In Europe it is usually consumed in its pickled form so it is ideally suited to being processed and packed in India. Accordingly, some big European firms have set up production units in India and get their supplies from contract farmers. The cultivation of gherkins is labour intensive: they have to be literally hand-picked. Since they grow fast, three crops may be harvested in one year. In 2004 India exported 100,000 tonnes of gherkins and earned US$ 63 million. Karnataka accounts for 60 per cent of this production; Andhra Pradesh and

Tamil Nadu produce most of the rest. There is an Indian Gherkins Exporters' Association which represents the thousands of peasants who have opted for this new crop. However, dependence on fluctuating prices abroad and power shortages at home affect the gherkin growers; their crop requires sprinkler irrigation and if power fails even for a short time, the gherkins may not grow.

The model of contract farming which has proved useful for the peasants growing gherkins is also applicable to other types of production for export. The firm which issues the contract knows the market and can provide technical advice and input. The peasant who accepts the contract has a guaranteed income. In fact, contract farming sponsored by big private sector firms has already become a major business in some parts of India and the government hopes for its expansion. The telecommunications wizard Sunil Bharti Mittal has teamed up with the Rothschild Group to establish Bharti Field Fresh with the slogan 'Link India's fields to the world'.[39] Since this is a joint venture with a foreign group, the new corporation is not permitted to engage in direct cultivation as the 'potato kings' of the Punjab do, who cultivate thousands of acres which they 'lease in', employing large numbers of temporary labourers. Bharti Field Fresh can only have contracts with individual peasants. But peasants often do not trust big corporations, as they may turn down their produce when the supply is ample and prices low. Such corporations may use the pretext of having to reject contracted produce because of low quality and then buy it more cheaply on the open market.[40] Enforcing contracts by resorting to the courts is impossible for poor peasants: they can only improve their bargaining position by forming associations of producers. The big corporations on the other hand would be well advised to cultivate the trust of the peasants by honouring their contracts and providing extension services as well as crop insurance. The majority of Indian peasants are not even aware of crop insurance and, according to a national sample survey, only 4 per cent of them have ever insured their crops.[41] In this respect the agricultural initiative of Reliance Industries may blaze a new trail. This is not yet aimed at production for export but at a guaranteed supply of the retail chain set up by Reliance. Initially Reliance also opted for contract farming and paid advances to the peasants. The results were disappointing, as many peasants spent the advances on consumption or on repaying old debts. Contract farming was then replaced by 'contact' farming, i.e. Reliance supplied inputs and guaranteed that it would buy the peasants' produce. This guarantee also included an element of crop insurance which has worked well and Reliance is extending its rural operations.[42] So far Reliance is only interested in the domestic market, but in due course 'contact' farming may also contribute to export production in the world's largest hothouse.

CHAPTER 11

THE GIANT'S SHACKLES: WATER, ENERGY AND INFRASTRUCTURE

The Menace of Water Scarcity

In trying to take further development in its stride, India is burdened by shackles whose weight increases with every step it takes. One of these shackles is the scarcity of water. The monsoon seems to supply India with abundant rain, even causing devastating floods almost every year. But this image of abundance is deceptive: much of the downpour runs off into the sea. Water harvesting is crucial, but it has been neglected. The forest is a great water harvester, but deforestation has progressed in India to an alarming extent. Official claims that about a fifth of India is still covered by forests are contradicted by the evidence of satellite photography according to which only about 10 per cent forest cover still exists. Moreover, soil erosion has increased with deforestation and is exacerbated by the characteristics of monsoon rainfall. The monsoon does not provide long periods of mild drizzle; it prefers sudden downpours. After the surface has been drenched, the penetration of the soil is stopped and further rain contributes to erosion. Altogether India receives an annual precipitation of 4,000 billion cubic metres, of which 80 per cent is concentrated in a period of about 10 weeks. The river systems of India distribute this wealth of rainwater rather unevenly. The northern plains which constitute only one third of India's land area command nearly two-thirds of its freshwater resources. The rest of the country is at a serious disadvantage in this respect.

Madhav Chitale, an engineer and civil servant who was awarded the Stockholm Water Prize in 1993 for his work on India's water problems, has categorized the regions of the country according to the degree of water scarcity. The stage of impending scarcity is defined as 'water stress'. This applies to regions whose renewable fresh water availability is below 1,700 cubic metres per capita per year. Water scarcity sets in when availability falls below 1,000 cubic metres. Absolute water scarcity affects regions with an availability

1 'Save Water' by Raghupathi Rao (2005)

of less than 500 cubic metres. India's average is at about 2,400 cubic metres, which is well above the level of water stress. But there are important regional disparities. The regions in the Ganges, Indus and Krishna basins face at the most some water stress. Along the east coast, the Mahanadi and Pennar valleys experience water scarcity and so do some of the areas of Kachchh and Kathiawar. The regions to the south of the Pennar valley all the way down to Kankyakumari face absolute water scarcity. Per capita water availability in this region is as low as 411 cubic metres.

Increasing the area under permanently irrigated agriculture in order to become independent of the vagaries of the monsoon has contributed to India's water problems. As mentioned earlier, about 40 per cent of cultivated land is by now under permanent irrigation. More than 50 per cent of this irrigation depends on the extraction of groundwater rather than on the use of surface water.[1] In many parts of India there are ancient tanks and other local irrigation works based on the collection of rainwater; sadly many of these old works have degenerated as the traditional institutions supporting them no longer exist. The great variety of such local irrigation works reflects the ecological practices closely followed by the local people. Sunita Narain, Director of the Centre of Science and Environment, New Delhi, has done a great deal to recover this traditional knowledge and to revive forms of community-based water harvesting,[2] and she received the Stockholm Water Prize for her work in 2005.[3] But it is difficult to overcome the colonial legacy in this field. The British colonial rulers were more interested in large-scale canal irrigation, which they introduced in the Punjab and in parts of the Gangetic plains. Canal irrigation was not always beneficial: if it was not managed properly, it could lead to waterlogging or to salinity of the soil, caused by the evaporation of water. The British emphasis on large-scale irrigation was inherited by independent India such that the Indian government took pride in building gigantic dams which could feed canal irrigation and also serve the purpose of power generation. Unfortunately, the building of these dams not only deprived many people of their habitat but also contributed to deforestation. With increasing erosion many of the reservoirs behind the dams silted up at a much faster rate than had been predicted by their planners. Moreover, some dams are located in areas threatened by earthquakes; if they break, thousands of people will die. The technocratic bias of politicians and bureaucrats favoured such conspicuous projects, but since they are devoted to surface irrigation groundwater irrigation – which is at least as important – is often neglected. Dams greatly reduce the replenishment of groundwater by rivers. They do contribute very visibly to surface irrigation, but diminish groundwater resources which are invisible and therefore do not attract attention. In spite of the emphasis on the building of dams, the per capita storage capacity of water amounts to only 262 cubic metres in India as compared to 1,111 in China and 6,103 in Russia.[4]

The extraction of groundwater by means of modern technology causes major problems. Traditionally, groundwater was tapped by wells dug only a few metres deep. Chains of buckets driven by animal power helped to lift the water. With a sinking water table, modern borewells which go down to 100 metres or more were used in great numbers. If such borewells are too close to each other there is a danger of the depletion of the sources of water available to one's neighbours. In fact, in some areas 'waterlords' have emerged who sell to their neighbours the water of which they have deprived them by digging the deeper well.[5] In earlier times tanks were maintained by the village community. The silt at the bottom of the tank had to be removed; it was then spread in the fields and served as manure. This was a collective effort and involved hard work. However, when peasants were able to access individual tubewells, they forgot about the tanks and their collective maintenance.[6] The Indian Easement Act of 1882 which assures the landowner of unrestricted property rights to the groundwater under his land is still valid and no attempt has been made to amend it. India's National Academy of Agricultural Sciences refers to 'state failure' with regard to the control of groundwater.[7]

State regulation of the access to water is necesssary, otherwise anarchy will prevail in this field. Unfortunately, this gives rise to a powerful water bureaucracy. Maharashtra is a case in point. After an initial Ground Water Act of 1993 further legislation was considered necessary. In 2005 a detailed act creating a Maharashtra Water Resources Regulatory Authority was passed.[8] The act empowered this authority to draw up an Integrated State Water Plan within whose framework it would allocate 'Aggregate Bulk Water Entitlements' to water users' associations.[9] Such associations were also established in other Indian states according to the general idea of participatory irrigation management (PIM). Whereas this type of legislation necessarily reflects a 'top down' approach, PIM embodies a development from below. It was not easy to make these two ends meet. The main problem is the payment of the charges for operation and management of the water supply. The state wishes to regulate access to these scarce resources, but it does not intend to foot the bill for operation and management. Faced with this dilemma, the state may privatize operation and management, as a private entrepreneur would certainly see to it that he gets paid for the service which he provides. However, this means that he would be vested with the control of a 'public good'. PIM is to be preferred to this alienation of scarce resources, but it must be made to work in a transparent and equitable manner.[10]

There is, of course, another option which pleases politicians and their rural voters: the state provides free water and free power and pays for this from general taxes. This was actually introduced in the Punjab in 1997.[11] It is an invitation to indulge in enormous waste: peasants would let their electrical pumps run day and night and exhaust the scarce water resources to their hearts' content. The only solution is for the local water users' associations to collect and retain the water charges and spend them on operation and management. But even this will not stop the depletion of groundwater resources. According to official figures, there are about 17 million wells in India and they extract twice as much groundwater from the soil than nature can provide as replenishment. The sinking of the water table indicates what is happening in the countryside.

The district of Sangrur in the Punjab provides alarming evidence of the rapid drop in the water table.[12] This district, which borders on Haryana, is inhabited by small and medium landholders who own on average some 4 hectares of cultivable land, almost all of which is irrigated. Several canals cross the district, but two-thirds of its irrigation depend on groundwater. The authorities concerned have found out that the water table is receding by 75 centimetres per year. It is now at a depth of 7 metres and the peasants are commissioning submersible pumps installed at a depth of about 100 metres to irrigate their fields. The over-exploitation of groundwater resources is mostly due to the cultivation of a particularly 'thirsty' type of rice and the area under rice (360,000 ha) is almost equal to that under wheat in this district. The local agricultural university has warned the peasants about the depletion of groundwater and has asked them not to transplant the PUSA-44 variety of rice, which requires up to four times more water than other varieties. However, this 'thirsty' rice yields 4,500 kg/ha and the peasants do not want to forgo such a rich harvest. It remains to be seen how long the peasants will be able to continue this type of cultivation.

The supply of groundwater is not only threatened by the sinking of the water table and the exhaustion of aquifers, it is also affected by pollution and contamination.[13] Pollution is man-made, it is caused by industrial effluents, by fertilizers and pesticides. Once these polluting materials enter the aquifers, they remain there for a very long time. Rivers change the composition of their water within a few weeks; aquifers take more than a thousand years to make such a change. In addition to man-made pollution, groundwater may be contaminated by elements such as arsenic which are present in the soil and absorbed by the aquifers to an increasing extent when groundwater is lifted by pumps and borewells. In West Bengal and adjacent Bangladesh there have been many cases where the population has suffered from the effects of arsenic in their drinking water. In coastal areas, aquifers which are depleted by pumping may attract sea water, the resulting salinity making the groundwater unsuitable as drinking water. Fluoride or heavy metals which cause various types of disease have also been found in many places in the groundwater. Water quality monitoring is of great importance, but the required technologies and the employment of qualified staff are expensive. Even more expensive are the methods of artificially recharging aquifers once they are found to be polluted and contaminated. In coastal areas it may even be less costly to desalinate sea water. Saudi Arabia depends to a large extent on such desalinated drinking water and has sponsored pioneering work in this field. In the near future India will have to do a great deal in this field, as its groundwater resources are deteriorating.

Although groundwater is such a vital asset to India, its exploration was taken up very late as a sideline to the work of the Geological Survey of India (GSI). This venerable institution started its operations in 1851 with the aim of exploring the coal and ore resources of India. Nobody thought of groundwater in those days. In the 1950s a groundwater wing of the GSI started preliminary explorations in some states, but it was only in the late 1960s that groundwater development was recognized as a priority area by the Indian government. Finally, in 1972, the Central Ground Water Board was carved out of the GSI and given independent status. It concentrates on experimental drillings, water quality testing and recently also on the use of remote sensing via satellite for the identification of suitable sites for further exploration. It now operates about 15,000 hydrographic stations all over India. But this board is not a statutory body with powers to regulate the exploitation of groundwater. It took another fourteen years and an injunction of the Supreme Court before a Central Ground Water Authority was established under Section 3 of the Environment (Protection) Act of 1986. Although this authority was given sweeping powers, it has hardly been able to stop the unjustified exploitation of groundwater.[14] The Government of Maharashtra had been ahead of the central government with regard to groundwater affairs, having established the Groundwater Surveys and Development Agency (GSDA) of Maharashtra in 1971. This agency had undertaken practical work in the countryside such as drilling about 178,000 borewells and installing 160,000 hand-pumps in 25,000 villages by 1999. Other state governments were not as active in this respect. Central government had circulated a model groundwater control and regulation bill to all state governments in 1970, and again in 1996 and in 1999, but by 2003 very few state governments had adopted this kind of legislation. India depends for half of its water use, for 70 per cent of its irrigation and 80 per cent of its domestic water supply on groundwater and yet this precious resource has been neglected. Groundwater management obtains less than 10 per cent of the public funds spent by the central and the state governments on water resources.[15]

In addition to irrigation, access to safe drinking water in Indian households has been of great concern to India's planners. In 1961 only 38 per cent of Indian households had such access. The urban/rural divide was glaring at that time: three-quarters of urban households were able to obtain drinking water but only one-quarter of rural households. This divide has been reduced very considerably. In 2001, 78 per cent of all households could get safe drinking water; in urban areas only 10 per cent had to live without direct access to drinking water while in rural areas nearly three-quarters of the population could get drinking water in their households. There were striking regional disparities. Kerala reported that just 16 per cent of rural households had a supply of drinking water; the others obviously depended on village wells. Low rates were also noted in the rural areas of tribal and remote regions such as Tripura, Meghalya, Manipur,

Mizoram, Nagaland and Jharkhand such that an Accelerated Rural Water Supply Programme was started in 1972 to address the problem. In recent years it has been carried on by the Rajiv Gandhi National Drinking Water Mission. By 2005 about 96 per cent of rural areas were reported as having access to drinking water. But at the same time it was also noted that sources were running dry and that the lowering of the water table had reversed the trend of steady progress in this field.[16] The menace of water scarcity remains a serious challenge to India's social and economic advancement.

There is an intractable political problem about water management in India. The federal constitution allocates this subject to the states. There is a central ministry dealing with water resources, but it can only commission reports and issue recommendations and at the most allocate some central funds for special projects. Everything else is left to the respective state governments. They often lack the political will to introduce measures which are resented by influential voters; and they may even adopt populist policies which lead to a greater wastage of water. The price is finally paid by the poor in dry areas who have to buy their water from a tanker while rich peasants elsewhere exploit water resources for which they do not have to pay.

The water resources of Indian rivers should also be taken care of in a constructive way. Unfortunately water disputes between lower riparian and upper riparian states have often vitiated the proper management of scarce resources. The Interstate Water Disputes Act of 1956 which was amended in 2002 provides for tribunals whose verdicts should be binding, but often states which were dissatisified with a particular verdict simply refused to implement it. The central government cannot force the recalcitrant state government to accept the verdict. It could only dismiss it and impose President's Rule, but although this has been done for other reasons, it has never been resorted to in a water dispute. In any case, it would not lead to a permanent solution of the conflict as the next state government would take up the same issue again. A better approach to conflict resolution would be the formation of inter-state water authorities to deal with the river basin in question in a comprehensive manner and the establishment of the Cauvery River Authority in 1998 seemed to be a step in the right direction. It has solved some short-term conflicts, but its work is obstructed whenever the chief ministers of Karnataka and Tamil Nadu are at loggerheads. The Indus Water Treaty concluded by India and Pakistan with the help of the World Bank in 1960 proved to be a success and could serve as a model for inter-state disputes within India. But even in the case of the adjacent rivers in India (Ravi, Beas) this model has not been adopted and the conflicts between the respective states drag on. All these river water conflicts are very costly as they impede the proper utilization of water resources and prevent the investment of funds which would help to improve the management of the river basins. Perhaps a powerful National River Water Commission as an apex body of regional river basin authorities would provide the institutional framework for dealing with India's precious water resources.[17]

The Increasing Demand for Energy

While stepping up its industrial development, India had to face the problem of securing an adequate supply of energy. In the recent past the demand for energy has grown at a higher rate than the rate of growth of GDP. Industry consumes about 50 per cent of the energy available to India; agriculture claims about 27 per cent. India's hunger for energy is, of course, minimal when compared to the enormous appetite of the USA: per capita consumption of energy is only 3 per cent of that in the USA. India has to spend a quarter of its import bill on petroleum, although it does have considerable indigenous resources of energy. Its most important asset in this respect is coal, of which there are supposed to be reserves of 206 billion tonnes. Unfortunately, this enormous wealth has not been exploited efficiently. Under British rule, the subsoil rights were vested in the landlords (zamindars) who issued contracts to British companies for the mining of coal.[18] Exploitation of the mines was carried on in a haphazard fashion with the actual work being left to raising contractors, that is, leaders of gangs of miners who were paid per tonne delivered at the pithead.

After independence, the British owners sold most of the mines to Indian coal traders. These traders were for the most part Gujaratis and Marwaris who continued to work with raising contractors and did not invest much in the mines.[19] Marwaris are traders from Marwar in Rajasthan who had swarmed all over India under British rule, usually working as rural money-lenders and grain dealers. They had also traded in coal in eastern India and had then emerged as mine owners. These new owners expected the mines to be nationalized; to them further private investment would have meant a waste of money. By 1970 the Indian coalfields were in a very bad condition. Underground fires were consuming a great deal of coal in mines which had been abandoned while in opencast mines one could see hundreds of women carrying coal in baskets on their heads. Production of coal amounted to 72 million tonnes. In 1973 the Coal Mines (Nationalization) Act was passed and Coal India Ltd took over all the mines – a change in ownership but not in the methods of management. Raising contractors continued to do most of the work. Until 1980 production had shown limited growth; from 1980 to 2000 it almost trebled and stood at 310 million tonnes in 2000. In recent years production has been stepped up, to reach 407 million tonnes in 2005.[20] Opencast mining has the lion's share of this increase, contributing about 70 per cent of the total. Now Coal India Ltd employs nearly 700,000 people, but 80 per cent of them work in underground mining which costs three to four times more than opencast mining. The coal mines are concentrated in Jharkhand and coal must be transported by rail to distant power stations. The railways carry about 70 per cent of the coal and this accounts for 45 per cent of their total goods traffic.[21] There is a perennial shortage of wagons and there is a great deal of loss through pilferage.

Indian coal has a high ash content; nearly three-quarters of it is of low quality. Coking coal is always in short supply and much of it has to be imported. Rather than transporting coal by rail, it would be much better to build modern power stations in the coalfield and feed the electricity into a national grid. There are now very efficient methods of converting coal into gas and generating electricity by means of turbines. One of these methods is pressurized fluidized bed combustion (PFBC) which is particularly suitable for coal with high ash content. In this process the coal is mixed with sorbents such as limestone in a pressurized boiler where jets of air stir the coal and sorbents, facilitating frequent interaction during combustion. Coal is gasified in this way and energy generated by a gas turbine. Surplus heat produces steam, which drives a steam turbine to generate additional energy.[22] Such installations require massive investment, which would yield good returns. For this, private sector participation is urgently required. Coal India Ltd does not have the resources for upgrading its production; for a long time it worked under the old 'cost plus' rules and did not even calculate its costs properly, practically supplying the market with coal below the cost of production. In 1996 the government deregulated the coal price and also lowered import duties on coal to introduce competition. Moreover, the old Nationalization Act of 1973 was amended in 1993 to allow private companies to establish 'captive mines' for producing their own supply. However, these captive mines were initially prohibited from selling their surplus in the open market. Considering the enormous amounts which India has to spend on importing petroleum, the investment in coal production and gasification should be stepped up.

Although India imports petroleum, it also has considerable resources of its own, but their exploration and exploitation leave much to be desired. In earlier times, oil exploration was almost exclusively the preserve of the big Western oil companies. They only looked for oil in places where people did not need it and were prepared to sell it at throwaway prices. Finding oil in India where it was needed for internal consumption was not good business from this point of view and it was only when the Soviet Union started helping the country with oil exploration in the 1960s that oil was found in several places. Before 1972 there was plenty of cheap oil in the world market and the Indian government preferred to bargain hard with the Western oil companies, keeping its own untapped reserves as a bargaining chip rather than exploiting them. When the oil crisis hit India, it could not step up its own production at short notice. From 1975 to 1985 Indian oil production from inland sources oscillated around 8 million tonnes per year. The real breakthrough came with the exploitation of offshore wells on the continental shelf near Mumbai (Bombay High). From very modest yields in the late 1970s, the production of these offshore wells rose from 5 million tonnes in 1980 to 21 million in 1985. In subsequent years further progress was made with Indian oil production reaching its zenith in 1989 at 34 million tonnes and then levelling off. Instead of using modern methods such as horizontal drilling in order to increase the yield, there was a widespread 'flogging' of wells, which increases output in the short run, but finally ruins the wells. Horizontal drilling works with mobile drilling heads which slither into oil-bearing layers like a snake into a hole. However, this technology is expensive and requires the type of investment for which public sector companies are not equipped.

The public sector oil companies are trapped in a system of cross-subsidies. In order to supply cheap kerosene to the masses, they must draw upon profits in other branches of their business. Thus they have no capital for investment in their upstream operations. The old cost-plus system combined with a regime of administered prices has prevented the oil industry from modernizing its operations and exploring the vast reserves which India is said to have. Nor have adequate incentives been given to foreign companies to go ahead with oil exploration, although the government has frequently promised to do something about it. The recent rise in the international oil price has burdened India's balance of payments, as 75 per cent of the country's energy resources must be imported. In 1990 India imported about 30 million tonnes of petroleum at a total price of US$ 6 billion; in 2004 it imported about 100 million tonnes at US$ 30 billion. In the following year the oil price increased by 47 per cent and India had to spend US$ 44 billion for its oil imports. In the meantime the dismal performance of the state electricity boards, which will be discussed later on, had forced more and more corporate consumers of energy to opt for 'captive energy', that is, diesel generators installed on their premises. This is an expensive method of electricity generation and amounts to a waste of scarce resources.[23]

India not only has oilfields but also large reserves of natural gas, which have been explored in recent years. Natural gas is often tapped while drilling oil wells. If there are no pipelines to channel this gas, it is flared to get rid of it, something that was done in India until the first major gas pipeline was constructed by the Gas Authority of India (GAIL).[24] This authority was established in 1984 and built the Hazira–Bijaipur–Jagdishpur (HBJ) pipeline in the mid-1990s. Hazira is located on the coast of Gujarat near Surat. Gas from Bombay High and from onshore gas resources near Hazira was transported by means of this pipeline via Bijaipur about 150 kilometres to the north of Bhopal in Madhya Pradesh to Jagdishpur in Uttar Pradesh – a distance of about 1,000 kilometres. It could supply power plants and fertilizer factories all along its course. GAIL had the monopoly of the transport of gas throughout India. Although it was not involved in exploiting or marketing oil, it had to contribute its share to the subsidy for kerosene supplied to the masses. The price of gas was dictated by the government until it was deregulated in 1997. In addition to its own natural gas, India imports a substantial amount of liquefied natural gas (LNG) from Qatar and other Gulf states. LNG is reconverted into gas in the ports and than transported via the pipelines. In 2003 India commissioned the first LNG port at Dahej which is equipped with a regasification plant.[25] Dahej is located at the mouth of the Narmada River. It has been connected with a direct pipeline to Bijaipur, where it meets the HBJ pipeline which has also been connected with Delhi. India's dependence on LNG may be considerably reduced when new sources of natural gas are tapped within the country. In recent years, Reliance, a major Indian industrial firm, has explored new gas sources in the Bay of Bengal near the Krishna-Godaveri delta.[26] These gas fields are located at a depth of about 2,000 feet and at a distance of about 30 kilometres from the coast. Reliance is eager to exploit this field and has even built a pipeline across India to Maharashtra and Gujarat that will be completed by the end of 2007. Chinese and Russian construction firms were hired to build it, the Chinese having just completed their own east–west pipeline and so were glad to use their equipment in India. The Bay of Bengal holds much promise for India's energy supply: it will be further explored in the near future.[27]

In addition to coal, oil and gas India also relies on the electricity generated by its dams and its nuclear reactors, albeit such additional sources are still of minor importance in terms of the country's total energy budget. In 2004 altogether 608 billion kilowatt-hours were generated by Indian utilities: the contribution of hydroelectricity was 101 and of nuclear reactors 17 kilowatt hours.[28] The generation of hydroelectricity was stepped up only recently. Earlier it had contributed only 75–80 billion kilowatt-hours.

Nuclear reactors, which were once supposed to emerge as a major source of energy for India, have not lived up to expectations. The problem of access to foreign technology in this field has been discussed earlier and is why India has been able to get ahead only very slowly in this respect. In 1990 the installed capacity of nuclear reactors amounted to 1,500 megawatts; by 2004 this had been expanded to 2,800 megawatts.[29] The nuclear deal concluded with President Bush in 2005 is supposed to mark a breakthrough in this field. However, there are inherent problems of safety here. Both dams and reactors can be affected by earthquakes, and India has experienced some rather devastating ones in recent years. The huge tectonic plate, of which most of India consists, still moves northward against the Himalayas. Earlier most earthquakes occurred in the zone of collision in the north. The recent quakes at Latur in Maharashtra in 1993 and Bhuj in Gujarat in 2001 have revealed a new pattern. Powerful earthquakes can now also affect the centre of the tectonic plate and its western rim. The Narmada dam, India's biggest and most controversial project of this kind, is located midway between Latur and Bhuj.

Alternative sources of energy such as wind and solar radiation have not yet been tapped by India to a significant extent. Wind energy has been harnessed by some Indian pioneers: its total potential in the country is estimated at 20,000 megawatts, of which only 2,500 had been utilized by the year 2004. India has some special zones which are particularly suitable for the generation of wind energy,[30] the most promising being the southern tip from the Nilgiris to Kanyakumari. Another prominent zone is the area from Kolhapur in Maharashtra to Chitradurga in Karnataka. In Gujarat the Kathiawar peninsula is swept by winds. In Rajasthan the desert around Jaisalmer would be suitable for the installation of a huge wind park. The desert is, of course, also an ideal place for the generation of solar energy. So far the generation of this energy has mostly been restricted to small projects in the countryside where normal energy supply is not available. However, a major solar energy plant is under construction at Mathania in Rajasthan[31] which will combine a 35 megawatt solar plant with a 105 megawatt thermal power station based on liquefied natural gas.

The cost of photovoltaic cells has so far impeded the rapid expansion of the generation of solar energy, but further research should bring this cost down. Indian research institutes have made significant contributions to so-called 'thin film' technology, but funds for such research are limited. Since sunshine is abundant in India, the generation of solar energy would yield wonderful results.[32] It has a potential of 20 megawatts per square kilometre. If only 1 per cent of Indian territory was equipped with solar cells it would add up to 600,000 megawatts, about four times the capacity installed in all conventional power stations at present. High oil prices have greatly increased the incentive for investment in solar energy in Western countries so joint efforts in achieving the production of inexpensive solar cells should be urgently promoted.

Another promising line of alternative energy generation is the production of biogas.[33] Again, this has been tried in small projects in the Indian countryside where *gobar* gas has been produced from cow dung. The dung is mixed with water and poured in a cylinder in which methane gas collects which can be used for heating stoves. The effluent is a better manure than the untreated dung. By now such small *gobar* gas plants are installed in many rural households. The next step would be to construct bigger biogas plants which can generate electricity. The technology is already available: it only requires widespread application. Moreover, the production of biogas is not restricted to extracting methane from cow dung. There are numerous other substances which are subsumed under the general term 'biomass'. One item is bagasse, the dry refuse emerging from the process of sugar-making.[34] Since India is the second-largest cane sugar producer in the world, there is a huge amount of bagasse available as biomass. There are estimates that the total potential of generating energy from biomass amounts to 20,000 megawatts.

Geothermal energy is a further source of alternative energy supply which has so far hardly been tapped or even recognized in India.[35] There are about 400 hot springs in India, some of them with a surface discharge at 90°C and more than 190 tonnes per hour. These springs are known; no costly prospecting has to be done in order to locate these sources of geothermal power. Whereas in many places of the world such springs have a moderate temperature (low enthalpy), there are places in the country such as Tattapani in Chhattisgarh where five wells spout boiling water in great quantities, making it an ideal place for a geothermic power station. In Austria such power stations are operated with great successs. Re-injection of water helps to secure a continuous stream.[36] China uses geothermal energy in a big way, although rarely for the generation of electricity. Experts estimate that the potential of geothermic energy in India amounts to 10,000 megawatts. Compared to the capacity of power generation installed in the country (2004) of about 137,000 megawatts this is not a negligible amount. However, the use of geothermal energy has been almost totally neglected in India so far.[37]

The exploration and exploitation of different sources of energy pose many problems. But these are dwarfed by the obstacles faced when it comes to generating and distributing electricity. In 1948 the Indian government adopted the policy of establishing state electricity boards (SEBs) with a monopoly on the generation, transmission and distribution of electricity.[38] It was stipulated that these SEBs should earn at least 3 per cent annually on the capital invested. But they were not only unable to achieve this modest aim; all of them have operated at a loss and have accumulated such losses to the great detriment of the budgets of the states.[39] In recent years their rates of return on capital investment have been around minus 25 per cent. All SEBs taken together employ nearly a million people and are grossly overstaffed with posts in these organizations often being treated as political sinecures. Political interests also prevail in the determination of the tariff structure. Peasants get their electricity at a very low rate, or even free of charge. Households pay about one rupee per kilowatt-hour, industrial consumers about twice that amount or more. They are thus forced to subsidize the energy required by other consumers. Moreover, power plants often work below capacity and there is a great deal of loss in transmission, including loss through widespread theft. In most countries long-distance transmission is effected at high voltages. India's transmission lines cover about 6.5 billion circuit kilometres, of this only 2.5 billion circuit kilometres are operated at tensions above 500 volts,[40] which means that the great majority of transmission lines operate at low voltages, which facilitates the theft of electricity. As far as distribution is concerned, the non-payment of bills has plagued all SEBs.

The result of all these operational problems are frequent power cuts that force corporate consumers to rely on captive power, the generation of which has far exceeded the electricity supplied to industrial firms by public utilities. From 1993 to 2001 this supply by public utilities stagnated at an average of 32,000 gigawatt-hours; in the meantime captive power supply forged ahead from 23,000 in 1993 to 54,000 in 2002. The Indian government has come to terms with this fact by deregulating captive power under the Electricity Act of 2003.[41] Many private households also keep a small generator at hand for dealing with the almost daily blackout. A solution to these problems has been sought by 'unbundling' the activities of the SEBs, separating the generation, transmission and final supply of electricity and entrusting it to different agencies which could then concentrate on their respective tasks. At all three levels, selective privatization could be tried, first of all at the level of generation, of course, which could attract private investment if the other agencies were prepared to guarantee a good price.

Unfortunately, the first major Indian experiment in attracting potent foreign investors in the field of energy generation turned out to be a disaster. In 1994, soon after the start of economic reforms, the Maharashtra SEB entered into a contract with the American firm Enron and established the Dhabol Power Company.[42] In order to attract foreign investment in this field, the central government provided a guarantee to the investor that it would foot the bill if the SEB defaulted on its payments. Enron was to build a thermal power station at Dhabol, a small port to the south of Mumbai. Naphtha (liquefied natural gas) was to be shipped from the Persian Gulf to this port as fuel for the thermal power station which was to have an installed capacity of 2,000 megawatts and a total investment of US\$ 3 billion. The boss of Enron had a great deal of influence on American presidents and political figures worldwide. After the Enron deal with India was clinched, Indian experts found out that Enron had built a power station in Great Britain of the same type as at Dhabol but at half the cost. There was a change of government in Maharashtra in 1995 and a new round of negotiations began. Finally the deal was reconfirmed, including even an expansion of the project (Phase II) which was supposedly more advantageous for the Indian side. The bone of contention was the fixing of the price at which the Maharashtra SEB had to buy the electricity generated by Enron. This price was far too high. After some years of wrangling, the government of Maharashtra terminated the contract. In the meantime Enron had gone bankrupt. The Dhabol project was hardly the cause of this bankruptcy: India was badly affected by the dramatic failure of this first major attempt at attracting foreign investment for the generation of energy. The Dhabol project remained in 'cold storage' for several years until it was revived in 2006. It was renamed Ratnagiri Power and Gas Private Ltd, to avoid the name 'Dhabol'; Ratnagiri being the name of the district in which Dhabol is located. Among the owners of the new company are the National Thermal Power Corporation, the Gas Authority of India Ltd and the Maharashtra SEB. The price of electricity which the company will have to charge still remains quite high. The Maharashtra SEB would probably have done better if instead of nurturing this white elephant it had imported electricity from the states of eastern India which generated more energy than they could consume. However, the existing lines of transmission did not exactly facilitate such imports.

The idea of a national grid which enables the transfer of energy from surplus to deficit states has been advocated in India for a long time. Such a grid would also help to deal with the peaks of electricity consumption which cause particular problems in India. However, this also raises the problem of payment for the electricity transferred from one SEB to another: since all SEBs are practically broke, such financial transactions have their problems. A central transmission company, the Power Grid Corporation of India Ltd, was established in 1989. It should have started operating a national grid by now, but in the *Economic Survey of 2005–2006*, the Finance Ministry states 'that [the grid] is envisaged to be developed in a phased manner' and announces its completion by 2012.[43] Whereas a national grid still remains a task for the future, some efforts have been made to amend the ancient Electricity Act of 1948 to provide for urgent changes in the organization of the SEBs. The new Electricity Act of 2003 scrapped the old cost-plus rule, made the unbundling of SEBs mandatory and aimed to eliminate cross-subsidies. It also opened the door to more private sector participation in the generation, transmission and distribution of electricity. Some of these measures appeared to be too radical and the new government which assumed office in 2004 passed an amended Electricity Act in 2005, in which the timetable for the unbundling was extended and the provision concerning the elimination of cross-subsidies was cancelled; only the need for their reduction was stressed.[44] Having won the elections with a 'pro-poor' agenda, the new government could not eliminate the cross-subsidies which benefit the peasants and poor consumers. However, the police is now empowered to investigate cognizable offences under the Act. Furthermore, the government commented that the provision of free electricity to the peasants was not desirable as it encourages wasteful use of electricity and contributes to the sinking of the water table. These were *obiter dicta* which could not be enforced.

Future amendments to the Electricity Act may be required to discipline consumers who are used to freeloading in this field. Facilitating private investment in this sector, which the Electricity Act is designed to do, is not compatible with cross-subsidies. Whereas a public sector company like GAIL can be forced to pay for cross-subsidies, as mentioned above, private investors cannot easily be persuaded to do so unless they are compensated in some other way. There is urgent need for central coordination of India's energy policies and this would require a powerful Ministry of Energy. At present different ministries deal with the respective resources such as coal, petroleum, etc. and they have their own agendas. Moreover, breaking the shackles of energy shortage will not be easy as it requires the political will to adopt unpopular policies. The same is true of the measures to be taken for the improvement of India's inadequate infrastructure. In all current debates on India's future growth, the problems are highlighted by everybody concerned. The term 'infrastructure' can cover a wide variety of institutional features of an economy with some experts even including the educational and judicial systems in their analysis. In the subsequent section only the more conventional components of infrastructure such as railroads, roads, ports, airways and the means of telecommunication will be discussed.

The Constraints of Infrastructure

Infrastructure everywhere is to a large extent a legacy of the past: it reflects the investment decisions of bygone days. The economist thinks in terms of the efficient allocation of resources guided by the forces of the market. This pattern of thought does not easily fit in with the analysis of infrastructure. The historian is called upon to explain the peculiar conditions of the evolution of infrastructure. Construction of the railways, a major part of India's infrastructure, is an interesting example of such historical development. The planning of this enormous venture started in the mid-nineteenth century. Lord Dalhousie, the Governor-General who ruled India at that time, had been a member of the British Railway Board before he was sent to India and it was he who drafted an outline of 5,000 miles (8,000 kilometres) of Indian railroads. By 1870 Dalhousie's target was almost reached; twenty years later there were 25,500 kilometres of railway lines. British investors were used to financing railways at home and abroad. The British–Indian government offered a guarantee of 5 per cent return on capital invested in Indian railroads. This was a high rate of return at that time and capital flowed freely to India for this purpose. Indian nationalists criticized the growth of the national debt owing to an investment which was not at all justified by the revenue earned by the railways. Indeed, with capital freely available, the British–Indian government did not have to worry about the economics of railway construction. Its initial aims were primarily strategic: railways would facilitate troop movements along the Gangetic plains to the north-western frontier. A secondary target was the connection of the ports of Karachi, Mumbai, Chennai and Kolkata with their respective hinterlands. A balanced development of cross-connections within India was not a major aim of British railway planning. Nevertheless, the railway network, combined with rapid steamer connections via the Suez Canal (after 1869), opened up India to the forces of the world market, effects that were not always beneficial: India supplied almost a quarter of British wheat imports by the end of the nineteenth century at a time when famines ravaged India. Moreover, the linkage effects of railway construction in India predicted by Karl Marx in 1853 did not materialize. With freight rates for sea transport coming down rapidly after the opening of the Suez Canal, all 'hardware' for the Indian railways was imported from Great Britain. Railway freight rates within India were determined in such a way as to benefit foreign rather than internal trade. Shipping goods by one line to and from the big ports was less expensive than the transhipment of goods via several lines within the country. Revenue from the transportation of goods via the railways caught up with the expenditure on their construction only by about 1910, by which time the period of rapid expansion had ended. Between the First and the Second World Wars further expansion of the network increased only at a moderate rate, from 55,000 to 65,000 kilometres. Hardly any new line has been added since independence except for the recent coastal railway line from Mumbai to Goa.

The use of the railways by passengers has increased continuously from the nineteenth century to the present. If one travels by rail in India one gets the impression that the whole nation is constantly on the move. The number of railway passengers increased from 1.2 billion in 1950 to 3.6 billion in 1980 and 5.4 billion in 2004.[45] Each passenger travelled on average 100 kilometres and paid about US$ 0.50 for this trip. Passengers enjoy cheap rates, but the transport of freight is comparatively more expensive as the government tends to subsidize passenger fares by means of higher freight rates.[46] The substantial modernization of the Indian railway network after independence consisted of its electrification, which progressed from a mere 400 kilometres in 1950 to 17,500 in 2004. The most rapid progress was from 5,000 kilometres in 1980 to 15,000 in 2000. Considering the fact that even now three-quarters of the Indian network requires diesel locomotives which consume a great deal of petroleum and whose degree of fuel efficiency is lower than that of locomotives powered by electricity, further electrification is an urgent task. In addition, the speeding up of traffic is essential as otherwise road traffic by truck remains the favourite option for all businesses. The goods traffic of Indian railways is still geared to the movement of bulk goods such as coal (45 per cent), cement (9 per cent), food grains (8 per cent), iron ore (6 per cent) and petroleum (5 per cent), making a total of 600 million tonnes. Such goods are moved at a slow pace. Moreover, the Indian railways with about 1.8 million employees is a colossus; its speed of operations cannot be improved in a short time. But this must be done, because road traffic by diesel trucks is comparatively more costly and puts an enormous stress on the Indian road network.

Road construction has only been taken up in earnest in recent years. The British did not do much for the Indian roads, as they relied on the railways. After independence some roads were designated as National Highways, but if one looked at them one could not quite see why they deserved this high-sounding title. With more than 3 million kilometres of roads, India has the largest road network of all nations. Only 65,000 kilometres are National Highways and of those the Golden Quadrilateral connecting Delhi, Kolkata, Chennai and Mumbai (5,800 kilometres) has been selected for priority treatment. By the end of 2005 about 5,000 kilometres of this Golden Quadrilateral had been equipped with four-lane highways[47] and the project was completed at a total cost of Rs 300 billion (US$ 6.6 billion) by the end of 2006. In a second phase the National Highways Authority of India (NHAI) has taken up the construction of a north–south highway from Srinagar to Kanyakumari, the southern tip of India. For this several BOT contracts have been given to private firms. B(uild)–O(perate)–T(ransfer) refers to an arrangement whereby the private firm invests the capital and recovers it by operating the highway as a toll road for an agreed period of time after which period the road is transferred to the government. It seems that the Indian government's experience with these arrangements has been very encouraging. In addition to road construction, NHAI now also pays some attention to 'corridor management' which includes the maintenance of the roads, their safety and the uninterrupted flow of traffic. For this, regular highway patrols are required. All this is financed by cess funds derived from a surcharge on petrol. In 2001–5 these funds provided an average annual income of about Rs 20 billion (about US\$ 440 million) and were augmented by external assistance. Road development has thus progressed very well in recent times.

The movement of goods and passengers on Indian roads increases steadily. By 2002 there were 3 million goods vehicles in operation. In addition to this there were about 670,000 buses carrying passengers.[48] In earlier years, the various state transport companies were in the vanguard of passenger transport, but in this as in so many other fields the private sector has expanded very rapidly. In 1975 there were 50,000 buses belonging to the public sector as against 63,000 in the private one. By 1995 the number of public sector buses stood at 110,000 and then more or less stagnated at that level. The number of private sector buses increased from 315,000 in 1995 to 554,000 in 2002.

In addition to rail and road, air traffic has been a major concern of India's planners.[49] The new Minister of Civil Aviation, Praful Patel, who took office in 2004 said in an interview: 'We have a country of over 1 billion people but we have just 150 aircraft for both domestic and international operations. It is ridiculous.' He has tried hard to change this and he has been concerned not only by the lack of aircraft but also by the inadequacy of the airports. The Airport Authority of India (AAI), established in 1995 after a merger of two separate authorities looking after the national and the international airports, was not exactly helpful in adopting new measures to upgrade the airports. AAI employees feared that they would be made redundant if the government went ahead with its plan to privatize major airports and to invite foreign investment for this purpose. The new congress-led coalition depended on the outside support of the communists, who were against the privatization of public sector enterprises. The BJP-led coalition government had opted for a 74 per cent cap on foreign direct investment in Indian airports. The communists considered this a sell-out.

Praful Patel scaled this down from 74 to 49 per cent and thus assuaged the fears of the communists but not those of the AAI employees who were still worried about their future. In trying to satisfy all parties concerned, Patel announced that the upgrading of airports would be managed by joint ventures in with AAI would participate.

The Bangalore airport, a greenfield project, was in a category of its own. Its construction was long overdue as the old airport which belongs to Hindustan Aircraft Ltd was totally inadequate for this software capital of India with its population of about 8 million inhabitants. The project to build a new airport at Devanahalli at a distance of 30 kilometres from the centre of Bangalore was conceived in 1991. A Tata-led consortium of private entrepreneurs was ready to take up this project but then withdrew because no progress could be made in getting the necessary clearances. One of the main obstacles was that AAI would remain in control of all user charges, which would preclude a proper BOT arrangement. A new beginning was made in 2000; bids were invited and in 2001 a Siemens-led consortium was selected. But even then there were innumerable delays. In 2002 Prime Minister Vajpayee performed the ground-breaking ceremony and after two years of inactivity, the Chief Minister of Karnataka performed a second ground-breaking ceremony. At last there seemed to be some progress and in 2005 the financial closure of the project could be achieved. Siemens Project Ventures, a subsidiary of Siemens of Germany, would contribute 40 per cent of the capital, a 13 per cent share was held by Unique Zurich Airport, the Indian engineering firm Larsen & Toubro would hold 17 per cent, and the rest will be in the hands of various Indian and Karnataka government agencies. The BOT agreement envisages a period of thirty years with the option of a renewal for another thirty years. Albert Brunner of Unique Zurich Airport is the CEO of the project and will be the director of the airport once it is in operation. Larsen & Toubro will do all the civil engineering work and Siemens will look after the electronic equipment of the new airport. In December 2006, Brunner announced that 42 per cent of the construction work had been completed and that the airport would start operating in April 2008.[50] With 53 per cent in the hands of foreign investors this exceptional project does not quite conform to the 49 per cent cap fixed by Praful Patel for foreign direct investment (FDI) in Indian airports. Perhaps Bangalore will set a pattern for other airport projects. The joint ventures for the renewal of Delhi and Mumbai international airports still have AAI with a share of 26 per cent and a cap of 49 per cent on FDI. It remains to be seen how these joint ventures will operate.

The acquisition of new aircraft is another field in which a great deal of progress has been made.[51] Air India, India's international carrier, has almost dwindled into insignificance in recent years. But the Indian government could profit from leasing the landing rights held by Air India to foreign airlines, which have to pay hefty charges for this 'cooperation'. Since India is well placed midway between Europe and East Asia, the Indian government could make money by being an 'air rentier' without the costs and risks of operating flights. Of course, this is not exactly an impressive role for a 'national carrier'. Now Air India is investing once more in modern Boeing aircraft. It has even started an additional discount line called Air India Express. Indian Airlines, the domestic carrier, has also been in the doldrums for quite some time. It is now adding new Airbus aircraft to its fleet. In 2007 the merger of Air India and Indian Airlines was finally achieved after it had been talked about for a long time. Since both airlines have lost market share it was high time that they pooled their resources.

The most surprising phenomenon in Indian skies is the sudden spurt of private airlines, which acquired altogether 51 new planes in 2005. Air Deccan founded by Captain Gopinath has been the most daring new enterprise.[52] It was started as a charter firm owning a fleet of helicopters. When Gopinath appeared in Toulouse, wanting to buy Airbus planes, he was initially not taken seriously. Now the Airbus sales team is bending over backwards to please him as he has become a good customer. He operates out of Bangalore and targets many smaller airports but also offers a 'software shuttle': hourly flights connecting Bangalore with the other IT centres Chennai and Hyderabad. By 2006 Air Deccan had 265 daily flights to 55 destinations. Gopinath was soon rivalled by brewery tycoon Vijay Mallya and his new Kingfisher Airline, named after his famous brand of beer. After early attempts at poaching each other's staff, Gopinath and Mallya concluded a pact not to do this. Mallya also made a clever deal with Indian Airlines, which now handles his services on the ground while he concentrates on the flights. Indian Airlines has plenty of staff, so both contracting partners profit from this arrangement. Trained staff, particularly pilots, are in short supply in India now, after this sudden expansion of air traffic. Mallya also made arrangements with foreign airlines, guaranteeing suitable connections for their passengers landing in India. In spite of all these clever deals, Kingfisher Airline suffered a loss of US\$ 53 million in 2005–6. But this did not shake Mallya's confidence in his new business. In May 2007 he arranged for the first flight of the giant Airbus A380 to India for the celebration of his airline's second anniversary. Mallya has already ordered five of these huge planes, obviously with a view to starting international flights in the near future and plans ahead even though in 2006 he had to admit that while he had once predicted that he would reach break-even point by 2008 he now felt that it might take a year longer.[53] Aggressive marketing does not guarantee immediate profits, but in due course Mallya's new airline may emerge as one of India's best.

Among the few pioneers of the 1990s to have survived are Jet Airways, founded in 1992, and Air Sahara, founded in 1993; they are also the first private airlines permitted to fly abroad. With the new entrants into the field, they will face tough competition, but the airlines are confident that Indian air travel will grow by leaps and bounds and yield them all healthy profits. However, the capacity of Indian airports is a headache for all airlines. Congestion forces them to waste fuel by circling in the air before getting permission to land. Therefore they want to add an air congestion surcharge to the price of their tickets. In addition to the congestion at airports, the Indian airlines face another bottleneck: the shortage of pilots. At present there are 2,940 pilots employed by all Indian airlines whereas 3,160 are needed. The expansion in air traffic projected for the next five years would require an additional 5,000 pilots.[54]

Next to airports, India's seaports require thoroughgoing modernization. The biggest and most famous of them all, Mumbai, has a notorious reputation for terrible delays and incompetent handling of goods. A few years ago, turnaround time was about eight days, regardless of the size of the vessel; this has improved somewhat but even now about four days are required to load or unload a ship.[55] This is due to deliberate negligence as the port earns more by collecting demurrage charges than by any other means. The trick of this trade is the stranglehold which Port Authority labour has on the loading and unloading of goods. In most other ports around the world, the port authority is merely a landlord, providing berths and cranes, etc. but no labour, with loading and unloading done by labour hired by the shipowner or his agent. The port authority with 'dedicated' labour is a British legacy. In British ports it may have made sense to retain a labour force specialized in loading and unloading ships, particularly in the past when most of this work was not mechanized. Nobody would have thought that delay rather than speed would be the result of retaining specialized labour. Making money on demurrage charges is, of course, a flagrant example of being penny-wise and pound-foolish. No shipowner in his right mind would enter a port such as Mumbai unless he absolutely has to because it is his destination. Bulk breaking is taking place elsewhere in efficient ports like Singapore or Colombo. Many a ship with only part of its load to be delivered to India would rather call at those ports than enter an Indian port. Jawaharlal Nehru Port across the bay from the old port of Mumbai is supposed to be somewhat more efficient than the old one, but it is first and foremost a container port under the management of the Indian railways and is thus not a direct competitor of the old port. Although

Jawaharlal Nehru Port is India's largest container port, it handles only about 10 per cent of the freight handled by Hong Kong, the world's largest port of this kind.[56] The inefficiency of Indian ports is not only delaying imports, it is also harming the export trade. In the old days of 'export pessimism' this was ignored, but now when producers in India wish to export some of their production to achieve economies of scale, they may give up such plans as their goods get stuck in the port.

Last but not least, telecommunications must be mentioned as an important part of Indian infrastructure. It has a venerable pedigree as it started with the building of telegraph lines across India in the early 1850s. William O'Shaughnessy, a medical doctor and professor of physics in Kolkata was the pioneer who managed to connect Kolkata with Delhi by 1853.[57] In 1854 the first Telegraph Act was passed which established a government monopoly in this field. In the same year an act was also passed in Australia for the same purpose. Telegraph lines including maritime cables spread around the globe very rapidly. The Mutiny of Indian soldiers which shocked the British in India in 1857 was quelled because news of the unexpected insurrection could be sent from northern India to the imperial capital at lightning speed. When a captured mutineer was asked why the mutiny had failed he said that the telegraph wire had strangled the mutineers.[58]

In 1885 the Telegraph Act was amended to make it more comprehensive and it has remained in force ever since. Its amendment in 2003 added only a provision for a Universal Service Obligation Fund (USO) which was supposed to finance the extension of telecommunication to rural and remote areas.[59] Telephones and wireless broadcasting were for a long time regarded as different incarnations of the telegraph. The old rule that all means of telecommunication should be controlled and operated by the government was strictly maintained with the Department of Telecommunication (DoT) of the Government of India being the sole arbiter of fate for all those who longed for connectivity in India. Getting a telephone connection in India was an arduous and time-consuming procedure. DoT tried to profit from the misery of the 'unconnected' by introducing a scheme called Own Your Telephone. The applicant had to shell out a handsome amount of money and then got his connection, hoping that it would work. But the 'owner' of his phone was subject to the same interruptions as all other clients of DoT.

Unlike the hapless SEBs which suffer from the non-payment of bills, DoT collects its dues efficiently because it is always prepared to cut the line. With a view to maximizing the government's telephone revenue, DoT created in 1986 the Mahanagar Telephone Nigam Ltd (MTNL), which is exclusively responsible for the two big cities (*mahanagar*) Delhi and Mumbai. It was a successful venture. The income of this new company dwarfed the combined municipal budgets of the two cities, which goes to show that the citizens of these two cities have plenty of money but do not want to be taxed by their municipalities. Of course, MTNL remained a public sector firm. It served as a model for Bharat Sanchar Nigam Ltd (BSNL) which was established in 2000 to take care of the rest of India. But by this time private sector firms had been permitted to enter the telecommunications business and had made great strides in capturing the growing telecommunications market.

The government had started auctioning licences to private companies in 1995 and had divided the country into telephone circles for this purpose. However, the government should have hired an expert in the theory of games in order to get proper advice on the auctioning procedure: it committed every conceivable mistake in playing this game. It should have stated for how many circles it would accept bids from one company; it should also have stated a reserve price, i.e. the minimum bid which would be acceptable. Moreover, it should have provided information on the revenue to be expected from the respective circles. It did nothing of the sort and invited the bidders to a free-for-all contest. One rather obscure but daring company managed to place the highest bids for nine circles – and won them. Struck by the 'winner's curse', the company concerned got cold feet and the government repeated the auction, specifying some of the essential conditions more carefully. The whole procedure was flawed by the fact that DoT was conducting the auctions although it was also among the bidders; as the incumbent DoT did not yield up its monopoly willingly.[60] The idea of establishing a Telecom Regulating Authority of India (TRAI) was mooted before the auctions were held. TRAI could have conducted these as an impartial umpire – but it did not yet exist and was established only in 1997. The beginning of this attempt at involving the private sector in the telecom business was certainly rather chaotic, but after the dust had settled, some major companies emerged which then did a great deal to increase 'teledensity' in India. All these big players belong to the major industrial houses of India such as Reliance of the Ambanis, the Tatas and Sunil Bharti Mittal.

The story of Sunil Bharti Mittal, who is now the biggest private operator in this field, is a good example of the rise of the new type of Indian telecom entrepreneur.[61] He is not related to the famous steel tycoon Lakshmi Niwas Mittal, and his rather unusual family name Bharti is made up. His father, who belonged to a caste of traders, married a woman of a higher caste. This inter-caste marriage was frowned upon at that time and the couple adopted the name Bharti. Sunil started making cycle parts in Ludhiana. In 1983 when many imports were still banned, he hit upon the idea of manufacturing push-button telephones and then launched his Airtel brand of mobile phones in 1995. From making phones it was only one further step to acquiring two mobile phone licences and one fixed net licence. Subsequently Mittal expanded his operations and now provides his services in all 23 mobile telephone circles of India in which field he has overtaken the public sector firm BSNL. In order to raise the capital for this relentless expansion he linked up with foreign investors. In 2001 the American firm Warburg Pincus acquired about 6 per cent of Bharti Televentures; later the Singapore firm SingTel and the British firm Vodafone also acquired shares in Mittal's company, but they are all minority share-holders. Meanwhile Sunil Mittal dominates the Indian telecom scene and continues to win prizes both in his personal capacity as an exemplary entre-preneur and for his company as the best in its field. He has also pioneered broadband connectivity in various fields and is always a step ahead in adopting new technologies. Mittal had started from scratch as an innovative entrepreneur. As he has stated, he was inspired by Mahatma Gandhi's words: 'First they ignore you, then they laugh at you, then they fight you, and then they lose.'[62]

If one considers the great variety of services offered by Mittal and his colleagues one can appreciate that legislation could not catch up with the telecom revolution. In 1995 a remarkable judgment of the Supreme Court had urged the government to go beyond the venerable Telegraph Act. This judg-ment will be dicussed in Chapter 17. The court had admitted that in view of the technology concerned, permitting access to the airwaves to everybody would create chaos and there was the need for a regulatory authority and also for a new broadcasting act. The first result of this judgment was the act creating TRAI in 1997. Unfortunately, this act was poorly drafted and soon became a victim of adverse judgments of the Delhi High Court.[63] When TRAI was swamped by many individual cases relating to dispute settlement, a Telecom Disputes Settlement and Appellate Tribunal was set up in the year 2000. However, a broadcasting bill which had been taken up in 1997 did not survive the fall of the National Front government. Under the new BJP-led administration, Pramod Mahajan became the Minister for Telecommunication and Information Technology and sponsored a communications convergence bill instead of a mere broadcasting bill. He rightly stressed that with the rapid progress of technology all means of telecommunication converge and new legislation should cover every aspect of this development. For instance, how do you regulate telephone communication via the internet (Voice over Internet Protocol = VoIP)? No doubt, the idea of a convergence bill was a good one, but the government tried to put too much into it by also including the control of the content of telecommunications. This, of course, raised fears of censorship. The bill became the subject of heated political debate and finally got nowhere. The new Congress-led government faced more urgent work and did not take any initiative in this matter. There was talk of introducing a broadcasting bill, but TRAI reminded the government of the urgent need to take up the convergence bill once more as broadcasting and telecommunications should be under the jurisdiction of a unified regulatory authority. TRAI was in a rather difficult position after all since it was supposed to regulate an ever more complex field of communications and still had to base its judicial decisions on the Telegraph Act. The pervasive legacy of British rule could not be demonstrated much better than by this recourse to an ancient act for regulating activities in an era of rapid technological progress. As Pradip Baijal, the third chairman of TRAI, has pointed out: 'Investors are looking for clarity on laws relating to convergence ... Technology specific licences have created confusion in the past and this should be cleared if we have to attract more investments.'[64]

In spite of this delay in the legislative sphere, connectivity increased in India very fast: BSNL extended a huge optical fibre network throughout India. Mobile phones too spread like wildfire: there were about 300 million in India by 2006. There was an agreement among all telecommunication providers to charge only 1 rupee (about US$ 0.02) per minute for all long-distance calls within India. Breaking free from shackles was very successful in this field, but in other areas the giant was still burdened by them.

CHAPTER 12

CASTE IN A CHANGING SOCIETY

Arranged Marriage and the 'Caste System'

The Indian caste system has fascinated social scientists; instead of having to project a taxonomy of their own onto a society, Indian society has supplied them with a detailed 'system' of social ranks and norms. These ranks and norms have been prescribed by Brahmins of the priestly caste, who were even more addicted to taxonomy than modern social scientists. The neat categories of the Brahmin texts were accepted by historians and social scientists as descriptive of social reality. In fact, these were norms prescribed so that people would follow them in practice; reality was often different. Moreover, the 'system' applied to the highly abstract division into the four castes (*varna*) of priests (*brahmin*), warriors (*kshatriya*), traders and cultivators (*vaishya*) and labourers (*shudra*). Social reality was more accurately reflected by the division into a plethora of sub-castes (*jati*). *Jati* means a community to which one belongs by birth. When the Portuguese came to India they translated *jati* quite accurately as *casta*. In Portuguese, *casta* means 'species'. On Portuguese wine bottles the type of grape, such as Riesling or Merlot, is listed as *casta*. Thus 'caste' in the Indian context really means *jati* and not the four *varna*.

Whereas it is easy to define the four *varna* as a system, it is impossible to do this for *jati*. Of course, it is held that each *jati* belongs to a particular *varna*. But any attempt to systematize such a classification is bound to fail. Herbert Hope Risley, a brilliant civil servant and self-trained anthropologist, made such an attempt when he was in charge of the Indian Census of 1901. People were asked by the census enumerators not only to name their *jati*, but also to define which *jati* was supposed to be higher or lower than their own. This caused a great deal of trouble; the question concerning lower and higher *jati*-classification was not repeated at the next census, in 1911. The last British–Indian census which contained references to caste was that of 1931. It adopted a peculiar system based on the assumption that 'caste' reflected professions and occupations.[1] This proved to be an artificial classification. In subsequent census operations, questions concerning caste were eliminated. All general statements on the caste composition of the contemporary Indian population are based on projections of the data of the 1931 census. Accordingly they are in many ways inaccurate.

Foreign observers not interested in social taxonomy are nevertheless fascinated – and appalled – by the caste system because of its blatant assertion of the inequality of human beings. In Western societies people are also aware of this inequality, but they hold that all men and women are equal before God and the law. Even this was denied by the Indian *dharmashastras* (law books) which prescribed different types of punishment for the same crime if committed by members of different castes.[2] Jawaharlal Nehru had criticized this neglect of equality in his presidential address to the Indian National Congress of 1929. When he was asked about this statement thirty-two years later, he gave an evasive answer. He said he had given many speeches in his lifetime.[3] It seemed that he did not want to be reminded of this theme. As a freedom fighter, he was forthright in his social criticism, but as the head of the Indian government he had learned to live with social contradictions.

The Hindu scriptures not only emphasized inequality as such but also prescribed the norms which would help to preserve it. Thus they contained rules concerning marriage which would prevent mixed marriages, since these would upset the social order.[4] There is a simple formula in Hindi: *Roti aur beti* (bread and daughter). It means that caste is defined by the rules which tell me with whom I am permitted to eat and to whom I should marry my daughter. The rule of commensality is of crucial importance for daily social life, although nowadays it is not observed as strictly as in earlier times. The rule of connubiality determines the life of the future generation. It is crucial for the maintenance of the caste system, because if marriages were no longer arranged by the parents and love marriages prevailed, caste would soon be irrelevant. Endogamy within the caste is thus the very foundation of the whole social order. It is amazing that even today many 'modern' young people in India prefer arranged marriages. Of course, the high rates of divorce in Western countries as contrasted with low rates in India may indicate that arranged marriages have some advantages after all. In India, the families on both sides support the marriage and see to it that it does not break up. Endogamy within the caste also goes along with common food habits, kinship systems and religious affiliations. It has made Hindus relatively immune to conversion to other religious creeds. Conversion means giving up the whole social context of one's life and thus amounts to much more than simply changing one's personal creed.

The coexistence of castes gave rise to a type of social federalism. In the course of time, communities of immigrants as well as various aboriginal populations have been absorbed as castes and have preserved their identity by means of endogamy. They maintained their own institutions and accepted royal authority as the arbiter of inter-caste conflicts. There is interesting evidence of this in medieval inscriptions. King Bukka of Vijayanagar documented his verdict on such a conflict in a stone inscription of 1368. Two communities, the Jains and the Vaishnavites, had appealed to him to settle their conflict and he had ruled that he considered both of them to be good communities and that they should live in peace. Such wise verdicts kept the balance in inter-communal relations and promoted social federalism. Of course, this kind of social order was not conducive to the emergence of social homogeneity.

There had been trends in Indian social history which challenged this order based on caste and endogamy. Buddhism and Jainism were social and religious movements founded on the quest for individual salvation. Both emerged as powerful spiritual forces in the fifth century BC and were spread by monks advocating their respective creeds. The Buddhist order of monks (*sangha*) established great monasteries which became centres of the new faith. They attracted royal patronage, which strengthened them but also contributed to the decline of Buddhism when it was withdrawn. Ashoka, who ruled the Maurya empire from 268 to 233 BC, had become a lay brother of the Buddhist *sangha* and had used the order very effectively for his imperial propaganda of universal peace.[5] The monks served as his emissaries and if Ashoka's successors had been able to preserve this empire, Buddhism might have become a universal religion in India, radiating from there to distant lands. It did radiate to South-East Asia, China and Japan, but it disappeared from India, where a Brahmin 'counter-reformation' struck at its roots.

The Brahmins were not monks, but householders. They established no expensive monasteries but formed small settlements at the invitation of kings. These Brahmins legitimized royal power and saw to it that ideas of caste spread among the people. In due course, the Brahmins absorbed Buddhist philosophy and could beat Buddhist monks in religious debate. Moreover, Brahmins were experts in producing mythological narratives which integrated local gods with those of the Hindu pantheon. They also tamed powerful indigenous mother goddesses by 'marrying' them to Hindu gods, thus ensuring patriarchal hegemony so that Hindu mythology became a fascinating panorama of manifold divine splendour. The development of the Hindu pantheon paralleled the social federalism of castes and communities. The mythological narratives also spread to distant lands in South-East Asia and have even penetrated modern media such as film and television. The

Hindu faith does not have any dogma; it depends on a vivid mythological imagination which captivates the mind.

Although it is not dogmatic, the Hindu faith does embody a definitive view of the right type of social order: *dharma*. The connotations of this term are manifold. It can mean cosmic law as well as the specific law regulating human conduct (cf. *dharmashastra*). It also means 'religion' in its outward manifestation. 'Hinduism' is a Western term not applied by Hindus to their 'religion';[6] they refer to it as *sanatan* (eternal) *dharma*. The social order sanctioned by 'religion' is described by the formula *varnashramadharma*.[7] The term *varna* has already been explained; *ashrama* stands for the stages of life: *brahmacharya, grihasta* and *vanaprastha*. The first stage is the life of the student, the second that of the householder and the third that of the old person who retires into the forest and leaves the world behind. Living according to the rules of one's caste and performing the duties associated with the stages of life one remains on the right path. But all this does not suffice for attaining *moksha* (salvation), which depends on one's individual penance and meditation. Of course, wilfully transgressing the rules of *dharma* does not help to achieve *moksha* unless one renounces the world and withdraws from it.

In order to understand the full meaning of Hindu 'religion' one must take note of a third term: *karma* (action). Just as a Hindu is responsible for his own salvation (*moksha*), he is also responsible for his good or bad actions (*karma*). There is no immediate reward or retribution in this life; *karma* determines the quality of the next life. This presupposes a belief in the transmigration of the soul, which reconciles the believer with his fate in this world as his life is conditioned by his actions in his previous life. But it does not imply predestination. One can always improve one's position and finally attain *moksha*.

Indian nationalists and social reformers have often argued that caste is not 'sanctioned by religion' but owes its existence merely to social custom. The very idea of caste is repugnant to national solidarity, therefore it had to be rejected by modern nationalists. But as the brief discussion of *dharma* has shown, the observance of caste rules is an integral part of *dharma*; however, these rules are not related to *moksha*. If one takes the quest for salvation as the essence of religion one could affirm that caste is not sanctioned by religion. But asserting that caste corresponds to social custom, i.e. that it is a habit which could be changed, does not explain its pervasive importance in so many aspects of life in India. In fact, instead of vanishing under the impact of modernization, caste as a 'social custom' has proved very adaptable and has produced new forms of social cooperation which were unknown in earlier times. For instance, one can find entire city blocks in a modern metropolis that are inhabited by a caste group which has formed a highly efficient housing society. Similarly, democratic politics has made caste affiliations a powerful tool for winning elections. The political use of caste has completely upset the hierarchical notions of a caste system. If a caste is 'high' but small in numbers it has no political clout. The large peasant castes, however, have become a dominant force in Indian politics. The fact that peasants have supported Indian democracy was discussed earlier, but while explaining the social order it must also be mentioned that peasant solidarity is both strengthened and fragmented by 'caste-consciousness'. It is strengthened by it wherever the regional peasantry belongs to the same caste or at least to the same cluster of more or less similar castes; it is fragmented wherever peasant castes exist whose competition in the political arena accentuates their respective caste identities. It is an irony of fate that the idea of positive discrimination introduced by the Indian state has led to inter-caste political competition. This kind of discrimination was meant to reduce social inequality by affirmative action, that is, the granting of special benefits to 'backward' communities so as to enable them to enter the mainstream of society. In concrete terms such affirmative action consists of the granting of scholarships and the reservation of posts in the public sector for members of such 'backward' communities. This requires the official classification of such communities. In this context belonging to a 'backward' community becomes an asset rather than a liability. Being a member of a 'forward' community (a term used for Brahmins and other high castes) but nevertheless being poor is a disadvantage, as one is definitely excluded from the benefits of positive discrimination.

The Political Role of Caste Groups: The Claims of 'Backwardness'

The communities which initially qualified for affirmative action were the 'Untouchables' and the tribal people who are referred to as the 'scheduled castes and tribes' because they are listed in a special schedule of the Indian constitution of 1950. Their problems will be discussed later in this chapter. Reserving nearly a quarter of all public sector positions for them (15 per cent for scheduled castes, 7.5 per cent for scheduled tribes) was already a source of social and economic conflict. To extend such reservations to 'other backward classes' would be even more controversial, but politicians might feel tempted to gain voters among those classes by advocating reservations for them. The matter was further complicated by the difficulty of defining criteria for inclusion in this rather vague category. Article 340 of the Indian constitution empowered the President to appoint a commission 'to investigate the conditions of socially and educationally backward classes'.

The first Backward Classes Commission was appointed in January 1953. Its chairman was the veteran nationalist and social reformer Kaka Kalelkar, an old associate of Mahatma Gandhi. The commission prepared a list of 2,399 backward communities of which 837 were classified as 'most backward'.[8] The commission also recommended that all women ought to be classified as backward and should therefore benefit from affirmative action. The report of the commission was submitted in March 1955 and was then shelved by the government. It was only the Janata government under Morarji Desai which took up this issue again and appointed the second Backward Classes Commission in January 1979 which was chaired by B.P. Mandal, a Member of Parliament, and was generally referred to as the Mandal Commission. It extended the list of castes to be considered as backward and recommended the reservation of 27 per cent of public sector posts for them (an earlier Supreme Court judgment had stated that not more than 50 per cent of such posts could be reserved). As 22.5 per cent were already reserved for scheduled castes and tribes, only 27 per cent were left for the communities taken into consideration by the Mandal Commission. Actually, the commission estimated that about 54 per cent of the population belonged to the backward castes. Adding to the 22.5 per cent already reserved for the scheduled castes and tribes, this would have amounted to 76.5 per cent, which would have exceeded the limit set by the Supreme Court judgment. The report of the Mandal Commission was submitted in 1980. By that time Indira Gandhi had returned to power. She shelved the report just as her father had shelved the previous one.

In 1990, Prime Minister V. P. Singh pledged to implement the recommendations of the Mandal Commission and raised a storm of protest in this way. He had political reasons for taking the Mandal report off the shelf. In the election campaign which he had engineered to bring about the downfall of Rajiv Gandhi, he had helped the Bharatiya Janata Party to gain a large number of seats, many of them in his own home state, Uttar Pradesh. His government depended on the support of the BJP from the outside: he was not happy with this and wanted to curtail the social base of the BJP and strengthen his own base at the same time.[9] Having been Chief Minister of Uttar Pradesh, he knew the politics of this huge state very well. The backward castes constitute a large part of the electorate of Uttar Pradesh. The BJP was mainly supported by the high castes; posing as a champion of the backward castes, Singh could hope to win their votes although he himself belonged to a high caste (Rajput, considered to be *kshatriya*). The BJP politicians were furious at Singh's stratagem but could not afford to show their anger. Singh wanted to provoke their protest so that they would alienate the backward castes. But he had to face a wave of protest nevertheless. Young students from the higher castes saw their career opportunities reduced by the impending reservations for the backward castes and immolated themselves in the streets of Delhi. In the meantime, the BJP played the Hindu card by stepping up its campaign for the restoration of a temple in Ayodhya which had presumably been destroyed at the time of the Great Mogul Babur and replaced by a mosque, the Babri Masjid. With this campaign, the BJP hoped to attract the Hindu sentiments of the backward castes, thus counteracting Singh's stratagem. At any rate, they brought down Singh's government in this way, because he had to stop their campaign in order to restore law and order. The BJP then withdrew its outside support and Singh had to resign.

Before Singh was toppled, his government had introduced the 27 per cent reservations for the backward castes in August 1990. The Congress government under Prime Minister Narasimha Rao had to live with this new rule and made no attempt to reverse it. It was soon faced with a landmark judgment of the Supreme Court in November 1992, which forced the government to establish a National Backward Classes Commission with quasi-judicial powers to determine the claims of castes for the recognition of their 'backwardness'. The judgment of the Supreme Court was due to a lawsuit initiated by some members of backward castes. The judges feared that they would be inundated with such suits and realized that they had no criteria by which to determine such cases. Moreover, they felt that litigants who were not at all backward as far as their economic situation was concerned would nevertheless try to obtain the benefits of affirmative action. The judgment of 1992 therefore included an injunction which obliged the government to define the criteria by which the 'creamy layer' of the backward castes would be excluded from such benefits.

The debate concerning the 'creamy layer' highlighted the problem created by the synonymous use of the terms 'caste' and 'class'. All official statements referred to 'backward classes' when they really meant backward castes, the term 'caste' being deliberately avoided as it referred to an undesirable aspect of Indian social life. However, caste and class are not at all identical. Many members of the high castes are poor labourers, whereas there are many rich people of low caste origin. Since speaking of a rich class among the members of the backward classes seemed to be incongruous, the term 'creamy layer' had to be used.

The National Backward Classes Commission was established by an act of Parliament (Lok Sabha) in 1993. Even before it was constituted, a special commission had reported on the problem of the 'creamy layer'. It was decided that the children of high government officials or of persons with an annual income above Rs 100,000 would not be entitled to the benefits of affirmative action. In 2004 this limit was raised to Rs 250,000 (approximately US$ 5,000). But whereas the 'creamy layer' could be defined in this way, it was much more difficult to fix the basic criteria for defining 'backwardness'. Of altogether 1,133 applications received from various communities during the period from

1993 to 2003, the commission accepted 682 for inclusion in the list of backward classes and rejected 451. In its report submitted in 2004, the commission admitted that it had to base its decisions on inadequate data and often had to fall back on the census of 1931 as it was the last one which contained information on castes.[10] The commission therefore recommended that future census operations should once more provide data on caste affiliations as it would otherwise be impossible to base affirmative action on reliable social data. It is doubtful whether the Indian government will follow this recommendation concerning census operations in view of the political trouble it might cause. Moreover, once it is known why such questions about caste are asked, interested parties would see to it that the respondents answered them in a suitable manner.

The problem of defining the criteria of 'backwardness' came up once more in 2006 when the Congress-led coalition government decided to extend the reservation for OBCs to educational institutions. The reservation of government jobs was controversial enough, but educational reservations cut even deeper as far as the career prospects of students from higher castes were concerned. Due to India's rapid economic growth, many students look for jobs in the private sector rather than for government posts. But whatever job one wants to get, access to higher education is the necessary precondition. Once more the Supreme Court played a decisive role. It asked the government to specify the criteria for OBC reservations. In addition, doctors launched a nationwide strike against this new policy since they are the only group of educated people whose strike really matters. The government stuck to its policy. The political equation is obvious: there are probably about 400 million OBCs in India and their vote will decide the outcome of the national elections which are due in 2009.

In the absence of census data, the National Sample Survey Organization finally supplied some relevant data in 2006 which were based on a sample survey of 125,000 households. According to this, the proportion of OBCs in the Indian population amounts to 41 per cent whereas the Scheduled Castes account for 20 per cent and the Scheduled Tribes for 8 per cent. As far as household expenditure was concerned, the survey showed that in the rural areas the OBCs attained about the same level as the 'forward communities' in this respect, whereas in the urban areas these communities were far ahead of the OBCs. Of the members of urban 'forward communities' 52 per cent spent Rs 1,100 per month whereas among the OBCs only 28 per cent reached that level.[11]

The politics of affirmative action has certainly strengthened the solidarity of the Other Backward Castes. In fact, the clubbing together of hundreds of such castes created this cohesion, which was absent in earlier days when each caste had to fend for itself in its specific local context. The Samajwadi Party of Uttar Pradesh owes a great deal to this newly established OBC solidarity. In fact, the OBC phenomenon is a peculiar feature of northern India where the high castes are also present in greater numbers than in the south. Brahmins constitute about 10 per cent of the population of Uttar Pradesh; in southern states their share in the population varies between 1 to 3 per cent and they are almost irrelevant in politics. The great peasant castes of the south, the Kammas and Reddys of Andhra Pradesh, the Marathas of Maharashtra and the Vellalas of Tamil Nadu have long since captured power in their respective states. They are not classified as OBC and they do not stake a claim to be included in this category because they are already in power and control the major political parties active in their states, where they also dominate the public sector. The members of higher castes have long since aspired to jobs in the private sector and have done well for themselves. For all these reasons in the south nobody got excited about the recommendations of the Mandal Commission.

The 'social federalism' of a caste-based society is also reflected in the pattern of regional parties whose rise was discussed in an earlier chapter. The notions of hierarchy associated with the caste system have vanished from political life where the manifold patchwork of regionally dominant peasant castes is much more important than notions of hierarchy and hegemony. But one particular element of stratification has survived in spite of all affirmative action: the stigma of 'untouchability'.

The Stigma of 'Untouchability'

The social practice of 'untouchability' is certainly the most offensive feature of a caste-based society. The stark reality behind this practice is the permanent relegation of the Untouchables to menial work such as scavenging, the removal of carcasses, etc. Association with this type of work meant that anybody not belonging to this underprivileged community would be defiled by touching them. However, only a small minority of Untouchables are really engaged in such work. Others are still regarded as untouchable even if their work is 'clean'. In independent India, the practice of untouchability has been made a cognizable offence, but since it is a matter of avoidance rather than of transgression, it is difficult to identify its practice as an offence. Only when Untouchables are, for instance, denied access to a village well and are forcibly prevented from drawing water can such an offence be punished.

National welfare schemes such as the Midday Meal Scheme (MMS) in primary schools or the Public Distribution System (PDS) which supplies the poor with food grain at subsidized prices through Fair Price Shops should actually benefit the Untouchables but whenever those in charge of such schemes belong to the dominant castes, the Untouchables may be denied access to such benefits by means which cannot be immediately identified as an offence. Only if the government involves active voluntary associations in administering such programmes can discriminatory practices be reduced. In Andhra Pradesh, for instance, women's organizations helped with MMS and saw to it that the Untouchables got their fair share. Untouchable cooks were hired to prepare meals for the MMS. Initially some parents belonging to dominant castes withdrew their children from those meals in protest, but when they saw that the government was not impressed by this behaviour, they permitted their children to share the meals. A determined political will is required to combat such social prejudices. Field studies have shown that in this way the right to food for the poor can be secured.[12]

The Untouchables constitute about one sixth of the Indian population. Keeping them in a subject condition and denying them ownership of land has always guaranteed the landowning peasantry a labour force which had to offer its services for minimal wages. Mahatma Gandhi campaigned for the improvement of the position of these people and called them 'Harijan' (People of God). But the politically conscious among them rejected this term and called themselves 'Dalit' (the broken people) in order to highlight their subjection. Dr B.R. Ambedkar, the political leader of the Untouchables, defied Gandhi in his quest for asserting their rights. Ambedkar was a legal luminary who had studied in the USA and Great Britain but still had to face the indignities his community suffered when he returned to India. In 1932 he almost succeeded in getting separate electorates for the Untouchables similar to those which the British had granted to the Indian Muslims in 1909. Gandhi then went on a fast to the death against this decision of the government. Ambedkar had to agree to a pact with Gandhi in which the separate electorates were converted into reserved seats which were to be filled by Untouchables standing for elections in joint electorates. Ambedkar feared that such candidates would be stooges of the majority of the electorate, but he could not defy Gandhi who was serious about staking his life on this issue. Gandhi felt that if there were separate electorates for the Untouchables the British would further subdivide the Indian nation and gain another social base for their rule.[13]

When Nehru became Prime Minister of India he appointed Ambedkar as Minister of Law although he was not a member of the Congress Party. Ambedkar was in charge of drafting the Indian constitution and helped Nehru in his effort to reform Hindu law, but in the end Ambedkar resigned because he was frustrated in his reformist endeavours.[14] He became an

embittered leader of his community and felt that it would always be discrim-
inated against by Hindus. Therefore he thought of changing the religious affiliation of the Untouchables, but as a nationalist he preferred an Indian religion
and did not consider conversion to Christianity or Islam. He toyed with the
idea of joining the Sikhs but then opted for Buddhism, to which he converted
with some of his followers in 1956 shortly before his death. Although only his
followers in his home state Maharashtra opted in large numbers for this new
creed, there are a few million New Buddhists in India now. But even those
members of Ambedkar's community who did not become Buddhists still
venerate him as their great leader.

Ambedkar had also established a party for the Untouchables, the
Republican Party, but under the prevailing majority election system such a
party did not have much of a chance. Instead the Untouchables had to look to
the Congress Party for political representation and Nehru did his best to
attract their votes. Affirmative action played an important role in this respect.
From those who benefited from it, there emerged in due course a 'creamy
layer' of Untouchables. Some prominent Untouchables were co-opted by the
Congress leadership. Among them was K.R. Narayanan from Kerala who had
joined the Indian Foreign Service and later on became Minister of Science in
Rajiv Gandhi's cabinet. He then rose to the position of Vice-President and
finally became President of India (1997–2002). He was an excellent president
and his community as well as the nation could be very proud of him. But, of
course, the rise of a Dalit to this eminent position did not mean that his
community would attain more political power. For this the success of Dalit
parties in democratic elections would be more important. The rise of the
Bahujan Samaj Party (BSP) showed that this could be achieved.

The BSP was founded in 1984 by Kanshi Ram, a consummate politician
who had earlier organized the government employees belonging to the
scheduled castes.[15] He belonged to a group of Punjabi Dalits who had been
converted to Sikhism and was employed in an ammunitions factory in Pune.
After reading Ambedkar's works he became an ardent advocate of the Dalit
cause and was dissatisfied with merely organizing government employees who
tended to forget about the fate of their community. His rhetoric became
strident in attacking the higher castes which constituted the minority of the
population and yet supressed the majority (*bahujan*). Accordingly, he called
his party Bahujan Samaj Party, extending its appeal to other backward castes
outside the Dalits.

Initially Kanshi Ram was not very successful, but then he recruited
Mayawati, a young law graduate belonging to a very large Dalit group, the
Chamars of Uttar Pradesh.[16] The Congress Party was in decline in this large
state and the Bharatiya Janata Party was damaged by its involvement in the

campaign which had led to the demolition of the Babri Masjid in 1992. At this juncture Mayawati led the BSP to victory at the polls and became the youngest Chief Minister of Uttar Pradesh in 1993. Her government was soon toppled, but then resurrected by forming a coalition with the BJP. Mayawati's volatile political career was stopped by her rival Mulayam Singh Yadav whose Samajwadi Party proved more attractive to the OBC but also to many of Mayawati's own followers, who left her in the lurch and rallied behind Yadav. She then decided to woo the Brahmins who make up about 10 per cent of the population of Uttar Pradesh and are for obvious reasons opposed to the OBC.[17] Mayawati pursued this new policy with resounding success. In the Uttar Pradesh assembly elections of 2007 she fielded 89 Brahmin candidates of whom 34 succeeded in winning seats. In earlier years both Kanshi Ram, the founder of the Bahujan Samaj Party, and Mayawati had viciously attacked the high castes, but as the Dalits supported her to the hilt, she could afford to turn around and woo the high castes without fear of losing the Dalit vote. Becoming Chief Minister of Uttar Pradesh with an absolute majority in her party she may now aspire to a role in national politics. Her party had staked a claim to the position of a national party even earlier: in the parliamentary elections of 2004 it had fielded 435 candidates in 25 states and Union Territories, but captured only 19 seats in Uttar Pradesh. The Samajwadi Party, which also put up candidates nationwide, obtained 38 seats (36 in Uttar Pradesh). The rise of parties supported by the backward classes in Uttar Pradesh shows that Indian democracy does produce social and political change. Once upon a time, Uttar Pradesh was a stronghold of the Congress Party. Of the ten prime ministers who governed India from 1947 to 2004, six had their home constituencies in Uttar Pradesh. Parties which make a mark in this state are bound to be of national importance.

In other Indian states, Dalit parties would still find it difficult to stake a claim of their own as the majority election system favours larger parties which are controlled by regionally dominant castes. But, of course, such parties would always have an eye on the Dalit vote and see to it that they put up candidates who would attract that vote. Just as the OBC have become conscious of a new type of solidarity which transcends the dividing lines of many local communities, the Dalits have also acquired a new consciousness. The widespread adoption of the term 'Dalit' shows this. There is even a special Dalit literature now. This helps to overcome the tendency to stress the differences which do exist among the Untouchables just as much as among other castes. Ambedkar's Mahars, who support the New Buddhist movement, and Mayawati's Chamars, who are more assertive than many other untouchable communities, maintain their own identity and do not necessarily fraternize with other backward classes unless the benefits of joint political action are clearly visible.

While the tradition of the subjection of a large part of the population cannot be easily overcome within a few decades, there has been considerable progress in recent times. The Dalits have asserted their rights with more confidence. In some rural areas of India this has provoked a backlash. Gangs of peasants have launched violent attacks against them in order 'to teach them a lesson'. But the Dalits can no longer be intimidated and know how to defend themselves. By and large the democratic process has contributed to this defence and violent encounters have remained local incidents.

Next to the Dalits, for a long time India's tribal population has suffered from oppression by the settled peasantry who have encroached on the land which they believed to be their domain. Most of the tribal people practised swidden cultivation, also referred to as 'slash and burn'. British forest officers who reported on it usually condemned this mode of cultivation as harmful and ensured that it was stopped. With a favourable land/man ratio in tribal areas, this mode of cultivation was actually not at all harmful. After cultivating an area which they had cleared for a limited period of time, the tribal people moved on. There was regeneration of the forest and the tribal people would not return to the same place for many decades. But with population growth in the plains settled by peasants a different type of land reclamation emerged. The peasants took over the land cleared and then left by the tribes and continued to cultivate it. Hard on the heels of the peasants, the British revenue officer appeared and saw to it that the land was registered and evaluated. Finally the tribes noted that the area of their operations was shrinking and they protested. There was still some tribal solidarity amongst them and this enabled them to launch violent rebellions. The Santal uprising of 1855 in an area which now belongs to Jharkhand was a major outbreak of this sort. The rebellion led by Birsa Munda at the end of the nineteenth century was another instance of tribal resistance. The British crushed these uprisings, the tribes lost much of their land and they had to be satisfied with whatever the revenue officers allocated to them. Finally many tribes turned into hardy miners in the coal mines. Unlike the Hindus, they were not afraid of working underground.

The tribal people in the north-eastern hills bordering Assam were not so easily subdued. Their resistance troubles the Indian government even today. The Nagas who earlier practised head hunting have become adept at modern guerrilla warfare. Their territory was made a federal state of the Indian Union in 1963, but they continue to struggle for greater autonomy. The Bodos of Bodoland are also restive and want to guard their territory against the invasion of migrants from the plains. The list of recalcitrant hill tribes is long.

The reaction of the Indian government oscillates between repression and concessions.

The neat social order which the ancient Brahmins had in mind when designing their 'caste system' has never worked in practice. India presents a vast panorama of thousands of communities which cooperate with each other but also experience many conflicts. So far conflict resolution has always prevailed over violence and social disintegration. A bloody civil war of the kind which has plagued Sri Lanka has never broken out in India. Social federalism combined with political federalism has helped India to maintain 'unity in diversity'.

CHAPTER 13

THE BOON OF A DEMOGRAPHIC DIVIDEND

Population Growth in Independent India

When India achieved independence in 1947 it had a population of 345 million; at the time of the census of 2001 it had 1,029 million people.[1] This increase of about 200 per cent in a period of 54 years seems to confirm the fears of those who speak of an Indian population explosion. But in fact population growth has dramatically declined in recent years in several Indian states. Since India is a young nation and new age groups are entering the reproductive phase, the population is bound to grow. According to various estimates, India will have a population of about 1.4 to 1.5 billion by 2050. This means a growth of the current population by 40 to 50 per cent. With the old growth rate of 200 per cent in half a century India would have 3 billion people by 2050.

The demographic transition usually begins with a decline in the death rate, which is then followed by a decline in the birth rate until a low-level equilibrium at the replacement rate is reached. This is in contrast with the earlier equilibrium at high death rates and high birth rates which prevailed for many centuries. The fall of the death rate in India was the result of advances in public health and modern medicine which eliminated epidemics. In the late nineteenth and early twentieth centuries there were deviations from this path due to famine and the toll taken by the so-called Spanish influenza (1918). From the 1920s to 2001 the death rate then fell from about 38 to 8 per thousand births, and in the same period the average life expectancy at birth rose from about 26.8 to 64 years. Infant mortality also showed a pattern of progressive decline. In 1951 and 1961 the infant mortality rate was 146 per 1,000 births. It slowly declined to 110 in 1981, and in the subsequent two decades it came down to 63, a fall which obviously reflects an improvement in medical care. The number of medical doctors increased from 62,000 in 1951 to 625,000 in 2004. While the doctors used to congregate in urban areas in earlier years, many of them now work in small towns in the countryside where they are accessible to the rural population. In 2005 the Indian government launched a National Rural Health Mission to accelerate the spread of medical care in the countryside.

While the death rate fell at a rapid rate, the birth rate responded to this trend very slowly. Initially it fell from about 47 in 1921 to 40 per thousand in 1941, but then started to rise once more, to 42 in 1961. The difference between the birth rate and death rate amounted to nearly 20 in 1961, causing the increase which was seen as a population explosion. After 1961 the birth rate fell again, but it kept its distance from the death rate at about 20 until 1991. The census of 2001, however, showed a narrowing of this gap; the birth rate had come down to about 25 while the death rate stood at 8 per thousand. Population density has increased in India in keeping with its population growth. In 1951 on average 117 people inhabited 1 square kilometre; in 2001 there were 324. Projections for 2026 show that by that time the average will be 448; four states will have more than 900 people per square kilometre: Bihar, Kerala, Uttar Pradesh and West Bengal.[2]

In spite of increasing population density, India has not yet attained a very high degree of urbanization; only about 28 per cent of people live in urban areas. As in many other countries there is a pull factor which attracts people to urban centres, but about 23 per cent of India's total urban population lives in slums. This means that the attraction of urban areas has its limits. The western and the eastern halves of India show a striking difference as far as the degree of urbanization is concerned. If one draws a line from Chandigarh in the north to Chennai in the south and looks at the distribution of the 35 Indian cities with more than a million inhabitants, one will notice that there are 20 cities in the west which have a total population of 76 million, whereas the 15 cities in the east have a total of just 31 million. The higher urbanization of the west is not necessarily a positive feature. In the biggest western metropolis, Mumbai, nearly half of the population lives in slums, whereas in Patna, a typical eastern city, there are hardly any slums at all. This does not mean that Patna is better off than other Indian cities; rather it is an indication of the lack of attraction of Patna for people looking for work. The future development of Indian urbanization will probably reconfirm the present pattern. It is estimated that there will be 74 'million plus' cities in India by 2026. The east – as defined above – will contain 20 of these cities.[3]

A peculiar feature of India's demographic profile is the female deficit.[4] In 2001 there were only 933 women per 1,000 men. Almost everywhere else in the world the male/female ratio is more or less balanced. The female deficit is caused by human intervention ranging from female infanticide to the neglect of young daughters-in-law. In recent years there has been an increase in abortions after medical diagnosis. Accordingly, determination of the sex of the foetus by such a diagnosis has been prohibited, but this may not prevent doctors from informing the parents if they insist on it. Asking for a dowry is also prohibited by law; nevertheless 'presents' may be given to the bridegroom. The expenditure on such presents is often too high for parents who have to marry several daughters. Therefore the birth of a daughter is considered to be a liability rather than an asset. Child marriage is also prohibited by law, but many girls are married in their early teens. Census data show this very clearly. A very young daughter-in-law can easily be replaced if she falls ill and dies early. While the parents would take their son to a doctor, they would not spend money on getting medical care for a daughter-in-law unless she has given birth to a son. The census data for northern India show that the female deficit increases in the second decade of life.

Female illiteracy is another indicator of the relative neglect of women in Indian society. According to the census of 2001 about 46 per cent of women were illiterate, as against 24 per cent of the male population. While literacy increased markedly from about 18 per cent in 1951 to 65 per cent of the total population in 2001, the gap between male and female literacy has more or less remained the same. Living in the atmosphere of a traditional Indian village, there is not much that would encourage a woman to learn how to read and write. There is a parallel here to medical care: just as one would take a son to a doctor one would also send him to school, whereas the education of a daughter or a daughter-in-law would be thought unnecessary. The urban middle class would see this differently, but as the great majority of the Indian people still live in the countryside, those who appreciate female education are in a minority. Taking this into consideration, the fact that by now more than half of India's female population is literate is no mean achievement.

Most demographers believe that female education encourages birth control and reduces the total fertility rate. As the next section of this chapter will show, a dramatic reduction in the fertility rate may also be achieved without an advance in female education, but in general it is true that educated women take a greater interest in family planning. The Indian government has pursued a very active programme of family planning since 1952. At the time of Indira Gandhi's 'Emergency' (1975–6) this took an ugly turn, as forcible sterilizations were conducted in many areas of northern India. It is said that at the time of the election campaign of 1977 when Congress politicians approached a constituency the opposition only needed to spread the rumour that the doctors were coming and the people would hide and not attend the Congress rallies. After this experience, the term 'family planning' was deleted from the official vocabulary and replaced with the more benign term 'family welfare'. During the sterilization campaign, many men had been forcibly sterilized (vasectomy). Initially this had been done with their consent. After 1977 the number of voluntary sterilizations of women (tubectomy) increased while male sterilization declined. Tubectomy is still the most common form of birth control adopted by Indian women, but it is usually done only after the woman has already given birth to two or three children. There is a striking difference between southern and northern India in this respect. A survey conducted in 1998 showed an All-India average of 34.2 per cent of currently married women as having been sterilized. All southern states were well above this national average. Andhra Pradesh with 52.7 per cent and Karnataka with 51.5 led the south, Kerala followed with 48.5 and Tamil Nadu with 45 per cent. Sterilization as the most effective means of birth control was universally known in south India.[5] Another factor which has an impact on the birth rate is the age at marriage. Here the national average for women was 16.4 years in 1998. In the south this age was higher than the average, but in northern India it was below it. Contraceptive methods other than sterilization have also been widely adopted in India: about 50 per cent of Indian women practise birth control using various methods of contraception. But there is still much scope for further propagation of 'family welfare', as the programme of birth control is called in official terminology.

The fertility reduction which has been quite noticeable in recent years has ushered in a phase of the demographic transition during which a 'demographic dividend' will accrue to India.[6] The young people who reach the age of employment will have to take care of fewer dependants and can thus save more of their income. Projections for the year 2011 show that by this time India will have a population of about 1.2 billion of which 65 per cent will be in the age group 15–64 and 29 per cent will be less than 15 years old; for 2001 the respective percentages were 60 and 35. The 'demographic dividend' will be even more obvious by 2026 when the respective percentages are supposed to be 69 and 23. Of course, there will also be an increase in the number of dependants above the age of 64 years. But this is comparatively small, from about 5 per cent in 2001 to about 6 per cent in 2011; by 2026 it is supposed to be 8 per cent. When the ageing population grows, the dividend turns negative. But this is a problem which India will not face for several decades. However, there are important regional differences. For Kerala and Tamil Nadu the dividend had already reached its highest point before 2001 and it will turn negative in 2011. By contrast Uttar Pradesh and Bihar may benefit only around 2026, when it has turned negative in most other states.

There are estimates that the dividend may enable India to add 3 per cent to its rate of economic growth per year. But this naturally depends on the gainful employment of the age group between 15 and 64 years. If the present trend of economic growth continues, it may actually be possible to find employment for all of them, provided that India escapes the trap of 'jobless' growth. This would require deliberate efforts to create more opportunities for employment because there has been a consistent decline in employment elasticity in recent years. A high elasticity means that an increase in economic growth would immediately be reflected in an increase in employment. Low elasticity may be due to the higher productivity of labour: i.e. those already employed would be able to cope with additional work. Agriculture, which had previously been able to absorb the additions to the labour force due to the increase of population, has recently shown zero elasticity. This is an ominous sign indicating a future rise in unemployment. Only a shift towards horticulture and animal husbandry may create more employment in the countryside. The total number of those who have to be employed in India in 2026 will amount to 925 million: this corresponds to 65 per cent of the population. From 1971 to 1991 this percentage had increased from 52 to 59 per cent of a much smaller population. The progress towards 65 per cent is a direct reflection of the 'demographic dividend'. The Planning Commission is aware of the problems faced by India in this respect: the paper on the approach to the eleventh Five Year Plan states: 'All avenues for increasing employment . . . must be explored. If we fail to do so, the demographic dividend can turn into a demographic nightmare.'[7] Perhaps the export of labour-intensive products offers the best prospects for the employment of India's huge labour force.

India's demographic transition is accompanied by an increase in life expectancy. This implies that there will be more people who require support in their old age. At present, India is far from being a welfare state, so it does not face the problem of providing pensions to most old people. However, there are about 17 million civil servants working for the central and state governments and they must be taken care of. Faced with a rising tide of such pensions, the Indian government has created a New Pension Scheme (NPS). Civil servants have to contribute 10 per cent of their salary and the government adds another 10 per cent. Others are free to join this scheme, but for them the government will not make any contribution. The NPS will be managed like some of the famous American pension funds, and experts estimate that the asset value of NPS will amount to US$ 95 billion by 2025. On reaching retirement age (60 years), the beneficiaries may spend 60 per cent of the amount of money according to their own wishes, but they are obliged to invest the remaining 40 per cent in annuities which provide them with a regular income. The NPS is hailed as a model to be emulated by other Asian countries.[8] It seems that demographic transition also gives rise to innovative ideas.

The Rapid Decline of Fertility in Southern India

The National Population Policy for the year 2000 had once more set a target for the achievement of the replacement level of the Indian population. The replacement level is defined in terms of the Total Fertility Rate (TFR) of 2.1 births per woman in the course of her life and should be reached by 2010. Demographic projections would prefer to assume 2016 as a more realistic date.[9] The average Indian TFR had come down from 6 in 1951 to 3 in 2001. To the great surprise of planners and demographers, several south Indian states have proved to be way ahead of the National Population Policy. Kerala registered a TFR of 1.71 in 2001, and Tamil Nadu was at almost the same level with 1.76, closely followed by Andhra Pradesh at 1.94. Karnataka was still above the replacement level, at 2.24; it was estimated that it would reach that level within a few years. Andhra Pradesh was the greatest surprise of them all: its TFR had dropped from 2.39 in 1997 to 1.94 in 2001. It has a high rate of female illiteracy and there has been no significant economic progress in this state. The major assumption of demographers that female education and economic progress would lead to a lower TFR was therefore contradicted by the experience of Andhra Pradesh.[10] Moreover, the decline in the TFR usually takes time and does not happen in such a dramatic fashion as it did in Andhra Pradesh. Perhaps it was an awareness of future deprivation rather than of economic progress which prompted even illiterate women to resort to birth control. This goes against all normal demographic assumptions, but there was a striking parallel to this development in Andhra Pradesh in East Germany at the time of German reunification.[11] The number of East German births dropped by 40 per cent at that time, which must have been due to apprehension of an uncertain future on the part of young East German women. This shows that perceptions of the future rather than long-term social and economic trends may influence the decisions of women. This is, of course, only one aspect of the rapid spread of birth control. Knowledge of the methods of contraception and the will to adopt them are also of great importance. Demographers who have studied the spread of adoption of contraceptives have noticed a snowball effect. After an initial phase when only a few women practise birth control, the demonstration effect catches on and others follow their example. In a strange reversal of the assumption that female education leads to birth control, it has been found that birth control may foster female education. Among illiterate women who adopted contraception there were many who would send their girls to school.[12] The correlation seems to be significant, but of course it does not necessarily indicate a causal relation.

Geographical studies of the diffusion of the decline in the TFR in southern India have pointed to clearly defined regional patterns. Scholars have been able to map such patterns, but they have been unable to explain them.[13] More detailed anthropological fieldwork is required to discover the motives of regionally concentrated communities. For instance, the Gounders of Kongunad whose activities in Tiruppur have been discussed in an an earlier chapter have shifted in recent times from paying a bride price to adopting a dowry system. The bride price was paid to the father of the bride because he lost a working member of his family; the dowry is paid by the father of the bride in order to acquire a suitable bridegroom. Adopting this custom was seen as a social advance – but it was expensive for the bride's family. The use of birth control therefore intensified in this community.[14] In other cases a general awareness of the rising level of expenditure may have had the same effect. In Andhra Pradesh where indebted peasants committed suicide in the 1990s the news of this desperate action would also have affected women's perceptions of the future.

The Peculiar Demographic Features of Northern India

The demographic profile of northern India is very different from that of southern India.[15] The female deficit discussed earlier is mainly a northern phenomenon; it is less in evidence in the south, where Kerala even has a female surplus. In ancient times, the Dravidian south was a region in which matriarchy prevailed, something which is still reflected today in the worship of mother goddesses such as Meenakshi of Madurai. In Kerala matrilinear patterns of inheritance still survive among some communities. The north, however, is the stronghold of patriarchy. In rural Uttar Pradesh, girls are still married early in spite of legal injunctions against child marriage. A young daughter-in-law is very insecure; only after the birth of a son is the young woman assured of the respect of the family into which she has married. This is a very ancient heritage which is reflected in the name of Ashoka, the great Maurya emperor. 'Ashoka' means 'without sorrow'. It was not he who was without sorrow but his mother, who gave him this name: she was a junior wife of the king and she had to live in fear of being rejected if she did not give birth to a son. The preference for sons is much more pronounced in the north than in the south. This means that having given birth to daughters women will still continue to bear children until they have a son.

The patriarchal custom of looking upon women mainly as agents for bearing children and giving them no scope for practising birth control according to their own wishes is an impediment to family planning. A high TFR and a slow rate of decline are characteristic of several north Indian states.

In Uttar Pradesh the TFR stood at 4.83 in 1997 and 4.33 in 2001. This was well above the national average of 3.49 and 2.89 respectively. The figures for Bihar were very similar to those of Uttar Pradesh: 4.89 and 4.40. Rajasthan with 4.41 and 3.54 also showed the same pattern, but here the rate of decline was much more pronounced than in the two other northern states. Projections for 2011, when the replacement rate should be reached throughout India according to the National Population Policy, show the following TFRs for the northern states: Uttar Pradesh 3.42, Bihar 3.49, Rajasthan 2.24. The fact that the national average of 2.1 may be achieved by 2011 would only be due to a compensation effect: the four southern states mentioned above would by that time have a TFR below the replacement rate, at about 1.7.

The discrepancy between north and south could actually lead to an intensified north–south migration which could have political repercussions because of the competition for jobs.[16] Uttar Pradesh is the greatest exporter of people in India and Delhi and Mumbai are the favourite destinations of UP migrants. Powerloom centres in Maharashtra such as Bhiwandi and Malegaon attract weavers from Uttar Pradesh. Bihar tends to send people to Kolkata, but in recent years this metropolis has proved to be less attractive than other Indian mega-cities. In addition to giving rise to migration the north–south discrepancy has another dimension which could precipitate political tensions. Parliamentary constituencies should have a similar number of voters throughout India. Theoretically each decadal census could lead to a revision of constituencies. The north would then get more parliamentary seats and the south would lose some. Those states which fail to reach the targets of the National Population Policy would thus be rewarded, while those that have met their target would be punished. In order to avoid a clash of interests, the number of constituencies was frozen in the 1970s.[17] After the 2001 census a revision would have been due, but then a new compromise was found: the delimitation of constituencies may be changed within states, but there will be no change in the number of parliamentary seats, which would be to the disadvantage of the states of southern India. As was pointed out in Chapter 3, a constitutional amendment has postponed the date of adjustment to 2026. By that time the contrast between the north and the south will be even more pronounced and the northern vote significantly 'devalued'. It will depend on the political power equation prevailing at that time whether there is an adjustment or not. Demography may become a political minefield.

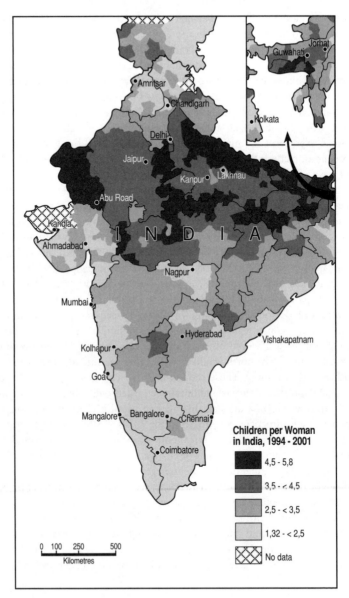

Map 4   Regional Differentiation of Fertility Rates
Source: Based on Data of C. Guilmoto and S. Irudaya Rajan (see bibliography)
Cartography: N. Harm, South Asia Institute, University of Heidelberg

CHAPTER 14

THE DEMAND FOR EDUCATION

The Colonial Legacy and the Neglect of Primary Education

Modern Indian education owes its origin to British colonial rule. Ancient Indian education had a long tradition. Its central institution was the *gurukul* (literally: family of the guru, or teacher). The pupil lived with his guru for many years. Much of the education consisted of learning sacred texts by heart. When the student became a teacher, he conveyed this knowledge to his pupils and thus participated in a *guruparampara* (line of tradition from guru to guru). Students who had studied with the same guru were attached to each other as *gurubandhu.* The medium of instruction was Sanskrit and the subjects taught could also include special fields of knowledge such as medicine, astrology and astronomy, and mathematics. Such education was, of course, reserved for a small elite but it did contribute to the enduring continuity of Indian culture throughout the ages.

The education which the British introduced in India created a new elite. The college was the main educational institution established by the Colonizers; some were government colleges, others missionary colleges run by various church organizations. The medium of instruction was English. This was not a foregone conclusion because some of the early British educationists in India favoured 'Oriental languages'. However, these 'Orientalists' were defeated by the 'Anglicists' who advocated English as the medium of instruction and were even supported in this by Indian scholars who felt that under British rule there would be career prospects for the Indians only if they mastered the language of their rulers.[1] Lord Macaulay, Law Member of the British–Indian government, settled the issue in 1835 in favour of English and by dismissing all oriental learning, of which he knew very little. He proclaimed that the British should educate Indian gentlemen who would be Indian in blood only but British in every other respect. British college education in India actually produced such people and the British were frightened when they encountered

Indians who knew their Shakespeare much better than they did and also behaved like proper gentlemen. Many British then felt that these products of their education were 'un-Indian' and not representative of their countrymen at all.

Macaulay's vision of breeding Indian gentlemen was geared to very practical purposes. The British needed clerks and other subordinate officials to run their Indian empire: for those people the education in a typical arts college was sufficient. There was no need to train scientists and engineers. The British believed in a 'trickle down' theory of education so there was no call for primary schools. The education of those who aspired to enter a college would be organized by the Indians themselves. In fact this did work, as parents who wanted to send their sons to college would hire private tutors. There would always be some college drop-outs or graduates who failed to get a government job who would be available as tutors. But no schooling system developed in this way. The colleges had a more or less uniform curriculum and syllabus governed by the rules of the University of London with the result that a common universe of discourse was spread throughout India. The authorities concerned did not stress a difference between education at home and in the empire: the same texts were prescribed everywhere. This is how Indians could imbibe the same liberal philosophy that was taught to their British contemporaries. The standardization of higher education in British India was enhanced by the establishment of the universities of Bombay (Mumbai), Calcutta (Kolkata) and Madras (Chennai) in 1857. These were affiliating universities setting the exams for colleges throughout their respective regions. Only at a later stage did they establish some postgraduate university departments.

In addition to arts colleges, the British also established law colleges in India. They thus produced swarms of law graduates who added an LLB to their BA. These people did not need to worry about getting government jobs: they could practise as lawyers in the ubiquitous British lawcourts. These courts yielded a handsome revenue to the British-Indian government, because court fees were high and covered much more than the expenditure on the judicial establishment. According to the British practice of recruiting judges from among the most brilliant lawyers ('from the bar to the bench'), Indians could even aspire to the post of judge at a High Court (with the coveted title 'Justice'). Some of the most eminent Indians of the nineteenth century belonged to this small group of High Court judges. The lawyers founded Bar Associations even in small district towns and these became centres of political debate and incipient nationalism.

Indian nationalists demanded at an early stage that the British–Indian government should do something for primary education. G.K. Gokhale, one of the leaders of the Indian National Congress, introduced an Elementary

Education Bill in the Imperial Legislative Council in 1912.[2] He wanted the government to provide compulsory primary education for boys aged 6 to 10 free of charge and argued that 'the whole of our future as a nation is inextricably bound up with it'. Knowing that there would be objections with regard to financing such a scheme, he suggested that the central government should only pay for part of it while local bodies should also contribute. He argued the case for primary education very persuasively but the bill was defeated nevertheless. The British–Indian government did not want to spend money on primary education and nothing was done about it as long as British rule lasted.

In independent India compulsory primary education was introduced and the government often published impressive statistics on the number of pupils attending primary school. The National Policy on Education announced in 1986 demanded that 6 per cent of GDP be spent on education. This target has not been reached; even in 2003 only 3.5 per cent of GDP was actually devoted to expenditure on education.[3] Primary education was affected by high drop-out rates. In the 1990s they still amounted to 73 per cent; by 2003 this had come down to 31 per cent. An important factor in the reduction of the drop-out rate was the provision of cooked midday meals in all schools paid for by central government. This is the largest school meals programme in the world and it has obviously made school attendance much more attractive.[4] Enrolment in primary schools (ages 6 to 14) has greatly increased: from 1961 to 2005 the number of pupils grew from 34 million to 209 million. The number of teachers grew from 0.7 to 3.6 million in the same period. This means that the staff/student ratio did not improve, as it changed from 48 to 58 students per teacher. In secondary schools (ages 14 to 18) the situation is somewhat better. Here the numbers of students grew from 3.4 to 35 million between 1961 and 2005. These schools have a more favourable staff/student ratio and their drop-out rates are lower. However, the number of students of secondary school age is much smaller than the number attending primary school. The ratio is about 1:3. Teachers are paid by the relevant state government. Primary school teachers, most of whom have to work in villages, often shirk their duty and do not show up in the village when they are supposed to teach their classes: surveys have shown that 25 per cent of teachers supposed to be on duty were absent.[5] The state authorities are far away and cannot check on their attendance and the local village council cannot discipline them.

Demand for education in India has risen enormously in recent years. Illiterate women who practise birth control and believe in improving the quality of their children's future prospects are eager to send them to school. Since the supply of teachers does not keep up with this demand, some local authorities have started employing 'para-teachers' (*shiksha karmis*, or educa-tion workers).[6] The state of Madhya Pradesh passed an Education Act in 2002 which actually declares the state-employed teachers to be a dying cadre to be replaced entirely by *shiksha karmis*.[7] These are untrained people employed at low salaries (e.g. Rs 1,000 a month) and with no permanent contract and there are probably about 400,000 such teachers throughout India by now. This is so to speak the informal sector of the education system. It has been reported that these para-teachers are better at their job than those paid by government. As their jobs are insecure and as they are paid directly by local bodies, they must work hard in order to retain their positions. The official teachers often devote more time to politics than to teaching and see to it that nobody can touch them even if they do not show up for their classes. Due to this official neglect, private schools have sprung up everywhere. Even poor people are prepared to pay fees if they can rely on efficient teaching. The growth of private schools in the field of rural primary education has been particularly strong in the huge state of Uttar Pradesh whose official education system is particularly bad. Teachers' unions are strong in this state. They ensure that salaries are increased, which results in a scarcity of funds for school buildings and so on. At the same time these unions campaign against the supervision of teachers by local bodies (*panchayats*) which could discipline them.[8] Holding the state education system to ransom, these unions practically force the parents to send their children to private schools.

Due to the increasing spread of education, India has been able to overcome the colonial legacy of limiting education to the privileged strata of the popu-lation. But the content of education and the methods of instruction are still very much influenced by the British legacy. In the course of the Indian freedom movement there were various attempts at introducing 'national education' only a few of which can be mentioned here. The earliest was inspired by the Arya Samaj, a reform movement founded in the late nine-teenth century by Swami Dayanand Saraswati whose followers established the Dayanand Anglo–Vedic Colleges which still exist in many parts of India.[9] 'Anglo–Vedic' is a peculiar term which indicates that the medium of instruc-tion is English and that in most subjects the syllabus and curriculum of the government colleges have also been adopted, but in addition there is an emphasis on Dayanand's interpretation of the ancient Vedas which according to him embodied the essence of Indian culture. A section of the Arya Samaj led by Mahatma Munshi Ram, alias Swami Shraddhanand, was more radical in its approach to 'national education'. Shraddhanand founded the Gurukul Kangri in 1900.[10] The village of Kangri is located near Hardwar, a holy place of the Hindus. Here the language of instruction was Sanskrit and the students had to observe strict discipline. 'Character building' was a main aim of this education and since this was also a guiding principle of many contemporary British educationists, British visitors were deeply impressed by this school. However, since the certificates of the school were not recognized by the British authorities, there were no career prospects for its students. Most of them ended up as humble practitioners of Ayurvedic medicine.

Rabindranath Tagore, India's famous poet, established an institution of national education on an estate of his family's near Bolpur in Bengal. His father Debendranath, leader of the Brahmo Samaj, a religious reform movement, had established an *ashram* there in 1863 and called it Shantiniketan (Place of Peace). Rabindranath, who was also inspired by the idea of establishing a *gurukul*, started a school at this place in 1901.[11] After receiving the Nobel Prize for Literature in 1913, Tagore toured many countries of the world spreading his message of universal peace. He also collected donations for Shantiniketan, which he wanted to develop as an international university with a special emphasis on the fine arts in its rather unorthodox curriculum. This university was officially started in 1921. In 1941 Tagore died at Shantiniketan and it was feared that the university would not survive after his death. But in independent India, Shantiniketan was made a central university and has continued its work under these auspices. It has remained unique and has not become a model for other universities, which still follow the pattern set by the British in the nineteenth century.

Mahatma Gandhi also sponsored a special type of national education in the context of his programme of constructive work for the improvement of India's villages.[12] He was joined by a young Muslim educationist, Zakir Hussain, who later on became President of India. Zakir Hussain drafted for Gandhi a scheme called 'Nai Talim' (New Education) which was submitted to the education ministers of the provincial governments formed under the Government of India Act of 1935. Gandhi hoped that the ministers would implement this scheme, but they had hardly any time to do so as their governments resigned in 1939. According to Gandhi's ideas, all pupils of village schools should receive practical training in some craft and also in the methods of agriculture so as to be able to improve their life in the village. Other Gandhian institutions of education were started by his followers, but none of them could issue certificates which guaranteed their students a 'normal' career. This was the same problem which the Gurukul Kangri had faced. Institutions of national education which did not follow official rules and regulations simply could not make a mark. In independent India, the government adopted the colonial legacy and retained the old rules and regulations; no unorthodox curriculum or syllabus had a chance of being accepted by the authorities concerned.

Scientific and Technical Education

The natural sciences were not favoured as academic subjects by the British in India. Some of the British openly stated that Indians had no aptitude for scientific thought. It was only when Indian assistants were required for British projects such as topographic survey work, the Geological Survey of India and public works such as roads and canals and the railways that academic institutions were established in these fields. First and foremost was the Civil Engineering College established at Roorkee, Uttar Pradesh, in 1848.[13] It was supposed to train sub-assistant executive engineers and overseers in civil engineering, and there were also some classes in survey work and in geology. This college did excellent work and continued to flourish in independent India. In 2001 it joined the ranks of the Indian Institutes of Technology which will be discussed later on. Following the precedent set by the college at Roorkee, similar colleges were established elsewhere, for example the Calcutta College of Civil Engineering founded in 1856 and the Madras College of Civil Engineering in 1858. Technical education of a very special kind was thus sponsored by the British-Indian government, but courses in natural sciences in the arts colleges did not follow until much later. Bombay University introduced a B.Sc. degree in 1879 but only 43 students took this degree over the subsequent 16 years primarily because the course of study was rather demanding and the career prospects very limited. British officials were appointed to the 'imperial grade' positions of the various scientific services such as the Botanical Survey, the Geological Survey, the Medical Service and the Trigonometrical Service. In 1880, there were altogether 212 imperial grade officials in these various scientific services and just 8 per cent of them were Indians. They received about half the salary of their British colleagues.[14]

Although career prospects were severely limited, there was a growing quest for scientific knowledge in India. Mahendra Lal Sircar (1833–1904) was one of the first leaders in this quest.[15] He joined a medical college which offered a course in experimental sciences and became only the second Indian to acquire the MD degree. He practised as a physician but also pursued his deep interest in the natural sciences. In 1879 he founded the Indian Association for the Cultivation of Science (IACS) in Kolkata, for which he received donations from many of the rich landlords of Bengal. Under the influence of the IACS, the University of Calcutta started M.Sc. courses. C.V. Raman, the Nobel Laureate in Physics, received his early scientific education in Kolkata. Ashutosh Mukherjee, the inspiring Vice-Chancellor of the University of Calcutta (1906–14) then took the initiative to introduce postgraduate research departments in the natural sciences in his university. The famous Indian chemist Profulla Chandra Ray served as the first professor of chemistry and

C.V. Raman as the first professor of physics in this new section of the University of Calcutta.

The great Indian industrialist Jamshetji Tata had a vision akin to that of Ashutosh Mukherjee. He too wanted to make India a centre of excellence in the sciences and devoted a large amount of his private wealth to the establishment of the Indian Institute of Science (IIS) in Bangalore.[16] The Johns Hopkins University in Baltimore served as a model for this institution, which is a great centre of excellence even today. Tata died before IIS was formally inaugurated in 1907 but his sons ensured that it remained well endowed. C.V. Raman joined IIS later on and contributed to its international fame. As mentioned earlier, both Homi Bhabha and Vikram Sarabhai were on the staff of IIS in the 1940s and Satish Dhawan served as its director from 1962 to 1981.

All these pioneering endeavours were due to patriotic Indians who had to struggle hard to get ahead in spite of the unsympathetic attitude of the British–Indian government. Lord Curzon, who was Viceroy of India at the time when Tata launched his scheme, poured scorn on such visionary plans. He felt that there was no need for Indian scientists. Nobody would want to hire them. Moreover, those who failed in their career would only add to the 'discontented hordes' of the educated unemployed. British attitudes changed only at the very end of British rule over India. In the midst of the Second World War, the British–Indian government founded the Indian Council of Scientific and Industrial Research (CSIR), which became the apex body of a large number of national scientific research institutes in independent India.

Except for such late endeavours as the establishment of the CSIR, the British institutional legacy to independent India in the field of scientific research and technical education was minimal. Of course, the imperial connection had induced some Indian scientists to study in Great Britain, but when they returned to India they rarely found favourable conditions for continuing their research work. When Jawaharlal Nehru became Prime Minister, he faced the challenging task of preparing the ground for India's rise to scientific and technical excellence. He especially encouraged the setting up of a large number of central or national research laboratories under the CSIR such that by the end of the Nehru era there were 23 institutions of this kind, employing thousands of scientists. However, the 'Council' form of organization was not very focused. In the quest for financial support the Department of Atomic Energy and the Department of Defence Research were more successful in the long run and by 1958 the CSIR had lost pride of place to them.

The various institutions mentioned so far conducted research but did not serve as centres of excellence in scientific and technical education. In this field the establishment of the Indian Institutes of Technology (IIT) was the major step ahead taken during the Nehru era. The model of the Massachusetts Institute of Technology (MIT) influenced the Indian planners. An erstwhile detention camp near Kolkata was selected as the site of the first IIT, Kharagpur, which was established in 1951 with the Vinod Gupta School of Management and the Rajiv Gandhi School of Law being established later on its campus. Many IIT graduates also like to acquire an MBA degree as it gives them better career prospects in Indian industry. The second IIT, established at Powai near Mumbai in 1958, benefited from cooperation with the Soviet Union and with Unesco. The Shailesh J. Mehta School of Management was later added to it. The third IIT was set up in Chennai (Madras) in 1959, aided by the government of the Federal Republic of Germany. In the same year the IIT Kanpur was started with aid provided by the USA. The Delhi College of Engineering, established in 1961, was made an IIT in 1963. This first group of five IITs was started in the Nehru era. In 1994 a sixth was opened in Guwahati, Assam, following a promise made by Rajiv Gandhi after student agitation in that state. Finally Roorkee, mentioned earlier, was made the seventh IIT in 2001. More IITs may be added to this list in due course.

Under the Indian Institute of Technology Act which was passed after the IIT Kharagpur was established and was then amended to accommodate the others, the IITs are designated as institutes of national importance and enjoy special privileges. Each of them is free to define its own curriculum. This enables the IITs to respond quickly to new challenges. There is a joint entrance exam for all IITs which must be passed by all those who want to be accepted for the undergraduate course (B.Tech.). Competiton is very keen: more than 300,000 take the exam and only about 3,900 can be admitted each year. There are various other tests for admission to graduate studies for M.Tech., M.Sc. and Ph.D. In earlier years there had been some criticism about the 'brain drain', as about half of all IIT graduates opted for careers abroad, particularly in the USA. However, with the country's recent economic growth, the number of graduates going abroad has dropped to about 30 per cent. Experienced IIT alumni who have worked for some years abroad return to India and gain good positions in Indian industry. There has also been some criticism of the limited output of patents and research papers by the staff of the IITs or their alumni. As far as patents are concerned, for a long time there were few incentives for Indian inventors to register patents in India. The procedure is lengthy and expensive and once the patent was registered, Indian industry took no interest in it as it mostly relied on imported technology. This criticism also implied that Indian industry did not invest much in research and development and would offer very limited career prospects for IIT graduates in R&D departments. The CSIR laboratories suffered from the same neglect of R&D by Indian industry; they often stood a better chance when offering their services to foreign firms, as Indian firms looked to those foreign firms rather than to their national laboratories when buying technology.

Next to the IITs, the Tata Institute of Fundamental Research in Mumbai deserves to be noted as an educational centre of excellence. As mentioned earlier, it was founded by Homi Bhabha in 1945. Initially it concentrated on nuclear physics and mathematics, but later biology and other branches of physics were added. From the very beginning TIFR also conducted a Ph.D. programme with degrees awarded by the University of Bombay. Recently TIFR has become a 'deemed university' and awards its own degrees. Nowadays the institution has an academic staff of 300 and accepts 20 new Ph.D. candidates every year who have to pass a stiff nationwide admission test. By now there are more than 600 alumni of this programme. TIFR has spawned many other institutes of fundamental and applied sciences in India. Its output of excellent scholars has helped to provide these institutes with competent staff.

At present the annual number of graduates of IITs and the TIFR amounts to about 5,000. In view of the enormous demand for scientific manpower, which is increasing by leaps and bounds, this output is insufficient. Private companies have started investing in scientific education in a big way in order to fill this gap. Infosys is a case in point. It hires about 28,000 IT specialists every year and has started its own corporate university in Mysore with an initial investment of US$ 300 million. This university is expected to produce 13,500 graduates annually.[17] Of course, the elite institutions are not the only ones to produce good graduates; it would be wrong to belittle the achievements of some of the good science departments of Indian universities and of several good engineering colleges. As the example of Narayana Murthy of Infosys (see Chapter 8) has shown, even such engineering colleges can produce brilliant graduates. The great danger in present times is that such colleges find it difficult to recruit good staff as the salaries paid by private firms are so high that in comparison the pay of a lecturer is a pittance. If this continues, the next generation will not be taught by competent teachers but will have to make do with those who have not been able to find a job elsewhere.

The Scope of Human Resources Development

The future of human resources development in India will depend on the attractiveness of teaching positions and the dedication of teachers to the ideals of their profession. This begins at the primary school level where the village schoolmaster should be a well-qualified teacher with good accommodation in the village who attends his classes regularly and is not overwhelmed by the number of pupils in his care. Given the figures quoted earlier, this means that there should be an increase of at least 30 per cent in the number of primary school teachers. If the target of spending 6 per cent of GDP on education is met, it should not be difficult to appoint these additional teachers.

It is not only primary education which suffers from a scarcity of funds in India. Post-secondary education also requires more investment. With 16 million students, India has the third-largest tertiary-level enrolment in the world, but this accounts for only 13 per cent of the relevant age group. India spends 0.37 per cent of GDP on higher education and is thus behind China, with 0.5 per cent.[18] India has to step up its investment in education if it is to succeed in the race for knowledge production. In addition to the provision of more funds, the content of education needs attention. Learning by rote is still widespread and there must be greater encouragement of independent and creative thinking. In higher education this implies participation in research. Mere training in research methodology is not enough: the students must be guided by teachers who are themselves actively engaged in research. While this is true for the advanced levels of higher education, a problem-solving approach should also be stressed in elementary education. Mahatma Gandhi's programme of practical training in village schools should be re-examined from this point of view. Some knowledge of the quality of the soil, the methods of water harvesting, of sprinkler irrigation, etc. should be transmitted in those village schools; many of the Indian peasants who committed suicide in recent years might still be alive if they had been taught these skills. But such a programme depends on dedicated teachers. They could help to improve the quality of life in the villages in many other respects: the village schoolmaster could also serve as registrar of the local cooperative, or help to run schemes of crop insurance, as recommended in the chapter on agriculture. In order to be able to do all this, the schoolmaster needs to be trained in these subjects. Human resources development in India should thus focus on producing the right type of schoolmaster. Prime Minister Dr Manmohan Singh recalls that when he grew up in a small village in the West Punjab, the schoolmaster, who was also the postmaster, was respected by everybody.[19] He wrote letters for the illiterate and was always available, whereas today village teachers are often conspicuous by their absence. The Prime Minister has written to the chief ministers and urged them to improve their education systems, for which the central government is willing to provide financial aid.

Similarly, the recruitment, training and conditions of service of college and university teachers should be a high priority for those who wish to advance human resources development in India. Teachers with special talents and qualifications should be attracted by more flexible pay scales so as to prevent their moving to the private sector. Academic salaries can never quite match such offers, but if the teacher can live in decent accommodation and is allowed to be creative in his field of work, he or she may still prefer academic life to a job in the private sector. One of the most crucial duties of an academic teacher is dissertation supervision as this sets the standards for the future generation. Foreign external examiners of Indian dissertations may often receive the impression that the Indian colleague who has supervised the dissertation has not even read it properly. If this were so, it would be a gross dereliction of a supervisor's duty. If the supervisor himself has been granted his doctorate by a negligent supervisor he will continue a negative tradition. Preserving high standards in dissertation supervision is one of the most crucial tasks in the field of human resources development.

India has a vast amount of human capital. With the 'demographic dividend' mentioned earlier there will be an increasing number of people in gainful employment who are less encumbered by dependants. They will find this employment only if they have been trained and educated properly. Starting with primary education, all levels of school and university education should be developed so as to prepare Indians well for the tasks they have to perform. As Gokhale said in 1912, the future of the nation is inextricably bound up with education.

CHAPTER 15

THE NEW MIDDLE CLASS: CONSUMERS AND SAVERS

The Upper Quintile of the Population as the 'Middle Class'

Since India embarked on a period of rapid growth in the 1980s, there has been talk of a new middle class variously estimated at 150 to 250 million people. This class is supposed to be in the vanguard of economic progress. Being able to spend more than the poor, it is also assumed to provide a large market for consumer goods. The term 'middle class' is actually misleading, as it should refer to the middle quintile of the population. But this third quintile consists of people who are just above the poverty line. They can make both ends meet, but they cannot spend much on consumer goods. The 'new middle class', however, belongs more or less to the uppermost quintile of the population. It includes the urban educated classes and the rich peasantry in the countryside which owns a disproportionately large part of the land. Within this first quintile of the population there is, of course, also a 'creamy layer' of industrialists, businessmen and rich professionals. They constitute an 'upper class' of about 1 per cent of the population. Unlike many other countries which are dominated by an upper class lording it over the poor masses, India does have a large number of well-to-do people who do not belong to the upper class but enjoy a higher living standard than the rest of the population. As they do not belong to the upper class, these people are defined as the middle class, although from a statistical point of view this would not be a correct classification.

The distribution of the national income among the five quintiles of the population is highly skewed. The upper quintile gets the lion's share at 46 per cent, the next quintile gets 20 per cent which is proportionate to its share of the population, the middle quintile is already underprivileged in this respect as it gets only about 15 per cent, and the next quintile gets 11 per cent. The lowest quintile has to be satisfied with 8 per cent of the national income. The skewed income distribution becomes even more obvious if one takes into consideration that the upper 10 per cent of the population get 33 per cent, so only 13 per cent is left for the other half of the upper quintile. This lower half of the upper quintile is thus only slightly ahead of the next quintile. Taking the lower 10 per cent of the first quintile and the second quintile together we would arrive at a stratum of 30 per cent of the population which is moderately well off. But only the upper 10 per cent is really in a position to spend money lavishly.

The income classifications mentioned so far are constructs of social scientists, they do not necessarily reflect the perceptions of the people concerned. Thus a schoolteacher earning a modest salary would think of himself as a member of the middle class while a factory worker whose wages dwarf the teacher's salary would still refer to himself as a member of the working class. On the other hand, a computer specialist with a high salary which would make him a member of what may be termed an upper class of the top 10 per cent would still think of himself as 'middle class'. As Thomas Friedman puts it: 'Middle Class is a state of mind, not a state of income.'[1] The new Indian middle class is relatively heterogeneous. It would include highly educated academics as well as millions of people who earn their living in the informal sector of the Indian economy. The owners of the powerlooms referred to earlier would belong to this latter group. They often own only a few looms and employ fewer than 10 workers whom they can hire and fire. Their workshop is usually only a shed and they have no over-heads. Nevertheless, their earnings would place them in the middle class. The same would be true of the small entrepreneurs of Tiruppur described in Chapter 8. Similarly, the peasants engaged in commercial agriculture mentioned in Chapter 10 would usually qualify for middle-class status. Most of them would have very little formal education, but many would aim at getting their children educated.

Analysts of the structure and the preferences of the new middle class usually stress their characteristics as a consuming class, but as far as the conditions of economic growth are concerned this class should also be seen as a 'saving class'. In the years from 2000 to 2004 gross domestic savings in the household sector increased from about US$ 991 billion to US$ 1,526 billion, i.e. from about 21.2 to 22 per cent of GDP.[2] A recent estimate (2005–6) shows total domestic savings of US$ 2,570 billion, of which US$ 1,771 billion are savings in the household sector. The latter amounts to 22.3 per cent of GDP.[3] It is difficult to figure out the class-specific origin of these savings, but since the lower quintiles of the population cannot save very much, they must be attributed to a large extent to the middle class. There is some indirect proof of this. In the early 1980s when economic growth had just started to move into a higher gear and the new middle class did not yet attract much attention, the savings rate was much lower. From 1980 to 1984 the average savings rate in the household sector only amounted to 13 per cent of GDP.

The savings of the middle class will increase with the demographic dividend mentioned earlier. For the working class in the informal sector this dividend will mean that low wages will suffice for families with fewer children. The middle class, however, which stands on the shoulders of this working class, will actually profit from higher incomes. It will spend a considerable part of its savings on the education of its children. The example of the IT economy, which so far encompasses a very small proportion of the middle class, has nevertheless shown that better education is a pathway to higher income. This will assure the growth of an educated workforce which will be India's most important asset in the immediate future.

The Aspirations of the New Middle Class

In assessing the aspirations of the new middle class, the investment in education is often neglected although it is of great importance. Middle class as a 'state of mind' encompasses ambitions for the advancement of the next generation. Consumption is curtailed for the sake of such ambitions. This implies a rising demand for qualified education, which has been discussed in Chapter 14. Those who stress the consumerism of the new middle class tend to forget these ambitions, but, of course, higher standards of consumption are also a characteristic feature of this new class. Better housing, easier communication and the improvement of urban neighbourhoods are high on the agenda of the middle class.

Social scientists who study the aspirations of India's middle classes tend to distinguish between the 'old' and the 'new' middle class. The old middle class is also called a 'national' one. It is inspired by Nehruvian values and is proud of belonging to a nation which has struggled for its freedom and has attained an important position internationally. Its members have college or university degrees, they read the national newspapers published in English and belong to the professions, the civil service, etc. In general, the members of this old middle class look down upon the new middle class, whom they regard as vulgar and uncultured. As far as Indian cultural traditions are concerned, the old middle class may be more conservative although its members would normally be modern in their lifestyle. The modernity of the new middle class would express itself in its shopping habits, its preferences for certain fashions – particularly among the young people – and for popular films. The members of this class would usually speak their vernacular language rather than English, but of course a smattering of English is also considered 'modern'. The rapidly expanding vernacular press caters to the tastes of this new middle class.

Another characteristic feature of this new middle class is the more assertive attitude of its women, many of whom earn salaries of their own. They have outgrown the traditionally submissive and self-effacing role of the woman who faithfully serves her husband. Of course, even in traditional families 'home government' often had a strong influence on the husband. But in the modern family this is no longer restricted to attempts to influence the behaviour of the husband but is aimed at a more open assertion of female self-determination. The novels of Shobha Dé offer interesting insights into this aspect of middle-class aspirations.[4] She is by far the commercially most successful Indian author writing in English. Serious literary critics would not mention her because they would regard her novels as pulp fiction, but social scientists turn to them as a source of information about the 'new Indian woman'. Shobha Dé is not a feminist; she is a rich socialite who rose to prominence as editor of a film magazine. The women she portrays are role models for her readers. Of course, such models reflect their aspirations and fantasies rather than their own behaviour in real life. Mumbai is the setting of all her novels and the attractions of the mega-city enrich her narrative. One of her first heroines was a girl with a provincial background who comes to Mumbai in search of a promising career and then gets enmeshed in a struggle for survival. Another heroine sleeps her way to stardom but is mercilessly exploited both by her own family and by the film industry. A further novel describes the life of two sisters in Mumbai's business world. Shobha Dé also dares to break the taboo of extra-marital relations when she describes a young woman's escape from the boredom of a suburban marriage by starting an affair with a young neighbour. There is not much psychological subtlety in her work, just as there is none in the Hindi films. But the types whom she creates come to life and there is a strong dose of realism in her work. She spices her dialogues with Hindi words, echoing the 'Hinglish' characteristic of middle-class conversations in Mumbai.

Whereas Shobha Dé does not include foreign settings in her narratives, recent Hindi films do this to an increasing extent. A trip to Switzerland, to London or, of course, to the USA provides the film directors with scenic locations as a backdrop for the adventures of the hero and heroine. Foreign settings also reflect the interest of the Indian middle class in foreign tourism, to which many of its members aspire and which growing numbers can actually afford. A less demanding adventure than a trip abroad is dining out in town. This has also become a favourite pastime for some members of the new middle class. In a novel with the appropriate title *Socialite Evenings* Shobha Dé has described this type of entertainment. While rich people may indulge in it often, for the middle class it is still an exceptional enjoyment and for this reason is more appreciated by them. From a traditional point of view, dining out is a rather revolutionary activity.[5] In India food has always been consumed at home and even while travelling people take along their own food and avoid eating out. In Mumbai even today thousands of *dabbawalas* – who carry head-loads of dozens of boxes which they deliver unfailingly to the husbands in their offices having collected them from their wives at home – show how important it is to eat food from home rather than eating out. Nevertheless, Mumbai probably has the greatest number and variety of restaurants of any Indian city. In recent years even a chain of restaurants serving pizzas has made a mark in Mumbai. Socialites may not frequent such restaurants, but young middle-class people flock to them.

The middle class is also the main supporter of the Indian media, which is discussed in Chapter 17. Television sets and video recorders are now essential items in any middle-class household. The income from advertisements is crucial for all media. In many ads a pretty, well-dressed middle-class lady, often surrounded by members of her family, shows off the products which are a must for her. Most middle-class people are still in a position to employ servants, but they do not appear in the ads. Dual-income families will often have a maid for the children and another servant who cooks and does the dishes. Invariably there is also a sweeper who comes once or twice a day and

N.S. Ponnappa | Bangalore | 2004

2   'Eating Out' by N. S. Ponnappa (2004)

cleans the floors and the bathrooms. Normally he or she serves several families in the neighbourhood. Only the very rich can afford to have servants'
quarters near their residence and servants of middle-class families often live
in slums and commute to their places of work. If there are about 40 million
middle-class households in India with about five members each, one can
assume that they depend on at least an equal number of households of
servants. The middle class is thus a major employer in the informal sector of
the Indian economy. When speaking of the middle class as a consuming class,
it is usually forgotten that one of the major items of its consumption is the
labour of the poor.

In recent years the middle class has also been able to acquire more cars and
scooters, items which were rarely available to the previous generation. When
the planned economy still prevailed, the production of cars for private transport was not considered a high priority. In the period from 1965 to 1975 the
annual production of cars stagnated at around 70,000. From 1980 to 1990 it
increased from 120,000 to 366,000.[6] With the economic reforms of 1991 car
production increased and even imported cars were more readily available.
Many foreign companies also started to manufacture their cars in India. At
present about 1.2 million passenger cars are sold in India annually.[7] However,
many members of the middle class cannot yet afford a car and have to rely on
two-wheelers (scooters and motorcycles), sales of which have reached about
9 million annually in recent times. The earlier generation of middle-class
people usually had to rely on bicycles, whose annual production rose very
gradually from 1 million in 1960 to 7 million in 1990; since then, annual
production has doubled. Riding a bicycle is no longer restricted to the middle
class: most middle-class people have graduated to the two-wheeler and would
regard the bicycle as an attribute of the poor.

The most easily available status symbol in India is the mobile phone.
Hardly any middle-class household is without one, and some households have
more than one. However, the Indian government has estimated that by
December 2006 only 190 million telephones, including mobile phones,
would be available in India,[8] which amounts to a teledensity of 16.8 per cent.
There is thus much scope for the further expansion of telephone ownership.
By the end of 2007 250 million telephones are forecast. The rates for calls
within India are now extremely cheap, having declined very rapidly over a
few years.

The more sophisticated members of the middle class also own personal
computers with about 70 per cent of Indian PC owners living in the two
mega-cities Mumbai and Delhi. A survey conducted in the year 2000 showed
that about 50 per cent of those owning a computer were also connected to the
internet.[9] Most of those interviewed had acquired their PC during the last two

years and those who used the PC were almost exclusively the younger male members of the family. In fact, the majority of the PC households consisted of single male graduates between 20 and 30 years old. Many of those who not only owned a computer but also used the internet belonged to higher income groups (about Rs 15,000–20,000 per month at that time). Obviously many of these people could be identified as 'Yuppies' (Young Urban Professionals). Nearly half of the PC owners also answered in the affirmative to the question of whether they would consider the PC to be a status symbol. They would not consider a TV set a status symbol any longer as its ownership is now widely taken for granted. In due course this will certainly also be true of the PC. By 2006 about 5 million out of 45 million middle-class Indian homes already had computers. PC sales had slumped in 2001 and 2002, but then they picked up again and in 2005 about 4 million PCs were sold in India. Most will have gone to offices rather than into homes. But home consumption will also increase, particularly as PCs become cheaper and the rates for internet connection are also reduced. This would correct the regional imbalance of PC distribution. As mentioned above, in 2000 Mumbai and Delhi accounted for about 70 per cent of PC households. By now other urban centres will have made great progress and some rural areas will also have PCs. Nevertheless, as in so many other fields, regional disparities are still very obvious in this sector.

Regional Concentrations of Purchasing Power

The regional disparities which have increased with economic growth are reflected by the concentrations of purchasing power.[10] The Business Intelligence Unit (BIU), Chennai, a private institute engaged in economic analysis, has constructed a relative purchasing power index according to which it has classified all districts of India. The purchasing power of the inhabitants of a district is graded in terms of its share of India's total purchasing power. The first study of this kind was done in 1999 and its data are used for Map 5 reproduced on page 204. Subsequent BIU studies have tended to reconfirm these findings. Only three grades of purchasing power are shown in the map. The highest grade (1 to 0.8) covers major urban centres and their hinterland. The medium grade (0.8–0.65) reflects concentrations of purchasing power above the average. The rest of the country is characterized by rather modest purchasing power.

The subsequent detailed commentary on the map follows the direction from north to south and from west to east. The first feature to be noted is a belt of high purchasing power from Amritsar and Chandigarh in the Punjab to the region around Delhi. Industrial as well as agricultural wealth is abundant in this region. It is paralleled by a broader belt of 'medium' purchasing power extending from the western districts of the Punjab via Haryana to northern Rajasthan, where the region around Jaipur belongs to the more affluent category. In Uttar Pradesh the only affluent districts are those in which the industrial cities of Kanpur and Lakhnau, the state capital, are located. In eastern India only Kolkata, the old metropolis, is of some importance and in Assam some districts in the fertile flood plains form isolated pockets of purchasing power. The vast central belt of India from Rajasthan to Orissa is a poor region. In southern Rajasthan, Sirohi district around Mount Abu has modest wealth. The prosperous state of Gujarat has several areas of relatively high purchasing power. The districts surrounding the Gulf of Kachchh with the port of Kandla at the centre show medium wealth, whereas the urban belt from Ahmadabad down to the Gulf of Khambat is the heart of prosperous Gujarat. The districts from Khambat to the east, including Anand and Vadodara, are also fairly well-off. South Gujarat around Surat is another fairly prosperous area. The large state of Maharashtra actually encompasses the contrasts of India within its boundaries. The state GDP is close to the national average, but coastal Maharashtra shows the largest concentration of high purchasing power. The Mumbai–Pune region is at the top, but the districts which surround this centre piece from Nashik in the north to Kolhapur in the south are also fairly well-off. The dry highlands in the middle of Maharashtra are extremely poor. In eastern Maharashtra, the region around the big city of Nagpur is again an area of noticeable purchasing power.

Southern India, which includes many districts with an index value between 0.6 and 0.649 that could not be shown on the map, is otherwise marked by only a few pockets of affluence. In Andhra Pradesh these pockets are located around the state capital, Hyderabad, and in the coastal area around the port of Vishakapatnam. Between Hyderabad and the east coast there is a belt of districts in the category 0.6–0.649. The southern part of Andhra Pradesh, however, is rather poor. In Karnataka the area around the state capital, Bangalore, the 'Silicon Valley' of India, is the only rich region, although there is a small area of medium quality near the port of Mangalore. In Tamil Nadu the state capital, Chennai, is rather affluent, and another well-off region is located around the industrial city of Coimbatore. Between Chennai and Coimbatore there is a bridge of districts of the index value 0.6–0.649. Similarly, almost the whole of Kerala consists of districts of this type, whereas the state has only a tiny pocket of high purchasing power around Cochin and Kottayam.

A comparison of the map showing the concentration of purchasing power with the map indicating population density demonstrates a striking contrast. In the western part of India (the region to the west of Delhi and coastal Gujarat and Maharashtra) there is a close correlation between areas of high purchasing power and high population density, but in the densely populated

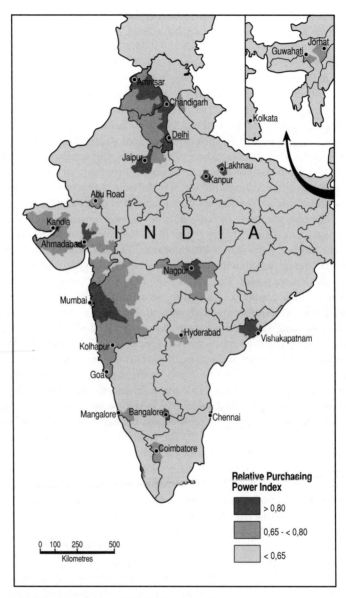

Map 5 Regional Distribution of Relative Purchasing Power
Source: J. Wamser (see bibliography)
Cartography: N. Harm, South Asia Institute, University of Heidelberg

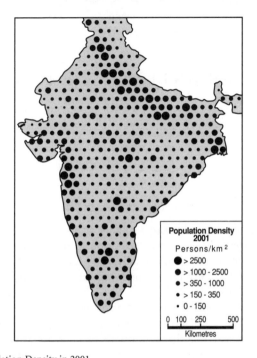

Map 6   Population Density in 2001
Source: Census of India, 2001
Cartography: N. Harm, South Asia Institute, University of Heidelberg

Gangetic plains to the east of Delhi concentrations of purchasing power are conspicuous by their absence.

If one equates the high incidence of purchasing power with the new middle class discussed above one is forced to conclude that this class is not spread at all evenly across the nation but is regionally concentrated around a few centres. This implies that this new class cannot impose a hegemony of its lifestyle and aspirations on the masses of India. The vast dimensions of India's poverty impede such an imposition. Mahatma Gandhi's vision of the 'Rise of All' (*sarvodaya*) still remains a hope for the future.

CHAPTER 16

THE PERSISTENCE OF POVERTY

Drawing the Poverty Line

The measurement of poverty varies with the standard of living of the society concerned. In an affluent society, a television set may be considered to be a basic necessity even for a household living on the dole. India, however, has tried to arrive at 'objective' criteria for drawing the poverty line. These criteria are nutritional ones, based on calculations of a minimum of calories plus marginal allowances for other basic needs. Some years ago, the Indian government proudly claimed that only 19 per cent of the population live below the poverty line, an assertion that gave rise to an acrimonious debate in which many eminent scholars participated. The officials of the Indian government were so intimidated by this quarrel that the *Economic Survey 2005–2006*, the most authoritative public document, had refrained from giving any figures concerning the poverty line and only referred to the 'intense debates' on the methodology of the respective surveys.[1] The paper outlining the approach to the eleventh Five Year Plan released by the end of 2006 finally mentioned specific figures which belied the earlier optimism: 27.8 per cent of the Indian people live below the poverty line and the absolute number of the poor amounts to 300 million.[2] These figures were repeated in the *Economic Survey, 2006–2007*.[3]

The Indian government adopted nutritional criteria at a very early stage. In 1962 a group of experts consisting of some of the most eminent economists of that time recommended these criteria, which were based on a report of a nutritional advisory committee of the Indian Council of Medical Research. Even at this stage, the experts should have taken health care and education into consideration, but it was clearly assumed that the state would guarantee rapid progress in those fields. The next major decision was taken in 1979 when the government adopted the recommendations of a Task Force on Projections of Minimum Needs and Effective Consumption Demand. The minimum

R. K. Laxman | Mumbai | 1984

3 'The Poverty Line' by R. K. Laxman (1984)

daily calorie intake was defined as 2,400 for rural and 2,100 for urban dwellers at that time and subsequent calculations were based on the price of food grains which would yield that amount of calories.[4] The database for these calculations was provided by the National Sample Survey Organization (NSSO) of the Government of India.

The NSSO is an excellent organization which was founded by the legendary Professor P. C. Mahalanobis (1893–1972) who also drafted India's first and second Five Year Plans. Mahalanobis was a pioneer in applied statistics and in the design of sophisticated sampling methods.[5] The quinquennial National Sample Surveys (NSS) cover about 500,000 households throughout India. They deal with many areas, such as unemployment, but the essential part is the household expenditure survey which contains detailed information on all items of expenditure. Initially, the period of recall for answering the questions was 30 days. Recently this has been shortened to seven days, when it was found that people could not easily remember what they had spent a month ago. For some items such as durable consumer goods, the period of recall was extended to one year. These changes have given rise to methodological debates concerning the comparability of recent NSS rounds with earlier ones.[6] This has an immediate relevance for estimating the reduction in the number of people below the poverty line. The latest figures on these, mentioned above, are based on the data of the 61st round of the NSS conducted in 2004–5 which became available only in 2006.

In addition to the methodological arguments, there were also questions raised about the very criteria adopted for the definition of the poverty line. First of all the reliance on food grains came under attack, as other items such as milk products had become more important and the overall consumption of food grains in India had declined. But of even greater relevance were the questions concerning the omission of shelter, clothing, health care and education. There had been a cutback in government expenditure on health and education in the reform period. Critics pointed out that if poverty was not just a matter of inadequate nutrition but also of lack of access to health care and basic education, the poverty line would have to be redrawn.

The drawing of this line is based on a head count of those who are below it in terms of average per capita expenditure (APCE). If large numbers of people are congregated in clusters close to this line, even modest changes in APCE may affect the headcount very significantly. This is what happened in the 1990s, but in that period poverty reduction might have progressed even further, if there had not been a substantial increase in inequality in India. Real wages in the rural areas rose very little, whereas urban incomes showed an upward trend.[7] It is, of course, a moot point whether the growth of the 1990s could have been achieved without an increase in inequality.

When extending the analysis of poverty to the phenomenon of inequality one can take access to land as a criterion for distinguishing the rural poor from the rest of the population. There are about 90 million peasant households in India and about 60 million other rural households. Of the latter only a small minority are traders and artisans who do not own land but have an income from their respective activities. The rest are landless labourers who have to work for the landowning peasants. Moreover, about half the peasant households are in debt: in Andhra Pradesh the figure is 82 per cent and in Tamil Nadu 75 per cent. While not every peasant in debt is poor, in general, indebtedness can be taken as an indicator of poverty. In the reform period, formal agrarian credit provided by the nationalized banks has been curtailed and the earlier policy of social and development banking has been abandoned. The new idea was to entrust NGOs and self-help groups with organizing micro-credit in the countryside. The system of regional rural banks which had been built up in previous decades was badly hit by this change of policy.[8] The new phenomenon of widespread suicides of indebted peasants was obviously due to 'credit starvation'.[9] Micro-credit could not fill the gap and the informal moneylenders who charge usurious interest rates expanded their business once more. As private agents of carefully 'supervised credit', the moneylenders are far more efficient than banks. But it is only they who benefit from this, whereas the debtors are exploited. Usually the moneylender is also the local grain dealer and pre-empts the harvest at a low price while charging high interest rates when the debtor returns to him later in the year in order to borrow cash or grain. In general, the moneylender is interested in keeping his debtors alive as he cannot expect repayment from the dead, but while he would save the debtor from starvation, he may not be able to prevent the desperate act of suicide.

The trend towards rural indebtedness is paralleled by a dwindling in the size of operational holdings in India. From 1970 to 1995 the number of operational holdings increased by about 64 per cent from 70 to 116 million, while the cultivated area remained more or less the same (163 million hectares). This means that by 1995 the average operational holding amounted to 1.4 hectares. If one looks at the details of land distribution one sees that the proliferation of holdings was accompanied by a rise in the number of small-holders who are prone to get indebted and/or are forced to earn wages by working for others.

Amartya Sen, India's Nobel Laureate in Economics, has highlighted the glaring incidence of poverty in India. He has pointed out that undernourishment of the poor is far more striking in India than in sub-Saharan Africa. This leads to anaemia among women and to the stunted growth of their children – and all this at times when the government is stockpiling food grain. He compares such policy failures which affect the poor to the casualties caused by 'friendly fire' in armed combat when troops inadvertently shoot their own comrades.[10] Amartya Sen has paid special attention to the poverty of children in India. In December 2006, he released the *Focus on Children under Six* report which highlights their plight. The scheme of integrated child development services is part of the Common Minimum Programme of the present government which is supposed to deal with such problems. The expenditure on this scheme should be improved, but the budget for 2007–8 shows no evidence of a sense of urgency in this respect.[11]

The various attempts at drawing the poverty line do not reflect the problems of specific groups of the population such as women and children. Moreover, the poverty line refers to a national average and masks the concentration of poverty in certain areas, something which a case study of Maharashtra illustrates very clearly.[12] Due to the industrial and commercial wealth of its coastal region, Maharashtra is one of the leading states of India. But some of its dry inland districts are very poor; rural household consumption amounts to only 45 per cent of urban consumption in this state. While the poverty line in Maharashtra is close to the national average, in some of the inland regions 30 to 40 per cent of the rural people are below this (official) line.

The disparities of Indian states with regard to the prevalence of poverty are very pronounced. Studies based on surveys (1999) have identified two distinct groups of states, of which the first is much better off than the national average of 29 per cent of people living below the poverty line and the second is very poor. The first group consists of Haryana and Punjab (11.8), Kerala (14.5), Gujarat (15.4) and Himachal Pradesh (17.5); the second includes Bihar (46.9), Orissa (46.3), Madhya Pradesh (36.8) and Uttar Pradesh (33). It is interesting to compare these figures with those for 1973. At that time the national average was 54.9 and the deviation from that average by some of the states just mentioned was less pronounced, e.g. Bihar 61.9, Kerala 59.8, Uttar Pradesh 57.1, Gujarat 48.2. Only the Punjab (28.2) and Himachal Pradesh (26.4) were comparatively well placed even then. Kerala registered rapid progess in the intervening period and Gujarat also did very well. This shows that there are not only persistent disparities but also striking differences in the trajectories of development. These trajectories, however, are again influenced by rather different circumstances. Gujarat, for instance, registered substantial industrial growth whereas Kerala benefited from the remittances of the many Keralites working in the Gulf states.

Attempts at drawing the poverty line usually focus on the chances of physical survival, but they should also encompass other features. In this respect the rate of illiteracy would be a suitable proxy. Not all illiterate people are poor and most are relatively well informed even if they cannot read the newspapers. Remaining illiterate often relates to the potential uses of literacy in daily life. Performing routine manual work in agriculture does not depend on the ability to read or write. Many children in rural areas are not sent to school because their parents need them for just such routine manual work in order to eke out a living. At present about 35 per cent of the Indian population are illiterate. The strong correlation of illiteracy and poverty is highlighted by the fact that India's poorest state, Bihar, has a rate of illiteracy of 53 per cent. Substituting the rate of illiteracy for the poverty line would thus yield a figure of 35 per cent. This would have to be slightly corrected, as female illiteracy is higher than male illiteracy and in more affluent households where the husband and sons are literate, the women may still be illiterate. Taking this into consideration, the poverty line based on the rate of illiteracy could be drawn at about 30 per cent.

This could be confirmed by looking at the share of the lower 30 per cent of the population in the Gross Domestic Product. In 2004, total GDP amounted to Rs 23,936 billion. In the previous chapter it was mentioned that the fourth and fifth quintiles of the population have a share of 11 and 8 per cent of GDP respectively. The share of the lowest 30 per cent of the population would thus amount to approximately 10 per cent, i.e. Rs 2,393 billion. India's population in 2004 was 1,029 billion. Accordingly, the per capita share of GDP of the lower 30 per cent would amount to about Rs 7,318 per year or Rs 20 per day. To sum up: India's poor make up about 30 per cent of the population, are illiterate and have a daily per capita income of US$ 0.43.

'Informal' Proletarians and Landless Labourers

The poor in India are a vast reserve army of cheap labour. Organized labour in the 'formal' sector of the economy is a comparatively small part of the total labour force. In 2003 the public and private sectors together employed 27 million workers. The private sector is the smaller one with 8.4 million but a greater share of the 'manufacturing' category with 4.7 million as against only 1.5 million in the public sector. According to the theory of W. Arthur Lewis, in a 'dual economy' (traditional and modern) there is a reserve army of labour in the traditional sector which supplies the modern one with a steady flow of new recruits. But the Indian economy is not a dual one: it consists of two parallel economies.[13] Since the reform of 1991, employment in the formal sector has practically stagnated; there has been only a slight shift from the public to the private sector, the first losing and the latter gaining 1 million employees. These figures would confirm the frequent comments on the phenomenon of jobless growth. But, of course, this refers only to the formal sector; the actual growth takes place in the informal sector. In fact, from 1978 to 2000, the share of the informal sector in the total labour force increased slightly from 91.3 to 92.4 million, although one would have expected a decrease of informal labour in a period of steadily increasing economic growth.[14] The wage differential between the two sectors is enormous. For employees in the public sector, official statistics show an average daily per capita rate of Rs 681. According to the National Sample Survey mentioned earlier, the daily wages for male casual labourers in urban areas are Rs 75 and in rural areas Rs 56; the rates for female labourers are Rs 44 and 36 respectively. The figure for the public sector would, of course, include the high salaries of the Class I officials, but they are a small minority when compared to the legions of humble Class IV officials who do manual work or errands for the higher-ups. Nevertheless, even these humble people are head and shoulders above the casual labourers in the informal sector. Moreover, their jobs are secure and permanent, unlike the 'informal' jobs, which are subject to the rule of 'hire and fire'.

Subjection to the rule of 'hire and fire' has increased with the growing casualization of informal labour. New forms of contracting labour have developed which permit the employer to shift the onus of hiring and firing casual labour to agents who are told how many workers are needed at any given time.[15] Casualization has particularly affected women workers who were previously not very active in the labour market but have joined it in recent years in increasing numbers.[16] Concerned social scientists have coined the term 'feminization of poverty' in order to characterize this phenomenon.

The 'informal' proletarians are not protected by any trade unions, which for good reasons concentrate on the organized sector of the economy. Very few of the recognized trade unions can depend on regular fees paid by their members. Accordingly, union leaders must look for other sources of income. They usually squeeze the employers by threatening to stir up trouble. There is no collective bargaining in India: wages are set by officially appointed tribunals and there are also tribunals which try the cases of individual workers who have been made redundant or have not been paid the wages due to them. Therefore most labour leaders are lawyers who spend their time pleading before those tribunals. The informal proletariat has no contact with such tribunals or lawyers.

The usual staff of a workshop in the informal sector consists of the boss and fewer than ten workers. In small firms which operate as subcontractors for manufacturers, the boss may even be an engineering graduate. Capital investment in such workshops is minimal so very often they band together and help each other out. One has a lathe, the other a drilling machine, etc.; if the piece of work requires both, it is carried from one shop to the other. The ignorant observer may think that this cluster of workshops is a slum, but on closer inspection he will be surprised to see the quality and variety of their products. Bigger firms rely on such subcontractors for two reasons: first of all, they can keep the number of workers and the investment in machines limited; and, secondly, if there is a slack in demand they can cut the orders farmed out to the subcontractors. This explains the phenomenon of jobless growth in the organized sector. The huge number of subcontractors who have the reserve army of labour on their doorstep shield the organized sector against risks but can also respond very quickly to increased demand. There is, however, a growing gap between labour productivity in the organized and in the informal sectors. In 1983 labour in the organized sector was about six times more productive than that in the informal one; by 1999 the differential had increased to nine times. This would also account for the wage differentials between the two sectors.

The wages paid by subcontractors, particularly if they work for manufacturers producing cars or machine tools, have to be higher than the wages of casual labourers mentioned above, but they would still be much lower than those in the organized sector. The qualifications of the informal proletariat working for subcontractors range from those of skilled workers to that of untrained people. The skilled workers in workshops would be the 'creamy layer' of the informal proletariat and they would be above the poverty line.

But the great majority of the reserve army of informal labour are quite poor, something that would be particularly true of the many landless labourers who are at the beck and call of the landowning peasantry. Earlier systems of permanent attachment of such labour to the households of their employers have long since disintegrated because the employer can always find casual labour and does not need to retain labourers in the off-season. Even at times when the harvest or other seasonal operations suddenly require additional labour, there are nowadays migrant labourers who make themselves available for seasonal employment. Workers from Tamil Nadu will show up in the Punjab or elsewhere at a distance of 1,500 kilometres from their home. Here, too, the informal proletariat shows its usefulness as a reserve army of labour. About 43 per cent of India's rural population are landless. If one deducts from this about 8 per cent for traders, carters, and so on there would still be 35 per cent of labourers who depend on their daily wages. In recent years milk production has emerged as an additional source of income for landless households, but only for those close to modern dairies.

While the poorest of the poor may be found among the landless labourers, the increase of casual labour in urban areas has contributed to the alarming phenomenon of urban poverty. Social scientists have turned their attention to this only in recent times. At present an 'Urban Poverty Report' is being prepared by a team at the Jawaharlal Nehru University in New Delhi.[17] Earlier studies of poverty in India concentrated on rural poverty and interpreted urban poverty as a spill-over from it. The classic study by Dandekar and Rath published in 1971 set the agenda for most subsequent work on this subject.[18] They advocated a big rural public works programme to be financed by taxing the rich, who should be interested in preventing the rural poor from swamping the cities and starting a violent revolution. Many of the subsequent government-sponsored programmes were inspired by this message. They aimed at 'poverty alleviation' in terms of relief measures so as to prevent the spill-over mentioned above. In recent years rural–urban migration has actually declined whereas urban poverty has increased. This has prompted social scientists to look at urban poverty as *sui generis*. The collapse of industries in the organized sector in the old textile centres of Ahmadabad and Mumbai has contributed to this kind of self-generated urban poverty. While some of the workers who had lost their jobs in the organized sector may have found employment in the sheds of the informal powerloom operators, many were left stranded in the cities and became victims of 'casualization', which usually means irredeemable poverty.

A striking manifestation of urban poverty are the huge slums which disfigure Indian cities.[19] It is estimated that about half of the population of New Delhi and Mumbai live in slums. Every so often the authorities start brutal campaigns of slum demolition, but usually the poor people reconstruct their ramshackle dwellings and hope that the demolition squad will not return for some time. The plight of these people defies the Indian nutritional norms of poverty. According to social scientists who have done fieldwork in the Mumbai slums only about 8 per cent of the people of Mumbai can be classified as below the poverty line. Many slum dwellers have television sets and refrigerators in their self-made huts, but they may not have a toilet or reliable access to drinking water. They may have an income well above the poverty line, but they cannot afford decent housing in a city like Mumbai.[20] In recent years Residents' Welfare Associations (RWAs) have arisen in many cities and have taken an active interest in improving their neighbourhoods.[21] But they are mostly found in gated communities, i.e. middle-class housing societies behind gates guarded by watchmen. These RWAs have no soft spot for slum dwellers; they usually urge the authorities to demolish any slums that encroach on their neighbourhoods. It is an irony of fate that the servants in the households of RWA members often live in those very same slums.

'Beat Poverty': Promising Government Programmes

Garibi hatao (Beat Poverty) was Indira Gandhi's election slogan in 1971 and ever since Indian governments have introduced impressive-sounding schemes which have promised to radically reduce rural poverty. All these programmes faced administrative problems in reaching the poor. The Public Distribution System of cheap food grain was mentioned earlier. Then there were the Food for Work programmes which were aimed at paying poor workers direct wages in the form of foodgrain for construction work immediately benefiting their villages (roads, irrigation, school buildings, etc.). These programmes were presumably 'self-targeting', that is, for the wages offered only poor people would show up for work. Since they received their wages in kind, there was supposed to be no scope for embezzlement and corruption. However, a case study of one such programme in Andhra Pradesh has shown how the recycling of rice was organized in this state.[22] The workers would be hired and paid by 'contractors' (entrepreneurs, but also village headmen). The contractors would get rice at subsidized rates through the outlets of the Public Distribution System, they paid the workers in cash and sold the rice to merchants, who in turn sold it to the Food Corporation of India whose job it is to procure and store rice and also to release it to the PDS.[23] The middle men made a good profit, but at least some money reached the poor and some constructive work was done. But due to faulty supervision and insufficient maintenance much of this construction did not last very long.

Andhra Pradesh was also the scene of a rather different scheme, the District Poverty Initiative Programme (DPIP) supported by the World Bank. It was started in six of the poorest districts of the state. Instead of the usual top-down approach, DPIP relied on local self-help groups at village level organized like those of the Grameen Bank of Bangladesh. The members of such groups agreed to save Rs 1 a day to build up a fund for small loans. Supervision and the training of bookkeepers was done by community coordinators who received monthly salaries of Rs 3,000 from DPIP and there was one coordinator for every group of 25 villages. This worked very well and the government proudly referred to the programme as *Telugu Velugu* (Telugu Shining); after the change of government in 2004 it was renamed *Indira Kranti Patham* (Revolutionary Path). The programme was extended to other districts of Andhra Pradesh. Its main aim was 'capacity building' among the poor so that they were empowered to help themselves rather than making them the target of official charity,[24] critics having pointed out that charity rather than the elimination of poverty had been the aim of most official programmes.[25] Since governments by their very nature tend to adopt a top–down approach, it was hoped that NGOs operating at the grass roots level would be able to do more for the empowerment of the poor.[26] But their efforts met with limited success. The bulk of the projects of poverty alleviation had to be sponsored by the government.

The numerous programmes funded by central government for all parts of India were known by some high-sounding names: *Jawahar Rozgar Yojana* (JRY), *Jawahar Gram Samridhi Yojana* (JGSY), *Sampoorna Grameen Rozgar Yojana* (SGRY), etc.[27] All referred to labour-intensive public works programmes aimed at providing the rural poor with additional income. JRY was launched in 1989, amalgamating two earlier programmes. JGSY then replaced JRY in 1999 with an emphasis on the creation of durable assets in the villages under the supervision of the village *panchayat*. SGRY was introduced in 2001: it absorbed JGSY but once more placed greater emphasis on wage employment of the Food for Work type. It was this latter programme to which the above-mentioned Andhra Pradesh case study of 'rice recycling' refers. Each time a new programme was announced, the financial allocations were raised and the relevant propaganda intensified. The largest and most recent programme has been launched under the National Rural Employment Guarantee Act (NREGA) of 2005,[28] legislation that was proposed in the Common Minimum Programme of the Congress-led coalition which assumed office in 2004. It took some time to pass the Act as the officials concerned tried to reduce the financial risks the government might face when implementing it.[29] For instance, it was suggested that it should be restricted to people below the poverty line. This would have introduced a great deal of bureaucratic hassle and was fortunately given up. Supporters of the Act trusted in the self-targeting nature of the guarantee, which promises 100 days of work at low wages to one member of each rural household (it was taken for granted that no members of well-off households would show up for such work). The limit of 100 days a year reflects the needs of most poor agricultural labourers who find only seasonal employment and have no work for the rest of the year. The onus of providing work is on the government; if no work is available, the worker who shows up has to be paid his wage nevertheless. Initially the scheme was to be implemented in the 200 poorest districts of India; after three years all districts were to be covered.

The design of this new scheme owes much to Jean Drèze, a brilliant development economist who was born in Belgium and came to India at the age of 20 in 1979 and has lived there ever since. In 2002 he became an Indian citizen. He has co-authored several books with the Nobel Laureate Amartya Sen. I met Drèze at the Delhi School of Economics and asked him about NREGA. He is shy and unassuming, but has an incisive mind and a deep commitment to the cause of the Indian poor. He has estimated that a fair implementation of NREGA throughout the country would involve an expenditure of about Rs 400 billion per year (at 2004 prices), assuming total participation of all households under the (official) poverty line, and a unit cost of Rs 100 per work-day. This would benefit 40 million rural households. The wage component of Rs 60 would provide an income of Rs 6,000 per year per worker. Drèze also observed that a net additional income of Rs 6,000 per year would lift about 75 per cent of poor rural households above the poverty line. Since total participation would not be achieved in the early phase with only 200 districts being included in the scheme, the cost would initially amount to about 0.5 per cent of GDP. Once full participation is achieved, the scheme might require 1 per cent of GDP. In March 2007, one year after the Act came into force in 200 districts, Jean Drèze pointed out that the levels of expenditure on NREGA in the better-performing districts were in line with these tentative calculations. In the country as a whole, however, the expenditure levels were much lower, as the scheme was still going through a prolonged learning phase.[30] When I talked to Prime Minister Dr Manmohan Singh about NREGA, he stressed that this Act in conjunction with the Right to Information Act would really help the rural poor, who would be entitled to protest if the amounts due to them did not reach them.[31]

There is a precedent for NREGA: the Maharashtra Employment Guarantee Scheme which was introduced after the great drought in that state in 1973. Those who have studied the impact of this scheme have arrived at the conclusion that it was successful as a relief measure but has not helped to eradicate poverty. Moreover, the area where the scheme has had the most productive results has been the richer coastal region, where much of the work done under the scheme has helped to prepare the ground for horticulture, which has experienced a boom in Maharashtra in recent years. The poor inland regions which actually needed the scheme much more have experienced no immediate impact from this measure.[32] Although the Maharashtra scheme has been in operation now for more than three decades, the state has scored poorly in inter-state comparisons of the proportion of people above the poverty line.[33] This may be a warning for the administration of the NREGA. Since the onus of providing work is on the government and the worker must be paid whether he works or not, there is a temptation to concentrate on projects which are readily to hand rather than to set up those which should be prioritized to eradicate poverty.

Dedicated civil servants can make all the difference in implementing the NREGA. Manju Rajpal is a young district officer in Dungarpur District, Rajasthan, a backward district located in the south-eastern corner of the state at the border with Gujarat. Two-thirds of its inhabitants are tribals. They trusted Manju Rajpal and agreed to work in the projects which she suggested, such as restoring irrigation canals. Within a short time about 165,000 families had one or two members, mostly women, earning wages in this way.[34] If this level of take up could be achieved in backward Dungarpur, other districts should be able to do even better. NREGA may thus prove to be a breakthrough in the struggle against poverty in India.

CHAPTER 17

THE SPLENDOUR OF THE MEDIA

The Importance of a Free Press

The spread of the print media had begun in India under British rule. The first printing presses were started by Christian missionaries, who also published the first vernacular newspaper, *Samachar Darpan* (Mirror of News), in Bengali at Serampore near Kolkata in 1818. In subsequent decades the vernacular press in India developed very rapidly and journalism contributed to the development of modern prose in all major Indian languages. Whereas once poetry had been the mainstay of Indian literature, prose now proliferated everywhere. New literary genres such as the novel, the short story, the critical essay or even satire flourished in India. However, the British colonial rulers were afraid that seditious propaganda might be spread by this new prose. Newspapers which they themselves could not read were suspect so they appointed 'oriental translators'. The 'reports on Native Newspapers' they prepared were printed and circulated as confidential papers to all British officers in India. But when incipient nationalism found its expression in the vernacular press, the British-Indian government was upset. In 1878 the Viceroy, Lord Lytton, suppressed the publication of newspapers in Indian languages by means of his Vernacular Press Act. This flagrant interference with the freedom of the press was soon countermanded, but in the meantime some vernacular papers had switched to publishing in English. The most prominent among them was *Amrita Bazar Patrika*, a Bengali paper started in 1868 which was then published in English from 1878 until 1986. In its heyday it was in the vanguard of Indian nationalism; Lord Lytton had unwittingly contributed to the launching of a nationalist Indian press published in English.[1]

When Mahatma Gandhi assumed the leadership of the Indian freedom movement he set high standards for Indian journalism in his own paper *Young India*. The 90 volumes of his collected works which were published in independent India contain innumerable articles in which he comments incisively on political and social issues. While he was a student in London in the 1880s he had avidly read the leading British papers of that time.[2] He appreciated their sober and analytical style and their serious investigative journalism. In his own writings he avoided empty rhetoric and hyperbole and concentrated on the essential points he wanted to convey to his readers and subsequently the press of independent India adhered to these standards. The major national newspapers such as the *Times of India*, the *Statesman* and the *Hindu* addressed a highly educated readership. There was no scope for tabloid journalism which would have been spurned by such readers. All national newspapers published in English also had vernacular editions in Hindi, Bengali, Marathi, Tamil and other languages.

In the early years of independent India, the national newspapers faced enormous logistical problems in reaching all their readers on the day of publication. The *Times of India* was published in Mumbai and Delhi, the *Statesman* in Kolkata and Delhi and the *Hindu* in Chennai, but they also had to reach readers elsewhere in India. This was achieved by dispatching the newspapers by air freight to centres from which they could be distributed to the surrounding area. When satellites became available, the logistics of newspaper distribution were simplified. The national papers set up printing presses in regional centres throughout India and the daily edition could be printed simultaneously by thoses presses due to the satellite connection. In recent years entrepreneurs have made use of this technology by publishing numerous local editions so as to cover large linguistic regions.

The 'newspaper revolution' which started in the late 1980s has changed the face of the Indian press. Even the *Times of India* now looks almost like a tabloid. Colourful photographs catch the reader's eye and a cheap price attracts buyers. Samir Jain, the paper's owner, started a price war in the 1980s. He called the low cost of his paper an 'invitation price':[3] it covered less than a quarter of the cost of production, but the increase in circulation multiplied advertising revenue. All Indian newspapers adopted the same strategy. The proliferation of pictures was a boon to the photographers who earlier had had to fight for every inch of space for their pictures. Raghu Rai, one of India's most famous press photographers, has described this earlier struggle for space.[4] But he also complains about the latest developments, which have led to a widespread reduction of quality photography and the dominance of advertising. Indian newspapers may finally follow the pattern of American newspapers in which advertisements take up so much space that the few columns left for printing text are aptly referred to as 'newshole' by American journalists.

Initially the 'national' press published in English dominated Indian journalism and attracted the largest amount of advertising revenue. In 1954 there were 330 dailies with a total circulation of 2.5 million of which 28 per cent were accounted for by the English-language press.[5] This has dramatically changed in recent years. The English-language press still has a total daily circulation of about 10 million, but it is far surpassed by the Hindi press, with 33 million. Other Indian languages are also well represented and, according to the Registrar of Newspapers, in 2004 altogether about 156 million copies of newspapers were published in India every day. The traditional English dailies mentioned above have more or less defended their turf until recently. A new venture was started in Mumbai in 2005: *Daily News and Analysis* (*DNA*). It is supported by the Dainik Bhaskar group, about which more will be said later, and by ZEE TV, a popular Indian television company. These sponsors have deep pockets and can afford to poach staff from the established press, especially from the *Times of India*. The newly recruited *DNA* staff were paid double the salary they had earned in their previous jobs. It seems that *DNA* is doing well and has tapped a new readership, because the circulation of the *Times of India* has not decreased owing to the rise of this competitor. However, the true circulation of *DNA* is difficult to ascertain as it is often distributed free of charge to attract new readers. Nevertheless, it seems to have made its mark in Mumbai. Prompted by this success story, the *Times of India* and its Delhi rival, the *Hindustan Times*, have teamed up to produce a new English paper in Delhi, the *Metropolitan*. It will be a tabloid aimed at the urban commuter who uses the new metro of the capital city. Yet while these additions to India's English press are certainly impressive, the real success story of recent years has been the rapid proliferation of vernacular papers.

The breakthrough of the vernacular press was due to the rising tide of money available for advertising in these media.[6] The new middle class grew and thus millions of consumers became targets of advertising campaigns. This class is more comfortable with papers in the vernacular and the circulation of those papers increased by leaps and bounds. Some had existed for quite some time, but their circulation was limited and they were not very attractive to advertisers. All this changed dramatically in the 1990s when the vernacular press really took off. A look at the rapid rise of the *Dainik Bhaskar* (Daily Sun), a Hindi newspaper, will illustrate this point.

The *Dainik Bhaskar* was established in Bhopal, Madhya Pradesh, in 1958 as a small provincial paper at quite a distance from the Hindi heartland. This heartland, Uttar Pradesh, was controlled by the *Dainik Jagran* (Daily Awakening), originally founded by a freedom fighter in 1942 in Jhansi and then based in Kanpur.[7] In spite of the existence of this older and weightier Hindi paper, the *Dainik Bhaskar* with its more dynamic and flexible policy managed to capture the fringes of the Hindi heartland by penetrating Rajasthan, the Punjab and Haryana and finally ending up with a Gujarati edition, *Divya Bhaskar*. The secret of its success was the close attention it paid to the preferences of its readers. The way it started its business in Chandigarh was typical of this policy. The editors were told that there was no scope for a Hindi paper in that city. They asked potential readers there and were told that 'Hinglish' (a mixture of Hindi and English) was the preferred medium of the Chandigarh middle class. The Chandigarh edition was then published in Hinglish and proved a great success. The phenomenal increase in the total circulation of the papers of the Dainik Bhaskar group further illustrates this success story. In 1994 circulation amounted to 228,000, by 1999 it had reached more than a million, within five years it was 2 million and in 2005 it attained 3.5 million The group publishes its papers from five centres in Madhya Pradesh, seven in Rajasthan, one in the Punjab and four in Haryana, five in Gujarat, two in Chhattisgarh and two in Maharashtra. In Uttar Pradesh it has only one centre, at Jhansi, otherwise it has refrained from challenging the *Dainik Jagran* on its turf. But this Hindi heartland paper has watched the rapid rise of the *Dainik Bhaskar* very carefully and has modernized its presentation accordingly. Its circulation is more or less the same as that of the *Dainik Bhaskar* and together they dominate the Hindi press.

There is a close parallel to the success story of the *Dainik Bhaskar* in Andhra Pradesh. In 1974 Ramoji Rao, who had worked in the advertising business, established a tiny paper called *Eenadu* (Today) in the big port city of Vishakapatnam which did not have its own newspaper at that time.[8] In 1976 he started the Hyderabad edition and subsequently set up centres throughout Andhra Pradesh, acquiring a circulation of about a million by 2004. He challenged the older Telugu papers and introduced novel features such as matrimonial advertisements which so far had not appeared in the Telugu press. He also launched district editions of *Eenadu*, covering village news. In his youth Ramoji Rao had been a communist, but when N.T. Rama Rao started the Telugu Desam Party (TDP), Ramoji Rao supported it wholeheartedly and for some time *Eenadu* was identified with that party. When the Congress Party toppled the TDP in 2004, Ramoji Rao once more veered to the left as he felt that the Communist Party of India (Marxist) would be a counterweight to the Congress Party. However, this did not mean that he neglected his capitalist ventures: he has invested huge sums in his film city near Hyderabad, which will be discussed in the next section.

Andhra Pradesh was a late-comer to the expansion of the vernacular press, but neighbouring Maharashtra had produced a paper like *Eenadu* even earlier. However, because it was started at a time when the vernacular press was not yet blessed with the kind of advertising revenue available in recent years, the Marathi paper *Sakal* (Morning) remained a more modest enterprise. This paper was founded by Dr N.B. Parulekar in Pune in 1932.[9] He had been awarded his doctorate at Columbia University, New York, and on returning home had started *Sakal*, which supported the freedom movement. After independence *Sakal* expanded its circulation. Parulekar died in 1973 and in 1985 his paper was bought by the family of a powerful politician, Sharad Pawar. When he took over, *Sakal* had a sales revenue of Rs 50 million; by 2002 its revenue was Rs 125 billion.[10] It is now printed in several centres in Maharashtra just as *Eenadu* is in Andhra Pradesh. Recently it has reached a total circulation of 580,000. The outreach of *Sakal* is restricted to western Maharashtra. *Lokmat* (People's Opinion) published from Nagpur with a circulation of 300,000 dominates the Vidarbha region of eastern Maharashtra. *Dina Thanthi* (Daily Express), the leading Tamil daily, had a career similar to that of *Sakal.* Originally established in Madurai in 1942, it soon spread throughout Tamil Nadu. Initially it owed its rapid spread to its association with the Dravidian movement in the 1950s but later it adopted a neutral position in politics. Nowadays it is published from 14 centres and has a total circulation of about 800,000. In a bold departure from its earlier editorial policy it struck up a partnership with the *Economic Times* and introduced a page with business news translated from material in this English-language paper. Readers appreciated this type of information presented in simple Tamil and the paper was able to attract more advertisements in this way.

In Kerala the newspapers published in the regional language, Malayalam, had a decisive advantage over the vernacular press in other regions. Kerala included the former princely states of Tranvancore and Cochin in which Malayalam was the language of administration. English had played no important role in those states. The leading Malayalam newspaper, *Malayala Manorama* (Malayala Entertainment), founded in 1890, was for a long time the vernacular paper with the highest circulation in India and has only recently been overshadowed by the Hindi press. However, unlike other vernacular papers, it has a significant circulation overseas, with five editions in the Gulf states. With its circulation of 1.3 million *Malayala Manorama* leads the lively press of Kerala, but it has a strong rival in *Mathrubhumi,* published from nine centres in the state and with a total circulation of 900,000. There is a third paper, *Kerala Kaumudi,* with a circulation of 150,000. Kerala's high rate of literacy explains the wide circulation of its thriving vernacular press.

Last but not least the largest Bengali paper, *Ananda Bazar Patrika,* should be mentioned. Founded in 1922, it is published from Kolkata and has a daily circulation of about 1.2 million.[11] Critics point out that it is mainly a city paper and has not tried to reach the countryside as *Eenadu* has done in Andhra Pradesh. In fact, setting its sights on the educated urban reader, *Ananda Bazar Patrika* even launched an English-language daily, the *Telegraph,* in 1982. Printed at five centres (Kolkata, Guwahati, Silguri, Ranchi and

Jamshedpur) it has attained a circulation of 300,000. In 2006 it won an international award as the Best Printed Paper from Asia. The leading English paper of Kolkata, the *Statesman*, lost some of its readership to the *Telegraph*. Perhaps it was the success of an English-language paper sponsored by a leading vernacular paper that encouraged the Dainik Bhaskar group to launch *DNA* in Mumbai. It is interesting to note that vernacular papers now sponsor English papers, whereas earlier vernacular editions were started by the major English papers when these vernacular editions were regarded as the 'poor cousins' of the rich national papers.

The rise of the vernacular press would have pleased Mahatma Gandhi. He disapproved of advertising and printed no ads in his papers. But perhaps he would have relented if he had realized that advertising revenue is the lifeblood of the vernacular press. When Gandhi reorganized the Provincial Congress Committees along linguistic lines in 1920, he did so because he was convinced that people must conduct their political debates in their mother tongue. The thriving vernacular press proves this point. Gandhi would also have been pleased by the national orientation of the vernacular press: none of the papers mentioned back any kind of secessionism.[12] This is also due to the fact that the 'print capitalists' who control the papers are very much aware of the benefits of an integrated national market. Another encouraging feature is that none of these papers are 'party papers' to the extent of being owned and operated by a political party. The private owners of the papers may sometimes back a particular party, as Ramoji Rao backed the TDP, but such alliances are temporary with the party depending on the 'print capitalist', not the other way round. In earlier times parties controlling the government could exercise considerable influence on newspapers by placing advertisements or withholding them. Nowadays revenue from commercial ads is far more important than that derived from government advertising and this has greatly enhanced the freedom of the press.

India's lively and free press is of great importance to the country's democracy. It is significant that the first big spurt in growth of the vernacular press was witnessed after Indira Gandhi's 'Emergency' had been terminated in 1977; her attempt at gagging the press by means of her emergency powers led to a pent-up demand for information.[13] Many people became avid readers when they had access to a free press once more. There is, of course, the more subtle method of influencing the press by co-opting journalists: giving them official importance or letting them know that their careers may depend on adopting certain political views fits in with this method. By now journalists earn good salaries and enjoy many perks, so the threat of forfeiting them might influence their views. But the large number of journalists would make it difficult to co-opt all of them: in 1950 there were only about 2,000 in India but by 1993 there were 13,000 officially registered journalists and there may have been many unregistered ones. At present there are probably more than 26,000.[14] As there are no powerful unions for journalists in India Indian journalism has no collective voice; but the large number and the great variety of journalists are in themselves guarantees of the freedom of the press.

Most Indian journalists are urban people who only occasionally show up in the countryside. But they have rural counterparts who are really behind the newspaper revolution which has swept India in recent years. These rural stringers are often graduates engaged in various activities in their locality. They may own some land or a repair shop and also serve as distributors of newspapers, as advertising agents and as part-time correspondents. They usually are not paid by the editors but send in their news items free of charge. If their contributions are printed, this enhances their reputation in the village and helps to increase the circulation of the paper which they distribute. In their own way, these people support the freedom of the press and it is mainly down to them that huge numbers of newspapers are sold in India every day.[15]

This freedom is also enhanced by the Right to Information Act passed by the Indian parliament in 2005. For a long time government officials could protect themselves against public scrutiny by citing official secrecy. While this may make sense if national security is at stake, it was even invoked when people were cheated by corrupt officials. For instance, in many Food for Work programmes a great deal of the money owed to the workers was withheld by such officials after they had recorded the payments to the workers in official lists and journalists who might have wished to take up such cases were debarred from examining the official files. A spirited campaign by the Mazdoor Kisan Shakti Sangathan of Rajasthan (Workers and Peasants Union) led by Aruna Roy, a former officer of the Indian Administrative Service, finally prompted the government to introduce a Freedom of Information Bill into the Indian parliament in 2000, but it took five years and many sessions of select committees before the Right to Information Act was put on the statute book. Hopefully it will prove to be a boon to investigative journalism in the interests of the people. Of course, the investigations of journalists may not always result in benefits to the people, as a story told by a prominent journalist indicates. Some corrupt police officers had set up unauthorized checkpoints and fleeced the people. A TV company, informed about this by a concerned citizen, sent an undercover film crew to film the illicit activities of those police officers, but instead of broadcasting the film, the team blackmailed the officers and extorted a large amount of money from them. Such abuse of the power of the media cannot be prevented, but it is probably an exception rather than the rule.

The Imaginative Production of Films

Indian civilization is characterized by its narrative power. Story-telling pervades all periods of Indian history and the great national epics, the *Mahabharata* and the *Ramayana* are treasure troves of imaginative stories. Most people in India, even the illiterate, are familiar with these stories and know about the prominent characters portrayed in the epics such that these characters and the situations in which they find themselves are often points of reference in current conversations. When Indians started making movies, they turned quite naturally to mythological themes.

Dhundiraj Govind Phalke (1870–1944), India's first prominent film director, set the trend with *Raja Harishchandra* in 1913.[16] While the story was taken from the *Mahabharata*, the style of its presentation owed much to folk theatre. Those were the days of the silent movie, but Phalke broke the silence by arranging that live recitations of texts and chants accompanied the showing of his film. It was a big success. Phalke was trained as a Sanskrit scholar and had then attended the J. J. School of Arts in Mumbai; he thus knew the classical texts well and was also a skilled artist. He was his own cameraman, director, producer and distributor. In 1917 he produced a second version of *Raja Harishchandra* on a grand scale and in the same year screened *Lanka Dahan* (Lanka in Flames) based on the episode in the *Ramayana* where the demon king, Ravana, abducts Sita to the island of Lanka. In 1919 he added *Kaliya Mardan* (The Slaying of the Demon Kaliya), a film in a lighter vein, showing the pranks of Baby Krishna played by his young daughter Mandakini. In those years he even experimented with animated film, which helped him to design special effects for *Kaliya Mardan*. The creativity of this 'Father of Indian Film' was boundless and he left a rich heritage for those who followed in his footsteps.

The next step in the history of Indian cinema was the rise of the 'Talkies', the first one being *Alam Ara* (Light of the World) screened in 1931. It was influenced by the popular Parsi theatre of Mumbai and its director was Ardeshir Irani, a Parsi. The Indian Parsis are a tiny community whose ancestors fled from Persia to Gujarat in the tenth century to escape from the threat of forcible conversion to Islam. Eventually they became close associates of the British and settled in Mumbai, where they engaged in trade and industry. Of the famous Indians mentioned in this book D. Naoroji, J.N. Tata and H. Bhabha were Parsis. The Parsis appreciate European literature and music and the Parsi theatre in Mumbai reflected these interests. Creative directors such as Ardeshir Irani adapted oriental themes to suit the taste of the Mumbai audience. His heroine, Alam Ara, was a princess, whose story provided him with a fairly simple plot. The success of the film was based on song and dance, which have ever since remained a characteristic feature of Indian films. The language of *Alam Ara* was a popular type of Hindi not yet affected by Sanskritization. In fact, this popular Hindi was very close to Urdu whose vocabulary (*dil* = heart, *kismet* = fate, etc.) predominated in Indian films for many years.[17] Initially the actors had to sing their own songs until playback singing was introduced in 1935. From then on the directors could employ expert playback singers, who established the reputation of Indian film music.

In independent India, the stars soon gained the greatest prominence in the film business. The earlier studio system declined; it had been ruled by producers and directors who employed actors and musicians. The stars were freelancers who could dictate their terms because the success of a film at the box office depended on them.[18] Films of great artistic merit such as those produced by the famous Bengali filmmaker Satyajit Ray were not commercially successful, but the Mumbai movies ('Bollywood') normally enabled their producers to earn a good deal of money. The financing of films was nevertheless a risky business and producers usually did not reveal how they achieved this. Black money and the underworld played their roles behind the scenes. Investing in a film was a good method of money laundering.

Filmmakers provide entertainment: they do not stress the message they want to convey to their audience. Indian films are not interested in the individual psychology of their characters; these characters are types rather than complex individuals and the tragic or comic situations in which they are involved are central to the development of the plot. The conservative parents, the ardent young lover, the coy or smart heroine, the sinister villain are present in almost every film. The family is, so to speak, the microcosm of the social universe. Tensions among its members may even reflect the fate of the nation.[19] Highbrow critics often belittle the content of Indian movies, but closer analysis shows that there are shifts of meaning which provide insights into the social history of India. The portrayal of the villains, for instance, is particularly revealing in this respect.[20] The character of the villain is rarely ambiguous: he has no redeeming features but is utterly bad. He may be a handsome and impressive man but the flaws in his character are easily recognized, because he is usually brutal and devious and takes pleasure in tormenting his victims physically or mentally. In the Nehru era, the villain was very often an unscrupulous profiteer who openly transgressed the socialist ethos of the time. After India had been attacked by China in 1962 and by Pakistan in 1965, the villain personified the 'foreign hand' which threatened national security. In the 1970s smugglers provided the role model for the bad characters in Indian films, and in the 1980s separatist terrorists were depicted as villains. In the 1990s, the traditional stereotype of the villain receded and the authoritarian patriarch who spoiled the plans of the young lovers emerged as the dominant negative character.

At the other end of the spectrum of characters is the mother who personifies everything that is good and noble.[21] Often depicted as suffering, usually at the hands of the villain, she is then defended by her son. Just as in real life in Indian society, the mother–son relationship is one of deep attachment. In this patriarchal society, the father embodies the law and the mother love and compassion. While the love of the mother for her husband is always tinged by the duty to serve him and to respect him, the love for her son is free from such considerations. The son is devoted to his mother. In a kind of allegorical transformation, the mother is sometimes equated with the nation and her son's devotion to her becomes a symbol of patriotism.

The male hero in Indian films is usually a young man, passionate and striving for a better future. In the 1970s, after the experience of the Emergency, the young hero might also be disillusioned or turn into the proverbial 'angry young man'. The actor who played this role most convincingly was Amitabh Bachchan.[22] He emerged as India's leading film star in the late 1970s and early 1980s. Right on the heels of the angry young man followed the vengeful woman in the 1980s. Earlier the female characters in Indian films were either loving mothers, devoted wives, coy girls or alluring vamps. The new vengeful women were powerful characters, and the vengeance they wreaked was usually for rape.[23] Either they themselves had been victims or they had to take revenge on behalf of a relative or friend. The most modern and shocking of these films was *Bandit Queen*, produced in 1994 and based on the life of Phoolan Devi who was a victim of gang rape and had then turned into a bandit leader. Phoolan Devi was a Dalit (Untouchable) and her fate and her resistance reflected that of her downtrodden community.[24]

Films like *Bandit Queen* are still the exception in the rather placid atmosphere of romance of the current Indian film. About 800 films are produced in India every year. The majority are Bollywood Hindi films, but films in other Indian languages have also proliferated. In the Tamil and Telugu cinema, the mythological genre has survived much longer than in Hindi films. Actors such as M. G. Ramachandran in Tamil films and N.T. Rama Rao in Telugu films were able to become chief ministers of their respective states because they descended as gods from the screen into the political arena. N.T. Rama Rao had also played the role of an honest forest officer (almost a contradiction in terms) in a Telugu film and in his election campaigns he appeared to good effect in the green uniform which he had worn in that film.

The Telugu film world has also given rise to the spectacular phenomenon of Ramoji Film City, founded by Ramoji Rao, proprietor of the *Eenadu* newspaper. He first started his own film company and then built his film city near

Hyderabad on a 2,000-acre plot. It houses the largest number of film studios in the world and has been included in the *Guinness Book of World Records*.[25] Welcoming filmmakers to this unique place, Ramoji promises them: 'Walk in with a script, walk out with a canned film.' His staff of 6,000 employees is ready to construct any set a filmmaker may need. There is even a lush green valley created in the midst of an arid landscape, which is an attractive setting for romantic scenes. There are tailors who can produce any costume required for a film. But first and foremost there are studios with the latest technological equipment for the post-production treatment of films. International filmmakers are already flocking to this film city, which offers much more than Hollywood and Bollywood – and at reasonable prices. Critics have written that Ramoji has bitten off more than he can chew with this project, but it seems that it will be a great success.

The Convergence of the Electronic Media

For a long time India's electronic media were under government control. All-India Radio (AIR) was the only agency which produced radio broadcasts and when television appeared on the scene it was also produced and transmitted by AIR. As mentioned earlier, the antiquated Indian Telegraph Act of 1885 protected government control of the airwaves. The challenge then emerged literally from below. Young men in big cities like Mumbai put cables into apartment houses and offered piped programmes to their customers for a reasonable fee. This business proliferated so rapidly that the authorities decided to clamp an entertainment tax on it. Only then did they notice that they were about to tax an illegal activity which contravened the Telegraph Act.[26] Further legislation was required in order to tackle the problem – and, in the meantime, the cable operators continued their business. They provided two films a day to their subscribers and each cable operator earned about Rs 70,000 per month. By 1990 there were about 3,500 cable operators in Mumbai. They also wanted to get access to encrypted programmes, but for this a special decoder was required which cost about Rs 24,000. This was too much for a single cable operator so they got together and financed multi-system operators (MSOs) who bought decoders and retailed the films to the cable operators.[27] Since the cable operators were in charge of the proverbial 'last mile' (the cables serving individual households), they controlled the revenue, of which the MSO and the broadcaster got only about 20 per cent. Moreover, cable operators did not reveal how many households they really served. The broadcasters and the MSOs therefore wanted to bypass the cable operators by supplying households directly: this would require special decoders in each household. The Cable Act of 2002 favoured this concept of direct supply but did not specify who should pay for the extra equipment.[28] This reflected the confusion prevailing when dealing with the new media.

Having been complacent about its control of the airwaves for a long time, the government was rudely awakened by a benchmark judgment of the Supreme Court in 1994. The Cricket Association of Bengal had broadcast an important cricket match and the government had filed a suit against it. The Supreme Court had then stated that 'the airwaves are not the monopoly of the Indian government. They are public property and have to be used to foster plurality and diversity of views, opinions and ideas.'[29] The right of free speech guaranteed by the constitution could be quoted in this context. Ever since this judgment, the government has tried to recover lost ground, their efforts culminating in the Communications Convergence Bill of 2001 which was supposed to be a comprehensive measure for the regulation of all kinds of electronic media. The rapid changes in communications technology have enabled entrepreneurs to provide content by using the airwaves in numerous ways. They can 'uplink', i.e. transmit messages to satellites, and 'downlink', or get messages via satellite in order to distribute them. Since the cost of satellite transmission has decreased very rapidly, uplinking and downlinking have proliferated. The problem with the attempts at legislation by the government is that it seems to be interested in the control of content and not just in regulating the traffic of the electronic media. So the Communications Convergence Bill has not yet been passed, as it has given rise to controversies that not only concern the control of content but also the danger of locking in a part of the electronic media by defining it in terms of a specific technology.[30] Since technological innovation constantly provides new possibilities, such locking in could easily strangle the communication industries, which depend on their ability to quickly adjust to new challenges. Legislating in this field is like aiming at moving targets.

A new challenge may arise if a powerful company aims at serving the communication needs of all households by joining radio, TV, broadband and telephone connections. Such a company would be interested in a comprehensive convergence bill to bridge the legal gap between services transmitted via airwaves and those transmitted by telephone lines. The proprietary control of such lines is not touched by the verdict of the Supreme Court on freedom of the airwaves. However, such proprietary control is already infringed by new technologies like Voice over Internet Protocol. This indicates that a Convergence Act is really overdue.

Transmission via the airwaves and the new methods of telecommunication are not the only fields in which there is rapid progress. The very terrestrial activity of recording and distributing music is also undergoing revolutionary change. The music cassette provided a cheaper medium than the old-fashioned record. This business did not involve government control but the copyright of private companies. Here the pioneer was Gulshan Kumar, the son of a fruit juice vendor, who discovered a loophole in the Indian Copyright Act and became a rich man in the 1980s.[31] Earlier the staid old gramophone company, His Master's Voice (HMV), held the copyright of most Indian film music. It sold expensive records while the production of cassettes would have been much cheaper. In fact, HMV sold its cassettes at artificially high prices so as to protect its records: this amounted to an invitation to challenge its monopoly. Instead of indulging in outright piracy, Gulshan Kumar hired new singers and reproduced the old tunes – thus circumventing the copyright. It was a roaring success. Knowing his father's business, Gulshan Kumar also found new ways of distributing his cassettes – they were sold by street vendors and in grocers. Gulshan Kumar amassed a fortune in this way and also entered the film business. Proudly he stressed that he was India's biggest taxpayer at that time. His company, Super Cassettes Industries, dwarfed its competitors. However, he was not prepared to accommodate them and this probably made him a target for hired hitmen, who gunned him down on his way to a temple in Mumbai in August 1997. His murderers were caught and confessed that they had been hired by gangsters from the Mumbai underworld. But who actually paid for Gulshan Kumar's assassination has remained a mystery. Had he lived longer he might also have branched out into the other communications industries like his younger contemporary Subhash Chandra, who emerged as India's media mogul in the 1990s.

Subhash Chandra was a rice trader in Haryana who made a fortune exporting rice to Russia. He also pioneered the manufacturing of laminated tubes in 1982. In 1990, by chance he visited a television studio of Doordarshan, the government's TV company. He seems to have realized at once that he could easily compete with Doordarshan, and set up his private company Zee TV in 1992.[32] Chandra cleverly circumvented the government's monopoly by teaming up with a company in Hong Kong and beaming his programme into India from abroad. Zee TV's Hindi programme soon became very popular. In 1995 Chandra started Siticable, providing cable TV to 6 million urban households. He also entered into a partnership with Rupert Murdoch's STAR TV, but the partnership did not last long because both partners felt constrained by it. For instance, STAR TV was not permitted to broadcast in Hindi as this remained the exclusive right of Zee TV. After the partnership was terminated in 1999, Chandra expanded his business very rapidly. He launched programmes in various other Indian languages and reaped a huge harvest in advertising revenues. He also entered the film business and took a special interest in the production of animated films. In 2003 he became the first provider of direct to home (DTH) services in India. By this means he could eliminate the middle men and attract customers by offering them individual access to all kinds of programmes and media. Other entrepreneurs had toyed with this idea, but had shied away from it because DTH requires expensive equipment in the home. It was left to Chandra to break the 'sound barrier' in this field. He also started the first online lottery in India. In addition to his media enterprises he has set up popular theme parks in several cities. Moreover, he has established TALEEM (Transnational Alternate Learning for Emancipation and Empowerment through Multimedia) to provide quality education to those who could otherwise not afford it.

Owing to his powerful position as a media mogul, in 2006 Chandra managed to join the board of directors of the United News of India (UNI).[33] This venerable institution, established in 1961, is a cooperative news agency serving the Indian press. The union of UNI employees was opposed to what they considered to be a takeover of UNI by Chandra; but the chances of UNI becoming an agency with a 'global footprint' will probably improve if Chandra takes an interest in it. He is a visionary entrepreneur and so far all his ventures have been highly successful. Chandra's rise is an indication of the convergence of the electronic media, a phenomenon which the government is still trying to encompass by means of suitable legislation.

CHAPTER 18

A DYNAMIC DIASPORA

The Export of Indian Labour under Colonial Rule and in Recent Times

The Greek word 'Diaspora' refers to 'scattered' people who live among strangers of different ethnic or religious identities. Such scattered people usually retain their language and their culture, whereas isolated individuals are absorbed by their host societies. The retention of the identity of a diaspora community may have different causes: it may be imposed by the host society because it despises the strangers or it may be consciously preserved by the members of the diaspora community as they value their culture and will not give it up. Disregard by the host society and the self-respect of the diaspora community may mutually reinforce the quest for a separate identity. On the other hand, there may also be privileged diaspora communities whose status in their host societies encourages them to take pride in their identity

The migration which leads to the rise of such scattered communities has many different causes. Abduction into slavery, emigration as contract labourers, the establishment of trading networks or the search for greener pastures may have led to permanent settlement abroad. Social and religious customs such as endogamy and adherence to specific rites may contribute to the cohesion of the diaspora community. For the Indian diaspora all these various features have been of relevance. In ancient times, colonies of Indian traders settled in many places on the shores of the Indian Ocean and established a far-flung trading network. But an organized mass exodus of Indians started only under British colonial rule when Indian indentured servants were shipped to plantations overseas in order to replace the African slaves after slavery was abolished in the early nineteenth century. These indentured servants were called 'coolies' from the Tamil word *kuli*, 'hired labour'. Initially this was a descriptive term, but it soon acquired an offensive connotation. The conditions of work of the indentured labourer were actually about the same as that of the slave. In fact, the plantation owner would be more interested in keeping a slave alive as he had invested capital in him whereas the death of an indentured labourer would not hurt him; he would even save the return passage to which the servant was entitled after the termination of his period of work specified in the contract.

The cultivation of sugar-cane in colonies such as Mauritius and the Natal province of South Africa, in Trinidad, Guyana and Surinam in the Caribbean and Fiji in the Pacific Ocean created settlements of Indian labourers as many stayed on as free labourers after their contracts had expired. In some of these places the Indians emerged as the majority of the population,[1] but with few exceptions they did not rise above the position of labourers. Therefore the diaspora in the ex-sugar colonies is not much of an economic asset to India. Mauritius is an exception to this rule. It has shown encouraging signs of economic growth and its Indian majority dominates the politics of the island but has maintained equitable relations with the other ethnic groups. Mauritius has become a major offshore banking centre for investors who channel their investments in India through the island. This has led to the strange phenomenon whereby tiny Mauritius ranks high among the nations investing in India. Being well aware of the benefits of good relations with Mauritius, India is even prepared to protect the maritime economic zone of the island with the help of its navy.

In spite of its global importance, the saga of Indian migration has hardly left any trace in creative writing. The one great exception is the work of the Nobel Laureate Vidiadhar Surajprasad Naipaul from Trinidad. His novel, *A House for Mr Biswas*, published in 1961, portrayed the life of an Indian family, the offspring of indentured servants. He had studied in Oxford and then looked at life in Trinidad through the prism of another diaspora experience in Great Britain. A few years later he made his first trip to India and published his account of this experience under the provocative title *An Area of Darkness*. Many took this as a reference to India as a land of darkness, but actually the darkness he was writing about was his feeling of not being able to get in touch with the land of his ancestors. As a meticulous and self-conscious observer he reflected the experience of the man from the diaspora who searches for his identity in the 'motherland' but only then becomes aware of a deep alienation. In fact, the first thing Naipaul experienced in India was the loss of his diaspora identity as he was seen as one among millions of Indians. It was as if a seismo-graph is swept away by an avalanche where nothing it records makes any sense. In his later books on India Naipaul shows a more balanced approach, but his work always reflects the tension between the diaspora man and his motherland. His great literary skills as a 'participant observer' were justly rewarded with the Nobel Prize in 2001.[2]

Naipaul visited India to observe the country, not to settle there. Other diaspora Indians did not even visit India but remained abroad for ever. The era of decolonization did not provide much scope for re-migration from the diaspora to India. Nor did the erstwhile colonial powers invite people of Indian origin to settle in their home countries. There were only two striking exceptions to this rule. The Netherlands became the target of a mass exodus of Indians from Surinam after that colony gained independence in 1975.[3] This was due to the fact that the Dutch had granted citizenship to the people of Surinam and since the Indians did not get along with the Afro-American majority, they left for the Netherlands before their right of citizenship could be revoked. A similar exodus of Indians from Uganda to Great Britain had taken place after Idi Amin had established his tyrannical rule in 1971. The Indians of Uganda were not the offspring of indentured servants but had followed the Uganda railroad. The workers who built that railroad had also come from India, but almost all of them had returned to their homes in the Punjab. The subsequent immigrants from India were for the most part literate Gujaratis who manned the administrative posts of the railway or set up shops in the hinterland which had been opened up by the railway. When these people were persecuted by Idi Amin and shifted to Great Britain they did very well there as a result of their business acumen. This group of the Indian diaspora is of considerable importance for India. But, of course, the Indians who came from East Africa are only part of the Indian diaspora in Great Britain, which also consists of Indian professionals and businessmen who migrated from India to the ex-imperial country in search of greener pastures.

Another post-colonial migration which had some similarity to the export of Indian manpower in colonial times was the recruitment of Indian labour by the countries along the Persian Gulf when those countries earned millions of petro-dollars. This recruitment benefited all South Asian countries. Most of them sent unskilled labourers to the Gulf; India had the lion's share of skilled administrative jobs. For quite some time the ample remittances of these skilled personnel filled the gap in India's balance of payments which was usually affected by a negative balance of trade. When the first Gulf War of 1991 disrupted this profitable connection, India was hit very hard, the more so as the disaster was sudden and unexpected. When Indira Gandhi was asked in 1981 whether she could envision an Indian exodus from the Gulf similar to that from East Africa precipitated by Idi Amin, she jauntily replied: 'The Arabs need us.'[4] Her successors also took this for granted and were rudely awakened by the Gulf War.

The Indian diaspora in the countries along the Persian Gulf was very different from that everywhere else. First of all it was of very recent origin. This diaspora had no second or third generation members born in the country of residence. Moreover, the Indians who came to the Gulf did not intend to settle there for any length of time. There were many educated people from Kerala among them who simply wanted to earn enough money to build a house back home. Busy construction work in the villages of Kerala provided striking evidence of this trend in the 1980s. Under such conditions there was hardly any incentive to establish Indian community centres in the Gulf countries. The Indian diaspora was not concentrated in any one place and its members fluctuated. Nevertheless, this was the diaspora which was most important for India, due to the economic effect of its remittances. Other Indian diasporas would be less inclined to send money to India as they would rather invest it where they lived. The occasional support of poor relatives in India did not give rise to substantial remittances.

In contrast to the Indian diaspora communities mentioned so far, the most prominent one – that in the USA – has an altogether different social structure, which is mainly determined by American immigration laws. These laws act as a filter through which only those migrants who have high educational qualifications can pass. The brain gain which has accrued to the USA in this way was initially deplored as a brain drain in India. Young Indians who had acquired their education in Indian universities at the expense of the Indian taxpayer not only deprived their nation of this educational capital but did not contribute to Indian development at home. There were suggestions that the Indian government should stop this brain drain by prohibiting this type of emigration. But wiser counsels prevailed and no attempt was made to restrict such emigration. Politicians were aware that the educated unemployed might easily become subversive elements, the more so if one prevented them from finding employment elsewhere. Positive measures such as creating a 'science pool' which would support unemployed Indian scientists until they could find a job in India were also phased out when they proved to be of no use. Recent developments have shown that these worries are no longer justified.

The Surprising Effects of the Brain Drain

In the vanguard of the brain drain were Indian medical doctors who flocked to the USA as early as the 1950s and 1960s. Their numbers were so substantial that it was said that if they all left the country the American health system would break down. At present, the American Association of Physicians of Indian Origin which was founded in 1984 has 42,000 members. Their 'drain' was particularly deplored at home, because doctors were scarce in India and hardly any were available in rural areas in the early decades after independence. The medical doctors were soon followed by natural scientists. There were some research institutes in the USA which were almost totally manned by Indian staff. Moreover, many colleges and universities offered attractive teaching posts. The Sputnik shock of October 1957 motivated the USA to invest more in scientific research and years of American complacency were abruptly ended by this first Soviet satellite. But the neglect of higher education in the natural sciences could not be overcome all of a sudden. Well-trained Indian scientists were welcome as they could fill this gap. The migration of medical doctors and scientists continued at a steady pace in the 1970s and 1980s, but then the IT revolution added a new dimension to the brain drain. It has been estimated that the loss to India caused by the emigration of its IT specialists amounted to about US$ 2 billion annually. The best IT specialists graduated from the five Indian Institutes of Technology (IIT). From 1951 to 2004 the IITs produced approximately 100,000 graduates, of whom a fifth live in the USA, as attested by alumni registers. In addition to the IIT elite, graduates of many Indian universities, engineering colleges and institutes of management found a new home in America.

Due to the criteria of selection of immigrants, their average income is much higher than that of other Americans and they can afford to contribute generously to institutions of the diaspora community. The Hindu temples in the Pittsburgh area illustrate this fact. The south Indians flock to the impressive Sri Venkateswara temple and the Gujaratis support an equally impressive Hindu–Jain temple. The latter is a unique construction which has no parallel in India: one aisle is devoted to a Hindu god and the aisle crossing it is devoted to a Jain Tirthankara. The young priest in charge is a Brahmin recruited in India and the temple is supported by 700 members of the community. There are about 200 Hindu temples in the USA whose addresses can be found on the internet.[5] Not all are as impressive as the two temples in the Pittsburgh area, but they are community centres which serve the resident Indians in many ways. Just like most American churches, these temples have kitchens and assembly halls in the basement. The Indian diaspora communities in the USA also take an active interest in politics and can influence elections if they jointly support a candidate. If an Indian wishes to run for political office, he needs the support of the majority of the voters. The success story of Bobby Jindal has shown that this is possible. Jindal was born in Baton Rouge, Louisiana, in 1971. His Punjabi parents had come to the USA to attend graduate school. Bobby was born as a Hindu but converted to Catholicism as a teenager. A brilliant student, he obtained an MA degree from Oxford University where he was a Rhodes Scholar. He held important positions in his home state and in Washington and was known for his work in reforming the health care system. In 2003 he narrowly failed in the election for Governor of Louisiana but 2004 won a seat in the House of Representatives in Washington on a Republican ticket. For many members of the Indian diaspora in America his success encourages them to make a mark in American politics.

Indian associations are very active in the USA, and often reproduce cultural and linguistic allegiances derived from their places of origin. The Telugus of Andhra Pradesh are a case in point. There are said to be 250,000 of them in the USA and they support two organizations, the Telugu Association of North America (TANA) and the American Telugu Association (ATA). TANA was established in 1977, while ATA was founded in 1991. These two organizations on American soil have reproduced the divide between two dominant caste groups, the Kammas and the Reddys of Andhra Pradesh. The Kammas were obviously too important in TANA, so the Reddys set up ATA. For special events such as hosting the visiting Chief Minister of Andhra, Dr Y. S. R. Reddy, the rivals share a common platform. Other regional groups of India have their own organizations, but there is also an apex body, the Global Organization of People of Indian Origin (GOPIO) founded in the USA in 1989. The activities of GOPIO are not restricted to America; it aims to represent the Indian diaspora worldwide.

In general the Indians in the USA are well integrated and, as Bobby Jindal's example shows, they may gain more and more political influence in that country. But unlike earlier immigrants who would not think of returning to their country of origin, having escaped misery and persecution, the Indians in the USA can seriously consider returning home. In fact, some of the most successful entrepreneurs, IT specialists and engineers have recently done just this. Their valuable connections with American partners make them an asset to any Indian company they choose to join. Very few of the Indian returnees go back because they have failed to make a mark in America; most return because they see India 'taking off' and want to participate in this new development. Some of these returnees are able to invest a considerable amount of capital in India. Among the more than 2 million Indians in the USA, there are about 200,000 dollar millionaires. There are no statistics showing the number of returning millionaires and the amount of capital they have 'repatriated', but it can be assumed that India's brain gain is accompanied by some capital gain.

Nowadays remittances to India from the diaspora Indians amount to about US$ 23 billion annually. These remittances have different origins. The Indians in the Gulf countries usually transfer all their savings to India as they intend to go home after having earned enough money. The affluent Indians in America who are more or less permanently settled there nevertheless do send some money back to India. They support economic development in the regions they come from by generous donations. As first generation emigrants they still have vivid memories of the villages they left behind. Surrounded by wealth in their new home they want to alleviate poverty in their places of origin and such aid is often far more effective than the foreign aid provided by Western countries in earlier years.

In addition to the Indians who have migrated to North America to pursue a specific career, there are by now some truly global Indians who live and work in different continents. I met such a man on a flight to India where he wanted to visit his old parents. He had been a captain of supertankers for many years and had settled with his family in Vancouver – not because he worked there but because he liked the city. At present he works in Africa where he is in command of a ship anchored at a distance off the coast. There he supervises offshore oil drilling and the shipment of oil. Flights from Africa to Canada and to India are routine for him and he enjoys his intercontinental lifestyle. In due course there may be more Indians like him who embody a new type of unlimited diaspora.

NRIs and PIOs: The Position of Overseas Indians

Overseas Indians are classified either as non-resident Indians (NRIs) or as persons of Indian origin (PIOs). The former are Indian citizens who retain their Indian passports but live more or less permanently abroad; the latter are Indians by birth or parentage who have acquired the citizenship of another country and have relinquished their Indian citizenship. Altogether these two goups of Indians living abroad are said to amount to about 25 million people. The number of the PIOs is, of course, much larger than that of the NRIs. About 70 per cent of the total Indian diaspora population consists of PIOs. In the former sugar colonies most Indians are PIOs. This is also true of other parts of South America, Africa and Asia, where PIOs by far outnumber NRIs. These regions have altogether about 8.6 million Indian inhabitants. In the Arab countries which do not grant citizenship to non-Arabs, the Indians living there are NRIs and amount to about 3.3 million. In Europe there are both PIOs and NRIs – in all about 1.7 million, of which 1.1 million live in Great Britain. According to a recent survey, 40 per cent of British Indians live in London. Only a third of the Indians in Great Britain came directly from India; 13 per cent came from East Africa and 46 per cent were born in Great Britain. Thus the majority of Indians in Great Britain are PIOs. In the USA the number of NRIs would be larger than that of the PIOs as Indian immigration has increased very rapidly only in recent years. There may be about 2 million Indians in the USA and more than 800,000 in Canada. Among the professionals the Indian doctors, many of whom came to the USA quite some time ago, are mostly PIOs. By now there is also a substantial group of second generation Indians who are American citizens by birth and thus PIOs. There is a nickname for them: ABCD (American Born Confused Desi). Desi is derived from *desh* (home country). The 'confusion' refers to being brought up by Indian parents in an American environment. In fact, the upbringing of ABCD kids is a major challenge for Indian fathers, who are particularly worried about their teenage daughters who start dating American boys. At that stage many a conservative father becomes highly motivated to return to India with his family.

In recent years the male NRI has become a standard type in Indian films. His brash self-confidence impresses those who have remained at home. At the same time there is a lurking anxiety that this NRI represents transnational social forces which challenge Indian identity. Actually most NRIs have nostalgic feelings about the motherland. Nevertheless, the filmmakers who portray these characters in their films are ambivalent about their identity. As consumers of Indian films the NRIs are becoming more and more important and this may in due course influence the attitudes of the filmmakers, who always have an eye on their audience.

The desire to maintain Indian identity is a distinctive feature of the life of NRIs and PIOs abroad. In fact, many of them have experienced being 'Indians' only when settling abroad. In India they had more or less unreflected multiple identities; living abroad they became self-conscious. In English usage 'self-conscious' can mean ill at ease as well as reflective. The feeling of being ill at ease when trying to determine one's identity in an alien environment is a typical diaspora experience. Thoughtful Indians living in the diaspora embarked on their own 'Discovery of India'. The streamlined version of Indian identity in terms of 'Hindutva' proved attractive to many of them. The Indian Nobel Laureate Amartya Sen has criticized this reductive approach to Indian identity which cuts off many branches of India's spacious cultural traditions.[6] Sen has also pointed out that the attraction of a reductive ideology has important economic implications as right-wing Hindu organizations receive large remittances from Indians abroad.[7] This motivates these organizations to take an active interest in the Indian diaspora whereas 'official India' had been indifferent to the diaspora for a long time.

The Indian government was, of course, interested in the remittances of overseas Indians as these helped to improve the balance of payments. Some special schemes were introduced which enabled NRIs to park their money at good interest rates in India. Such funds could be freely reconverted into foreign currency. This also meant the risk of a sudden withdrawal of NRI money when India faced a balance of payments crisis. Fortunately this has happened only once, in 1991, and since then the NRIs have again filled their Indian accounts. The PIOs were not entitled to such privileges; however, in recent years the Indian government has paid some attention to them and in 2002 a measure was introduced which permitted these people to acquire PIO cards. These guarantee visa-free entry into India for a period of fifteen years. There is a fee of US$ 310 for such a card so only frequent travellers will find this an attractive offer. Nevertheless, the issuing of PIO cards is a significant political gesture as it shows that the Indian government wants to keep in touch with the vast Indian diaspora. PIOs are also entitled to buy property in India. The new initiatives resulted from the recommendations of the High Level Committee on the Indian Diaspora which was appointed by the Government of India in September 2000 and submitted its report in December 2001. The numbers of overseas Indians quoted above are derived from this report. They add up to about 17 million overseas Indians[8] (there may be some illegal Indian immigrants who do not show up in the statistics). Nevertheless, the figure of 25 million which is often quoted seems to be exaggerated. However, even about 17 million overseas Indians would be of great significance, the more so as the total social product of these people would be very considerable. There are claims that this social product would approximate to about half of India's GNP. If this is true India would certainly be well advised to cultivate the Indian diaspora not only for cultural but also for economic reasons.

With all their structural differences, the Indian diasporas have one feature in common: enthusiasm for cricket. This British game has recondite rules which are known only to the initiated – of whom there are millions. The captains of national cricket teams are often much more famous than prominent politicians. Cricket teams such as those of the (Caribbean) West Indies are popular in India as well as in many other countries, and fans everywhere know that if there is something unfair in this world: 'That's simply not cricket.'

EPILOGUE

The Giant's Next Steps

With 9 per cent growth in recent years and the potential for double-digit growth, India seems to face a bright future. But in order to proceed on this growth path, India will have to divest itself of the shackles of water scarcity, inadequate power supply and deficiency of infrastructure. With concerted efforts these problems can be solved. The abundance of the monsoon can be harnessed by methods of water harvesting. Impending advances in the field of solar energy will contribute to an ample supply of electricity. But electricity must be distributed in a reasonable manner. The free supply of electricity to the peasants in some parts of India only leads to a waste of energy and a depletion of groundwater by excessive pumping. Moreover, while this electricity is provided free of charge for some time, it may not be available when the peasant needs it most. A Punjab peasant who was asked about this replied that he would rather pay for electricity if he could be assured of its supply when he needed it. The private sector would probably do a better job at generating and distributing energy than the moribund state electricity boards while the division of the electricity sector into separate units for generation, transmission and supply would improve this situation. The same is true of the provision of adequate infrastructure. Toll roads give private firms an immediate return on the capital invested: they already exist in many places in India. BOT (build, operate, transfer) arrangements attract private capital and ensure the future control of the roads by the state which guarantees their continuing maintenance. The Indian railways are another very important element of infrastructure. So far only part of the vast network has been electrified; this has to be extended very rapidly so as to save the fuel consumed by the diesel locomotives. The recent turnaround of the railways, whose operations are now very profitable, augurs well for their further development.[1]

Indian manufacturing will have to be improved by using the latest technology. There are pioneers in India such as Ace Designers Ltd in Bangalore which produces numerically controlled machine tools of world standard.[2]

This example should be followed by manufacturers throughout India. The application of IT to machine building offers great prospects for India. So far the big Indian IT firms have done excellent work in producing software for financial and management solutions; they also design software for CAD (computer aided design) and CAM (computer aided manufacturing) for many customers abroad. These skills are applicable to Indian manufacturing and will certainly proliferate in the immediate future.

Another field in which India may show excellent results is the life sciences and their application to industrial production. Reliance Industries has established an impressive Life Science Department. The immediate aim of this company is the production of inexpensive generic drugs for the Indian masses and the development of new drugs and medicines based on the company's own research is a long-term project which should turn into a profitable venture in due course.[3] Backed by India's richest man, this project will certainly be a success. Big international firms like Dupont have also opted for India as a breeding ground for new ideas and new products in the life sciences. The Dupont Knowledge Centre, to be built in Hyderabad, will concentrate on plant biotechnology and crop genetics.[4]

All this requires great efforts in human resource development. India has a wealth of educated manpower but the recruitment of future generations depends on a broad base of universal primary education. As pointed out earlier, this has been India's aim for a long time. But there are great gaps in the implementation of this programme: a school in every village with a qualified teacher in residence is still a dream. Many teachers behave like absentee landlords: they draw their salary from the state government but do not show up in the village since they are not under the jurisdiction of the village *panchayat*. *Panchayati raj,* the democratic structure of village government, has been strengthened by constitutional amendments. Elections of the office holders have been conducted conscientiously. However, this political empowerment at the local level has not been accompanied by the devolution of financial powers. If the teacher drew his salary from the local government, he would not dare to neglect his work in the village.

An active teacher in the village would also be an asset beyond the immediate sphere of the school. When F. W. Raiffeisen established the rural co-operatives named after him in Germany in 1848 he could rely on the village teachers as trusted and competent voluntary accountants. Early Indian nationalists praised Raiffeisen's work and recommended it as a model for India. But they were not aware of the crucial role played by the teachers in this scheme. In Indian villages, the teacher can be the friend, philosopher and guide of the peasants in many respects. To cover his salary and other essential services in the village, the administration of land revenue should be transferred to the *panchayat*. Land revenue was once the mainstay of Indian state finance and even today the district officer in most Indian districts is called 'collector', because collecting the land revenue and maintaining the relevant records used to be his main duty in times gone by. Under British rule, the land revenue was transferred to the provincial governments and it has remained under the jurisdiction of the Indian federal states. However, under the impact of the Great Depression, land revenue withered away as its burden was resented by the peasants. In independent India, land revenue was not revised. In many states the cost of its collection was higher than the amount collected. It should have been abolished, but the peasants did not want that, because the revenue receipt is usually the only land title available to them. If the land revenue administration is turned over to the village, the *panchayat* can revise it and the peasants should be willing to pay enhanced rates once they are convinced that the money will be spent on communal services in the village.

A comprehensive reconstruction of local government in the countryside would not only benefit the maintenance of common services but also encourage the full development of the potential of Indian agriculture. As has been pointed out, this potential is enormous. However, the Indian government has mostly thought of rural India in terms of the need to alleviate rural poverty. In the absence of real political power at village level, benevolent schemes guided from above have often been ruined by corruption and administrative inefficiency. An empowered village government, also armed with the right to information which it can invoke to make all authorities at higher levels accountable, could transform the life of the peasants and unleash the growth of agricultural productivity.

The life of a large part of the Indian peasantry has become more difficult in recent times due to the fragmentation of land-holdings caused by population growth. Uneconomic holdings abound and their owners must work for others in addition to cultivating the tiny plots they have inherited and many would prefer to sell their land in order to be able to earn a living elsewhere. But the Indian land market is treacherous terrain because of the absence of a proper record of rights in most parts of the country. The British revenue authorities were usually satisfied with recording the land; they could disregard the rights of ownership. If the revenue was not paid, the land would be sold at auction by the authorities. There was no need to worry about the intricacies of ownership in this context. Independent India thus inherited land records without a record of rights. Some states have recently computerized their land records, but unless these contain a conclusive record of rights, they do not provide a basis for a transparent land market. The consolidation of economic land-holdings urgently requires a reliable record of rights. The preparation of such a record will be a costly affair, but this work must be undertaken very soon so as to improve the productivity of Indian agriculture.[5]

Politically India is a modern nation state just like Great Britain, France or Germany, but in its vast dimensions it dwarfs the European Union to which those nations belong. It is far ahead of the European Union in terms of institutional integration. But, of course, it still lags behind the European Union in its economic power. In this respect it will soon catch up as its growth rates are three or four times as high as those of major European nations. Having been economically isolated for a long time, India still has to find its place in a new world order in which it will be one of the few major global players. As a giant, it does not need to adjust to the rules of the game but can participate in making these rules. Indian legal experts have been pioneers in formulating international law concerning the seabed and outer space. India has also played a leading role in the peacekeeping operations of the United Nations. In spite of its economic isolation, India has gained a great deal of experience in the international arena and its influence will continue to grow in this field. This influence will generally be directed to the maintenance of stability in world affairs. India is rightly called a 'status quo' power as it has no ambitions to extend its reach beyond its territory. Any future steps India takes will thus be devoted to the preservation of the status quo.

India faces a unique political and social task in dealing with its large Muslim minority. The Muslims of India amount to about 140 million, which is more or less the same as the total population of Pakistan and dwarfs the population of most Muslim nations of the world. The social and political position of Muslims in India is therefore important for the development of Islam in a global context. Hinduism and Islam are not just creeds, they are ways of life. The Hindu attitude of inclusive tolerance, stressing the equal value of all religions, is an insult to an orthodox Muslim who believes that Islam is the only true religion. Nor is the concept of secularism derived from the Western experience of the separation of Church and state quite applicable to the Indian situation. Neither Hindus nor Muslims have a church. Moreover, 'secularization' can be interpreted as a denigration of the Hindu or Muslim way of life and would thus have a negative rather than a positive connotation. However, the impartiality of the state in maintaining law and order is a principle which can be easily understood by all citizens, but this impartiality must be demonstrated by active intervention and not only by passive non-interference. It was mentioned earlier that quelling Hindu– Muslim riots requires preventive intervention at the right moment. Deploying the army may be a means of last resort: it should be avoided as far as possible as the army is trained to shoot at the enemy rather than to control riots. And since the local police is often suspected of being partisan, India should concentrate on special police units trained in riot control. They could be deployed in small groups dressed in plain clothes rather than in conspicuous uniforms. India has a special police force dressed in black uniforms and referred to as 'Black Cats'. These are well-trained people but they are mostly responsible for the security of VIPs. There is also the Rapid Action Force mentioned earlier. Its deployment by central government in the case of communal riots may have to be ensured by special legislation.

The political fortunes of India are also deeply influenced by the fate of the Dalits (Untouchables) most of whom are extremely poor and underprivileged. According to various estimates their numbers amount to between 170 and 200 million. Affirmative action by the state has improved the position of some of them, but it could not reach the masses in the countryside where most of the Dalits live. There is recent evidence of an amazing political mobilization of the Dalits which may set the pace for the further development of Indian politics. A Dalit party has won an absolute majority in the legislative assembly of Uttar Pradesh, India's largest state.[6] This was achieved by means of a political alliance with representatives of the high castes (Brahmins and Rajputs). Although this is only a regional success, it may well have an impact on national politics in the near future.

In the cultural sphere India is casting its magic spell globally. The earlier interest in Indian wisdom was usually restricted to an elite of scholars. Indian spirituality attracted esoteric circles who would flock around Indian gurus who visited many countries. But nowadays Bollywood and other elements of popular Indian culture have reached younger people everywhere and their influence will probably spread in the years to come. This type of popular culture will attract ever more foreign tourists. India is a hospitable country and individual tourists who are patient and enjoy organizing their own trip have usually returned with pleasant memories. The usual tourist, however, who buys a package tour which fits in with a restricted vacation period is often taken by travel agents to other destinations, because these agents depend on logistics such as predictable flight schedules in the country, an ample supply of suitable hotel rooms, etc. In India travel agents often experience logistical problems. But there has been a great deal of change in India in recent years. New hotels have been built everywhere and numerous airlines now offer reliable flights to many places. Growing familiarity with India among people abroad will not only enhance the country's income from tourism but also foster better political and economic relations. Visitors to India will come to know that the Indian giant is a friendly one who does not threaten others, but aims at peaceful coexistence.

NOTES

Chapter 1: Building a Democratic Nation

1. J. D. Kelly and M. Kaplan, *Represented Communities. Fiji and World Decolonization*, Chicago 2001, p. 156.
2. D. Rothermund, *Die politische Willensbildung in Indien*, Wiesbaden 1965, p. 17 ff.
3. L. Zastoupil, *John Stuart Mill and India*, Stanford 1994.
4. K. T. Telang, 'Free Trade and Protection from an Indian Point of View', in K. T. Telang, *Writings and Speeches*, Bombay 1916, pp. 97–187.
5. D. Naoroji, *Poverty and Un-British Rule in India*, London 1901.
6. Rothermund, *Politische Willensbildung*, p. 37.
7. Interview with J. Nehru, January 1961.
8. D. Rothermund, 'Traditionalism and Socialism in Vivekananda's Thought', in D. Rothermund, *The Phases of Indian Nationalism and Other Essays*, Bombay 1970, pp. 57–64.
9. D. Rothermund, *Mahatma Gandhi. Der Revolutionär der Gewaltlosigkeit*, Munich 1989, p. 67.
10. Ibid., p. 146.
11. G. B. Moore, *Social Origins of Democracy and Dictatorship. Lord and Peasant in the Making of the Modern World*, Boston 1966.
12. D. Rothermund, *Government, Landlord and Peasant in India. Agrarian Relations under British Rule, 1865–1935*, Wiesbaden 1978.
13. D. Rothermund, *India in the Great Depression, 1929–1939*, New Delhi 1992.
14. Ibid., p. 125 ff.
15. Rothermund, *Politische Willensbildung*, p. 171 ff.
16. Ibid., p. 173.
17. A. Jalal, *The Sole Spokesman. Jinnah, the Muslim League and the Demand for Pakistan*, Cambridge 1985.
18. M. A. K. Azad, *India Wins Freedom*, Madras 1988, p. 226.
19. R. Tagore, *Mein Vermächtnis*, trans. and ed. R. P. Das, Munich 1997, p. 47; the original Bengali text of 1901 is reprinted in *Rabindra Racanabali*, Kolkata 1978, pp. 485–9.
20. Rothermund, *Mahatma Gandhi*, p. 424.
21. R. Sachar et al., *Social, Economic and Educational Status of the Muslim Community of India. A Report*, Prime Minister's High Level Committee, Cabinet Secretariat, Government of India, November, 2006.
22. Ibid., p. 52.
23. Ibid., p. 73 f.
24. Ibid., p. 77.

25. P. Brass, *The Production of Hindu–Muslim Violence in Contemporary India*, Seattle 2003, p. 231.

26. Ibid., p. 219 ff.

27. K. S. Subramaniam, 'Police and the Minorities: A Study of the Role of the Police during Communal Violence', in A. A. Engineer and A. S. Narang (eds), *Minorities and the Police in India*, New Delhi 2006, p. 130.

28. A. Varshney, *Ethnic Conflict and Civic Life. Hindus and Muslims in India*, New Haven 2002, p. 175.

29. Brass, *Production of Hindu–Muslim Violence*, p. 385 ff.

30. Varshney, *Ethnic Conflict*, p. 255 ff.

31. A. Teltumbde et al., *Glimpse of Gujarat in a Martyr's City. A Fact-finding Report on Sholapur Communal Riots*, Delhi, 10 November 2002.

32. Varshney, *Ethnic Conflict*, p. 294.

Chapter 2: The Emergence of National Coalitions

1. Rothermund, *Politische Willensbildung*, p. 58 f.

2. Rothermund, *Mahatma Gandhi*, p. 145.

3. Ibid., p. 438.

4. E. Luce, *In Spite of the Gods. The Strange Rise of Modern India*, London 2006, p. 355.

5. Rothermund, *Politische Willensbildung*, p. 227.

6. H. Kulke and D. Rothermund, *A History of India*, 4th edn, London 2004, p. 335.

7. Interview with E. M. S. Namboodiripad, February 1965.

8. T. Zinkin, *Reporting India*, London 1962, p. 148 ff.

9. Interview with M. Desai, August 1978.

10. C. Jaffrelot, 'The BJP and the 2004 General Election: Dimensions, Causes and Implications of an Unexpected Defeat', in K. Adeney and L. Sáez (eds), *Coalition Politics and Hindu Nationalism*, London 2005, p. 238.

11. Ibid., p. 238.

12. Ibid., p. 243.

Chapter 3: The Tensions of Federalism

1. D. Rothermund, 'Constitution Making and Decolonization', in *DIOGENES*, 53/4 (212), London 2006, pp. 9–17.

2. Rothermund, *Politische Willensbildung*, pp. 164 f., 183.

3. Ibid., p. 216.

4. Ibid., p. 215.

5. K. Adeney, 'Hindu Nationalists and Federal Structure in an Era of Regionalism', in Adeney and Sáez, (eds), *Coalition Politics*, p. 110.

6. M. G. Rao and N. Singh, *Political Economy of Federalism in India*, New Delhi 2005, p. 90.

7. Rothermund, *Mahatma Gandhi*, p. 143.

8. Rothermund, *Politische Willensbildung*, p. 225.

9. Rothermund, *Mahatma Gandhi*, p. 144.

10. Rothermund, 'Probleme des indischen Föderalismus', in W. Draguhn (ed.), *Indien 2001*, Hamburg 2001, pp. 59–78.

11. Interview with M. S. Ahluwalia, March 2007.

12. Adeney, 'Hindu Nationalists and Federal Structure', p. 102.

13. Rothermund, *India in the Great Depression*, p. 219 f.

14. D. Rothermund (ed.), *Liberalizing India. Progress and Problems*, New Delhi 1996, p. 13.

15. Rothermund, *India in the Great Depression*, p. 220.
16. Rao and Singh, *Political Economy*, pp. 188, 199 f.
17. Ibid., p. 172 f.
18. Ibid., pp. 55, 198, 213.
19. Interview with M. S. Ahluwalia, March 2007.
20. Interview with M. Govinda Rao, March 2007.
21. Rao and Singh, *Political Economy*, p. 359.
22. Interview with S. D. Tendulkar (member of the Fifth Pay Commission), March 2007.
23. Government of India/Ministry of Finance, *Report of the Twelfth Finance Commission (2004–2010)*, New Delhi 2004, p. 488 f.
24. A. K. Dasgupta, 'Value-added Tax in the States', in K. Basu (ed.), *Oxford Companion to Economics in India*, New Delhi 2007, p. 543 ff.
25. Rao and Singh, *Political Economy*, p. 296.
26. Ibid., pp. 57, 138, 166.
27. Ibid., p. 338.

Chapter 4: A Role in World Affairs

1. G. H. Jansen, *Afro-Asia and Nonalignment*, London 1966, pp. 182 f., 279.
2. Kulke and Rothermund, *A History of India*, p. 354.
3. Government of India/Ministry of External Affairs, *Notes, Memoranda and Letters Exchanged and Agreements Signed between the Governments of India and China, 1954–1959. White Paper*, New Delhi 1959.
4. Kulke and Rothermund, *A History of India*, p. 355.
5. D. Rothermund, *The Routledge Companion to Decolonization*, London 2006, p. 227.
6. Kulke and Rothermund, *A History of India*, p. 356 f.
7. R. C. Horn, *Soviet–Indian Relations. Issues and Influences*, New York 1982.
8. Kulke and Rothermund, *A History of India*, p. 360.
9. D. Rothermund, *Indien und die Sowjetunion*, Tübingen 1968.
10. Kulke and Rothermund, *A History of India*, p. 363.
11. J. N. Dixit, *Across Borders. Fifty Years of India's Foreign Policy*, New Delhi 1998, p. 214.
12. Ibid., p. 132.
13. J. Chiryankandath and A. Wyatt, 'The NDA and Indian Foreign Policiy', in Adeney and Sáez (eds), *Coalition Politics*, p. 205.
14. D. Rothermund, *Krisenherd Kaschmir. Der Konflikt der Atommächte Indien und Pakistan*, Munich 2002, p. 98 ff.
15. Ibid., p. 105 f.
16. S. Talbott, *Engaging India. Diplomacy, Democracy and the Bomb*, Washington, DC 2004, p. 160 f.
17. Rothermund, *Krisenherd Kaschmir*, p. 108 f.
18. D. Rothermund, 'Die Europäische Union und Indien', in W. Weidenfeld (ed.), *Europa-Handbuch*, Gütersloh 2004, pp. 596–607.
19. D. Kux, *Estranged Democracies. India and the United States, 1941–1991*, New Delhi 1993, pp. 243 f., 255 f.
20. Ibid., p. 305.
21. Rothermund, *Krisenherd Kaschmir*, p. 116 f.
22. Ibid., p. 128 f.
23. D. Banerjee, 'Die Verteidigung', in D. Rothermund (ed.), *Indien. Ein Handbuch*, Munich 1995, p. 433.
24. H. White, 'Great Power Gambits to Secure Asia's Peace', *Far Eastern Economic Review*, 170(1), Jan./Feb. 2007, pp. 7–11.

Chapter 5: The Argument of Power: Atom Bombs and Rockets

1. D. Rothermund, *Mahatma Gandhi. An Essay in Political Biography*, New Delhi 1991, p. 107.
2. Ibid., p. 114.
3. I. Abraham, *The Making of the Indian Atomic Bomb: Science, Secrecy and the Postcolonial State*, New Delhi 1998, p. 43.
4. Ibid., p. 48 f.
5. Ibid., p. 86 f.
6. Ibid., p. 74 f.
7. G. Perkovich, *India's Nuclear Bomb. The Impact on Global Proliferation*, Berkeley 2001, p. 26.
8. Ibid., p. 35.
9. Ibid., p. 36.
10. Abraham, *Indian Atomic Bomb*, p. 84 f.
11. Ibid., p. 123.
12. Ibid., p. 114 f.
13. Ibid., p. 126.
14. Perkovich, *India's Nuclear Bomb*, p. 60 f.
15. Ibid., p. 98.
16. Ibid., p. 122.
17. Abraham, *Indian Atomic Bomb*, p. 133.
18. Ibid., p. 164 f.
19. Perkovich, *India's Nuclear Bomb*, p. 190.
20. Ibid., p. 143.
21. Ibid., p. 196.
22. Ibid., p. 242 f.
23. Ibid., p. 235.
24. Ibid., p. 273.
25. Talbott, *Engaging India*, p. 37 f.
26. Ibid., p. 50.
27. Interview with A. Kakodkar, November 2006.
28. Talbott, *Engaging India*, p. 100.
29. Ibid., p. 172.
30. Ibid., p. 180.
31. Perkovich, *India's Nuclear Bomb*, p. 154 f.
32. Talbott, *Engaging India*, p. 29.
33. A. Tellis, *India's Emerging Nuclear Posture. Between Recessed Deterrent and Ready Arsenal*, Santa Monica 2001, p. 568.
34. Ibid., p. 98.
35. Ibid., p. 234.
36. R. Menon, *A Nuclear Strategy for India*, New Delhi 2000, p. 95.
37. Ibid., pp. 100, 114.
38. Tellis, *Nuclear Posture*, p. 381.
39. Ibid., p. 387.
40. Menon, *A Nuclear Strategy for India*, p. 226 f.
41. Tellis, *Nuclear Posture*, p. 578.
42. Ibid., p. 637.
43. Menon, *A Nuclear Strategy for India*, p. 303.
44. Tellis, *Nuclear Posture*, p. 760.
45. Luce, *In spite of the Gods*, p. 283.
46. Interview with A. Kakodkar, November 2006.
47. *The Hindu*, 18 November 2006.

Chapter 6: Liberalizing a Hidebound Economy

1. Rothermund, *India in the Great Depression*, p. 169 f.
2. Ibid., p. 142 ff.
3. D. Rothermund, *An Economic History of India*, London 1993, p. 120 f.
4. B. Zachariah, *Developing India. An Intellectual and Social History, ca. 1930–1950*, New Delhi 2005, p. 216.
5. Ibid., p. 156 ff.
6. Rothermund, *An Economic History of India*, p. 124.
7. G. D. Parikh and M. N. Roy, *Alphabet of Fascist Economics – A Critique of the Bombay Plan of Economic Development for India*, Calcutta 1944.
8. Rothermund, *An Economic History of India*, p. 125.
9. S. Marathe, *Regulation and Development. India's Policy Experience of Control over Industry*, New Delhi 1986, p. 289 ff.
10. Ibid., p. 45 f.
11. Rothermund, *India in the Great Depression*, p. 146 ff.
12. Ibid., p. 205 f.
13. Rothermund, *An Economic History of India*, p. 133.
14. Ibid., p. 138 ff.
15. I. J. Ahluwalia, *Industrial Growth in India. Stagnation since the Mid-Sixties*, Delhi 1985.
16. Rothermund, *An Economic History of India*, p. 154 f.
17. S. Lall, *Learning to Industrialize. The Acquisition of Technological Capability by India*, Basingstoke 1987.
18. S. D. Tendulkar and T. A. Bhavani, *Understanding Reforms. Post-1991 in India*, New Delhi 2007, p. 23.
19. I. N. Gang and M. Pandey, 'Small-scale Industries', in Basu (ed.), *Oxford Companion to Economics in India*, p. 485.
20. Rothermund (ed.), *Liberalising India*, p. 12.
21. V. Krishna, 'Raj Krishna', in Basu (ed.), *Oxford Companion*, p. 324.
22. Rothermund (ed.), *Liberalising India*, p. 13.
23. V. Joshi and I. M. D. Little, *India. Macroeconomics and Political Economy, 1964–1991*, Washington, DC 1994.
24. Tendulkar and Bhavani, *Understanding Reforms*, p. 81.
25. Interview with M. Singh, October 1995.
26. Tendulkar and Bhavani, *Understanding Reforms*, p. 88.
27. Inaugural Address by Manmohan Singh, Finance Minister, in Rothermund (ed.), *Liberalizing India*, pp. 21–8.
28. Tendulkar and Bhavani, *Understanding Reforms*, p. 113.
29. Government of India/Ministry of Finance, *Economic Survey, 2005–2006*, New Delhi 2006, p. 132 ff.
30. Ibid., p. 123 f.
31. T. N. Srinivasan, 'Unfinished Reform Agendum: Fiscal Consolidation and Reforms', unpublished paper, 9 October 2006, p. 10 ff.
32. Government of India/Ministry of Law and Justice, *Gazette of India*, 23 June 2005, The Special Economic Zones Act, 2005.
33. Government of India/Ministry of Commerce and Industry, *Gazette of India*, 10 February 2006, The Special Economic Zones Rules, 2006.
34. Interview with M. Singh, November 2006.
35. *The Hindu*, 21 March 2007.
36. Interview with M. Ambani, February 2007.
37. Interview with M. S. Ahluwalia, March 2007.
38. M. Govinda Rao, 'SEZs: Boon or Bane', *Business Standard*, 5 September 2006.

Chapter 7: Sick Mills and Strong Powerlooms

1. S. Aiolfi, *Calicos und gedrucktes Zeug: Die Entwicklung der englischen Textilveredelung und der Tuchhandel der East India Company, 1650–1750*, Stuttgart 1987.
2. K. Specker, *Weber im Wettbewerb. Das Schicksal der südindischen Textilhandwerker im 19. Jahrhundert*, Stuttgart 1984.
3. Rothermund, *An Economic History of India*, p. 53.
4. Rothermund, *India in the Great Depression*, p. 167.
5. Rothermund, *Mahatma Gandhi. An Essay in Political Biography*, p. 129.
6. S. Leadbeater, *The Politics of Textiles. The Indian Cotton Mill Industry and the Legacy of Swadeshi*, New Delhi 1993, p. 167 f.
7. Ibid., p. 218.
8. T. Anant and O. Goswami, 'Getting Everything Wrong. India's Policies Regarding "Sick" Mills', in D. Mookerjee (ed.), *Indian Industry. Policies and Performance*, New Delhi 1995.
9. D. D'Monte, *Ripping the Fabric: The Decline of Mumbai and its Mills*, Delhi 2002.
10. Government of India, *Report of the Fact-Finding Committee (Handlooms and Mills)*, Delhi 1942.
11. Rothermund, *An Economic History of India*, p. 147.
12. Lall, *Learning to Industrialize*, p. 131.
13. T. Roy, 'Market Resurgence, Deregulation and Industrial Response. India's Cotton Textile Industry in the 1990s', *Economic and Political Weekly*, 25 May 1996, M31–M41.
14. Government of India, *Economic Survey*, 2005–2006, p. S–16.
15. Ibid., p. 110 f.
16. Government of India/Ministry of Finance, *Economic Survey, 2006–2007*, New Delhi 2007, p. S–86.

Chapter 8: Diamonds, Garments and Software

1. *Journal of the Gem & Jewellery Machinery & Accessories Association*, 4(4), Sept.–Oct. 2004.
2. Government of India, *Economic Survey, 2005–2006*, p. 143.
3. *The Hindu*, 21 December 2006.
4. Government of India, *Economic Survey, 2006–2007*, p. 119.
5. Ibid., p. S–86.
6. P. Ananthakrishnan and S. Jain-Chandra, *The Impact on India of Trade Liberalization in the Textiles and Clothing Sector*, Washington, DC 2005 (IMF Working Paper WP/05/214) p. 25 ff.
7. S. Chari, *Fraternal Capital. Peasant Workers, Self-made Men and Globalization in Provincial India*, Stanford 2004.
8. Ibid., p. 243.
9. G. De Neve, 'Weaving for IKEA in South India: Subcontracting, Labour Market and Gender Relations in a Global Value Chain', in J. Assayag and C. J. Fuller (eds), *Globalizing India. Perspectives from Below*, London 2005, pp. 89–119.
10. R. Jhabvala and R. Kanbur, 'Globalization and Economic Reform as seen from the Ground: SEWA's Experience in India', in N. K. Basu (ed.), *India's Emerging Economy*, Cambridge, Mass. 2004, pp. 293–312.
11. *Daily News and Analysis* (Mumbai), 23 August 2005 ('Raymond wants to be a billion dollar global fashion house').
12. *Business Standard*, 2 April 2006 ('Raymond aims to be outsourcing giant').
13. *Economic Times*, 5 June 2006.
14. A. Sheshabalaya, *Rising Elephant. The Growing Clash with India over White-Collar Jobs and its Challenge to America and the World*, Monroe, Maine 2005, p. 150.

15. Interview with D. Mehta, April 2000.
16. Sheshabalaya, *Rising Elephant*, p. 115.
17. T. Friedman, *The World is Flat. The Globalized World in the Twenty-first Century*, London 2005, p. 128, 133.
18. Ibid., p. 240.
19. Sheshabalaya, *Rising Elephant*, p. 35.
20. Ibid., p. 109.
21. Friedman, *The World is Flat*, p. 282.
22. Sheshabalaya, *Rising Elephant*, p. 112.
23. M. Landler, 'A New Type of Software Company for India', *New York Times*, 26 March 2001.
24. Friedman, *The World is Flat*, p. 218.
25. S. Warrier, 'Making Maths Fun, Worldwide', in *rediff.com*, 10 October 2005.
26. Sheshabalaya, *Rising Elephant*, p. 61 f.
27. Friedman, *The World is Flat*, p. 526 f.
28. S. Gokarn et al., *The Rising Tide – Employment and Output Linkages of IT–ITES*, New Delhi: NASSCOM–CRISIL, February 2007.
29. M. Fromhold-Eisebith, 'Infotech Industries and Regional Disparities in India', in S. Raju, S. Kumar and S. Corbridge (eds), *Colonial and Post-Colonial Geographies*, New Delhi 2006, pp. 162–81.
30. *The Hindu*, 18 December 2006.

Chapter 9: The Quest for Supercomputers

1. C. Christensen, *The Innovator's Dilemma: When New Technologies Cause Great Firms to Fail*, Boston 1997.
2. A. Parthasarathy, 'Target: Teraflops', *Frontline*, 22, 14 January 2005.
3. G. Taubes, 'The Rise and Fall of Thinking Machines', *Inc. Magazine* (New York), September 1995.
4. B. Jagadeesh (ed.), *Anupam Supercomputer Systems*, Mumbai: Bhabha Atomic Research Centre 2003.
5. A. Parthasarthy, 'Fastet Academic Computer to Vie for Top Spot', *The Hindu*, 28 April 2004.
6. J. Venkatachari, 'A Global Winner', in: *domain-b.com*, 12 February 2003.
7. A. Jhunjhunwala et al., 'n-Logue: The Story of a Rural Service Provider in India', *Journal of Community Informatics*, 1(1), 2004, pp. 30–8.
8. J. Paul, 'What Works: n-Logue's Rural Connectivity Model. Deploying Wireless-Connected Internet Kiosks in Villages throughout India', in *World Resources Institute/Digital Dividend*,Washington, DC December 2004, pp. 1–27.
9. Sheshabalaya, *Rising Elephant*, p. 227.
10. Ibid., p. 224.
11. P. Sunderarajan, 'Here Comes the No-frills, Mobile Computer System', *The Hindu*, 11 May 2005.

Chapter 10: Agriculture: Crisis or Promise?

1. Government of India, *Economic Survey 2005–2006*, p. 155.
2. J. Witsoe, 'India's Second Green Revolution? The Sociopolitical Implications of Corporate-Led Agricultural Growth', in D. Kapur (ed.), *India in Transition: Economics and Politics of Change*, Philadelphia 2006, p. 8.

3. Government of India/Planning Commission, *Towards Faster and More Inclusive Growth. An Approach to the 11th Five Year Plan*, New Delhi, 9 December 2006, p. 5 f.

4. A. Kundu, 'Changing Agrarian System and Rural Urban Linkages', in S. Ray (ed.), *A Handbook of Agriculture in India*, New Delhi 2007, pp. 183–202.

5. D. Gupta, 'How Rural is Rural India? Rethinking Options for Farming and Farmers', in Ray (ed.), *Handbook of Agriculture*, pp. 207–31.

6. Rothermund, *Government, Landlord and Peasant*, p. 41 ff.

7. Interview with M. S. Ahluwalia, March 2007.

8. Rothermund, *An Economic History of India*, p. 134 f.

9. Ibid., p. 140 f.

10. Government of India, *Economic Survey 2005–2006*, p. S-20.

11. Ibid., p. S-24.

12. V. K. Ramachandran and M. Swaminathan (eds), *Financial Liberalization and Rural Credit in India*, New Delhi 2005.

13. Government of India, *Economic Survey 2005–2006*, p. S-17.

14. Ibid., p. 5–17.

15. Ibid., p. 166.

16. Ibid., p. S-16.

17. Ibid., p. S-85 f.

18. Z. Nazir, 'Cane Farmers Protest Export Ban as Prices Fall', *Indian Express*, 8 December 2006.

19. *The Hindu*, 5 January 2007.

20. G. Chandrashekar, 'World Sugar Market to Remain Firm on Ethanol Demand', *Business Line*, 1 November 2005.

21. Government of India, *Economic Survey 2005–2006*, p. S-21.

22. Ibid., p. 172.

23. *The Hindu*, 7 January 2007.

24. Rothermund, *Government, Landlord and Peasant*, p. 12 f.

25. Government of India, *Economic Survey 2005–2006*, pp. 94 and S-22.

26. Witsoe, 'India's Second Green Revolution?' p. 4.

27. Government of India, *Economic Survey 2005–2006*, p. 96.

28. Ibid., p. 161.

29. Ibid., p. 162.

30. Ibid., p. 158.

31. Ibid., p. 158.

32. Ibid., p. 164.

33. Ibid., p. 159.

34. Ibid., p. 166 f.

35. Ibid., p. 160.

36. *The Hindu*, 28 November 2006.

37. A. Gulati, 'High Time for High-Value Agriculture', *Economic Times*, 29 November 2006.

38. P. Ilavia, 'From the Vine to the Bottle at Grover's', *Deccan Herald*, 28 June 2004.

39. *Businessworld*, 4 October 2004.

40. J. Witsoe, 'India's Second Green Revolution?' p. 21.

41. Ibid., p. 10.

42. Interview with M. Ambani, February 2007.

Chapter 11: The Giant's Shackles: Water, Energy and Infrastructure

1. A. Gulati, R. Meinzen-Dick and K. Raju, *Institutional Reforms in Indian Irrigation*, New Delhi 2005, p. 18.
2. A. Agarwal, S. Narain and A. Sharma (eds), *Green Politics*, New Delhi 1999.
3. *The Hindu*, 27 August 2005.
4. R. P. S. Malik, 'Water and Poverty', in J. Briscoe and R. P. S. Malik (eds), *Handbook of Water Resources in India*, New Delhi 2007, p. 142.
5. B. Vira, R. Iyer and R. Cassen, 'Water', in T. Dyson et al. (eds), *Twenty-first Century India. Population, Economy, Human Development and the Environment*, New Delhi 2004, p. 317.
6. Communication from Professor Gunnar Jacks, February 2007.
7. National Academy of Agricultural Sciences, *Emerging Issues in Water Management – The Question of Ownership* (Policy Paper 32), New Delhi 2005.
8. Maharashtra Act No. XVIII of 2005, Chapter II.
9. Ibid., Chapter III.
10. Gulati et al., *Institutional Reforms*, p. 138 ff.
11. Ibid., p. 115.
12. *The Hindu*, 12 June 2006.
13. M. Kumar and D. Shah, 'Groundwater Pollution and Contamination in India: The Emerging Challenge', in *The Hindu Survey of the Environment 2004*, pp. 7–12.
14. Centre for Water Policy, *Some Critical Issues on Groundwater in India*, New Delhi 2005, p. 4.
15. T. Shah, 'Institutional and Policy Reforms', in Briscoe and Malik (eds), *Handbook of Water Resources*, p. 323.
16. Government of India, *Economic Survey 2005–2006*, p. 219 f.
17. Govinda Rao and Singh, *Political Economy*, pp. 224–42.
18. D. Rothermund and D. C. Wadhwa (eds), *Zamindars, Mines and Peasants. Studies in the History of an Indian Coalfield and Its Rural Hinterland*, New Delhi 1978.
19. G. Ruths, 'Entrepreneurs in the Coalfield', in D. Rothermund et al. (eds), *Urban Growth and Rural Stagnation. Studies in the Economy of an Indian Coalfield and its Rural Hinterland*, New Delhi 1980, pp. 403–52.
20. Government of India, *Economic Survey 2006–2007*, p. S-25.
21. Government of India, *Economic Survey 2005–2006*, p. S-28.
22. B. P. Banerjee, *Handbook of Energy and the Environment in India*, New Delhi 2005, p. 107 f.
23. *TERI Energy Data Directory and Yearbook (=TEDDY) 2003–2004*, New Delhi 2004, p. 113.
24. Ibid., p. 70.
25. Ibid., p. 51.
26. Ibid., p. 52.
27. Interview with M. Ambani, February 2007.
28. *TEDDY 2003–2004.*, p. 123.
29. Ibid., p. 146 (Table 1.74).
30. Ibid., p. 166 f.
31. Ibid., p. 170.
32. Ibid., p. 173 f.
33. Ibid., p. 171.
34. Ibid., p. 163 f.
35. J. Lund and D. Freeston, 'World-wide Direct Uses of Geothermal Energy 2000', *Geothermics*, 30, 2001, p. 45.
36. Ibid., p. 49.
37. Banerjee, *Handbook of Energy*, p. 214.

38. *TEDDY 2003–2004*, p. 1.
39. Ibid., p. 134 (Table 1.63: Financial Status of SEBs).
40. Ibid., p. 140 f. (Table 1.69).
41. Ibid., p. 115 f.
42. A. Katakam, 'The DPC Chronicle', *Frontline*, 19(4), 16 Feb.–1 March 2002.
43. Government of India, *Economic Survey 2005–2006*, p. 179.
44. Ibid., p. 181 f.
45. Ibid., p. 195.
46. S. Gokarn, 'Railways', in Basu (ed.), *Oxford Companion*, p. 441 f.
47. Government of India, *Economic Survey 2005–2006*, p. 188.
48. Ibid., p. S-29.
49. Ibid., p. 193 f.
50. *The Hindu*, 21 December 2006.
51. Government of India, *Economic Survey 2005–2006*, p. 194.
52. *Business Line*, 26 July 2006.
53. *The Hindu*, 24 December 2006.
54. *The Hindu*, 18 March 2007.
55. Government of India, *Economic Survey 2005–2006*, p. 192.
56. Ibid., p. 191.
57. S. Sangwan, Science, *Technology and Colonisation. An Indian Experience 1757–1857*, Delhi 1991, p. 91 ff.
58. Ibid., p. 95.
59. A. V. Desai, *India's Communications Industry. History Analysis, Diagnosis*, New Delhi 2006, p. 130.
60. Ibid., p. 35 ff.
61. J. Johnson, 'Profile: Sunil Bharti Mittal', *Financial Times*, 27 November 2006.
62. S. Mittal, *India's New Entrepreneurial Classes: The High Growth Economy and Why It is Sustainable*, Philadelphia (Center for the Advanced Study of India) 2005, p. 7.
63. Desai, *India's Communications Industry*, p. 53.
64. *Business Line*, 21 March 2006.

Chapter 12: Caste in a Changing Society

1. D. Rothermund, 'Gebundene Gesellschaft: Soziale Schichtung und Emanzipation in Indien', in U. Engelhardt (ed.), *Soziale Bewegung und politische Verfassung*, Stuttgart 1976, pp. 394–414.
2. P. Kane, *History of Dharmasastra*, Vol. I, Poona 1930, p. 141 f.
3. Interview with J. Nehru, January 1961.
4. P. Kane, *History of Dharmasastra*, Vol. II, Part I, Poona 1941, p. 447 ff.
5. R. Thapar, *Early India*, London 2002, p. 100 f.
6. H. von Stietencron, 'Hinduism: On the Proper Use of a Deceptive Term', in G. Sontheimer and H. Kulke (eds) *Hinduism Reconsidered*, New Delhi 1997, p. 32 ff.
7. Kane, *History of Dharmasastra*, Vol. II, Part I, p. 416 f.
8. *Indian Express*, 8 April 2006 ('The ABC of OBCs').
9. Kulke and Rothermund, *A History of India*, p. 344.
10. *The Hindu*, 30 January 2004.
11. *Hindustan Times*, 1 November 2006.
12. J. A. Dohrmann and S. Thorat, 'Right to Food: Food Security and Discrimination in the Indian Context', *Asien. The German Journal on Contemporary Asia*, 102, January 2007, pp. 9–31.
13. Rothermund, *Mahatma Gandhi. An Essay in Political Biography*, p. 78 ff.
14. Kulke and Rothermund, *A History of India*, p. 329.

15. *The Hindu*, 10 October 2006 ('Kanshi Ram passes away').
16. A. Waldman, 'An Opulent and Pugnacious Champion of India's Outcasts', *New York Times*, 4 May 2004.
17. *Hindustan Times*, 11 November 2006 ('Mayawati new saviour of Brahmin community').

Chapter 13: The Boon of a Demographic Dividend

1. This is the revised figure published in *Census of India 2001: Population Profiles*, New Delhi: Office of the Registrar-General, 2004.
2. T. Dyson, 'India's Population – The Future', in Dyson et al. (eds), *Twenty-first Century India*, p. 98.
3. T. Dyson and P. Visaria, 'Migration and Urbanization: Retrospect and Prospects', in Dyson et al. (eds), *Twenty-first Century India*, p. 122.
4. T. Dyson, 'Population', in Dyson et al. (eds), *Twenty-first Century India*, p. 25.
5. S. Krishnanmoorty et al., 'Causes of Fertility Transition in Tamil Nadu', in C. Guilmoto and S. Irudaya Rajan, *Fertility Transition in South India*, New Delhi 2005, p. 238.
6. S. Acharya et al., 'The Economy – Past and Future', in Dyson et al. (eds), *Twenty-first Century India*, p. 217 f.
7. Government of India/Planning Commission, *Approach to the 11th Five Year Plan*, p. 6.
8. M. Asher, 'India's Innovative Pension Plan', *Far Eastern Economic Review*, 170(4), May 2007, pp. 54–7.
9. Dyson et *al.,Twenty-first Century India*, p. 346.
10. L. Visaria, 'The Continuing Fertility Transition', in Dyson et al. (eds), *Twenty-first Century India*, p. 69.
11. J. Witte and G. Wagner, 'Declining Fertility in East Germany after Unification. A Demographic Response to Socioeconomic Change', *Population and Development Review*, 21 (2), 1995, pp. 387–97.
12. G. Kingdon et al., 'Education and Literacy', in Dyson et al. (eds), *Twenty-first Century India*, p. 139.
13. C. Guilmoto, 'Fertility Decline in India: Maps, Models and Hypotheses', in Guilmoto and Irudaya Rajan, *Fertility Transition in South India*, p. 411.
14. S. Vella, 'Low Fertility and Female Discrimination in South India: The Puzzle of Salem District', in Guilmoto and Irudaya Rajan (eds), *Fertility Transition in South India*, p. 277.
15. A. Bose, 'Demographic Transition and Demographic Imbalance in India', *Health Transition Review*, Supplement to Vol. 6, pp. 89–99.
16. T. Dyson and P. Visaria, 'Migration and Urbanization', in Dyson et al. (eds), *Twenty-first Century India*, p. 112 f.
17. Dyson et al. (eds), *Twenty-first Century India*, p. 345.

Chapter 14: The Demand for Education

1. Kulke and Rothermund, *A History of India*, p. 254 f.
2. T. Parvate, *Gopal Krishna Gokhale*, Ahmedabad 1959, p. 337 ff.
3. Government of India, *Economic Survey 2005–2006*, p. 210.
4. Ibid., p. 211.
5. D. Majumdar, 'Teacher Absenteeism', in Basu (ed.), *Oxford Companion*, p. 513.

6. G. Kingdon et al., 'Education and Literacy', in T. Dyson et al. (eds), *Twenty-first Century India*, p. 141.
7. World Bank, *Reforming Public Services in India. Drawing Lessons from Success*, New Delhi 2006 pp. 46–53 ('Decentralizing Teacher Management').
8. Kingdon et al., 'Education and Literacy', in T. Dyson et al. (eds), *Twenty-first Century India*, p. 147.
9. Kulke and Rothermund, *A History of India*, p. 276 f.
10. H. Fischer-Tiné, *Der Gurukul Kangri oder die Erziehung der Arya-Nation. Kolonialismus, Hindureform und 'nationale Bildung' in Britisch-Indien (1897–1922)*, Würzburg 2003.
11. E. Thompson, *Rabindranath Tagore. Poet and Dramatist*, London 1926, p. 188 ff.
12. Rothermund, *Mahatma Gandhi. Der Revolutionär der Gewaltlosigkeit*, p. 336.
13. Sangwan, *Science, Technology and Colonisation*, p. 60 f.
14. A. Basu, 'The Indian Response to Scientific and Technical Education in the Colonial Era, 1820–1920', in D. Kumar (ed.), *Science and Empire. Essays in Indian Context*, Delhi 1991, p. 129.
15. Ibid., p. 132.
16. Ibid., p. 133.
17. N. Mahajan, 'The Cream of India's Colleges Turns Sour', *Far Eastern Economic Review*, 170(1), Jan./Feb. 2007, pp. 62–5.
18. P. Altbach, 'Fostering Asia's Brightest', *Far Eastern Economic Review*, 170(1), Jan./Feb. 2007, pp. 53–7.
19. Interview with M. Singh, November 2006.

Chapter 15: The New Middle Class: Consumers and Savers

1. T. Friedman, *The World is Flat*, p. 461.
2. Government of India, *Economic Survey 2005–2006*, pp. 12 f., S-6.
3. Government of India, *Economic Survey 2006–2007*, p. S-6.
4. R. Dwyer, *All You Want is Money, All You Need is Love. Sexuality and Romance in Modern India*, London 2000, p. 202 ff.
5. F. Conlon, 'Dining Out in Bombay', in C. Breckenridge (ed.), *Consuming Modernity in Contemporary India*, Minneapolis 1995, p. 90 ff.
6. Rothermund, *An Economic History of India*, p. 152.
7. Government of India, *Economic Survey 2005–2006*, p. S-31.
8. Government of India, *Economic Survey 2006–2007*, p. 188.
9. A. Venkatesh, *Computers and New Technologies in Indian Households: Based on a Study of Eight Major Cities in India*, Irvine 2000.
10. J. Wamser, *Standort Indien. Der Subkontinentalstaat als Markt und Investitionsziel ausländischer Unternehmen*, Münster 2005.

Chapter 16: The Persistence of Poverty

1. Government of India, *Economic Survey 2005–2006*, p. 205.
2. Government of India/ Planning Commission, *Towards Faster and More Inclusive Growth*, p. 75.
3. Government of India, *Economic Survey, 2006–2007*, p. 207.
4. R. Radhakrishna and S. Ray (eds), *Handbook of Poverty in India*, New Delhi 2005, p. 1 ff.
5. A. Rudra, *Prasanta Chandra Mahalanobis. A Biography*, New York 1996.

6. A. Deaton and J. Drèze, 'Poverty and Inequality in India: A Re-Examination', *Economic and Political Weekly*, 7 September 2002, p. 3729 ff.

7. Ibid., pp. 3734 f., 3739 f.

8. Ramachandran and Swaminathan (eds), *Financial Liberalization and Rural Credit in India*.

9. R. S. Deshpande, 'Farmer Distress and Suicides', in Basu (ed.), *Oxford Companion*, p. 170 ff.

10. A. Sen, *The Argumentative Indian*, London 2005, p. 212 ff.

11. J. Drèze, 'Empty Stomachs and the Union Budget', *The Hindu*, 9 March 2007.

12. S. Mishra and M. Panda, *Growth and Poverty in Maharashtra*, Mumbai 2006.

13. A. K. Ghose, 'Informal Labour', in Basu (ed.), *Oxford Companion*, p. 291.

14. Ibid., p. 290.

15. H. Streefkerk, *Tools and Ideas. The Beginning of Local Industrialization in South Gujarat, 1970–2000*, New Delhi 2006, p. 131 ff.

16. Ibid,, p. 139.

17. Government of India–UNDP, *Urban Poverty Report, First Draft*, 18–19 February 2007.

18. V. M. Dandekar and Nilakantha Rath, *Poverty in India*, Bombay: Economic and Political Weekly (for Indian School of Political Economy), 1971.

19. G. A. Menon, 'Slums', in Basu (ed.), *Oxford Companion*, p. 480 f.

20. Interview with A. Pethe, February 2007.

21. D. Kundu, 'Participatory Urban Governance – The Issue of Elite Capture with Special Reference to Metro Cities', in Government of India–UNDP, *Urban Poverty Report, First Draft*.

22. P. Deshingkar and C. Johnson, *State Transfers to the Poor and Back: The Case of the Food for Work Programme in Andhra Pradesh*, London 2003, p. 5.

23. Ibid., pp. 17, 24.

24. Interview with B. Rajsekhar, Indian Administrative Service, November 2006.

25. Radhakrishna and Ray (eds), *Handbook of Poverty*, p. 67.

26. Ibid., p. 119 ff.

27. Government of India, *Economic Survey 2005–2006*, p. 206 f.

28. Ibid., p. 204.

29. V. Sridhar, 'Empowering the Rural Poor' *Frontline*, 22(19), 10–23 September 2005.

30. J. Drèze, 'Empty Stomachs and the Union Budget', *The Hindu*, 9 March 2007.

31. Interview with M. Singh, November 2006.

32. Mishra and Panda, *Growth and Poverty in Maharashtra*, p. 31 f.

33. S. Venkitaraman, 'Job Schemes Must Affect Grassroots Changes', *Business Line*, 13 December 2004.

34. P. Nandi, 'Working Model', *Sunday Express*, 5 November 2006, p. 14 f.

Chapter 17: The Splendour of the Media

1. Kulke and Rothermund, *A History of India*, p. 286.

2. Rothermund, *Mahatma Gandhi. Der Revolutionär der Gewaltlosigkeit*, p. 27.

3. V. Sanghvi, 'Making of a Newspaper', in U. Sahay (ed.), *Making News. A Handbook of the Media in Contemporary India*, New Delhi 2006, p. 56.

4. R. Rai, 'News Pix Lack Sparkle', in Sahay (ed.), *Making News*, p. 72.

5. R. Jeffrey, *India's Newspaper Revolution. Capitalism, Politics and the Indian Language Press, 1977–1999*, London 2000, p. 27.

6. Ibid., p. 51 ff.

7. Ibid., p. 85 f.

8. V. Kohli, *The Indian Media Business*, New Delhi 2003, p. 35.

9. Jeffrey, *India's Newspaper Revolution*, p. 45.

10. Kohli, *The Indian Media Business*, p. 28.
11. Jeffrey, *India's Newspaper Revolution*, p. 213.
12. Ibid., p. 217 f.
13. Ibid., p. 39.
14. Ibid., p. 140.
15. S. Ninan, 'Rural Revolution', *The Hindu*, 23 June 2002.
16. Kohli, *The Indian Media Business*, p. 114.
17. J. Virdi, *The Cinematic ImagiNation. Indian Popular Films as Social History*, New Brunswick 2003, p. 19 f.
18. Kohli, *The Indian Media Business*, p. 118 f.
19. Virdi, *The Cinematic ImagiNation*, p. 4 f.
20. Ibid., p. 87 ff.
21. Ibid., pp. 90, 122 f.
22. Ibid., pp. 15, 107.
23. Ibid., p. 160 ff.
24. Ibid., pp. 22, 175 ff.
25. *Business Line*, 3 August 2003.
26. Kohli, *The Indian Media Business*, p. 97.
27. Ibid., p. 72 f.
28. Ibid., p. 75.
29. Ibid., p. 95 f.
30. Ibid., p. 97.
31. Ibid., p. 156 ff.
32. Ibid., pp. 70, 76 f.
33. *Business Line*, 27 September 2006.

Chapter 18: A Dynamic Diaspora

1. Rothermund, *Routledge Companion to Decolonization*, p.196 ff.
2. R. Donadio, 'The Irascible Prophet: V. S. Naipaul at Home', *New York Times*, 7 August 2005.
3. Rothermund, *Routledge Companion to Decolonization*, p. 205 f.
4. Interview with I. Gandhi, February 1981.
5. www.hindutemples.us.
6. Sen, *The Argumentative Indian*, p. 75 f.
7. Ibid., p. 74.
8. Government of India, *Report of the High Level Committee on the Indian Diaspora/ Estimated Size of Overseas Indian Community: Countrywise*, New Delhi 2002.

Epilogue: The Giant's Next Steps

1. *The Hindu*, 15 March 2007.
2. *Business Line*, 22 August 2002.
3. Interview with M. Ambani, 20 February 2007.
4. *The Hindu*, 15 March 2007.
5. Interview with Dr Montek Singh Ahluwalia, Deputy Chairman, Planning Commission, 2 March 2007.
6. *The Hindu*, 12 May 2007.

BIBLIOGRAPHY

Abraham, Itty, *The Making of the Indian Atomic Bomb. Science, Secrecy and the Postcolonial State*, New Delhi: Orient Longman, 1998.

Adeney, Katharine and Lawrence Sáez (eds), *Coalition Politics and Hindu Nationalism*, London: Routledge, 2005.

Agarwal, Anil, S. Narain and A. Sharma (eds), *Green Politics*, New Delhi: Centre for Science and Environment, 1999.

Agarwal, Pradeep et al., *Policy Regimes and Industrial Competitiveness: A Comparative Study of East Asia and India*, Houndsmill: Macmillan, 2000.

Ahluwalia, Isher J., *Industrial Growth in India, Stagnation since the Mid-Sixties*, Delhi: Oxford University Press, 1985.

Aiolfi, Sergio, *Calicoes und gedrucktes Zeug. Die Entwicklung der englischen Textilveredelung und der Tuchhandel der East India Company, 1650–1750*, Stuttgart: Steiner, 1987.

Anant, T. and O. Goswami, 'Getting Everything Wrong: India's Policies Regarding "Sick" Mills', in Dilip Mookerjee (ed.), *Indian Industry, Policies and Performance*, New Delhi: Oxford University Press, 1995.

Ananthakrishnan, P. and S. Jain-Chandra, *The Impact on India of Trade Liberalization in the Textiles and Clothing Sector*, Washington, DC: IMF, 2005 (IMF Working Paper WP/05/214).

Assayag, Jackie and C.J. Fuller (eds), *Globalizing India. Perspectives from Below*, London: Anthem Press, 2005.

Azad, Maulana Abdul Kalam, *India Wins Freedom*, Madras: Orient Longman, 1988.

Bajpai, Kanti P. and Amitabh Mattoo (eds), *Securing India: Strategic Thought and Practice*, New Delhi: Manohar, 1996.

Banerjee, Bani P., *Handbook of Energy and the Environment in India*, New Delhi: Oxford University Press, 2005.

Basu, N. Kaushik (ed.), *India's Emerging Economy. Performance and Prospects in the 1990s and Beyond*, Cambridge, Mass.: MIT Press, 2004.

Basu, Kaushik (ed.), *The Oxford Companion to Economics in India*, New Delhi: Oxford University Press, 2007.

Brass, Paul, *The Production of Hindu–Muslim Violence in Contemporary India*, Seattle: University of Washington Press, 2003.

Breckenridge. Carol A. (with Arjun Appadorai) (ed.), *Consuming Modernity: Public Culture in a South Asian World*, Minneapolis: University of Minnesota Press, 1995.

Breman, Jan, *The Labouring Poor in India. Patterns of Exploitation, Subordination and Exclusion*, New Delhi: Oxford University Press, 2003.

Briscoe, John and R. P. S. Malik, *Handbook of Water Resources in India*, New Delhi: Oxford University Press, 2007.

Chari, Sharad, *Fraternal Capital. Peasant Workers, Self-Made Men and Globalization in Provincial India*, Stanford: Stanford University Press, 2004.

Christensen, Clayton, *The Innovator's Dilemma: When New Technologies Cause Great Firms to Fail*, Boston: Harvard Business School Press, 1997.

Desai, Ashok V., *My Economic Affair*, New Delhi: Wiley, 1993.

Desai, Ashok V., *India's Communications Industry. History, Analysis, Diagnosis*, New Delhi: Sage, 2006.

Deshingkar, P. and C. Johnson, *State Transfers to the Poor and Back: The Case of the Food for Work Programme in Andhra Pradesh*, London: Overseas Development Institute, 2003 (Working Paper 222).

Dixit, J.N., *Across Borders. Fifty Years of India's Foreign Policy*, New Delhi: Picus, 1998.

D'Monte, Darryl, *Ripping the Fabric: The Decline of Mumbai and its Mills*, Delhi: Oxford University Press, 2002.

Dwyer, Rachel, *All You Want is Money, All You Need is Love: Sexuality and Romance in Modern India*, London: Cassell, 2000.

Dyson, Tim, Robert Cassen and Leela Visaria (eds), *Twenty-first Century India: Population, Economy, Human Development and the Environment*, New Delhi: Oxford University Press, 2004.

Engineer, A. A. and A. S. Narang (eds), *Minorities and the Police in India*, New Delhi: Manohar, 2006.

Fischer-Tiné, Harald, *Der Gurukul Kangri oder die Erziehung der Arya-Nation. Kolonialismus, Hindureform und 'nationale Bildung' in Britisch-Indien (1897–1922)*, Würzburg: Ergon, 2003.

Friedman, Thomas L., *The World is Flat. The Globalized World in the Twenty-first Century*, London: Penguin, 2005.

Fromhold-Eisebith, Martina, 'Infotech Industries and Regional Disparities in India', in Raju, Kumar and Corbridge (eds), *Colonial and Post-Colonial Geographies*, pp. 162–81.

Gokarn, Subir, et al., *The Rising Tide – Employment and Output Linkages of IT–ITES*, New Delhi: NASSCOM-CRISIL, February 2007.

Gordon, Sandy, *India's Rise to Power in the Twentieth Century and Beyond*, London: Macmillan, 1995.

Government of India, *Report of the High Level Committee on the Indian Diaspora*, New Delhi, 2002.

Government of India, *Report of the High Level Committee on the Social, Economic and Educational Status of the Muslim Community of India*, New Delhi, 2006 (Sachar Report).

Government of India/Ministry of External Affairs, *Notes, Memoranda and Letters Exchanged and Agreements Signed between the Governments of India and China, 1954–1959*, White Paper, New Delhi, 1959.

Government of India/Ministry of Finance, *Report of the Twelfth Finance Commission (2004–2010)*, New Delhi, 2004.

Government of India/Ministry of Finance, *Economic Survey 2005–2006*, New Delhi: Government of India Press, 2006.

Government of India/Ministry of Finance, *Economic Survey 2006–2007*, New Delhi: Government of India Press, 2007.

Government of India/Planning Commission, *Towards Faster and More Inclusive Growth. An Approach to the 11th Five Year Plan*, New Delhi, 9 December 2006.

Guilmoto, Christophe and S. Irudaya Rajan, *Fertility Transition in South India*, New Delhi: Sage, 2005.

Gulati, Ashok, Ruth Meinzen-Dick and K. V. Raju, *Institutional Reforms in Indian Irrigation*, New Delhi: Sage, 2005.

Hansen, Thomas Blom, *Wages of Violence: Naming and Identity in Postcolonial Bombay*, Princeton: Princeton University Press, 2001.

Hansen, Thomas Blom, *Urban Violence in India. Identity Politics, 'Mumbai' and the Postcolonial City*, New Delhi: Permanent Black, 2001.

Harriss-White, Barbara, *India Working. Essays on Society and Economy*, Cambridge: Cambridge University Press, 2003.

Heeks, Richard, *India's Software Industry: State Policy Liberalisation and Industrial Development*, New Delhi: Sage, 1996.

Horn, Robert C., *Soviet–Indian Relations. Issues and Influences*, New York: Praeger, 1982.

Imhasly, Bernard, *Abschied von Gandhi ? Eine Reise durch das neue Indien*, Freiburg: Herder, 2006.

Jagadeesh, B. (ed.), *Anupam Supercomputer Systems*, Mumbai: Bhabha Atomic Research Centre, 2003.

Jalal, Ayesha, *The Sole Spokesman. Jinnah, the Muslim League and the Demand for Pakistan*, Cambridge: Cambridge University Press, 1985.

Jansen, G.H., *Afro-Asia and Nonalignment*, London: Faber & Faber, 1966.

Jeffrey, Robin, *India's Newspaper Revolution: Capitalism, Politics and the Indian Language Press, 1977–1999*, London: Hurst, 2000.

Jhabvala, R. and R. Kanbur, 'Globalization and Economic Reform as Seen from the Ground: SEWA's Experience in India', in Basu (ed.), *India's Emerging Economy*, pp. 293– 312.

Joshi, Vijay and I. M. D. Little, *India: Macroeconomics and Political Economy, 1964–1991*, Washington, DC: World Bank, 1994.

Kane, Pandurang V., *History of Dharmasastra*, Poona: Bhandarkar Oriental Research Institute, Vol. I, 1930; Vol. II, Part 1, 1941.

Kapur, Devesh (ed.), *India in Transition: Economics and Politics of Change*, Philadelphia: Center for the Advanced Study of India, 2006.

Kelly, J. D. and M. Kaplan, *Represented Communities. Fiji and World Decolonization*, Chicago: Chicago University Press, 2001.

Kishwar, Madhu P., *Deepening Democracy. Challenges of Governance and Globalization in India*, New Delhi: Oxford University Press, 2005.

Kohli, Vanita, *The Indian Media Business*, New Delhi: Response Books, 2003.

Krueger, Ann (ed.), *Economic Policy Reforms and the Indian Economy*, Chicago: Chicago University Press, 2002.

Kulke, Hermann and D. Rothermund, *A History of India*, London: Routledge, 2004.

Kumar, Arun, *The Black Economy in India*, New Delhi: Penguin, 1999.

Kumar, Deepak (ed.), *Science and Empire. Essays in Indian Context*, Delhi: Anamika Prakashan, 1991.

Kux, Dennis, *Estranged Democracies. India and the United States, 1941–1991*, New Delhi: Sage, 1993.

Kux, Dennis, *The United States and Pakistan, 1947–2000: Disenchanted Allies*, Washington, DC: Woodrow Wilson Center Press, 2001.

Lall, Sanjay, *Learning to Industrialize. The Acquisition of Technological Capability by India*, Basingstoke: Macmillan, 1987.

Leadbeater, S. R. B., *The Politics of Textiles. The Indian Cotton Mill Industry and the Legacy of Swadeshi*, New Delhi: Sage, 1993.

Luce, Edward, *In Spite of the Gods. The Strange Rise of Modern India*, London: Little, Brown, 2006.

Marathe, Sharad S., *Regulation and Development. India's Policy Experience of Control over Industry*, New Delhi: Sage, 1986.

Mattoo, Amitabh, *India's Nuclear Deterrent*, New Delhi: Har Anand, 1999.

Menon, Raja, *A Nuclear Strategy for India*, New Delhi: Sage, 2000.

Mishra, S. and M. Panda, *Growth and Poverty in Maharashtra*, Mumbai: Indira Gandhi Institute of Development Research, 2006.

Mittal, Sunil Bharti, *India's New Entrepreneurial Classes: The High Growth Economy and Why it is Sustainable*, Philadelphia: Center for the Advanced Study of India, 2005.

Mohan, C. Raja, *Impossible Allies: Nuclear India, United States and the Global Order*, New Delhi: India Research Press, 2006.

Moore, G. Barrington, *Social Origins of Democracy and Dictatorship. Lord and Peasant in the Making of the Modern World*, Boston: Beacon Press, 1966.

Naoroji, Dadabhai, *Poverty and Un-British Rule in India*, Delhi: Bharatiya Kala Prakashan 2006 (reprint).

Nayar, Baldev Raj, *Globalization and Nationalism: The Changing Balance in India's Economic Policy,1950–2000*, New Delhi: Sage, 2001.

Nayar, Baldev Raj and T.V. Paul, *India in the World Order. Searching for Major-Power Status*, Cambridge: Cambridge University Press, 2003.

Pai Panandiker, V.A. and A.K. Mehra, *The Indian Cabinet*, New Delhi: Konark, 1996.

Parikh, G. D. and M.N. Roy, *Alphabet of Fascist Economics – A Critique of the Bombay Plan of Economic Development for India*, Calcutta 1944.

Parvate, T., *Gopal Krishna Gokhale*, Ahmadabad: Navajivan, 1959.

Perkovich, George, *India's Nuclear Bomb. The Impact on Global Proliferation*, Berkeley: University of California Press, 2001.

Radhakrishna, R. and Shovan Ray, *Handbook of Poverty in India*, New Delhi: Oxford University Press, 2005.

Raju, Saraswati , S. Kumar and S. Corbridge (eds), *Colonial and Post-Colonial Geographies*, New Delhi: Sage, 2006.

Ramachandran, V. K. and Madhura Swaminathan (eds), *Financial Liberalization and Rural Credit in India*, New Delhi: Tulika Books, 2005.

Rao, M. Govinda and Nirvikar Singh, *Political Economy of Federalism in India*, New Delhi: Oxford University Press, 2005.

Ray, Shovan (ed.), *A Handbook of Agriculture in India*, New Delhi: Oxford University Press, 2007.

Rothermund, Dietmar, *Government, Landlord and Peasant in India. Agrarian Relations under British Rule, 1865–1935*, Wiesbaden: Steiner, 1978.

Rothermund, Dietmar, *Mahatma Gandhi. Der Revolutionär der Gewaltlosigkeit*, Munich: Piper, 1989.

Rothermund, Dietmar, *Mahatma Gandhi. An Essay in Political Biography*, New Delhi: Manohar, 1991.

Rothermund, Dietmar, *India in the Great Depression, 1929–1939*, New Delhi: Manohar, 1992.

Rothermund, Dietmar, *An Economic History of India*, London: Routledge, 1993.

Rothermund, Dietmar (ed.), *Liberalising India. Progress and Problems*, New Delhi: Manohar, 1996.

Rothermund, Dietmar, *The Role of the State in South Asia and Other Essays*, New Delhi: Manohar, 2000.

Rothermund, Dietmar, *Krisenherd Kaschmir. Der Konflikt der Atommächte Indien und Pakistan*, Munich: Beck, 2002.

Rothermund, Dietmar, 'The Industrialization of India: Technology and Production', in Binay Bhushan Chaudhuri (ed.), *Economic History of India from Eighteenth to Twentieth Century*, New Delhi: Centre for Studies in Civilizations, 2005, pp. 437–523.

Rothermund, Dietmar, *The Routledge Companion to Decolonization*, London: Routledge, 2006.

Rothermund, Dietmar and D. C. Wadhwa (eds), *Zamindars, Mines and Peasants. Studies in the History of an Indian Coalfield and its Rural Hinterland*, New Delhi: Manohar, 1978.

Rothermund, Dietmar et al. (eds), *Urban Growth and Rural Stagnation. Studies in the Economy of an Indian Coalfield and its Rural Hinterland*, New Delhi: Manohar, 1980.

Rudra, A., *Prasanta Chandra Mahalanobis. A Biography*, New York: Oxford University Press, 1996.

Sahay, Uday (ed.), *Making News. A Handbook of the Media in Contemporary India*, New Delhi: Oxford University Press, 2006.

Sangwan, Satpal, *Science, Technology and Colonisation. An Indian Experience, 1757–1857*, Delhi: Anamika Prakashan, 1991.

Sen, Amartya, *The Argumentative Indian*, London: Penguin, 2005.

Sheshabalaya, Ashutosh, *Rising Elephant. The Growing Clash with India over White-Collar Jobs and its Challenge to America and the World*, Monroe, Maine: Common Courage Press, 2005.

Singh, Jasjit (ed.), *Nuclear India*, New Delhi: Knowledge World, 1998.

Singh, Jaswant, *Defending India*, New York: St. Martin's Press, 1999.

Sontheimer, Günther Dietz and Hermann Kulke (eds), *Hinduism Reconsidered*, New Delhi: Manohar, 1997.

Specker, Konrad, *Weber im Wettbewerb. Das Schicksal der südindischen Textilhandwerker im 19. Jahrhundert*, Stuttgart: Steiner, 1984.

Sridharan, Eswaran, *The Political Economy of Industrial Promotion: Indian, Brazilian and Korean Electronics in Comparative Perspective*, Westport, Conn.: Praeger, 1996.

Stern, Robert W., *Changing India: Bourgeois Revolution on the Subcontinent*, Cambridge: Cambridge University Press, 1993.

Streefkerk, Hein, *Tools and Ideas. The Beginning of Local Industrialization in South Gujarat, 1970–2000*, New Delhi: Manohar, 2006.

Talbott, Strobe, *Engaging India. Diplomacy, Democracy, and the Bomb*, Washington, DC: The Brookings Institution, 2004.

Tata Energy Research Institute (TERI), *TERI Energy Directory and Yearbook (TEDDY), 2003–2004*, New Delhi: TERI, 2004.

Telang, Kashinath Trimbak, 'Free Trade and Protection from an Indian Point of View', in K. T. Telang, *Writings and Speeches*, Bombay: Manoranjan Press, 1916, pp. 97–187.

Tellis, Ashley, *India's Emerging Nuclear Posture. Between Recessed Deterrent and Ready Arsenal* (Project Air Force, RAND), Santa Monica: RAND, 2001.

Teltumbde, A. et al., *Glimpses of Gujarat in a Martyr's City. A Fact-finding Report on Sholapur Communal Riots*, Delhi: People's Union for Civil Liberties, 10 November 2002.

Tendulkar, Suresh and T. A. Bhavani, *Understanding Reforms. Post-1991 in India*, New Delhi: Oxford University Press, 2007.

Thapar, Romila, *Early India*, London: Allen Lane, 2002.

Varshney, Ashutosh, *Ethnic Conflict and Civic Life. Hindus and Muslims in India*, New Haven: Yale University Press, 2002.

Venkatesh, A., *Computers and New Technologies in Indian Households: Based on a Study of Eight Major Cities in India*, Irvine: Center for Research on Information Technology and Organization, University of California, 2000.

Venkateswaran, G., *Bhubha and his Magnificent Obsessions*, Hyderabad: Universities Press, 1994.

Virdi, Jyotika, *The Cinematic ImagiNation. Indian Popular Films as Social History*, New Brunswick: Rutgers University Press, 2003.

Wamser, Johannes, *Standort Indien. Der Subkontinentalstaat als Markt und Investitionsziel ausländischer Unternehmen*, Münster: Lit Verlag, 2005.

Witsoe, J., 'India's Second Green Revolution? The Sociopolitical Implications of Corporate-Led Agricultural Growth', in D. Kapur (ed.), *India in Transition: Economics and Politics of Change*, Philadelphia: Center for the Advanced Study of India, 2006.

Zachariah, Benjamin, *Developing India. An Intellectual and Social History, ca. 1930–1950*, New Delhi: Oxford University Press, 2005.

Zastoupil, Lynn, *John Stuart Mill and India*, Stanford: Stanford University Press, 1994.

Zinkin, Taya, *Reporting India*, London: Chatto & Windus, 1962.

INDEX